Islamic Ethos and the Specter of Modernity

ANTHEM MIDDLE EAST STUDIES

The Anthem Middle East Studies series is committed to offering to our global audience the finest scholarship on the Middle East across the spectrum of academic disciplines. The twin goals of our rigorous editorial and production standards will be to bring original scholarship to the shelves and digital collections of academic libraries worldwide, and, to cultivate accessible studies for university students and other sophisticated readers.

KEY ISSUES IN MODERN SOCIOLOGY

Anthem's **Key Issues in Modern Sociology** series publishes scholarly texts by leading social theorists that give an accessible exposition of the major structural changes in modern societies. These volumes address an academic audience through their relevance and scholarly quality, and connect sociological thought to public issues. The series covers both substantive and theoretical topics, as well as addressing the works of major modern sociologists. The series emphasis is on modern developments in sociology with relevance to contemporary issues such as globalization, warfare, citizenship, human rights, environmental crises, demographic change, religion, postsecularism and civil conflict.

Islamic Ethos and the Specter of Modernity

Farzin Vahdat

ANTHEM PRESS

Anthem Press India
An imprint of Wimbledon Publishing Company India Private Limited (WPCIPL)
WPCIPL is a subsidiary of Wimbledon Publishing Company Limited (UK)

This edition first published in India 2015
by ANTHEM PRESS INDIA
www.anthempress.co.in

First published in UK and USA 2015
by ANTHEM PRESS
www.anthempress.com

ISBN-13: 978 93 80601 73 1 (Hbk)
ISBN-10: 93 80601 73 5 (Hbk)

FOR SALE IN SOUTH ASIA ONLY

Digitally Printed at Replika Press Pvt. Ltd

CONTENTS

ACKNOWLEDGMENTS

In the process of writing this book, I have benefited from many people. I am especially thankful to Bryan S. Turner for his support in this project. Ali Gheissari read several chapters of this book and provided me with very helpful insights. I greatly appreciate his friendship and his input. In writing this book I have received encouragement, support and comments from many friends. I thank Roy Mottahedeh, Houchang Chehabi, Ramin Jahanbegloo, Abbas Amant, Mohamad Tavakoli-Targhi, Touraj Atabaki and Afshin Matin-Asgari, among many, who gave me moral and intellectual support in this and other projects. I have learned and benefited from my friendships with Shahla Haeri and Valentine Moghadam. I am also thankful to the staff at Anthem Press, Tej Sood, Brian Stone and Lori Martinsek, for their cooperation and teamwork.

A NOTE ON TRANSLITERATION

I have transliterated Persian and most Perso-Arabic terms in the Persian style. If I determined a Perso-Arabic term possesses a more Arabic sense, I have used the Arabic style. For Arabic terms, I have used the Arabic style.

INTRODUCTION

There are compelling reasons as to why the binary question of Islam and modernity constitutes one of the major issues that the contemporary world faces today. Islam, as a world religion, has shaped the lives and consciousnesses of a large segment of humanity for centuries and created a world civilization that runs in many ways parallel to Western civilization. The rise of social and political movements in the Islamic world in the past few decades is in many ways a response to the negative forces of modernity, such as colonialism and the related problems of economic and political development. At the same time these movements are, in one way or another, faced with new ideas and institutions such as individual and citizenship rights, political participation by the populace, gender equality, economic development and tolerance of difference. The emergence of Islamic movements in the 20th century has been marked, on the one hand, by militant action and reaction against the colonial legacy that is often marred by fanaticism, xenophobia and misogyny. On the other hand, these movements have called for the mobilization of the masses and large-scale political and social participation of the populace in some parts of the Islamic world. The actions and reactions against modern colonialism (e.g., the formation of Muslim Brotherhood in early 20th century Egypt and the 1979 Islamic revolution in Iran) inspired by Islam, or more accurately by interpretations of Islam, and the responses from the West, have created volatile situations in many parts of the world. Simultaneously, the galvanization and mobilization of the masses in these parts of the world by Islamic movements have the potential to forge the foundations of mass democracy. Once a population has been mobilized and encouraged to participate in the social and political affairs of its community, it is probable for it to develop a sense of agency and feel entitled to determine its own affairs, which constitutes the foundation of mass democracy and creation of a public sphere in which individuals have the equal right to discuss and determine their community's political and social issues. The role of Islam, or in fact interpretations of Islam, has been crucial to this process. Islamic political movements in Egypt, Pakistan and Iran, to mention a few, have all been based on interpretations of Islamic foundational sources such as the Qur'an, the Hadith, the Sufi traditions and sometimes Islamic philosophy and theology. At the same time, these movements and their ideological foundations have been in many ways embedded and articulated in the context of the forces and conditions of the modern world. Thus, in order to understand the contemporary Islamic movements and the consciousness of the millions of Muslims involved in or affected by these movements, it is necessary to study the complex relationships between contemporary readings of Islam and modernity in various Islamic social contexts.

This study directly speaks to both sides of this question by examining different aspects of modernity and contemporary interpretations of Islam *together*. Modernity is indeed another complex category that defies facile and simplistic approaches that are prevalent in the literature and current studies of Islam and the Muslim world. In this study, I engage in a close reading and in-depth analysis of the discourses of some of the most prominent 20th- and 21st-century thinkers who identified themselves as Islamic and who grappled with the questions that lie at the core of modern world and their relations to Islam and Islamic civilization. I have chosen nine Islamic thinkers who lived in the 20th century (or are still living) because of the significance of their thought as it regards the notions and conditions of the forces that make up the modern world in relation to Islamic civilization. Since the last century, these thinkers have played crucial roles in shaping the consciousness of many in the Muslim world, and their discourses in turn reflect, to a significant degree, the different paradigms of political and social cultures in some very important parts of the Islamic regions. In many parts of the world, the work of leading intellectuals reflects the concerns, apprehensions, frustrations, desires, and aspirations of a society, while their discourses immensely influence the public's views and values. This is even more so in societies that are in process of change and conflict, like Muslim societies since the mid-19th century. Their chief intellectuals, poets and artists to a large extent absorb the feelings and concerns of the population and respond to them to fashion new solutions and paths for change in these societies. These influential intellectuals have contributed to the formations of frames of mind that extensively condition the attitudes and behaviors of millions of people in Islamic societies. Their discourses have often led to the formation of large and small social and political movements as well as the undermining and even destruction of old institutions and creation of new ones.

Most of the thinkers analyzed here are well known in the Muslim world and outside, and some are mostly known in their own countries or among the scholarly community. For all of them, the ideas and conditions related to the forces of modern world are pivotal, regardless of whether they are sympathetic toward modernity or harbor antipathy toward it. But before I briefly discuss these thinkers and political actors and present the outline of the chapters in this book, it is necessary to examine the notion of modernity briefly.

Modernity and Contemporary Islam

Modernity is a contested and convoluted category. There is not much consensus among the scholars who have addressed the issue since the early nineteenth century. Yet, in the tradition of Critical Theory, from Immanuel Kant and G.W.F Hegel, to Max Weber, the Frankfurt School and Jürgen Habermas, the discussion of modernity has occupied a central place. In this tradition, the notion of human subjectivity is the pivotal concept in the phenomena we associate with modern times. Modern social, political, economic and cultural institutions are all built upon human subjectivity. Subjectivity itself is indeed a complex phenomenon and a fleeting concept. But, put in simple language, it refers to the idea of human empowerment and agency. Modernity begins, from this point of view, when a critical mass of a society abandons the life of passivity and acquires a sense of assertiveness, vigor, volition, resolve and action. In a nutshell, modern people are not passive and possess agency and power. They act upon the world. Moderns' intervention in and acts upon nature constitute the fundaments of technology that has, to some extent, liberated humans from the whims of nature and at the same time brought us close to the destruction of nature and ourselves. Modern people also act upon society and politics as they assert their individual and collective power over political processes and the social world. These aspects of human agency and empowerment underlie the democratic institutions of modern societies. Democracy in the modern world is not possible without these fundamental transformations in the psyches of the members of a given society. We can establish all the institutions of a modern democracy, such as a parliament, a free press, elections and separation of powers, but without a critical mass in the society that has a sense of subjectivity, agency and empowerment, these institutions would not be able to survive. This happened in Iran (not to mention other countries) in the early 20th century, when the Constitutional Revolution of 1906 laid the foundations of a constitutional and restricted monarchy, a parliament, a more or less free press and elections. Because this sense of agency and empowerment had not developed among the bulk of Iranian people, all of these institutions failed and in fact were used by the despotic Pahlavi kings to promote their heavy-handed rule.

From this perspective, the idea of human subjectivity is the very cornerstone of modernity. As the term cornerstone implies, the idea is that when large numbers of individuals are empowered to assert their will on nature and social and political spheres, then the conditions for advanced technology, political democracy and societal activity, including modern proactive economic action, can emerge. When a sense of agency and empowerment is initiated among a critical mass of a population, a dynamic process that would not only increase the sense of agency in individuals but also disperse and disseminate it further in society might develop. When the individual develops a sense of agency and empowerment in his or her psyche and comes to realize that other individuals in the society are entitled to the same agency, then the foundations of universal rights are created, which in turn can give rise to a democratic ethos among a large number of people. The development of a *democratic ethos* is, I contend, the necessary precondition for the emergence of one of the most desirable features of modernity: flourishing democratic institutions.

The transformation from the state of passivity to subjectivity and agency among a populace does not occur extemporaneously or easily. Human populations must necessarily go through a long and arduous process to achieve this transformation. In fact, one of the major reasons for the prolongation and difficulty of the process of subject formation is that it is necessarily accomplished by means of disciplining the body and psyche of the subject. Power and empowerment cannot be achieved without individuals having been trained to overcome and control, to a large degree, their instinctual inclinations and the desire for pleasure and comfort. The modern subject begins its career as an ascetic who imposes her or his will on the inner and outer nature. Thus the repression directed inward that is part and parcel of self-control in the formation of human subjectivity has constituted the core of discipline in the formation of agency and subjectivity in the modern history of the West, starting with the Protestant Reformation and especially its Puritan variation. We can witness a similar strong emphasis of the disciplining of the body and the soul among some of the Islamic thinkers discussed in this volume.[1]

One of the most important aspects of modern discipline is its impact on women and sexual norms. The subjectivity that is established by means of discipline typically entails the domination of men over women and proliferation of masculinst heteronormativity.[2] The power and empowerment that are the goals of subjectivity do not develop in a vacuum. At least during the early stages of the formation of subjectivity and agency, power is always exercised over something or someone. As the beneficiaries of the early stages of subjectivity, men find themselves in positions of power and exercise it over women while promoting a culture of masculinity and heteronormativity. As we will see in the chapters to follow, these issues of agency (especially its particular form among Muslim

---

1. What made modern discipline successful in the West was the fact that it was, by and large, a voluntary undertaking by the agents and not entirely imposed from outside. In the conclusion of his meticulous analysis of Calvinism, Michael Walzer wrote that among the Puritans, "discipline was not to depend upon the authority of paternal kings and lords or upon the obedience of childlike and trustful subjects. Puritans sought to make it [discipline] voluntary [...] the object of individual and collective willfulness. But voluntary or not, its keynote was repression." Continuing the passage, Walzer also correctly points out the importance of discipline for later phases of modernity, i.e., liberalism, that is laid during the earlier Puritanical phase: "Liberalism also required such voluntary subjection of self-control, but in sharp contrast to Puritanism, its politics was shaped by an extraordinary confidence in the possibility of both a firm sense of human reasonableness and of the relative ease with which order might be attained. Liberal confidence made repression and the endless struggle against sin unnecessary; it also tended to make self-control invisible, that is, to forget its painful history and naïvely assume its existence. The result was that liberalism did not create the self-control it required. The Lockean state was not a disciplinary institution as was the Calvinist holy commonwealth, but rather rested on the assumed political virtues of its citizens. It is one of the central arguments of this conclusion that Puritan repression has its place in the practical history of that strange assumption" (Michael Walzer, *The Revolution of the Saints: A Study in the Origins of Radical Politics* (New York: Atheneum, 1974), 302.). To what extent this disciplinary exercise in the Muslim world is voluntary and to what degree it is imposed by a politicized elite cannot be determined at this time.
2. In the early modern West, we find very similar developments. For example, "In the Puritan family," wrote Sally Kitch, "male dominance was mandated in the covenant model of Calvinism. Husbands were supposed to be the loving rulers of their voluntarily submissive wives, just as God lovingly rules His voluntarily submissive children" (Sally Kitch, *Chaste Liberation: Celibacy and Female Cultural Status* (Urbana: University of Illinois Press 1989), 36.). On the same theme, Michael Walzer wrote, "The tendency of Puritan thought was to turn fatherhood into a political sovereignty and the family into a 'little commonwealth.' The brethren produced a fairly large literature on family life, but they rarely discussed the traditional themes of alliance and misalliance, and they dealt curtly with the degrees of natural affinity that made marriage impersonal. In their treatises, neither nature nor love played much of a part. Their concern was almost entirely with the 'government' of the household; they wrote prolix chapters with such as titles as 'How women ought to be governed,' and 'How children owe obedience and honor to their parents" (*The Revolution of the Saints*, 187–88).

thinkers), discipline and the dominatory position of men and masculinity constitute some of the most important themes in the discourses of a number of Islamic thinkers in the contemporary period.

As I said before, modernity is complex and confusing. One of the reasons for this complexity and confusion is that it consists of "phases" and "stages": the early modern period, high modernity and late modernity (or as some may dub it, "postmodernity") need to be distinguished, albeit without making them watertight entities without any relation to one another.[3] In fact, in my view, we should understand these stages in a dialectical relation to one another. The early phase of subject formation with its harsh emphasis on disciplined agents is very different from the more liberal stages of modernity. Yet they are dialectically related in that without the formation of the very strong character of the disciplined subject of the earlier phase, the more moderate and tolerant stage is not conceivable. The Puritan saint of 16th and 17th centuries and the somber and austere Islamist of today may appear anything but modern, but without the agency that they carry and disseminate among the multitudes, the more salutary stage of modernity does not seem possible.

Theoretically speaking, the most important feature of the early phases of modernity, in both the western and Islamist incarnations, is its peculiar notion of human agency and subjectivity. The notion of human subjectivity here is indirect and circuitous. First, the essential characteristics of power, such as omnipotence, omniscience and volition, are projected to the divine entity, and then these very same attributes are partially re-appropriated by humans. In this scheme, humans possess power and agency because they are affiliated with God. The same goes for knowledge and the will to act upon the world. Thus the Puritans saw themselves as God's instruments.[4] The Islamists often refer to humans as God's successors on earth (*Khalifatullah fi al-ard*). I have referred to this

3. See, for example: Giddens, Anthony, *Modernity and Self-identity: Self and Society in the Late Modern Age* (Stanford: Stanford University Press, 1991).
4. Max Weber described this circuitous path to subjectivity, or what I call "mediated subjectivity," in the following manner: "A real penetration of the human soul by the divine was made impossible by the absolute transcendentality of God compared to the flesh: *finitum non est capax infiniti* [the finite cannot contain the infinite]. The community of the elect with their God could only take place and be perceptible to them in that *God worked (operatur) through them and that they were conscious of it.* That is, their action originated from the faith caused by God's grace, and this faith in turn justified itself by the quality of that action. Deep-lying differences of the most important conditions of salvation which apply to the classification of all practical religious activity appear here. The religious believer can make himself sure of his state of grace either in that he feels himself to be the vessel of the Holy Spirit *or the tool of the divine will*. In the former case his religious life tends to mysticism and emotionalism, *in the latter to ascetic action*; Luther stood close to the former type, Calvinism belonged definitely to the latter" (Max Weber, *The Protestant Ethic and the Spirit of Capitalism*, New York: Routledge, 2001, 68; emphasis added). As Walzer has observed, Girolamo Saonarola (d. 1498) had claimed that "God moves all men [...] 'as the saw is moved by the hand of the craftsman.'" This metaphor "would naturally appeal to a Calvinist preacher. The image of the divine instrument was so frequently used in Puritan literature that it came near to replacing the much older image of man as God's child" (*The Revolution of the Saints*, 166).

phenomenon as "mediated subjectivity."[5] In this schema, human subjectivity is indirect and derived from God's absolute Subjectivity.

Hegel referred to this indirect and mediated subjectivity as Unhappy Consciousness (*das unglückliche Bewusstsein*, sometimes translated as Contrite Consciousness) in which humans aspire to achieve divine attributes as empowerment and attaining agency.[6] In this scheme, the human conceives of itself as a duality, man and God simultaneously. God is perceived to be the real and man unreal. At the same time, the human feels that his or her mundane selfhood must be cancelled out, and the attributes of the divine or "changeless" assumes a form of elevation from low to the high.[7] But in actuality, the human is the real agent who acts upon the world by toiling and deep down knows it, yet does not explicitly acknowledge his or her agency and subjectivity. Human agency, as manifested in our faculties and powers, is hidden in God's agency, which is viewed as an external and alien gift from the otherworldly divine for the benefit of humankind.[8] What is important is that humans in this paradigm attribute all their power to the divine as the absolute power and think of themselves as nullity, while it is they who act upon the world and move things in it.[9]

In fact, Hegel was very critical of this indirect attempt of humans to achieve agency and subjectivity. For him, this path signified the surrendering of self-will, freedom, and a sense of autonomous selfhood, as well as resorting to a mysterious act to attain subjectivity and empowerment. "Through these moments—the negative abandonment first of its own right and power of decision, then of its property and enjoyment, and

5. See Farzin Vahdat, *God and Juggernaut: Iran's Intellectual Encounter with Modernity* (Syracuse University Press, 2002).
6. In Jean Hyppolite's words, "Man humbles himself and poses himself as nonessence, and then seeks to rise indefinitely toward a transcendent essence" (Jean Hyppolite, *Genesis and Structure of Hegel's Phenomenology of Spirit*. Evanston: Northwestern University Press, 1974, 198).
7. Hegel describes humans' finding their subjectivity in God as follows: "Consciousness of life, of its existence and action, is merely pain and sorrow over this existence and activity; for therein consciousness finds only consciousness of its opposite as its essence—and of its own nothingness. It is, therefore, immediately consciousness of the opposite, viz. of itself as single, individual, particular [God]." (Hegel. G.W.F. *The Phenomenology of Mind* (New York: Harper and Row, 1967), 252.)
8. As Hegel puts it, "Consciousness, on its part, appears here likewise as actual, though, at the same time, as internally shattered; and this diremption shows itself in the course of toil and enjoyment, to break up into a relation to reality, or existence for itself, and into an existence in itself. That relation to actuality is the process of alteration or acting, the existence for itself, which belongs to the particular consciousness as such. But therein it is also in itself; this aspect belongs to the unchangeable "beyond." This aspect consists in faculties and powers: an external gift, which the unchangeable here hands over for the consciousness to make use of" (*The Phenomenology of Mind*, 260).
9. In Hegel's words, "This consciousness [human], to which the inherent reality, or ultimate essence [God], is an 'other,' regards this power (which is the way it appears when active), as 'the beyond,' that which lies remote from its self. Instead, therefore, of returning out of its activity into itself, and instead of having confirmed itself as a fact for its self, consciousness reflect back this process of action into the other extreme [God], which is thereby represented as purely universal, as absolute might, from which the movement in every direction started, and which is the essential life of the self-disintegrating extremes." (*The Phenomenology of Mind*, 261.)

finally the positive moment of carrying on what it does not understand—it [the human] deprives itself completely and in truth, of the consciousness of inner and outer freedom, or reality in the sense of its own existence for itself. It has the certainty of having in truth stripped itself of its Ego, and of having turned its immediate self-consciousness into a 'thing,' into an objective external existence."[10] Yet, despite his bitter lamentation regarding this type of circuitous path toward agency, Hegel thought that it would lead to autonomous human subjectivity and empowerment. While rendering thanks, and acknowledging the Other (the divine) as the real Subject, and reducing its own ego to nullity, the human has still been acting upon the world, which would supply the consciousness of its self as an autonomous subject. "For consciousness, no doubt, in appearance renounces the satisfaction of its self-feeling [*Selbstgefühls*; "self-feeling" or "self-assurance; satisfaction of being an autonomous self"], but it gets the actual satisfaction of that feeling, for it *has been* desire, work and enjoyment; qua consciousness it has willed, has acted and enjoyed. Its thanks similarly, in which it recognizes the other extreme [the divine] as its true reality, and cancels itself, is itself its own act, which counterbalances the action of the other extreme and meets with a like act the benefit handed over [by the divine]."[11]

---

10. *The Phenomenology of Mind*, 265–66.

11. *The Phenomenology of Mind*, 261–62. In Jean Hyppolite's reading of Hegel, the paradigm of Unhappy Consciousness can be summarized as humans' vicarious attempt to attain subjectivity through a circuitous and *dialectical* path: "Active consciousness [the human] merely appears to act. Inside and outside it, God acts, just as the master was the true subject of the slave's action. 'For what the slave does is, properly speaking, the action of the master; being for-itself, essence, are the master's alone.' Both in its withdrawal into itself and in its action in the world, unhappy consciousness merely experiences the transcendence of its own essence. Its action is reflected beyond it. It is not genuinely autonomous, as self-consciousness claims to be. The truth of its self-certainty is a transcendent goal [God], which condemns it no longer to contain its own certainty. The relation of master to slave reappears here within consciousness itself. Human consciousness poses itself as slave consciousness; its essence, mastery, is beyond it in God, whom Hegel here still calls the immutable, or the universal. Does unhappy consciousness, then, not realize concretely its communion with its beyond? On the one hand, indeed, the immutable offers itself to it and allows it to act; on the other hand, unhappy consciousness recognizes its dependence with respect to the immutable, as the slave recognized the master; 'it forbids itself the satisfaction of consciousness of its independence and attributes the essence of its action to the beyond rather than to itself.' [...] Acting consciousness humbles itself in its thanksgiving, in the recognition of God. Does it not, then, achieve communion with the transcendent? Hegel especially emphasizes this humiliation of unhappy consciousness which reaches communion with God through its recognition of him. Man, who poses himself as autonomous insofar as he is active being, man who works on the world and draws his enjoyment from it, nonetheless recognizes himself as passive. This recognition of God, who alone acts, is man's essential action. As the slave recognized the master and posed himself as slave, so human consciousness poses itself as passive and dependent. It renounces its domination. But through a dialectical reversal which we have already seen several times, the humiliation of man, who attributes everything to grace and grants himself nothing, is in fact an elevation. For it is man himself who poses God. Man recognizes the master, but that recognition emanates from him. In posing himself as the lowest he is the highest. Thus, self-consciousness fails to divest itself of its freedom, fails truly to alienate it. Self-consciousness glorifies God and denies man's freedom, but that, precisely, is its

From this perspective, while mediated subjectivity is a form of "false consciousness" whereby humans attribute their subjectivity to an "alien" entity, i.e., the divine, its outcome could be quite different, because once even a rudimentary form of human agency is attained in a society on a large scale, it can create a dynamism of its own that can bring about a state of self-sustaining and autonomous human subjectivity.

The condition that Hegel refers to as Unhappy Consciousness and I describe as mediated subjectivity (and which constitutes the crux of the present study with regard to the Islamic world) also corresponds to what Louis Dupré has described as the general worldview during the Baroque era in Europe. In this period, humans attempt to achieve empowerment and agency is mediated by the absolute power of the divine. Thus, in Dupré's words:

> With its unprecedented tensions, social as well as religious, the Baroque appears a dubious model of an integrated culture. My justification for introducing it here is that, despite tensions and inconsistencies, a comprehensive spiritual vision united Baroque culture. At the center of it stands the person, confident in the ability to give form and structure to a nascent world. But—and here lies its religious significance—that center remains vertically linked to a transcendent source from which, via a descending scale of meditating bodies, the human creator draws his power. This dual center—human and divine—distinguishes the Baroque word picture from the vertical one of the Middle Ages, in which reality descends from a single transcendent point, as well as from the unproblematically horizontal one of later modern culture, prefigured in some features of the Renaissance. The tension between the two centers conveys to the Baroque a complex, restless and dynamic quality.[12]

There is very little doubt that in many respects the Europe of the Baroque period cannot be compared to that parts of the Muslim world studied in this volume in the twentieth and twenty-first centuries. Yet, the core worldview in the Baroque period, what

---

grandest act—which is why it does not allow itself to be duped by its thanksgiving" (*Genesis and Structure of Hegel's Phenomenology of Spirit*, 211–12).

In his earlier writings, Hegel presented a somewhat different version of the notion of Unhappy Consciousness. Before the *Phenomenology*, he thought of this idea as humans' attempt to separate and extirpate themselves from nature and become dominant over it. In this sense, Hegel thought, we had to endure the pain of being separated from nature. As Hyppolite has observed, "Hegel had reflected on the unhappiness of consciousness from the time of his first theological works. We can even say that the essential preoccupation of those early works was to describe the unhappiness of consciousness in its most diverse form in order to define the essence of that torment. At the time, Hegel was preoccupied with extraindividual entities with the spirit of a people, or with a religion—and he envisaged the Greeks as the happy people of history and the Jews as the unhappy people. He also viewed Christianity as one of the great forms of unhappy consciousness. The Jewish people is the unhappy people of history because it represents the first total reflection of consciousness away from life [nature]. Whereas the Greek people remain in the bosom of life and attain a harmonious unity of self and nature, transposing nature into thought and thought into nature, the Jewish people can only oppose itself constantly to nature and to life" (*Genesis and Structure of Hegel's Phenomenology of Spirit*, 191).

12. Louis Dupré, *Passage to Modernity: An Essay in the Hermenutics of Nature and Culture* (New Haven: Yale University Press, 1993), 237.

I have called mediated subjectivity, seems to be at heart of the operating *weltanschauungs* in many parts of the Muslim world. And it indeed exhibits a complex, restless and dynamic quality whereby it can change culture, society and politics in these societies.

This indirect path to subjectivity, both in Western experience and now in many parts of the Islamic world, has made some contemporary thinkers deny any form of subjectivity in the current Islamic discourses and, by extension, Muslim cultures. Prominent among these thinkers is Bassam Tibi, who is cognizant of the importance of human subjectivity for modernity, yet does not recognize that subjectivity in its fully developed form cannot appear overnight. Tibi thus blames the Islamic discourses in their current configuration for the negation of human agency and subjectivity: "Contemporary Islamism, though modern, adopts the Arabic vocabulary replete with religious rituals of fatalism. Religious language signifies the belief that man has little control over human destiny. The most popular formula is '*insh'a Allah* (*Inshallah*)/ if Allah is willing.' When a Muslim is asked whether a job will be done, he or she responds with '*Inshallah*' and thus denies the will of the self. If a traditional Muslim faces a challenge or is required to accomplish a task, the formula traditionally used is '*tawakal 'ala Allah*/rely on God.' This mindset of fatalism needs to be changed through religious reform."[13] Lamenting the negation of "humanism" in contemporary Islamic discourses, Tibi further asserts, "The belief that knowledge is based on a fundamental and absolutist 'Allah's will' is essential to this breakdown [of human-centered knowledge]. In contrast, Cartesianism helps man to realize an awareness of himself as *res cogitans*. In epistemological terms, this is the 'principle of subjectivity' (Habermas), which establishes a foundation for the shift from religious worldview to the modern worldview. Political religions dismiss this worldview, and in consequence, result in irrationalism. This is the case with the intolerable views of all religious fundamentalisms, revealing the limits of pluralism with regard not only to society and polity but also to knowledge and epistemology."[14]

As we can see in the above excerpts, there is a strong inclination on the part of some thinkers, especially among "secularists" from Muslim origins such as Tibi, to depict contemporary Islamic discourses as lacking any element of subjectivity. What these thinkers tend to ignore is the dialectical development of subjectivity and agency that proceeds from what I have called mediated subjectivity. From their perspectives, therefore, the only path to modernity is through a cultural reform from above, a transformation in culture that would bring about reason, human rights and other fundaments and trappings of modernity.[15] No one can deny the

13. Bassam Tibi. *Islam's Predicament with Modernity: Religious Reform and Cultural Change* (London: Routledge, 2009), 57.

14. *Islam's Predicament with Modernity*, 83.

15. In Tibi's words, "An Islamic reform has to be guided by an effort at enlightenment in order to promote cultural change and religious reform. This is a requirement for the introduction of the concept of individual human rights. Muslims need to beware of stranding themselves in familiar apologetics by claiming that Islam includes all concepts of human rights and has no need of borrowing from other cultures [...] The writings of Islamic modernists since Afghani are characterized by the fact that they utterly fail to rethink the inherited religious dogma. In

importance of cultural change in contemporary Muslim world, but cultural things do not change by mere edicts and intellectual exhortation. It is true that intellectuals can facilitate the path toward cultural change, but real change in peoples' attitudes is largely the result of experience wherein they participate in political, social and cultural *activities* that engage them in transforming their society and themselves. On the ideational level, of course, a discourse that promotes such a participation is essential.

Thus, I contend that the formation of subjectivity is a long process of *experience* that a critical mass of society needs to go through first hand, while its starting point could be, or often is, in an inchoate and elementary form, or what I call mediated subjectivity. We should be aware of the difficulties and perils that lie in the path of development from this inchoate subjectivity to full subjectivity and, in fact, intersubjectivity. Subjectivity and agency, prosaically put, entail empowerment of those who have been historically denied power. And whenever power and empowerment are involved, conflict and struggle are also part and parcel of the process of empowerment. Thus, the processes of subject formation have been realized in revolutions, wars and struggles of various types, including class struggle as well as struggle between ethnicities and races with genocidal outcomes. As such, it is quite likely that the process of modernity in the Muslim areas would be similarly characterized by parallel or even worse perils.

In this book I have closely examined the discourses of nine prominent and influential Islamic thinkers whose discourses have, in one way or another, major bearings on the conditions and notions of modernity in the Muslim world, as well as reflecting and echoing them. In chapter one I closely examine the thought of Muhammad Iqbal (Indian subcontinent, 1877–1938), who was well versed in modern Western thought as well as in the Islamic discourses. His notion of the Islamic "self" as the modern subject and his extensive elaborations on it constitute a crucial step in the broaching of the seminal ideas pertaining to modernity that have influenced other thinkers we encounter in this volume. Chapter two is devoted to Abul Ala Maududi (Pakistan, 1903–1979), who was the founder and main ideologue of the influential Jamaat-e-Islami in Pakistan and India. At the core of Maududi's activities and thought stands a cosmology and theory of an Islamic state that has had far-reaching implications for many Islamist movements around the world. Sayyid Qutb (Egypt, 1906–1966), the focus of chapter three, is another highly influential thinker of the 20th century whose thought has had a major impact on contemporary radical Islamist discourses and movements, especially in their relations with the West. Qutb's discourse is one of the most influential and comprehensive attempts by an Islamist revivalist to create a neo-Islamic civilization to compete with, and eventually replace, not only modern authoritarian states in Muslim lands, but also modern welfare state of liberal democracies as well as the now-defunct communist system. In chapter four I analyze and discuss Fatima Mernissi, (Morroco, 1940) whose discourse has had a

other words, one can assume a lack of willingness on the part of Islamic scribes to engage in topical reasoning. In Islamic history they were never committed to real cultural change through religious reform. The *ulema* would never come to terms with the Islamic predicament with modernity because their minds are closed." (*Islam's Predicament with Modernity*, 123–24).

significant impact on the conceptualization of gender relationships in some parts of the Muslim world.

In chapter five I closely examine the thought of Mehdi Haeri Yazdi (Iran, 1923–1999). His expert knowledge in Islamic philosophy and other Islamic fields of knowledge, and very importantly, his formal training at doctoral level in modern western philosophical traditions in the west enabled Haeri to investigate the fundamental issues of modernity and Islam to a remarkable depth. In chapter six my focus is on the Mohammad Mojtahed Shabestari (Iran, b. 1936), who has taken the debate on Islam and modernity to a higher level through a sophisticated attempt to reconcile human subjectivity and God's sovereignty. In chapter seven, I discuss the thought of Mohammad Khatami (Iran, b.1943), Iran's ex-president, which embodies the dilemmas and contradictions of the Islamic modernity and democracy, as well its promises.[16] Seyyed Hossein Nasr (b. 1933) has devoted much of his voluminous work, written primarily in English after his exile from Iran and move to the United States after the revolution of 1979, to oppose modernity in its roots and branches. Chapter eight discusses Nasr's efforts to deconstruct modernity and its humanism. The final chapter is devoted to Mohammed Arkoun (Algeria/France, 1928–2010) who attempted to promote the idea and ideals of liberal democracy in the Muslim world for decades.

The chapters in this book are all independent essays that can be read individually. For this reason, in the beginning of some essays, I have expanded on the theoretical tools used to shed light on our understanding of modernity. This can complement my discussion of the main features of the modern world that I have presented here in the introduction.

16. In this volume I do not discuss the discourses of other prominent Iranian Islamic thinkers such as Ali Shariati, Ayatollah Khomeini, Morteza Motahhari and Abdulkarim Soroush because I have analyzed their discourses in my previous work. See *God and Juggernaut.*

Chapter One

SIR MUHAMMAD IQBAL: THE DIALECTICIAN OF MUSLIM AUTHENTICITY

Muhammad Iqbal, who was knighted by the British in 1922, was one of the most important intellectual architects of the Islamic revival in the twentieth century. While he wrote most of his considerable output as Persian poetry, he neither considered himself a poet, nor could he easily engage in a conversation in Persian. By his own admission, his thought was vastly influenced by European philosophy, and yet his discourse is one of the largest and most profound bodies of work attempting to construct a Muslim selfhood ever produced. To be sure, Iqbal's discourse is replete with tensions and contradictions, but as I will try to show below, these contradictions are not primarily the result of his mixing European philosophy and Islamic thought, and therefore he should not be accused of bad eclecticism. As with many other social and political philosophers, some of these contradictions were the consequences of the development of his thought in their different stages. But many other contrarieties in his writings, as I argue below, were caused by his attempt to construct an Islamic subjectivity that he wished to build by invoking the monotheistic Godhead. Like many of his Islamist cohorts, Iqbal insisted that human agency is possible only if it is derived from the Divine Agency; and this, I will argue, is at the core of some of the most elemental tensions in his thought. However, this is not to dismiss the significance of his discourse in the creation of Muslim selfhood and agency. In the history of Western modernity, a very similar process of projecting the desired attributes of human empowerment and agency onto an image of a powerful omniscient God and then re-appropriating these attributes for humans has laid the foundations of the modern world in the West. A very analogous process has been at work in the Islamic world since mid-nineteenth century, producing dialectical tensions in the discourses of most of its prominent modernist thinkers, and the work of Iqbal is no exception in this regard. In fact, this type of contradiction is a source of dynamism in the Islamic world, which carries within itself the seeds of major changes in the cultures and polities of the Muslim regions involved.

Iqbal himself viewed his role as very much akin to that of "prophecy." Thus, in one of his most important works, *Javidnameh*, he prophesied a resurrection for the East wherein "jewels" would emerge from its rocks and its mountains would be shaken.[1] In the same

1. Iqbal, Muhammad. *Javidnameh* (Lahore: Sediqi, 1972), 37.

book he asserted that if the intention of "poetry" is forging of human subjects [*adam gari*], then poesy is the heir to prophethood.[2]

Muhammad Iqbal was born, apparently in 1877, at Sialkot, a border town in Punjab and near Kashmir, now an area of contention between Pakistan and India.[3] Iqbal's grandfather Shaikh Rafiq left the ancestral village of Looehar in Kashmir some time after 1857 and settled in Sialkot, working as peddler of Kashmiri shawls. Iqbal's father, Shaikh Nur Muhammad, was a pious Muslim and while not formally educated, was close to Sufi orders and interested in mystical pursuits. He made a living as a tailor and embroiderer. Iqbal's mother, Imam Bibi, was also devout, came from a working class family and, beyond an elementary knowledge of the Qur'an, had no formal education. Iqbal's father's business experienced some ups and downs, but on the whole, Sheikh Nur Muhammad's income was not sufficient to support a proper education for the children. Only the fact that Iqbal's elder brother acquired training as an engineer by joining the British Indian Army and then secured a supervisory job in the same army catapulted the family into the middle class and paved the way for Iqbal's education.

Iqbal graduated from high school in 1892, having already been tutored by a religious scholar who was well versed in Arabic and Persian literatures. A year later Iqbal entered the Scotch Mission College, a junior college that had been established in 1889 in Sialkot by European missionaries. As he graduated from high school, his parents married him to Karim Bibi. This marriage was a source of unhappiness and frustration for Iqbal, and he eventually broke it off in 1916. Having excelled in his studies, in 1895 Iqbal's father, encouraged by his teachers, decided to send him to Government College, a prestigious institution in Lahore. He graduated *cum laude* from Government College, receiving a Bachelor of Arts degree in 1897, and was awarded a scholarship toward a Master's degree in philosophy. At about the same time, his talents in poetry began to be recognized, and by the time he received his Master's degree in 1899, his reputation as a talented young poet was established among the intellectual circles of Lahore.

One of Iqbal's British professors at the Government College, Sir Thomas Arnold, a scholar of Islam and of modern Western philosophy, had a lasting influence on him. It was with Arnold's guidance and friendship that Iqbal developed the interest and preliminary skills to combine Islamic and modern Western ideas. It was also Arnold who persuaded Iqbal to pursue further post-graduate studies in Europe.

From the time of his graduation until 1905, Iqbal engaged in some junior academic positions and tried to enter the legal profession in Lahore. But he found the academic career unsatisfactory and failed the preliminary examinations for a career in law. In 1905, with the financial and moral support of his brother, Iqbal left India for England, where he studied to qualify for the Bar. He also enrolled in an undergraduate program at the Trinity College of Cambridge University, although he had already obtained a master's degree in India. Apparently Iqbal wished to benefit from the lectures of John McTaggart

2. *Javidnameh*, 44.
3. Most of the information on Iqbal's biography is based on accounts by Hafeez Malik and Lynda P. Malik, Muhammad Daud Rahbar and Iqbal's son, Javid Iqbal, in *Iqbal: Poet-Philosopher of Pakistan*, ed. Hafeez Malik (Columbia University Press, 1971).

and James Ward, two Hegel scholars, as well as those of prominent scholars of Iran and the Persian language, Edward G. Browne and Reynold A. Nicholson, all of whom were in Cambridge at that time. At the same time, Iqbal made an arrangement with Munich University in Germany to submit a dissertation on Philosophy for a doctoral degree. His dissertation, which was accepted for the fulfillment of his doctorate in 1907, was published a year later in London under the title *The Development of Metaphysics in Persia*, which laid the foundations for much of his subsequent intellectual output.

During the years that Iqbal spent in Europe, he met and befriended 'Atiya Begum Faizee, a wellborn young and educated Indian Muslim woman with a free spirit. They seem to have developed close intellectual and romantic bonds, but for unexplained reasons, they did not marry. After Iqbal's return to India in 1908, however, his family arranged a second marriage to Sardar Begum. This marriage seems to have gone sour because of anonymous letters Iqbal received tarnishing Sardar Begum's character. Eventually Iqbal's suspicions lifted; he married Sardar Begum and the couple had three children. Back in India, Iqbal started a professional career as an attorney at law with his British law degree while declining academic appointments, apparently because he thought an academic career would restrict his intellectual autonomy and because of its meager financial rewards. Yet his law practice, which officially existed until 1934, never thrived either, mostly because of Iqbal's lack of enthusiasm while he tried to maintain sufficient leisure time for his intellectual activities. Iqbal wrote most of his philosophical works after he settled in India in the form of poetry and in the Persian language. One of the most seminal of these books was *asrar-i khudi* (*Secrets of the Self*), published in 1915. Two years after this book was translated into English by Nicholson, in 1922, and while the significance of his thought had already became known in Europe, Iqbal was knighted by the British government. Iqbal visited Europe twice more in 1931 and 1932, when he met with diverse individuals as Henry Bergson, the Spanish scholar of Islamic thought Miguel Asin Palacios and the French orientalist and scholar of Sufism, Louis Massignon. In Italy he also met with Benito Mussolini before he invaded Ethiopia. In October and November 1933, Iqbal visited Afghanistan at the invitation of Muhammad Nadir Shah. It was after this journey that his health started to deteriorate gradually, and he died on April 20, 1938 in Lahore.

A New Muslim Subjectivity: The Self as the Pivot of the Universe

In his groundbreaking work the *Secrets of the Self*, Iqbal asserted that the very "form of existence" is there because of human selfhood.[4] It is because of human selfhood that the world reveals itself to us and the power and firmness that underlies the movement of the universe is a result of human selfhood.[5] The Persian term that Iqbal used to render the concept of selfhood was *Khudi*, literally meaning "I-ness" or selfhood. To be sure this term was not a neologism coined by Iqbal, but had been relatively rarely used in

4. Muhammad Iqbal, *Asrar-i Khudi* (Tehran: Moaseseh Farhang va Amuzesh-e 'Ali, 1991), 16; trans., 34.
5. *Asarar-i Khudi*, 18.

classical Persian literature. When it had been used, *Khudi* and its various synonyms had strong negative connotations of selfishness, narrow self-interest and egotism. Similarly, Iqbal was not the first person who used the concept of *selfhood* in a positive light, but his treatment of the concept remains the most elaborate among the various Muslim thinkers of modernity.

What Iqbal meant by the notion of selfhood was very closely related to the notion of subjectivity that is often considered to be the foundation of modern world. He used the term subjectivity in his early work, *The Development of Metaphysics in Persia*, which is basically an *étude* in Iranian thought seen through the lens of Western philosophy that he had been studying in Europe.[6] Nevertheless, what Iqbal had in mind by the notion of selfhood or *Khudi* is closely related to the idea of human subjectivity and agency. *Khudi* for Iqbal was synonymous with will and volition. As early as *The Development of Metaphysics in Persia*, Iqbal wrote, "The Semitic formula of salvation can be briefly stated in the words 'Transform your will'—which signifies that the Semitic looks upon will as the essence of the human soul."[7] The ability of the individual to make moral decisions through volition was a basic tenet of Islam according to Iqbal. "It is therefore evident," he wrote, "that Islam, so to speak, transvaluates the moral values of the ancient world and declares the preservation and intensification of the sense of human personality to be the ultimate ground of all ethical activities."[8] As such, subjectivity was real for Iqbal. Even though one may assume that the entire universe does not exist in its materiality, and that it is all but an illusion, Iqbal postulated, *Khudi* is not delusion. And once it reaches the state of maturity, subjectivity becomes indelible.[9]

Goal achievment was another very important attribute of selfhood for Iqbal. Thus he wrote in a poem:

Life is preserved by purpose;
Because of the goal its caravan-bell tinkles.
Life is latent in seeking …
Rise, O thou
Rise O thou who art strange to Life's mystery.
Rise intoxicated with the wine of purpose
A purpose shining as the dawn,
A blazing fire to all that is other than God,
Wining, captivating, enchanting men's hearts,
A destroyer of ancient falsehood,

6. See Muhammad Iqbal, *The Development of Metaphysics in Persia; A Contribution to the History of Muslim Philosophy* (Lahore: Bazm-i Iqbal, 1964), 38. In later years, this book was translated by the one of the intellectual gurus of the Iranian left, Amir-Hossein Arianpour, into Persian under the title *Sayr-i Falsafah dar Iran*. Tehran, Negah 2001. I thank Ali Gheissari for bringing this to my attention.
7. *Development of Metaphysics in Persia*, 82–83.
8. Iqbal, Muhammad. *Islam as an Ethical and a Political Ideal* (Lahore: Muhammad Ashraf, 1940), 69.
9. *Gulshan Raz-i Jadid*. N.D.NP. (attachment to *Zabur-i Ajam*), 170–71.

Fraught with turmoil, an embodiment of the Last Day.
We live by forming purposes
We glow with the sunbeam of desire.[10]

What motivates humans to seek goals is, according to Iqbal, desire (*arezoo*). It is quite possible that Iqbal chose this concept under the influence of the Hegelian notion of Desire (*Begierde*).[11] Again we see that Iqbal took a concept such as *arezoo*, which traditionally was considered a cognate of the notions of appetite and lust and disparaged, and gave it a new and positive meaning. Desire for Iqbal was what gave life to the material world and motivated the subject. It is the desire that give birth to understanding (*'aql*), social organization, customs, laws and novelties of sciences.[12] In a word, desire is the very foundation of the preservation of the self, and without cultivating desire in our hearts, we will be trampled by others.[13]

As such, Iqbal believed in the domination of nature by humans. He posited that humans were originally enmeshed in nature from which they have to extricate themselves.[14] Humans have been associated with nature for thousands of years and this association has caused them alienation from selfhood and subjectivity. As such, our destiny is to overcome the idol of nature, which we have carved out ourselves, and shatter it.[15] The self in Iqbal's philosophy could even lasso the sun and the moon:

Drunk with selfhood like a wave
Plunge into the stormy lave;
Who commanded thee to sit
With thy skirts about thy feet?

---

10. *Asrar-i Khudi*, 20–21; trans., 38–41 (translation slightly modified).
11. See Hegel, *The Phenomenology of Mind*. For example, "Self-consciousness is Desire. Convinced of the nothingness of this other [nature], it definitely affirms this nothingness to be for itself the truth of this other, negates the independent object, and thereby acquires the certainty of its own self, as true certainty, a certainty which it has become aware of in objective form." G.W.F Hegel, *The Phenomenology of Mind*, trans. J.B. Baillie (Harper and Row, 1967), 225. See also Kojeve's interpretation of Hegel's notion of Desire: "Philosopher must—Man must—in the very foundation of his being not only be passive and positive contemplation, but also be active and negating Desire. Now, if he is to be so, he cannot be a Being that *is*, that is eternally *identical* to itself, that is self-*sufficient*. Man must be an emptiness, a nothingness, which is not a pure nothingness (*reines Nichts*), but something that is to the extent that it annihilates Being, in order to realize itself at the expense of Being and to nihilate in being. Man is negating *Action*, which transforms given Being and, by transforming it, transforms itself." (Alexander Kojève. *Introduction to the Reading of Hegel: Lectures on the Phenomenology of Spirit* (Basic Books, 1969), 38.)
12. *Asrar-i Khudi*, 20.
13. Muhammad Iqbal, *Pas che bayad kard Ey Aqvam-i Sharq* (Lahore: Sediqi, 1972), 60. It should be noticed that using the concept of *arezoo*, Iqbal did not approve of closely related notions such as *havas* (lust), as we will see below, see, for example, *Asrar-i Khudi* 25, where he denounces *havas* as an idol to be broken.
14. In the *Zabur-i Ajam*, for example, Iqbal exhorts his reader to look into, "the meaning of [being] human... Man is still enmeshed in Nature, but he will be "cultivated" [*mozun*] one day" (112).
15. Muhammad Iqbal, *Payam-i Mashriq* (Lahore: Sediqi 1972), 65.

Let the tiger be thy prey:
Leave the mead and flowers gay,
Out toward the mountain press,
Tent thee in the wilderness.
Cast thy strangling rope on high,
Circle sun and moon in sky,
Seize a star from heaven's sphere,
Stitch it on thy sleeve to wear.[16]

In his *Javidnameh*, Iqbal proposed that since the entire heavens and the earth, are the property of God, the moon and the Pleiades are human hereditament.[17] The earth and the heavens are to obey the commands of the subject: "If you say do this, don't do that, they'd oblige."[18] As early as 1932, long before the United States sent exploratory missions to the moon, Iqbal was suggesting that sooner or later we would observe the moon's conditions and its caves and mountains.[19]

In a similar vein, Iqbal believed that whatever is not human is for conquest and nothing more. In his *Rumuz-i Bikhudi* (*Mysteries of Selflessness*), which was published in 1918 and was meant to complement the *Secrets of the Self*, Iqbal declared that conquest of the Other is deeply rooted in human psyche,

O You! Who has a Covenant
With the Invisible Being,
And who, like a Flood,
Is free from the boundary
Of a Shore!

Now, grow from the Soil
Of this Garden,
Like a Plant!
Attach your Heart
To the Invisible Being,
And fight against
The visible world!

The *visible* things
Of the world,
Describe the Power of the *Invisible*,

16. Muhammad Iqbal, *Zabur-i Ajam* (N.P.N.D.), 72; trans., 68.
17. He could justify this because in the Qur'an Adam is designated as God's successor on earth (2:30–34).
18. *Javidnameh*, 31.
19. *Javidnameh*, 32.

And they become a Preface
To its conquest!

Every thing Other
Exists here to be *conquered*,
And its breast is a Target
For your Arrow! [...]
Are you a dew drop?
Then possess the Sun!

If you can work wonders,
Then melt this Lion of ice
With your warm Breath!

Whoever was able
To conquer the visible things,
He built a world
From a single mote![20]

What underlies the notion of conquest for Iqbal is the notion of power. For him, power is the "manifestation" (*shu'ar*) of conquest, as conquest and domination are signs of strength.[21] In this view, life is nothing but power. Power even determines right and wrong:

Life is the seed and power the crop:
Power explains the mystery of truth and falsehood
A claimant, if he be possessed of power,
Needs no arguments for his claim.
Falsehood derives from power the authority of truth.
And falsifying truth deems itself true.
Its creative word transforms poison into nectar;
It says to Good, "Thou art bad," and Good becomes Evil[22]

On the other hand, power makes humans ethical, respecting the subjectivity of others. In a lecture that Iqbal delivered in 1908, he contended that weakness is the cause of evil, and that once a person develops a keen appreciation of his or her own sense of selfhood, he or she will, "respect the personalities of others and become perfectly virtuous."[23]

20. Iqbal, Muhammad. *Rumuz-i Bikhudi* (Tehran: Moaseseh Farhang va Amuzesh-e 'Ali, 1991), 131–32; trans., 157–59. Translation slightly modified. It must be noted that Iqbal set limits for his notion of conquest. For example in *Asrar-i Khudi* (59), he rejected *jihad* waged in the interest of "hunger for land" (*ju' al-ard*).

21. *Asrar-i Khudi*, 30; trans., 53.

22. *Asrar-i Khudi* 50; trans., 80.

23. *Islam as an Ethical and a Political Ideal*, 67.

Islam, he argued, in contrast to Christianity and Buddhism, does not approve of "self-renunciation, poverty and slavish obedience," which are concealed "under the beautiful name of humility and unworldliness."[24] In his 1930 book *The Reconstruction of Religious Thought in Islam*, which was a collection of six lectures he had delivered in Madras, Hyderabad and Aligarh, Iqbal invoked the Qur'an to say that it is natural for the self to maintain itself, and that to do so it seeks knowledge, self-multiplication and power. This was so, Iqbal argued, because the very first *sura*, or chapter of the Qur'an that was revealed to the Prophet, relates to the human need for knowledge and the second to the desire for power and the propagation of the human species.[25]

Master/Slave Dialectic and *Ressentiment*

Power for Iqbal possessed a historical dimension in which he saw the struggle between the powerful and the powerless, propelling the powerless to create a religion of renunciation and rejection of subjectivity. In his *Asrar-i Khudi* (*Secrets of the Self*), Iqbal wrote a poem relating the tale of a sheep who claims to be prophet and converts the lions by preaching the harms of eating meat, which led to the lions losing their teeth and claws:

> The weak, in order to preserve themselves,
> Seek devices from skilled intelligence.
> In slavery, for the sake of repelling harm,
> The power of scheming becomes quickened
> And when the madness of revenge gains hold,
> The mind of the slave meditates rebellion.

As a result of the sheep's preaching, the lion becomes like the sheep:

> He that used to make sheep his prey
> Now embraced a sheep's religion.
> The lions took kindly to a diet of fodder:
> At length their lion nature was broken.
> The fodder blunted their teeth
> And put out the awful flashing of their eyes.
> By degrees courage ebbed from their breasts,
> The sheen departed from the mirror.
> [...]
> They lost the power of ruling and the resolution to be independent,
> They lost reputation, prestige, and fortune.
> Their paws that were as Iron became strengthless;
> Their souls died and their bodies became tombs.
> Bodily strength diminished while spiritual fear increased:

24. *Islam as an Ethical and a Political Ideal*, 68.
25. Iqbal, Muhammad. *The Reconstruction of Religious Thought in Islam* (Lahore: Ashraf, 1999), 86.

Spiritual fear robbed them of courage.
Lack of courage produced a hundred diseases—
Poverty, pusillanimity, low-mindedness,
The wakeful lion was lulled to slumber by the sheep's charm:
He called his decline Moral Culture.[26]

The above tale, Iqbal believed, is the story of the Muslims who used to be like the lions, but by accepting the religion of weakness, they had lost all their power in historical time. He blamed the Sufi tradition and Plato, whose alleged influence on Sufism he bitterly decried.[27] He called Plato a member of the "ancient flock of sheep" whose obsession with the world of the "invisible" (*na-mahsus*) led him to reject the real world we live in. Plato, in this view, is responsible for the slumber and the "drowsy dream" of Muslims conditioned by a world steeped in opium for centuries. Sufism and its teacher, Plato, Iqbal believed, had robbed the Islamic world of its ability to act upon the world, leaving Muslims bereft of the desire to be active agents.[28]

In order to remedy this deplorable state of affairs, Iqbal prescribed a life lived dangerously. Following Hegel's idea that fear of death is responsible for the slavery of the bondsman in the slave/master struggle, Iqbal advised his readers not to live the life of a slave in fear of death. Each moment the slave dies from fear of death. The freeman has dignity, and his willingness to die bestows a new life upon him. The freeman as a subject is not apprehensive of death since he possesses *self*-consciousness and his death is but an instant.[29] To live dangerously, Iqbal argued, is decreed by God. Religion asks the Muslim to become a flame and pierce the rock when engaged in battle.[30] Thus, following the tradition of animals relating stories in Persian literature, Iqbal concocted a conversation between two gazelles, one of whom proposes seeking a life of security by taking refuge in sanctuary. The other gazelle objects by arguing that living in danger "brings out the best" in the subject.[31]

However, for Iqbal, living dangerously was not confined to the physical realm, as it was also a psychic phenomenon. In a poem called Paradise (*behesht*), Iqbal taunted paradise for not posing any challenge to humans. In heaven, Joseph would be a stranger to the pain of prison, Abraham wouldn't know the ordeal by fire, and Moses would not have a spark in his soul. But more importantly, in paradise, "Certainty is not assailed by doubt," and the comfort of "union" [*vesal*] is not plagued by separation's fear. How can one enjoy a path that is straight, fixed and clear? Iqbal then exhorts the reader, "Never live in a world devoid of flair and zest.//Where God exists, but Beelzebub doesn't exist."[32]

26. *Asrar-i Khudi*, 30–32; trans., 53–57.
27. It is interesting that despite his close familiarity with Western philosophy, Iqbal, like the early Muslims interested in Greek philosophy, conflated Neo-Platonic thought with that of Plato himself.
28. *Asrar-i Khudi*, 33–35; trans., 57–60.
29. *Javidnameh*, 185; trans., 134.
30. *Rumuze Bikhudi*, 120; trans., 119.
31. *Payam i Mashriq* 123; trans., 85–86.
32. *Payam-i Mashriq*, 131–32; trans. 91–92. Translation slightly modified.

Iqbal went as far as claiming that an external enemy is very helpful for the formation of the subject:

> I will declare the truth: thine enemy is thy friend;
> His existence is your prosperity.
> Whosoever knows the state of the Self
> Considers a powerful enemy to be a blessing from God.
> To the seed of Man the enemy is a rain-cloud;
> He awakens his potentialities.[33]

In a similar vein, Iqbal thought that struggle and warfare (*jang*) ripens the self into hard rock.[34]

Disciplining the Muslim Subject

The reason why the Muslims have lost their original subjectivity, according to Iqbal, is that they have lost their penchant for discipline. As a result of Sufi influence, the Muslims have become slothful: "'Tis pampered case hath made thee so wretched// A disgrace to Islam throughout the world. One can bind thee with the vein of a rose,// One can wound thee with a zephyr." Following Ibn Khaldun's diagnosis of the decline of the Muslim empire as a result of luxury, Iqbal also lambasted the Muslims for having indulged themselves in a life of comfort.[35] For a long time, Iqbal argued, the Muslim has lazed about in a bed of silk and "danced on tulips." Now it is time to get accustomed to rough burlap.[36]

In order to achieve his disciplining of the subject, Iqbal proposed a three-stage regiment. Apparently borrowing Nietzsche's notion of the camel as the first stage of human development, Iqbal posited that service and travail constitute the necessary first stage on the path toward selfhood and subjectivity. At this stage the self "eats seldom, sleeps little, and is inured to toil." Obedience and compulsion bring about the sweet fruit of liberty (*ikhtiar*).[37] At the second stage, discipline (*aiin*) makes the "un-self" (*na-kas*) into a self, as the subject who endeavors to conquer the moon and the Pleiades must first become regimented. The undisciplined self, like the camel, only cares for its corporeal self. It can only become human by bringing its halter into its own hands. In the hands of the Muslim subject, prayer is a dagger used to kill fornication, sedition and evil—the impediments on the path toward discipline. The most effective scheme for discipline, Iqbal often insisted, must be found in Islam. The very existence of the Muslim is dependent on the discipline

33. *Asrar-i Khudi*, 52; trans., 83. Translation slightly modified. Based on such a principle, one wonders if Iqbal would have thought that the Arab-Israeli conflict has paved the way for the Arab sense of subjectivity.
34. *Asrar-i Khudi*, 55; trans., 87.
35. See, for example, Ibn Khaldun, *The Muqaddimah; An Introduction to History* (Pantheon Books, 1958) vol. II, 119–22 for how luxury undermines a civilization.
36. *Asrar-i Khudi*, 40; trans., 66.
37. *Asrar-i Khudi*, 41; trans., 67–68.

of Islam, which constitutes the core of its creed. Just like in melodious music, "discipline" and order (*zabt*) are essential to the harmony of the community of Muslims.[38] Thus, fasting makes an assault on hunger and thirst, breaching the citadel of slothfulness. [39] The third stage is achieved when the "camel" of the self has come under control, which makes the subject rule the world and "wear the crown of Solomon." It is the stage when humans will become God's vicegerents and will exercise sway over the elements. In one word, it is at this stage, according to Iqbal, that humans will achieve subjectivity as God's successors on earth, and will dominate the universe and bring about a new world.[40]

As such, the body for Iqbal was something that had to be conquered. Earlier in his career, when he was not yet an ardent anti-rationalist, it was the mind that had to achieve the conquest. In a poem in the *Secrets of the Self*, Iqbal invoked the character of Ali, the cousin and son-in-law of the Prophet, to convey this idea. Iqbal used one of Ali's epithets, Bu Turab, to make the point. In Arabic, Bu Turab literally means the "father of earth,"

38. *Rumuz Bikhudi*, 115; trans., 101.

39. *Asrar-i Khudi*, 41–44; trans., 67–71. It seems that at some points Iqbal expressed some ambivalence toward the impact of discipline on the human self. In referring to the Qur'anic idea (33:72) of God offering the burden of "trust" in His vicegerency first to the Heavens, the earth and the mountains, which refuse, and then offering it to humans, as a symbol of their subjectivity and its burdens, Iqbal wrote: "Shall we, then, say no or yes to the trust of personality with all its attendant ills? True manhood [subjectivity] according to the Quran, consists of 'patience under ills and hardships.' At the present stage of the evolution of selfhood, however, we cannot understand the full import of the discipline which the driving power of pain brings. Perhaps it hardens the self against the possibility of dissolution." *The Reconstruction of Religious Thought in Islam*, 88.

40. *Asrar-i Khudi*, 44–46; trans., 71–75. It is worthwhile to quote more of Iqbal's rather hyperbolic description of human subjectivity in this poem:
God's vicegerent is as the soul of the universe,
His being is the shadow of the Greatest Name.
He knows the mysteries of part and whole.
He executes the command of Allah in the world.
When he pitches his tent in the side world,
He rolls up this ancient carpet [the universe as it is].
His genius abounds with life and desires to manifest itself;
He will bring another world into existence.
A hundred worlds like this world of parts and wholes
Spring up, like roses, from the seeds of his imagination.
He makes every raw nature ripe,
...
When that bold cavalier seizes the reins,
That steed of Time gallops faster.
His awful mien makes the Red Sea dry
He leads Israel out of Egypt,
At his cry, "Arise," the dead spirits
Rise in their bodily tomb, like pines in the field.

He gives a new explanation of Life,
A new interpretation of this dream.
...

connoting having mastery over earth and by extension over the "matter," including the human body:

> The Apostle of God gave him [Ali] the name Bu Turab;
> God in the Koran called him [Ali] the "Hand of Allah"
> Every one that is acquainted with Life's mysteries,
> Knows what is the inner meaning of the names of Ali
> The dark clay, whose name is the body—
> Our reason is ever bemoaning its tyranny.
> On account of it our lofty thought is earth-bound;
> It makes our eyes blind and our ears deaf.
> It has in its hand a two-edged sword of lust:
> Travelers' hearts are broken by this brigand.
> Ali, the Lion of God, subdued the body's clay
> And transmuted this dark earth to gold.
> Murtaza [Ali], by whose sword the splendour of Truth was revealed,
> Is named Bu Turab for his conquest of the body.[41]

This control over the body also extended to human sexuality. Sexuality, Iqbal argued, is necessary for the propagation of the species, and as such it is approved by the Qur'an.[42] However, he believed that the strong Ego must gain domination over the sexual impulses. In his *Reconstruction of Religious Life in Islam*, Iqbal engaged with Freud and interpreted him in a way that said that the forces of the disciplined self are chiefly in control of the entire psychic system.[43] In fact, one of the chief aims of religion, according to Iqbal, is the reconstruction of the "finite ego" by redirecting it away from "sex imagery" and toward a contact with God, as an "external life-process, and thus giving him [the finite ego] a metaphysical status of which we can have only a partial understanding in the half-choking atmosphere of our present environment."[44]

Freedom of the Disciplined Self

Whenever the notion of subjectivity is broached, the idea of personal freedom is also raised. In Iqbal's discourse, the relations between these two categories are indeed complex and susceptible to the tensions that characterize his thought in general. On a religious basis, Iqbal believed in a philosophical notion of human freedom. In the *Reconstruction of Religious Life in Islam*, he pointed to the Qur'anic account of Adam's expulsion from the Garden because of his disobedience of God's decree not to eat the fruit of the forbidden tree of eternal life, as an indication of deep human freedom:

41. *Asrar-i Khudi*, 47; trans., 76. Translation modified.
42. *Reconstruction of Religious Life in Islam*, 87.
43. *Reconstruction of Religious Life in Islam*, 24.
44. *Reconstruction of Religious Life in Islam*, 194.

Man's first act of disobedience was also his first act of free choice; and that is why, according to the Qur'anic narration, Adam's first transgression was forgiven; it is the self's free surrender to the moral ideal and arises out of a willing co-operation of free egos. A being whose movements are wholly determined like a machine cannot produce goodness. Freedom is thus a condition of goodness.[45]

One of the themes that Iqbal consistently posited was the notion of free will (*ikhtiyar*) and rejection of necessitarianism (*jabr*) and predestiny (*taqdir*). In a poem in the *New Gulshan-i Raz*, Iqbal seems to acknowledge the reality of both human freedom and necessity, but in the same poem he encourages the reader to transcend the realm of necessity and enter the realm of freedom:

What should I say about its [ego's] character?
Outwardly it is determined, inwardly it is free.
Such is the saying of the Lord of Badr [Muhammad],
That faith lies between determinism and indeterminism.
You call every creature to be determined,
To be confined to the chains of "near" and "far."
But the [human] soul is from the breath of the Creator,
Which lives in privacy with all its [Creator's] manifestations.
Determinism with regard to it is out of question,
For soul without freedom is not a soul.
...
From determinism it passed over to freedom.
When it (ego) removes from itself the dust of determinism,
It drives its world like a camel.
The sky does not revolve without its [ego's] permission,
Nor do stars shine without its grace[46]

Speaking through the voice of one his characters, the "Martian Sage," Iqbal proposes an even more forceful notion of humans having their destiny in their own hands:

If your heart bleeds on account of one destiny,
petition God to decree another destiny;
if you pray for a new destiny, that is lawful,
seeing that God's destinies are infinite.
Earthlings have gambled away the coin of selfhood,
not comprehending the subtle meaning of destiny;
its subtlety is contained in a single phrase—
'If you transform yourself, it too will be transformed.'

---

45. *Reconstruction of Religious Life in Islam*, 85.
46. *The New Gulshan-i Raz*, 164; (English trans., by Bashir Ahamad Dar. Lahore, Institute of Islamic Culture, 1964, 41).

Be dust, and fate will give you the winds;
be a stone, and it will hurl you against glass.
Are you a dew-drop? Your destiny is to perish;
are you an ocean? Your destiny is to endure.[47]

Iqbal's strong belief in subjectivity predisposed him to equate freedom often, but not always, with the domination over nature. In his *Persian Psalms* he wrote:

Happy is the day when you conquer this world
And pierce the bosom of the skies.
The moon will prostrate before you
And you throw over it a lasso of waves of smoke.
[At last] You will be free in this ancient world."[48]

This approach led Iqbal to condone what later we have come to know as instrumental rationality. In this view, the subject living in a complex environment is forced to reduce nature to a system that would provide him a form of control over the vagaries of natural phenomena. "The view of the environment as a system of cause and effect" is therefore "an indispensable instrument of the ego." In fact by viewing nature in this manner, the subject "understands and masters its environment and thereby acquires and amplifies its freedom."[49]

Iqbal seems to have harbored very ambivalent feelings on the freedom of thought. In one of his Urdu books, *The Rod of Moses* [*zarb-e Kalim*], he wrote that Muslims "own" the right of free thinking.[50] Freedom of thought is a gift from God, which cannot be restrained. However, a few pages later in the same book, he wrote that free thought can lead to the ruin of those with "low and mean" thoughts.[51] In light of his partially anti-democratic sentiments, as we will see below, by those with "low and mean" thoughts he must have meant the "masses." There seems to be little doubt that this type of ambivalence was closely related to Iqbal's viewing himself in a pedagogic role for the entire Muslim world, and his often bitter complaints that the Muslims were not yet ready for his message or for the construction of their own selfhood.

Yet, on an ontological level, Iqbal was prepared to declare that, "Man is a free responsible being; he is the maker of his own destiny; his salvation is his own business. There is no mediator between God and man. God is the birth right of every man."[52] This, however, in Iqbal's discourse, did not easily translate into the personal, social, cultural and political freedom of the individual of the late modern period. Thus, as early as 1908, wrote Iqbal, that, "It must, however, be confessed that the Muslims with their

47. *Javidnameh* (Arberry), 85; Persian, 107.
48. *The New Gulshan-i Raz*, 150; English trans. Bashir Ahamad Dar, 12.
49. *The Reconstruction of Religious Thought in Islam*, 108.
50. Iqbal, Muhammad. *The Rod of Moses* (Lahore: Iqbal Academy, 1983), 36.
51. *The Rod of Moses*, 46.
52. *Islam as an Ethical and a Political Ideal*, 69.

idea of individual freedom, could do nothing for the political improvement of Asia."[53] In fact, in his last book, *Armaghan-i Hijaz*, he bitterly complained about the freedom in the late modern period, contending that there are "a thousand shackles in its freedom."[54]

Mothering the Muslim Self

Iqbal's message for constructing a Muslim subjectivity was primarily addressed to men, as evidenced by his frequent use of the Persian term "*mard*" for man in much of his poetry. Yet, he also expressed some significant views on women.[55] In a poem, Iqbal declared Fatima, the Prophet's daughter, a perfect role model for Muslim women, because she was first, the daughter of the Holy Prophet; secondly, because she was the wife of Ali and thirdly, because she was the mother of Hassan and Hussein, the grandsons of the prophet.[56] The poem ends by claiming that the primary task of Fatima was to produce a Hussein to rejuvenate the Islamic community.[57] This type of "derivative" subjectivity was generally what Iqbal had to offer the Muslim women. Thus, in another couplet in the same poem, while Iqbal made the angels and the *jinn* obedient to the will of Fatima, "her will," he asserted, "was lost in the will of her husband."[58]

On the other hand, Iqbal found in women the "lost flame" of love that, as we will see below, was missing in the modern West. Thus, in a poem in *Javidnameh* he wrote:

man and woman are bound one to the other,
they are the fashioners of the creatures of verve [*shauq*].
Woman is the guardian of the fire of life,
her nature is the tablet of life's mysteries;
she strikes our soul's fire for us
and it is her substance that makes of the dust a man.
In her heart lurk life's potentialities,
from her glow and flame life derives stability;
she is a fire from which the sparks break forth,
body and soul, lacking her glow, cannot take shape.
What worth we possess derives from her values
for we are all images of her fashioning;

---

53. *Islam as an Ethical and a Political Ideal*, 95.
54. Iqbal, Muhammad. *Armaghan-i Hijaz* (Lahore: Sediqi, 1972), 95.
55. On Iqbal's muddled personal relations with women see his biography by Hafez Malik and Lynda P. Malik (Op. cit.). He married three women, one of them twice. While he did not marry the women he seems to have loved, he did not seem to have loved his married wives.
56. *Rumuz-i Bikhudi*, 138; trans., 184.
57. In anther poem in *The Rod of Moses* (57–58), Iqbal praised women for giving birth and nurturing great men such as Plato.
58. Yet, in another poem where Iqbal praised the mothering role of women, he admonished the men not to view women as their maid-servants which he thought was contrary to the teachings of the Qur'an.
(*Rumuz-i Bikhudi*, 136; trans., 177–78.)

if God has bestowed on you a glance aflame
cleanse yourself, and behold her sanctity.[59]

Here we can observe that even though Iqbal accords women an originary status, that of providing the passion that is necessary for the construction of his ideal male self, the woman herself is not a subject per se.

Accordingly, it is not surprising that Iqbal expressed notoriously negative views on women's emancipation in the West as well as it impacts on Islamic societies. It is very interesting that in his personal life he seems to have been enamored by ʿAtiya Begum Faizee, an intelligent, free-spirited Indian Muslim woman whom he met in Europe when he was a student. Yet, in his *Javidnameh*, Iqbal created a character, a "Martian damsel" whom he mocks as a false "prophetess." This character closely resembles the first wave western feminists who challenged Muslim women to reject traditional values. Thus, in a poem, Iqbal first gives voice to the "Martian damsel" expressing feminist ideas and then proceeds to denounce these ideas:

Women! Mothers! Sisters!
How long shall we live like fond darlings?
To be a darling here is to be a victim,
to be a darling is to be dominated and deprived.
We idly comb out our tresses
and think of men as our prey;
but man is a hunter in the guise of a quarry
and circles about you to lasso you.
[...]
To be his consort is a torment of life,
union with him is poison, separation from him sugar.
A twisting serpent he [is] - flee from his coils,
do not pour his poisons into your blood.
Maternity pales the cheeks of mothers;
O happy, to be free and without husband![60]

After these lines, Iqbal makes the "prophetess" celebrate the prospect that, as result of modern technology, it is now possible not only to screen the fetus and kill the undesired ones, but also to do away with pregnancy, childbirth and men altogether. Thus, according to Iqbal, by fighting against nature, women delude themselves that they are able to be freed from the tyranny of nature and the miseries that it imposes on them. In the next segment of the poem and in response to such views, Iqbal animated Rumi to express bewildered chagrin about the "new-fangled" modern age in which women fantasize about

59. *Javidnameh*, 69; trans., 60. Translation modified.
60. *Javidnameh*, trans., 88.

liberation.[61] Yet, in some other poems Iqbal expressed ambivalence toward women's situation. On the one hand, he opined that women's "first and foremost aim," should be procreation, and on the other hand, he implied that it would cause the oppression of women, a puzzle that he professed he could not resolve.[62]

On the question of women's veiling, Iqbal does not seem to have expressed clearly articulated views. In one poem he used one of the epithets of Fatima, *Batul*, which means chaste and "covered," as the most appropriate position for women.[63] Similarly, and very much in conformity with his disciplinary attitude toward the human body, he was clearly against women paying attention to their appearance and the use of make up.[64] Thus, he praised the "rustic woman" who is "illiterate, short-statured, fat, ugly," and "lacking in manners," but is "keeping her eyes down, mute and simple," and who is "very much sensitive about the responsibilities of motherhood." By way of contrast, he denounced the westernized woman, "that delicate 'modern' woman whose lap is empty," and who causes "many a tumult by her [coquettish] glances." Her shameless freedom, he declared, is a source of mischief.[65]

Some of Iqbal's other pronouncements on women were even more contradictory. In *The Reconstruction of Religious Thought in Islam*, while he was very critical of the legal inability of Muslim women to divorce their undesirable husbands, he fully supported the inheritance system with regard to women.[66]

The Self and God

Iqbal believed that the construction of the subject would be impossible without God. In *The Reconstruction of Religious Thought in Islam*, he argued that humans are bound to shape their own destiny as well as the destiny of their environment, by either adjusting themselves to its forces or by putting these forces to work for them. However, in this process, God acts a "coworker" with them, provided that they take the initiative.[67] Iqbal then proceeded to

61. *Javidnameh*, 111–12; trans., 88–89. It is very interesting to note that a few pages after this, Iqbal, by way of adulation, quoted a famous poem by Tahira Qurat al-'Ayn, the Babi woman who in the mid-19th century defied traditional religious values regarding women to such an extent that it led to her execution by the Qajar government in Iran in 1852 (*Javidnameh*, 118, 125; trans., 92, 96). Throughout his career, Iqbal had nothing but admiration for Tahira.
62. *The Rod of Moses*, 59.
63. *Armaghan-i Hijaz*, 94.
64. *Armaghan-i Hijaz*, 92.
65. *Rumuz-i Bikhudi*, 137; trans., 180–81.
66. *The Reconstruction of Religious Thought in Islam*, 169–70. The inconsistencies and contradictions of Iqbal, especially regarding women, are indeed bewildering. But, we should always be mindful of contradictions of the paradigm of mediated subjectivity, to which Iqbal's discourse belongs. Human subjectivity in this paradigm is derived from that of God, and often it comes to be perceived as negating God's subjectivity. For this reason, this paradigm is replete with contradictions. With regard to women, this contradiction is intensified, at least partly because women's bodies are thought to be obstacles and snares for men's discipline, which is necessary for the process of subjectification. See more on this issue in the chapter on Maududi.
67. *The Reconstruction of Religious Thought in Islam*, 12.

quote the Qur'anic verses (2:30-33) of human vicegerency to God, wherein God places Adam as his successor on earth by virtue of Adam's conceptual ability to name objects, despite protests from the angels. For Iqbal, like many of the modernist Islamic thinkers, this was the only path toward selfhood and subjectivity. Iqbal argued that the vicegerency verses in the Qur'an have bestowed on humans enormous potentialities and powers, and as a result humans will become their own "Imam, prayer and sanctuary." In the vicegerency paradigm, Iqbal thought, man becomes "himself the Ink, himself the Book and the Pen." Little by little, human potentialities will be realized and become visible.[68]

Consequently, Iqbal's path to human empowerment and subjectivity, entailed the Divine Subject whom he considered to be the real Self, and from whom human selfhood is derived. In this view, humans are merely trustees, and the real proprietor is God.[69] Iqbal expressed the same idea even more forcefully and explicitly when he had Rumi say: "Man is a sword, and God is the Swordsman; the world is the whetstone for this sword."[70] In his "pantheistic" moments, Iqbal elaborated on this very important theme:

> I have conceived the Ultimate Reality as an Ego; and I must add now that from the Ultimate Ego only egos proceed. The creative energy of the Ultimate Ego, in whom deed and thought are identical, functions as ego-unities. The world, in all its details, from the mechanical movement of what we call the atom of matter to the free movement of thought in the human ego, is the self-revelation of the "Great I am." Every atom of Divine energy, however low in the scale of existence, is an ego. But there are degrees in the expression of egohood [subjectivity]. Throughout the entire gamut of being runs the gradually rising note of egohood until it reaches its perfection in man. That is why the Quran declares the Ultimate Ego to be nearer to man than his neck-vein. Like pearls do we live and move and have our being in the perpetual flow of Divine life.[71]

Sometimes Iqbal gives the impression that the entire purpose of God is the forging of human subjectivity. For example, in one of the poems of *Javidnameh* that Iqbal attached to the end of *Reconstruction of Religious Thought in Islam*, he urged us to view our "egohood" (the term he often used to render subjectivity) through that of God:

See thyself, then with God's light.
If thou standest unshaken in front of this light,
Consider thyself as living and eternal as He!
That man alone is real who dares—
Dares to see God face to face!
What is 'ascension'? only a search for a witness
Who may finally confirm thy reality—
A witness whose confirmation alone makes thee eternal[72]

---

68. *Javidnameh*, 68; trans., 59–60.
69. *Javidnameh*, 108; trans., 86.
70. *Javidnameh*, 36; trans., 40. Translation slightly modified.
71. *The Reconstruction of Religious Thought in Islam*, 71–72.
72. *Reconstruction of Religious Thought in Islam*, 198.

Iqbal even considered the "climax of religion," to be the "discovery of the ego as an individual," which, he asserts, is deeper than a selfhood which could be constructed conceptually through philosophy. In fact, it is only in "contact with the Most Real that the ego discovers its uniqueness, its metaphysical status, and the possibility of improvement in that status."[73]

An Action-Oriented Ego

Iqbal's version of human subjectivity via Divine Subjectivity is action-oriented. In his *Secrets of the Self*, he excoriates the poet who has given up the passion for life. Such a poet, Iqbal insists, destroys the life of a people. One of the gravest sins of such a poet, in Iqbal's estimation, was that, "He plunges thee in a sea of contemplation//And makes thee a stranger to action."[74] Thought, for Iqbal, was primarily a vehicle to action. As such, in the realm of philosophy, he preferred Kant's emphasis on action, in contrast to Descartes' alleged emphasis on thought:

> It is in the ego's effort to *be* something that he [the ego] discovers his final opportunity to sharpen his objectivity and acquire a more fundamental "I am" which finds evidence of its reality not in the Cartesian "I think" but in the Kantian "I can." The end of the ego's quest is not emancipation from the limitations of individuality; it is on the other hand, a more precise definition of it. The final action is not an individual act, but a vital act which deepens the whole being of the ego, and sharpens his will with the creative assurance that the world is not something to be merely seen or known through concepts, but something to be made and re-made by continuous action. It is a moment of supreme bliss and also a moment of the greatest trial for the ego.[75]

This frame of mind led Iqbal to articulate quite negative views on theory, philosophy and intellectualism, despite his own strong penchant for all three. In his early work, namely *The Development of Metaphysics in Persia*, Iqbal was very much favorably inclined toward Islamic and Iranian philosophers such as Ibn Sina (Avicenna; d. 1037). But later in his work, he became very critical of the philosophical tradition for its alleged discouragement of action, among other things. Thus, in a poetic conversation that Iqbal contrived between a "bookworm" and the proverbial "moth" of Persian poetry, he poked fun at the two giants of Islamic philosophy, Ibn Sina and Farabi:

I hear that in my library one night
A bookworm spoke thus to a moth:

---

73. *Reconstruction of Religious Thought in Islam*, 184. In a similar vein, in *Armaghan-i Hijaz* (121), Iqbal wrote:
"The self received its being from God's Self,
The self's manifestation is from God's Manifestation.
About this shining pearl [human ego] I know not where,
It could be then without the Ocean there."
74. *Asrar-i Khudi*, 37; trans., 62. Translation slightly modified.
75. *The Reconstruction of Religious Thought in Islam*, 198.

"I have lodged in [Ibn] Sina's tomes
And have consumed much of Farabi's manuscripts.
About life's mystery,
And am just as much in the dark
About it as before."

The half-burnt moth gave it a fine reply:
"You will not find life's mystery
Explained in books.
However, here it is:
What gives to life intensity
Is ardency (*tapesh*)
It lends life wings
With which to fly."[76]

For Iqbal, the distaste toward theory was closely related to his orientation toward action and its correlate, the notion of perpetual change. In *The Reconstruction of Religious Thought in Islam* he wrote:

> The Qur'an opens our eyes to the great fact of change, through the appreciation and control of which alone it is possible to build a durable civilization. The cultures of Asia and in fact, of the whole ancient world, failed because they approached Realty exclusively from within and moved from within outwards. This procedure gave them theory without power, and on mere theory no durable civilization can based.[77]

In the same book, Iqbal criticized what he considered to be the detrimental impact of Greek philosophy on Muslims because of its alleged "speculative nature," which enjoyed theory at the expense of being "neglectful of fact." Thus, according to Iqbal, the Greek speculative and deductive cosmology retarded the practical Arabs' temperament from realizing its potential for two centuries. [78] This approach led Iqbal to propose a theory of

---

76. *Payam-i Mashariq*, 103; trans., 63–64. Translation slightly modified.
77. *The Reconstruction of Religious Thought in Islam*, 14–15. On page 146, Iqbal further wrote, "As a cultural movement Islam rejects the old static view of the universe and reaches a dynamic view." Yet, Iqbal was facing the classical dilemma of the tension between change and permanence in religion. "The ultimate spiritual basis of all life, as conceived by Islam, is eternal and reveals itself in variety and change. A society based on such a conception of Reality must reconcile, in its life, the categories of permanence and change. It must possess eternal principles to regulate its collective life, for the eternal gives a foothold in the world of perpetual change. But eternal principles when they are understood to exclude all possibilities of change, which, according to the Qur'an, is one of the greatest "signs" of God, tend to immobilize what is essentially mobile in its nature. The failure of Europe in political and social science illustrates the former principle [lack of eternal principles], the immobility of Islam in the last 500 years illustrates the latter [lack of change]. What is the principle of movement in the nature of Islam? This is known as 'Ijtihad'," 147–48.
78. *The Reconstruction of Religious Thought in Islam*, 128–31.

knowledge that was hyper-pragmatist in its nature. He wrote, for example, "Knowledge must begin with the concrete. It is the intellectual capture of and power over the concrete that makes it possible for the intellect of man to pass beyond the concrete. As the Qur'an says: 'O company of *djin* and men, if you can overpass the bounds of the Heaven and the Earth, then overpass them. But by power alone shall ye overpass them.'"[79]

Toward an Autonomous Ego

Unlike many other Islamist modernists, Iqbal's discourse, in significant instances and manners, transcends the paradigm of mediated-subjectivity (human subjectivity that is contingent upon Divine Subjectivity) and approaches the notion of the self-sufficient subject. As we have seen above, Iqbal often advocated the construction of human subjectivity through a process of proximation toward the Divine, what can be described as "theomorphic subjectivity". However, he expressed serious concerns about the loss of the human self in this process, "The only danger to which the ego is exposed in this Divine quest is the possible relaxation of his activity caused by his enjoyment of and absorption in the experiences that precede the final experience. The history of Eastern Sufism shows that this is real danger [...] And the reason is obvious. The ultimate aim of the ego is not to see something, but to be something."[80] In a similar vein, Iqbal was very critical of the widely accepted notion of *tavakkol* (Ar. *tawakkul*), meaning delegation of human agency to God, and as such, living a life of passivity. The concept of *tavakkol* was traditionally viewed as a highly virtuous approach to life in many parts of the Muslim world in medieval period.[81] Iqbal blamed the Iranians and the Persian culture for infusing this attitude among the Arabs and, by implication, the Muslims.[82]

Thus, with some minor exceptions, throughout his career Iqbal fought against a deterministic view of life which negated the notion of human agency: "The world regarded as a process realizing a pre-ordained goal is not a world of free, responsible moral agents; it is only a state on which puppets are made to move by a kind of pull from behind."[83] The positing of human agency has brought many modernist Islamic thinkers face to face with the conundrum of choosing between human subjectivity and agency and that of God's. In contrast to many of his fellow modernists, Iqbal opted for confirming human agency in this difficult quandary: "No doubt, the emergence of egos endowed with the power of spontaneous and hence unforeseeable action is, in a sense, limitation of the freedom of the all inclusive Ego [God]. But this limitation is not externally imposed. It is born out of His own creative freedom whereby He has chosen finite egos to be participators of His life, power and freedom."[84] In fact, according to

79. *The Reconstruction of Religious Thought in Islam*, 131.
80. *The Reconstruction of Religious Thought in Islam*, 197–98.
81 Tawakkul: "Verbal noun of *mūdur* of form V of *wakala* 'to entrust [to someone], have confidence [in someone]', a concept in Islamic religious terminology, and especially that of Ṣūfism, with the sense of dependence upon God." *Encylopedia of Islam*, Third Edition.
82. *Rumuz-i Bikhudi*, 120–21; trans., 121–22.
83. *The Reconstruction of Religious Thought in Islam*, 54.
84. *The Reconstruction of Religious Thought in Islam*, 79–80.

Iqbal, the human ego, "shares in the life and freedom of the Ultimate Ego Who, by permitting the emergence of a finite ego, capable of private initiative, has limited this freedom of His own free will."[85]

This scheme of sharing subjectivity between God and humans was deeply rooted in Iqbal's analysis of Sufi tradition. As we saw before, Iqbal forcefully rejected the world-renouncing aspects of Sufism. Yet, he had nothing but praise for some of the "extravagant" concepts in that tradition. Unlike many of the Islamist theorists who had first sought human subjectivity through a theomorphic path, only later to announce the annihilation of the human subject in the "Oceanic" Being, Iqbal's human subject is enduring: "In the higher Sufism of Islam, unitive experience [communion with God] is not the finite ego effacing its own identity by some sort of absorption into the infinite Ego; it is rather the Infinite passing into the loving embrace of the finite."[86] In the *New Rose Garden of Mystery*, Iqbal advised the proverbial "traveler" [*musafir*] of the Sufi path to God, to be "enduring" [*javdan zi*] since "To be lost in His sea is not our destiny // And if you absorb Him, it is not annihilation."[87]Indeed Iqbal interpreted the famous pronouncement of Hallaj (d. 922) "I am the Truth" as the positing of human subjectivity and the reality of the ego that is not to be effaced, even vis-à-vis God's visage.[88] In *Javidnameh*, Zindehrud, who is Iqbal's own persona, asks Hallaj if the end of the theomorphic path is "not-being [*fana*]?" To which Hallaj responds, "not being is to be ignorant of the Gnostics' path," since "non-being can never discover Existence."[89]

Iqbal's very positive attitude toward human subjectivity was also manifested in an unusual interpretation of the notion of the finality of revelation. Among the orthodox, this idea has normally meant that Muhammad was the last emissary of God, often signifying the idea that Islam is the most perfect religion and there would be no prophet after Muhammad. But for Iqbal, the finality of revelation meant the maturity of the human subject and its self-sufficiency:

> In Islam prophecy reaches its perfection in discovering the need for its own abolition. This involves the keen perception that life cannot forever be kept in leading strings; *that in order to achieve full self-consciousness man must finally be thrown back on his own resources.* The abolition of priesthood and hereditary kingship in Islam, the constant appeal to reason and experience

---

85. *The Reconstruction of Religious Thought in Islam*, 108. In the next page Iqbal wrote: "It cannot, however, be denied that the idea of destiny runs throughout the Qur'an. This point is worth considering, more especially because Spengler, in his *Decline of the West*, seems to think that Islam amounts to a complete negation of the ego." Iqbal also stated that as a matter of historical factuality, fatalism has prevailed in the Islamic world for many centuries, which he contended was far removed from the spirit that Islam originally imparted to its followers. P. 110.
86. *The Reconstruction of Religious Thought in Islam*, 110. Ali Shariati and Ayatollah Khomeini, for example, attempted to propound a form of human subjectivity through similar theomorphic paths. However, eventually both effaced the subject. See my *God and Juggernaut: Iran's Intellectual Encounter with Modernity*, Chapter 4.
87. *Gulshan-I Raz-i Jadid*, 159; Trans., 22–23.
88. Iqbal, Muhammad. *Speeches and Statements of Iqbal* (Lahore: Al-Manār Academy, 1948), 152.
89. *Javidnameh*, 132; trans., 101.

> in the Qur'an and the emphasis that it lays on Nature and History as sources of human knowledge, are all different aspects of the same idea of finality.[90]

This position in turn led Iqbal to posit a very anthropocentric and humanist view at times. Thus, in a poem in the *Persian Psalms*, he placed humans as the center of the universe, even slyly questioning the centrality of the Divine,

> What is the world? The temple of my thought,
> The seen projection of my wakeful eye;
> Its far horizons, I capture by a glance,
> The circle of existence, by my spinning compass wrought.
>
> Being and Nothingness is an effect of my seeing and not seeing;
> Time and space, [reflect] the audacity of my mind,
> Movement and repose, are my heart's wizardry
> Whereby are secrets known, and mysteries taught.
>
> That other world, where reaped is all our sown [next world],
> Its light and fire are of my rosary made;
> I am fate's instrument, and hold a hundred songs
> Wherever thought is played, it is from my instrument.
> Where is Thy sign? In Thee my life is lasting;
> *Where is Thy world? These twain [this world and next] are mine alone.*[91]

In another instance of unabashed humanism, Iqbal wrote:

> "Rise up! The hour is here
> For Man's epiphany;
> The stars bow, as they must,
> To this handful of dust.
>
> The Secret that was
> Hidden in Being's breast,
> By the audacity of Clay and Water [human],
> Became quarrelsome.[92]

In a poem in the *New Rose Garden of Mystery*, Iqbal went even as far as claiming that the universe exists because of humans:

> Between us and the world there is a secret tie;
> For every object owes its being to a seeing eye.

90. *The Reconstruction of Religious Thought in Islam*, 126 (emphasis added).
91. *Zubur-i Ajam,* 17; trans., 11. Translation modified (emphasis added).
92. *Zabur-i Ajam,* 63; trans., 55. Translation modified

It is all lost if no one sees it,
When seen, [then] it is hills and seas.
A plant entirely nurtured by our sight,
Along with us it grows in height.
Strange is the mutual bond of seen and seer.
In every mote's heart is this prayer:
"O seer, see me, see me,
And make me be."
For everything it is the perfect state
To be in someone's sight.
It is a loss for it to be concealed from us
And not be lit up by our consciousness.
This world is nothing but our own self-revelatory experience,
For how could light or sound without us be?[93]

Individual or Collective Subject (Ego)?

Throughout most of the different phases of his intellectual career, Iqbal was both a fervent supporter of the individual and the collectivity virtually simultaneously. He was convinced of the significance of these two categories for a functioning modern society. In the first book where he seriously elaborated on the notion of human subjectivity, *The Secrets of the Self*, Iqbal's emphasis was on the construction of subjectivity, or what he called "egohood," without explicitly emphasizing the individual or the collectivity as its carrier. Yet, because of the Persian term he used to render the notion of subjectivity, namely *khudi*, meaning selfhood, it can easily be interpreted that his emphasis was on the individual. In the sequel to *Secrets of the Self*, which he called *The Mysteries of Selflessness* (alternatively translated as *The Secrets of Collective Life*), Iqbal placed more emphasis on the collectivity, seemingly attempting to balance out his stress on the idea of the individual. This alternation continued in most of Iqbal's later work, signifying the impossibility of exclusively opting for one at the expense of the other in the contemporary world.

Theologically, and in conformity with the monotheistic eschatology, Iqbal believed that each person will encounter God as an individual. Quoting the Qur'anic verses (19: 93-95) that said, "and each one of them shall come to Him on the day of Resurrection as a single individual," Iqbal argued that, "It is with the irreplaceable singleness of his individuality that the finite ego will approach the infinite ego to see for himself the consequences of his past action and to judge the possibilities of his future."[94] In fact, Iqbal emphasized that in Islam the individual is responsible for his or her own deeds, and no other individual can be held responsible for the deeds of others:

93. *Gulshan-i Raz-I Jadid*, 152; trans., 12–13. Translation slightly modified.
94. *The Reconstruction of Religious Thought in Islam*, 117.

> The Qur'an in its simple and forceful manner emphasizes the individuality and uniqueness of man, and has, I think, definite views of his destiny as a unity of life. It is in consequence of this view of man as a unique individuality, which makes it impossible for one individual to bear the burden of another, and entitles him only to what is due to his own personal effort, that the Qur'an is led to reject the idea of redemption [in contrast to Christianity].[95]

In his more "psychological" reasoning, Iqbal also believed that the integrity of the individual was essential to the notion of subjectivity and selfhood: "The nature of the ego is such that, in spite of its capacity to respond to other egos, it is self-centered and possesses a private circuit of individuality excluding other egos other than itself. In this alone consists its reality as an ego."[96] The unique experiences of each individual made him or her, in Iqbal's view, the foundation of free choice. Thus, despite his rejection of liberal individual freedom, Iqbal was ironically laying down its very philosophical foundations:

> The dentist may sympathize with my toothache, but cannot experience the feeling of my toothache. My pleasures, pains and desires are exclusively mine, forming a part and parcel of my private ego alone. My feelings, hates and loves, judgments and resolutions, are exclusively mine. God himself cannot feel, judge and choose for me when more than one course of action is open to me.[97]

Historically, Iqbal argued, the growth of the individual was stunted because of the conservative forces that took the upper hand in the Islamic lands. The devastation of the Mongol invasion of the Muslims' lands forced them to put their emphasis on the integrity of the collectivity, at the expense of the individual. Thus in response to the desolation brought about by the Mongols and:

> [f]or the fear of further disintegration, which is only natural in such a period of political decay, the conservative thinkers of Islam focused all their efforts on the one point of preserving a uniform social life for the people by a jealous exclusion of all innovations in the law of Shari'at as expounded by the early doctors of Islam. Their leading idea was social order, and there is no doubt that they were partly right, because organization does to a certain extent counteract the forces of decay. But they did not see, and our modern Ulema do not see, that the ultimate fate of a people does not depend so much on organization as on the worth and power of individual men. In an over-organized society, the individual is altogether crushed out of existence [...] The only effective power, therefore, that counteracts the forces of decay in a people is the rearing of self concentrated individuals. Such individuals alone reveal the depth of life.[98]

At the beginning of his *Mysteries of Selflessness*, however, Iqbal attempted to even out his foregrounding of the individual as the carrier of his notion of "egohood." This section is worth quoting at length:

---

95. *The Reconstruction of Religious Thought in Islam*, 95.
96. *The Reconstruction of Religious Thought in Islam*, 72.
97. *The Reconstruction of Religious Thought in Islam*, 100.
98. *The Reconstruction of Religious Thought in Islam*, 151.

Close association of an Individual
With his Community,
Is a great blessing for him!
His nature achieves perfection
By the "Community"!

As much as possible
Make friends with your community,
And enhance the strength
Of free people with your help!

Never forget the saying
Of the Holy Prophet:
"Satan keeps himself away
From the Community!"

The "Individual" and the "Nation"
Are Mirror for each other!
They are like the String and the Pearl,
And the Milky Way and the star!

Just as an Individual is honoured
By his association with the Community,
Similarly a Nation takes form[99]
From the Individuals!

When an Individual is lost
Into the Nation,
He is like a Drop,
Expanded into the Sea!

Then he is a representative
Of the character
Of his good Forefathers,
And the "Past" and the "Future"
Reflect themselves in his Person!

99. The word that Iqbal often used for community was *millat*, which in pre-modern times meant a religious creed and the community of its followers. In modern times *millat* has come to mean the nation-state. Iqbal was very much against the notion of the modern nation-state and his use of "nation" referred to a religious community. For Iqbal's negative views on modern nationalism see, for example, Muhammad Iqbal, *Speeches and Statements*, 38. Yet, in the realpolitick milieu of his later years, Iqbal advocated the creation of Pakistan as an independent nation for the Muslims of the subcontinent.

In other words, the "Past"
And the "Future" are united
In his being,
And like Eternity,
His Times are endless!

In his heart
The desire to blossom
Is from the Nation!
And the reward of his deeds
Is from the Nation!

His Body as well as his Soul
Is from the Nation!
His external condition
As well as his internal condition
Is from the Nation!

Whenever he speaks,
He speaks by the Tongue of his Nation!
Until in reality,
He becomes the Nation!

In fact, his Singularity
Is strong and stable
From the Plurality,
And the plurality
Becomes a Singularity
In his being!

For example, if a word
Is taken out of a verse,
The beauty of its real meaning
Is lost!
[...]
An Individual
So long as he is an "Individual"
Can't be conscious of an "Ideal",
And his physical and spiritual powers
Are inclined to decay!

As a matter of fact,
It is the Nation, which instructs him
With "Discipline" and "Self-control"

And tames him to go
As soft as the morning-breeze!

The Nation compels
him to stand still at a certain Spot
Just like the Cypress!
It binds together his hands and feet,
To make him free![100]

As we can see in this poem, even though Iqbal emphasizes the collectivity, he does not attempt to obliterate the individual. In a very Durkheimian manner, his objective seems to be to bring these two categories to some sort of reconciliation. For example, just like Durkheim, who attempted to show that the individual by itself is not capable of forming his or her own thought processes, Iqbal in this poem points out that the individual alone is not capable of forming social ideals and social goals.[101] In fact, in the second poem in *Mysteries of Selflessness*, again just like Durkheim, Iqbal contended that without the community the individual is incapable developing cognitively.[102]

Near the end of his life, however, it seems Iqbal placed more weight on the community without annihilating the individual. Thus, in his *Armgaghn-i Hijaz*, which was published in 1938, he wrote, "'I am the truth' [*analhaq*] is but the station of the Almighty. Is the gallows his [one who proclaims "I am the truth," as Hallaj did] desert or not? If an individual utters it, it is better to reprove him, but if the collectivity claims it, it is not wrong."[103]

Subjectivity as Authenticity

Iqbal's notion of egohood was, as we have seen, in many ways deeply influenced by the Western notion of subjectivity (even though he used primarily Islamic sources and symbols to articulate it). This entailed the construction of a Muslim self which stood in strong opposition to an "other," i.e., the West, which he contended was the source of much of the misery among the Muslims. Yet, Iqbal was very critical of the actual state of Muslims in recent history. He expressed these ideas in a poem in *The Persian Psalms*:

The East that holds the heavens in its imagination
Is alienated from itself,
The flames of its desire [*arezoo*] have died.

The burning glow of living birth
Pulses no more in its dark earth;

100. *Rumuz-i Bikhudi*, 89–90; trans., 9–12.
101. In *The Elementary Forms of Religious Life* one of the most significant contentions of Durkheim was to demonstrate the crucial role of community in the formation of the individual in its sociological, linguistic, and cognitive dimensions.
102. *Rumuz-i Bikhudi*, 92.
103. *Armaghan-i Hijaj*, 70.

It stands upon the river side
And gazes at the surging tide.

The fire in its temple is dead!
Its Magian still holds a cup in his hand,
But stale the wine is in his glass.
[...]
The East is waste and desolate,
The West is more bewildered yet
The ardent quest inspires no more,
Death reigns supreme the whole world o'er.[104]

In a couplet in *Armaghan-i Hijaz*, Iqbal described the material conditions of Muslims as "poverty-stricken" (*faqeh-mast*) and "tatterdemalion" (*jhendehpush*).[105] In the *Persian Psalms*, he likened the East to the dust of a roadway whose groaning is silent and whose sigh has no vigor.[106]

Similarly, in two long poems published in a book under the title *Complaint and the Answer* (*Shikwa va Javab-i Shikwa*) Iqbal lamented the desolate state of Muslims and even took God to task for having abandoned the Muslims in their unhappy state, to which God responds that the Muslims themselves are at fault:

The only people in the world of every skill bereft are you.
The only race which cares not how it fouls its nest are you,
Haystacks that within them concealed the lightning's fire are you.
Who love by selling tombs of their sires are you.
If as traders of tombstones you have earned such renown,
What is there to stop you in trading in gods made of stone?[107]

Yet despite all his self-critique, Iqbal's attempt to reconstruct the Muslim self entailed an "other" very much in conformity with what later came to be known as "identity politics" Thus, in a poem in *The Mysteries of Selflessness*, Iqbal declared that to be independent, a community has to abandon foreign mores and culture (*shu'ar*). Once the Muslims' collective mind is forfeited to foreigners, their spirit would leave them, and the spiritless spirit of foreigners would replace it. As a result, Muslims' discourse is not their own, and their wants and desires are all borrowed from the "other." He then advised the Muslims to come back to "themselves."[108]

Really you are a Sun;—
Therefore, look into yourself,

104. *Zabur-i Ajam*, 49–50; trans., 40–41. Translation modified.
105. *Armaghan-i Hijaz*, 15
106. *Zabur-i Ajam*, 81.
107. *Complaint and Answer*, 70.
108. *Rumuz-i Bikhudi*, 144.

And don't borrow light
From another's Star!

You've inscribed the picture
Of a stranger in your Heart;—
Thus you've lost Elixir,
And gained the dust only![109]

Iqbal then asserted that the lowest ranking among the Muslims is equal in value to one hundred men from another community.[110] To be sure, the "other" that Iqbal had in mind was the West, and in the construction of his ipseity, he went as far as recommending, for example, Ayurvedic and *Unani* medicine over modern medicine, neglecting the fact that *Unani* (Ionian) medicine was Greek in origin and that Ayurvedic medicine was Hindu.[111]

Othering the Occident

By his own admission, what Iqbal was doing was a re-interpretation of Islam in light of modern Western philosophy.[112] Yet, his construction of the Muslim self very much resulted in creating an alterity called the "West". His criticism of the Occident went as far back as the ancient Greeks. As we saw before, Iqbal assailed the Greeks for their alleged anti-empirical and "speculative" cosmology. To this he added the criticism that their understanding of time was circular, as opposed to linear, and as such obstructed any notion of progress in history. Iqbal thought Muslim thinkers had a very different and progressive perception of time. Thus, Ibn khaldun's chief merit, according to Iqbal:

> [L]ies in his acute perception of and [giving] systematic expression to, the spirit of the cultural movement of which he was the most brilliant product. In the work of this genius, the anti-classical spirit of the Qur'an scores its final victory over Greek thought; for with Greeks time was either unreal, as in Plato and Zeno, or moved in a circle, as in Heraclitus and the stoics. Whatever may be the criterion by which to judge the forward steps of a creative movement, the movement itself, if conceived as cyclic, ceases to be creative. Eternal recurrence is not eternal creation; it is eternal repetition. We are now in a position to see the true significance of the intellectual revolt of Islam against Greek philosophy. The fact that this revolt originated in a purely theological interest shows that the anti-classical spirit of the Qur'an asserted itself in spite of those who began with a desire to interpret Islam in the light of Greek thought.[113]

---

109. *Rumuz-i Bikhudi*, 145; trans., 204.
110. *Rumuzi-i Bikhudi*, 145; trans., 204.
111. *Speeches and Statements of Iqbal*, 73.
112. For example, in *Compliant and Answer* (8) Iqbal wrote, "Most of my life has been spent in the study of European philosophy, and that viewpoint has become my second nature. Consciously or unconsciously I study the realities and truth of Islam from the same pont of view. I have experienced this many times, that while talking in Urdu, I cannot express all that I want to say in that language."
113. *The Reconstruction of Religious Thought in Islam*, 142.

More bitterly, and for very good reasons, Iqbal was very critical of the violence the modern West has visited upon the rest of the world, and on its own inhabitants. In a sardonic poem, Iqbal satirized the violent nature of the modern West by relating the story of a man who suffers a painful death at the hands of the clumsy Angel of Death and asks God to send the Angel of Death to the West to develop his killing skills.[114] In fact, in Iqbal's view, the nature of the modern West lies in the exploitation and murder of the weak:

Unless people understand the significance of a lawfully earned food,
life of society becomes miserable.
Alas! Europe is not aware of this principle,
her eyes do not see through God's light;

---

114. *Payam-i Mashriq*, 125–26 (trans., 87–88):
The story goes that in Iran
A worthy man,
Intelligent and wise,
Died, suffering great agonies.
Departing with a heart
Full of distress and smart,
He went up to God's throne
And said: "God I am one
Grieved at the way that I
Was made to die.
Your Angel of Death is
Supposed to be a specialist,
And yet he has no expertise,
No knowledge of the new skills that exist
In the fine art of killing. He
Kills, but does it so clumsily.
The world is going rapidly ahead,
But his growth has stopped dead.
The West develops wonderful new skills
In this as in so many other fields.
Fine are the ways it kills,
And great are its skill's yields.
It has encompassed even thought with death.
Death is all its philosophies' life-breath
It is what all its sciences devise.
Its submarines are crocodiles,
With all their predatory wiles.
Its bombers rain destruction from the skies.
Its gases so obscure the sky
They blind the sun's world-seeing eye.
Its guns deal death so fast
The Angel of Death stands aghast,
Quite out of breath
In coping with this rate of death.
Dispatch this old fool to the West
To learn the art of killing fast – and best."

she does not know lawful from unlawful,
her wisdom is immature and all her activities defective
One nation preys on another,
one sows the seed, another takes away the harvest.
It is "wisdom" to snatch food from the weak!
And to rob their body of the soul!
The way of the modern culture is to murder people;
and this killing is done under the garb of commerce.
These banks, the result of clever Jews' thinking,
have taken away God's light from the heart of man.
Unless this system is destroyed completely,
knowledge, religion and culture are mere empty names.[115]

Despite his painstaking efforts to construct a modern self among the Muslim populations, Iqbal was very critical of modern Western egohood. As such in *The Reconstruction of Religious Thought* in Islam he wrote:

> The modern man with his philosophies of criticism and scientific specialism finds himself in a strange predicament. His Naturalism has given him an unprecedented control over the forces of nature, but has robbed him of faith in his own future [...] Thus, wholly overshadowed by the result of his intellectual activity, the modern man has ceased to live soulfully, i.e., from within. In the domain of thought he is living in open conflict with himself; and in the domain of economic and political life he is living in open conflict with others. He finds himself unable to control his *ruthless egoism* and his infinite gold-hunger, which is gradually killing all higher striving in him and bringing him nothing but life-weariness.[116]

What lies behind the West's violence, according to Iqbal, is the predatory nature of its brand of subjectivity. The very act of the Western subject to know its object is by nature predatory, according to him. In a poem in *Javidnameh*, Iqbal animated Tolstoy to complain to Christ that modern Western knowledge, which "resolves the enigma of objects" with its thought, is marauding in essence, just like "Genghis Khan."[117] This way of looking at the issue, in turn, has its roots in the way Iqbal viewed the relations between the subject and the object, humans and nature, in Islam and the West. According to Iqbal, in the West there is a total and un-reconcilable separation between the subject and the object, the soul and the body that is rooted in Christianity (in turn inherited from Manichaeism) and more forcefully articulated since Descartes. [118] These separations are ultimately responsible, according to Iqbal, for what might be termed the "predatory" nature of the Western subject. In the Islamic world, to be sure, there is a separation between these categories, but the division is not absolute, and even though

115. *Pas Che Bayad Kard Ey Aqwam-i Sharq*, 29–30; trans. 80–81. Translation slightly modified.
116. *The Reconstruction of Religious Thought*, 186–87. Emphasis added.
117. *Javidnameh*, 53; trans.,50. See also page 190 (Persian), where Iqbal describes the knowledge of the westerners as "plundering" (*gharatgari*).
118. *The Reconstruction of Islamic Thought in Islam*, 9–10; 104–6.

the subject is dominant over the object, and the soul is superior to the matter, ultimately they are reconciled:

> With Islam the ideal and the real [subject and object, humans and nature] are not two opposing forces, which cannot be reconciled. The life of the ideal consists, not in a total breach with the real, which would tend to shatter the organic wholeness of life into painful oppositions, but in the perpetual endeavor of the ideal to appropriate the real with a view eventually to absorb it, to convert it into itself and to illuminate its whole being. It is the sharp opposition between the subject and object, the mathematical [the mind] without the biological [nature] within that impressed Christianity. Islam, however, faces the opposition with a view to overcome it. This essential difference in looking at a fundamental relation determines the respective attitudes of these great religions towards the problem of human life in its present surroundings. Both demand the affirmation of the spiritual self [subjectivity] in man, with this difference only: that Islam, recognizing the contact of idea [subject] with the real [nature], says "yes" to the world of matter and points the way to master it with a view to discover a basis for a realistic regulation of life.[119]

What, in essence, Iqbal was proposing is the desire to transcend the chasm that exists between the subject and the object, between humans and nature, a goal that the West has failed to achieve.[120] What Iqbal was not explicitly expressing was that this was the same goal that some movements and thinkers, such as the German Romantic movement, Hegel and some of his followers, and various socialist and utopian movements and thinkers, such as Bergson, were pursing in the West itself.[121]

Iqbal's othering of the West seemed inevitable, given the history of brutal western colonialism and imperialism that he set out to fight as an essential component of the formation of Muslim subjectivity. For this reason he was very much critical of those

---

119. *Reconstruction of religious Thought in Islam*, 9–10. This does not mean that Iqbal rejected a critical attitude toward knowledge. In the introduction to *The Reconstruction of Religious Thought in Islam* (v-vi) he specifically mentioned a wish to maintain an "independent critical attitude" toward knowledge, but also the desire of reconciling it with the Islamic approach, without mentioning the specifics.

120. In his religious mood, which occurred more in his poetry than prose, Iqbal thought that the absolute dominatory attitude of the West over nature and the other was a result of its secularism and its claim to direct subjectivity and rejecting God's primary subjectivity. In *Javidnameh*, Iqbal wrote that,
"He [the European] became a stranger to the station of being God's servant,
Revelation embraced him, yet he knew it not,
Like a fruit all farther from the roots of the Tree.
His eyes desired no other vision but man;
Fearlessly he shouted 'Where is Man?'" *Javidnameh*, 153; trans., 113. Translation modified.
On the issue of the reconciling the human soul and the body, Iqbal, was not as enthusiastic, mainly because in Islamic metaphysics, despite Iqbal's denial, there is a strong emphasis on the soul in overcoming the "crass materiality" of the body, which even Iqbal could not overcome. See, for example, *Javidnameh*, pp. 24; 102; 163; 207, where Iqbal, in the tradition of much of Islamic metaphysics, contemns the body.

121. For the "dialogues" between Iqbal and Marx, Hegel, Nietzsche and Bergson among others, see for example, *Payam-i Mashriq*, pp. 196–210.

Muslims who blindly followed western patterns and manners.[122] Yet, his project did not end just here. He had much larger plans to introduce a type of Muslim subject that, in his view, was not condemned to live in a world devoid of passion and emotion.

Sublimated Dionysianism

Iqbal's remedy for the ills of modern selfhood can be best described as an effort to infuse passion and exuberance into the barren life of the rational subject. In this sense he closely followed western thinkers of 19th and 20th century, particularly Nietzsche and Bergson. Yet, this was a type of passion that was, for the most part, devoid of sexual and "sensual" elements. Iqbal had little tolerance for late modern desublimated sexuality as well as Hafiz's Anacreontic sensuality:

> Beware of bibulous Hafiz,
> His cup is filled with deadly poison
> He worships the goblet, just like the wine
> He seeks religion in the lute, harp and reed.
> He left behind only the chalice and the cupbearer (*saqi*)
> He left behind only the reveling of the debauchees[123]

Yet, he often used the term "love" (*'ishq*) to convey his version of rarified Dionysianism. In poem after poem he praised love for its magical engendering of effervescence and ebullience in the individual and its ennobling effect on human life,

> My heart is lit up by an inner flame;
> Tears of blood lend my eyes a cosmic frame.
> May he stray farther from life's mystery
> Who thinks that madness is Love's other name.
> [...]
> Love's music found its instrument in man.
> Man unveils mysteries, though he himself is a mystery
> God made the world fair; man made it more fair,
> Is man God's colleague and companion?[124]

For Iqbal, the subject acquires substance from love. Love is responsible for passion and enthusiasm, which he thought was lacking in the modern western subject. Thus in the

122. In this regard Iqbal introduced the concept of *afrangzadegi*, literally meaning being stricken by the Europe. It is quite interesting that a few decades later, Iranian anti-imperialist intellectuals such as Jalal-e Al-Ahmad, promoted the notion of *gharbzadegi* (literally meaning stricken by the West and often translated as Westoxication), which is peculiarly close to Iqbal's idea and terminology. See *Rod of Moses*, p. 15. Urdu original: http://www.allamaiqbal.com/works/poetry/urdu/zarb/scanned/index.htm.

123. *Asrar-i Khudi*, 38. In the first edition of the *Asrar-i Khudi*, Iqbal strongly attacked Hafiz whom he had admired earlier in his life. As a result of protests by the admirers of Hafiz, Iqbal dropped the section on Hafiz in later editions.

124. *Payam-i Mashriq*, 27–28; trans. 3–5. Translation modified.

third poem in his *Secrets of the Self*, which he labeled "Showing that the Self Receives Stability from Love," he wrote:

> The luminous point whose name is the Self,
> Is the life-spark beneath our corporeal body.
> By Love it [the Self] is made more lasting,
> More living, more ardent, more glowing.
> From Love proceeds the radiance of its being
> And the development of its unknown possibilities.
> Its nature gathers fire from Love,
> Love instructs it to illumine the world.
> Love fears neither sword nor dagger,
> Love is not born of water and air and earth.[125]

In fact, Iqbal thought that his brand of *'ishq* was capable of remolding human beings:

> "Come, O Love [*'ishq*], the Secret of our Heart.
> Come, O our cultivation and harvest.
> These men, empty of soul, who have grown far too old.
> You can refashion a new man from their clay bold. [126]

Alternatively, Iqbal utilized the concept of "heart" using various Persian and Arabic terms, *qalb, del,* or *fu'ad,* to round off and tame the subject of modernity. Early in his career, by invoking Hegel and the medieval Muslim philosopher and mystic, Abdulqadir Jilil (1077–1166), Iqbal proposed to transcend the European type of subjectivity and agency:

> Here [at the end of the third stage of human "perfection"] is the end of our author's [Jili's] spiritual ethics; man has become perfect, he has amalgamated himself with the Absolute Being, or has learned what Hegel calls the Absolute Philosophy. "He becomes the paragon of perfection, the object of worship, the preserver of the Universe." He is the point where man-ness and God-ness become one and result in the birth of god-man [...] But the means of achieving this perfection is the "heart" and not intellect, according to Jili: "This characteristic of the agency [associated with perfection] differentiates it from the intellect, the object of which is always different and separate from the individual exercising that faculty."[127]

Similarly, in one of his *ghazal* poems in *Payam Mashriq*, Iqbal praised the "glowing ardor" that arises from the heart (*del*). Without it, human existence is nothing but a handful of clay, and the world would be mere dark dust.[128]

---

125. *Asra-i Khudi*, 21; trans., 41. Translation modified.
126. *Payam-i Mashriq*, 55; trans., 21. Translation modified.
127. *The Development of Metaphysics in Persia*, 129.
128. *Payam-i Mashriq*, 171–72.

Realizing that matters of the "heart" are connected to the sphere of nature, and despite his metaphysical penchant in favor of domination over nature, which is a part and parcel of human subjectivity, Iqbal, attempted to reconnect the "heart" with nature:

> The naturalism of the Qur'an is only a recognition of the fact that man is related to nature, and this relation, in view of its possibility as a means of controlling her forces, must be exploited in these interests, not of unrighteous desire for domination, but in the nobler interest of a free upward movement of spiritual life. In the interests of securing a complete vision of Realty, therefore, sense perception must be supplemented by the perception of what the Qur'an describes as "Fuad," or "Qalb," i.e., heart.[129]

Iqbal's emphasis on passion, ardor and fervor, which he associated with love, entailed a strong interest in movement and dynamism. As we saw before, he was very much in support of action, and his emphasis on movement was closely related to his idea of action. Thus while he described the slave as idle, motionless and subjected to natural immobility, the free person is always innovating and avoiding replication. The slave is constantly engrossed in the past and caged by time, while the free person has mastery over time.[130] The Muslim self that Iqbal was striving for was very much characterized by an existential penchant for movement. He told the Muslims that they are nothing but a "perpetual escape" (*ram-i payham*), and since life is not a "stationary bird," its nature is flight.[131] In *The Reconstruction of Religious Thought in Islam*, he wrote: "Hard his lot and frail his being, like a rose-leaf, yet no form of reality is so powerful, so inspiring, and so beautiful as the spirit of man! Thus in his inmost being, man, as conceived by the Qur'an, is a creative activity, an ascending spirit who, in his onward march, rises from one state of being to another"[132] In fact Iqbal often used images of the sea and the wave and its opposite, the shore, as metaphors to encourage his ideal egos to follow and avoid—i.e., to follow the restlessness of the sea and the wave, and avoid the immobility of the shore.[133]

Iqbal extrapolated his lively cosmology to form a dynamic view of Islamic jurisprudence (*fiqh*). He was, with a notable exception, very critical of the so-called closing gates of Ijtihad in the Sunni world and promoted the idea of change in the Sharia:

> And I have no doubt that a deeper study of the enormous legal literature of Islam is sure to rid the modern critic of the superficial opinion that the Law of Islam is stationary and incapable of development. Unfortunately the conservative Muslim public of this country is not yet quite ready for a critical discussion of "Fiqh," which, if undertaken, is likely to displease most people, and raise sectarian controversies.[134]

129. *The Reconstruction of Religious Thought in Islam*, 15.
130. *Asrar-i Khudi*, 69–70.
131. *Rumuz-i Bikhudi*, 125.
132. *The Reconstruction of Religious Thought in Islam*, 12.
133. See, for example, *Payam-i Mashriq*, 64; 128.
134. *The Reconstruction of Religious Thought in Islam*, 164. The term Ijtihad refers to the exercise of independent judgment by a Muslim jurisconsult in Islamic law to arrive at new interpretations of a legal or ethical principle or points. In the Sunni jurisprudence, it is said that since the 10th century C.E., "the gates of Ijtihad are closed," meaning that among the Sunni's the

This outlook of perpetual change, Iqbal interestingly argued, also constitutes the Qur'anic cosmology, and therefore, "the Qur'an cannot be inimical to the idea of evolution."[135]

Iqbal's emphasis on the Dionysian elements, and the élan that he was trying to derive from it in his construction of Muslim subjectivity, exhibited a strong inclination against reason, or so it may seem. As we saw before, he expressed quite strong sentiments against philosophy, theory and intellectual pursuits. Similarly his discourse is replete with diatribes against reason (*'aql*) and rationality, often expressed through the pen of Rumi. Thus Iqbal made a comparison between reason and love:

Reason is confused
In the riddle of "Causes,"
But Love is a Player
In the field of *Action*!

Love can catch his Prey
By the strength of his own *Arm*
But Reason, being cunning,
Can only throw her *Net*!

The only Substance with Reason
Is "Fear" and "Doubt";
But a firm Faith and Determination
Are indispensable to "Love!"

Reason builds a certain thing
To destroy it,
But Love first destroys it,
To rebuild it!

Reason is as cheap
In the world as wind,
But Love is very *rare*,
And its price is very high!

Reason is strengthened
On the basis of "How?"
And "How many?"
But Love would never wear
Such old and rotten garments!

---

practice of Ijtihad did not continue, in contrast to the Shia jurisprudence. At some points, Iqbal argued that Ijtihad at a time of decadence is not appropriate since it creates more uncertainty in the community.

135. *The Reconstruction of Religious Thought in Islam*, 166.

Reason says: "Surrender yourself
To your enemy!"
But Love says: "Strike hard
And test your *Strength*!"

Reason makes friends
With others rather than herself,
But Love, by his extensive Knowledge,
Is always *Self-checking*!

Reason says: "O Man!
Be always happy,
And enjoy your Life to its lees!"
But Love says:
"Be *obedient* to God
And then enjoy a perfect *Freedom*!"

In short, the greatest Pleasure
For Love is "Freedom,"
And Its real guide is Freedom![136]

As we can see from the above, Iqbal attributed action, power, certainty and determination, "constructive destruction," nobility, courage and freedom to "love," and the opposite traits to reason. He even went as far as changing the Cartesian dictum to, "I love, therefore I am."[137] Yet, despite his harsh criticisms of reason and rationality, there are a number of significant instances in his discourse when Iqbal articulated much more positive views of these categories. For example, in *The Reconstruction of Religious Thought in Islam*, he wrote:

> Now during the minority of mankind psychic energy develops that I call prophetic consciousness—a mode of economizing individual thought and choice by providing ready-made judgments, choices and ways of action. With the birth of reason and critical faculty, however, life in its own interest, inhibits the formation and growth of non-rational modes of consciousness through which psychic energy flowed at an earlier stage of human evolution. Man is primarily governed by passion and instinct. Inductive reason, which alone makes man master of his environment, is an achievement; and when once born it must be reinforced by inhibiting the growth of other modes of knowledge.[138]

Similarly Iqbal praised the notion of critical scrutiny, which he attributed to Islam:

> Just as the first half of the formula of Islam has created and fostered the spirit of a critical observation of man's outer experience by divesting the forces of Nature of that Divine character

136. *Rumuz-i Bikhudi*, 107–107; trans., 69–71. Translation slightly modified.
137. *Payam-i Mashriq*, 152. In Persian: در بود ونبود من اندیشه گمان ها داشت از عشق هویدا شد این نکته که هستم من.
138. *The Reconstruction of Religious Life in Islam*, 125–26.

with which earlier cultures had clothed them. Mystic experience, then, however unusual and abnormal, must now be regarded by a Muslim as a perfectly natural experience, open to critical scrutiny like other aspects of human experience. This is clear from the Prophet's own attitude toward Ibn-i Sayyad's psychic experiences.[139]

Iqbal also expressed very positive views on consciousness and criticized the vulgar Marxist approach toward the activities of mind: "To describe it [consciousness] as an epi-phenomenon of the processes of matter is to deny it as an independent activity, and to deny it as an independent activity is to deny the validity of all knowledge, which is only a systematized expression of consciousness. Thus consciousness is a variety of the purely spiritual principle of life, which is not a substance, but an organizing principle, a specific mode of behaviour essentially different to the behaviour of an externally worked machine."[140] In fact, deep in Iqbal's thought, I would argue, lies an attempt to *transcend* reason and rationality with the force of what he called "love" and not just totally dismiss it. In *Payam Mashriq*, Iqbal set up a dialogue between knowledge and "love" in which he tacitly recognizes the validity of science while criticizing it for severing itself from love:

Knowledge:
My eye sees the whole spectrum of material things.
It captures the world in its comprehensive net.
My field of vision is this side of heaven: I have
Nothing to do with those celestial happenings.
My instrument creates a thousand melodies,
And I put on the market all my mysteries.

Love:
Your evil magic sets the ocean's waves ablaze,
And shrouds the atmosphere in a foul gaseous haze
When you were friends with me, you were incarnate light;
But since you broke with me, your light is a dread blight;
You were born in the sacred shrine of the Divine
But you got yourself firmly caught in Satan's twine.
Come make this dusty waste a garden once again.
Rejuvenate this ancient, time-worn, ailing world.
Come take from me a little of my Passion's pain,
And under the skies build a lasting Paradise.
From the first we have kept each other company:
We are the treble and bass of one grand harmony.[141]

139. *The Reconstruction of Religious Thought in Islam*, 127.
140. *The Reconstruction of Religious Thought in Islam*, 40–41.
141. *Payam-i Mashriq*, 57; trans., 97–98. Emphasis added.

On one hand, in a sense this is a synthesis between knowledge and reason and what Iqbal called "love," and on the other, it was an attempt on the part of Iqbal to sublate what he considered to be the stultified modernity of the West:

For Westerners intelligence is the stuff of life,
for Easterners love is the secret of all being.
Only through love intelligence gets to know God,
love's labours find firm grounding in intelligence;
when love is companioned by intelligence
it has the power to design another world.
Then rise and draw the design of a new world,
mingle together love with intelligence.
The flame of the Europeans is damped down,
their eyes are perceptive, but their hearts are dead;
they have been sore smitten by their own swords,
hunted down and slaughtered, themselves the hunters.
Look not for fire and intoxication in their vine;
not into their heavens shall rise a new age.
It is from your fire that the glow of life comes,
and it is your task to create the new world.[142]

Since Iqbal closely connected "love" with revelation, his idea of transcending knowledge entailed reconciling it with revelation as well. He thought that knowledge without love and revelation was idol worship (*taghut*), but with love it becomes Godly.[143] As such he thought that knowledge must be "converted" to revelation and Islam:

Knowledge takes up residence in the thought,
love's lodge is the unsleeping heart;
so long as knowledge has no portion of love
it is the mere playhouse of thoughts.
This stage show is the Samiri's conjuring-trick;
knowledge without the Holy Ghost is mere diabolism.
Without revelation no wise man ever found the way,
he died trampled by his own imaginations;
Without revelation life is a mortal sickness,
reason is banishment, religion constraint.[144]

---

142. *Javidnameh*, 65; trans., 57–58. Translation slightly modified. On at least one occasion, Iqbal alluded to a larger scheme of a Hegelian type of synthesis between consciousness and "life." In The *Reconstruction of Religious Thought in Islam* (p. 57), he wrote: "In conscious experience life and thought permeate each other. They form a unity. Thought therefore, in its true nature, is identical with life."

143. *Javidnameh*, 76.

144. *Javidnameh*, 10; trans., 23. In the Qur'anic account, Samiri was responsible for the Israelites switching to the worship of the golden calf (20:87–88).

Islamizing Science and Technology

Iqbal's approach to modern science and technology also exhibited a similar pattern, as he exhibited a very ambivalent attitude to these emblems of the modern world. Thus, in *Secrets of the Self*, he likened modern science (*danesh*) to an idol-worshiping infidel that creates a barrier between the Muslim and God, because it is devoid of the glow and flame of love.[145] In a similar vein, Iqbal often excoriated modern technology. It seems that he was quite fascinated with the newly developed technology of aviation, as he occasionally mentioned airplanes with marveling overtones. Yet, Iqbal was very critical of the devastation that these machines had brought to humans and nature: "Science without the heart's glow is pure evil, for then its light is darkness over sea and land, its rouge renders the whole world black and blind, its springtide scatters the leaves of all being, sea, plain and mountain, quiet garden and villa are ravaged by the bombs of its aeroplanes."[146] It is interesting to note that in his description of his utopian city, for which he chose the unfamiliar name of Marghadin, Iqbal depicted an environ that is free from the "demon of machine" (*div-e mashin*) and the dark clouds of industrial smoke.[147]

Despite his severe criticism of modern science and technology, Iqbal did not reject them as such. Rather his intention was to "Islamize" them. Science, as long as it is under the "Islamic" control is good and vital (*kimia, elixir*) for the Muslims, a condition that would make the impact of science in Islamic lands different than that of Europe. Thus after bitterly lamenting the atrocities that Europe has visited on humans by the means of its science and technology, Iqbal claimed that science is of divine origin in Islam. The "knowledge of the object" (*hikmat-i ashya'*), he contended, is rooted in the Qur'an, since it encourages people to observe natural phenomena (Qur'an 88: 17). Thus, in a poem, Iqbal exhorted the reader that the East should take away this "sword" from the Frankish "thief" and breathe the soul of the Orient in its body.[148] He even went one step further and claimed that the origin of modern science is not in fact European, as they took it from the Muslims:

> The knowledge of things is not European in origin,
> its root is the eagerness for creation.
> If you see well, it owes its existence to the Muslims,
> this pearl has fallen from our hands.
> When the Arabs spread their wings in the West,
> they laid a new foundation for science and knowledge.
> The seed was sown by these dwellers of the desert,
> but the harvest was reaped by the Europeans.
> This fairy [science] sprang from the glass of our ancestors;
> win her again because she flew from our Clime.[149]

145. *Asrar-i Khudi*, 65; trans., 101.
146. *Javidnameh*, 74; trans., 64.
147. *Javidnameh*, 106; trans., 84.
148. *Pas che bayad kard*, 43–44; trans., 120–24.
149. Iqbal, Muhammad. *Mathnavi Musafer* (Lahore: Sedigi, 1972), 83–84.

As such, Iqbal considered science and technology not an end itself, but a means to attain selfhood and subjectivity for Muslims:

> The object is not knowledge of science and art,
> [...]
> Science is an instrument for the preservation of Life.
> *Science is a means of invigorating the Self.*
> Science and art are servants of Life[150]

On some occasions, Iqbal pointed out that the power of the West was derived from modern knowledge. Then he criticized those modernizers in the Islamic world who erroneously believed that the power of the West lay in its libertinism and indulgence in music, fashion and "dance and unveiled women." Neither, he asserted, was the might of the West because of its irreligiousness or its Latin script. The power of the Europeans came from science and technology only.[151] In fact, in one important poem, Iqbal viewed technology as the embodiment of human empowerment and praised it as the logical development of our agency, which serves as a fortress and protector. In this poem, he reiterated the notion of humans as God's vicegerents on earth, which, in his view, legitimated their mastery and domination over nature and their relation to modern technology:

> The steed of your Thought
> Has the speed of a Parrot,
> And it can reach Heaven
> By a single pace!
>
> The necessities of Life
> Become its *Spur*,
> And, in spite of being
> On Earth,
> Goad it to fly in the Heavens;
>
> So that, by the conquest
> Of the *Forces*
> Of this world,
> Your Craftsmanship
> Should attain its *perfection*!
>
> In fact, "Man" is the
> "Vicegerent of God" on Earth,
> And his command is perfect
> On all the *Elements*!
> Thus your weakness

150. *Asrar-i Khudi*, 20; trans., 41. Translation slightly modified. Emphasis added.
151. *Javidnameh*, 187; trans., 129.

Transforms into strength
In the world,
And all your "plans"
Acquire *material Form*
In the *world*!

Now, be a Rider
On the back of *Air*—
That is control
This she-camel!

Let your hands be red
With the blood of a Mountain
And bring Streams of Pearls
From the bottom of Sea!
[…]
By the rays of each Sun
Make *visible*, what has been
Invisible hitherto,
And reveal the Secrets
Of the Unintelligible!

All the Stationary
And Moving Heavenly Bodies—
Those gods of the ancient Nations

Are really your servants
And Maid-servants,
O lord of the creation [humans]
[…]
He who has thrown his lasso on objects [Westerners]
Has created a steed from Lightning and Heat.
He makes his words fly like a Bird,
And causes Tunes in his instrument without a Plectrum!

O You! Whose Donkey
Has become lame [Muslims]
Due to the difficult journey
Of Life, and who is Unaware
Of the Tumults
Of the Battle of Life:

Your companions [Westerners]
Have reached the Destination,
And they have taken away
The coveted prize

But you are still wandering
In the Desert exhausted and helpless!

In fact, the science
Of Naming [of things],
Is a great *Validation* for Man
And the knowledge
Of the Objects,
Is a fortress for Man![152]

It should be noted that, on at least one occasion, Iqbal went as far as embracing a positivistic approach toward modern science and technology. Thus in one of his short essays, in a very uncharacteristic fashion, Iqbal attempted to confirm the Islamic belief in corporeal resurrection at the End of Time by invoking modern scientific research.[153] Yet, despite his mostly negative depiction of modern science and technology, and a very rare instance of the opposite, in general it is fair to say that what Iqbal had in mind was a project to synthesize what he considered to be the cold and heartless, but necessary, spirit of modern science and technology, with the warmth and zest of what he called "love," as we saw above.

Politics, Economics, Aesthetics

Iqbal was politically quite active, although his practical views and statements do not always match his more theoretical positions. Yet, he consistently emphasized the value of equality as basic for his view of politics—at least among the Muslims. Thus, even though Iqbal believed that the form of prayer in Islam and its direction should not be a subject for dispute, he thought that the choice of a particular direction in Muslim prayer signifies the unity of believers and the sentiment that worship is an effective means of creating social equality and elimination of rank and racial superiority.[154] The Islamic emphasis on

152. *Rumuz-i Bikhudi*, 132–33; trans., 160–66. Translation modified. It is noteworthy that in this poem Iqbal praises the advent of radio in poetic codes as "birds of sound" taking flight while chastising Muslims for falling behind the Europeans in modern science and technology.

153. Iqbal wrote, "The noteworthy point in this passage is how modern science and philosophy, becoming more and more exact is furnishing rational foundations for certain religious beliefs which the eighteenth and nineteenth centuries' science rejected as absurd and incredible. Further the Muslim reader will see that the argument in support of corporeal resurrection advanced in this passage is practically the same as put forward in the Quran over thirteen hundred years ago." *Speeches and Statements of Iqbal*, 156–59.

154. *Reconstruction of Religious Thought in Islam*, 93. It is significant to note that based on this interpretation of prayer in Islam, Iqbal posited a notion of universality that went beyond Islam: "The Islamic form of association in prayer, besides it cognitive value, is further indicative of the aspiration to realize this essential unity of mankind as a fact in life by demolishing all barriers which stand between man and man." (94).

equality, Iqbal also pointed out, was responsible for the great political power of Muslims in their early history, when it worked as a leveling force and thus elevating the socially deprived classes. And along these lines, he often emphasized that the success of Islam in the Indian subcontinent was because of its egalitarian spirit.[155]

Yet, despite his unequivocal support for equality, Iqbal exhibited quite contradictory views on the notion of democracy and republicanism. Early in the development of his discourse he expressed quite positive views on the idea of democracy. "The best form of government," for Muslim community, he wrote, "would be democracy, the ideal of which is to let a man develop all the possibilities of his nature by allowing him as much freedom as possible."[156] Even in the later phases of his discourse, Iqbal praised the idea of a parliament that would run the affairs of an Islamic state, which he thought was rooted in the Islamic institution of *ijma'* (consensus). Thus in the *Reconstruction of Religious Thought in Islam*, he wrote:

> The third source of Mohammedan Law is Ijma, which is in my opinion, is perhaps the most important legal notion in Islam [...] Possibly its transformation into a permanent legislature institution was contrary to the political interests of the kind of absolute monarchy that grew up in Islam immediately after the fourth Caliph. It was, I think, favorable to the interest of the Omayyad and Abbaside Caliphs to leave the power of Ijtihad to individual Mujtahids rather than to encourage the formation of a permanent assembly, which might become too powerful for them. It is, however, extremely satisfactory to note that the pressure of new world forces and the political experience of European nations are impressing on the mind of modern Islam the value and possibilities of the idea of Ijma. The growth of republican spirit, and the gradual formation of legislative assemblies in Muslim lands constitute a great step in advance.[157]

In his poems, on the other hand, Iqbal articulated quite hostile views on democracy and the republican form of government, which seems to contradict his views expressed in prose. Thus in his *New Gulshan-i Raz*, he excoriated the West along with its republican system and its technology:

> The West has set up the rule of democracy [*jumhuri*],
> It has thus set free a demon.

155. *Islam as an Ethical and a Political Ideal*, 99.

156. *Islam as an Ethical and a Political Ideal*, 94. It is significant that at this relatively early stage in the development of his discourse, Iqbal had very positive views of the British involvement in India and thought it was spreading democracy there: "Democracy has been the great mission of England in modern times, and English statesmen have boldly carried this principle to countries which have been for centuries groaning under the most atrocious form of despotism. The British Empire is a vast political organism, the vitality of which consists in the gradual working out of this principle [democracy]. The permanence of the British Empire as a civilizing factor in the political evolution of mankind is one of our greatest interests. This vast Empire has our fullest sympathy and respect since it is one aspect of our own [i.e., Muslims'] political ideal that is being slowly worked out in it." (96) To be sure, later, as we have seen, Iqbal developed very different views about the West, including the British.

157. *The Reconstruction of Religious Thought in Islam*, 173.

It does not possess sound without plectrum and musical instruments,
Without a flying machine it does not possess the power of flying.
A desolate field is better than its garden,
A desert is better than its city.
Like a marauding caravan it is active,
Its people merely busy to satisfy their hunger.
Its soul became dormant, and its body awoke;
Art, science and religion all became contemptible.
Intellect is nothing but fostering of unbelief.
The technology of the West is nothing but man-killing.
A group lies in ambush against another group,
Such a state of affairs is sure to lead to disaster.
Convey my message to the West
That the ideal of democracy is a sword out of its sheath:
What a sword that it kills men
And does not make a distinction a between believer and an unbeliever!
If it does not remain in the sheath for a little more time,
It will kill itself as well as the world.[158]

On a somewhat different register, Iqbal also expressed multifarious thoughts on social revolution, Marxism and Bolshevism. On numerous instances in his poetry, Iqbal took the side of the downtrodden and blamed the rich and powerful for the plights of the former.[159] Writing shortly after the October Revolution in Russia and during the tumultuous conditions in Europe, Iqbal seems to have believed that the era of exploitation and domination had expired, and the world was ready for a revolution on behalf the powerless. Using the characters of Farhad and Parviz from classical Persian poetry to represent the slave and the master respectively, Iqbal versified the struggle between the powerful and powerless and celebrated the victory of the latter:

The royal crown has passed into the hands of highwaymen.
Hushed is the song of Darius; mute is Alexander's flute.
Farhad has changed his pickaxe for the scepter of Parviz.
Gone are the joy of mastership, the toil of servitude.
Freed from his bondage, Joseph sits on Pharaoh's high throne:
The tales and wiles of Potiphar's wife cannot win her suit.
Old secrets that were veiled stand unveiled in the marketplace:
No longer are they subjects of debate for the elite.

158. *The New Gulshan-i Raz*, 167–68; trans., 35–36. Translation slightly modified. In another poem Iqbal derisively depicted a republic as a barn of donkeys and asserted that Muslims should "Run away from the republican way [...] [since] from the brains of two hundred asses [i.e., a republic] human thought does not arise." *Payam-i Mashriq*, 135.

159. See for example his *Payam-i Mashriq*, pp. 215–16, in which Iqbal portrays the oppression of the factory workers as well as the other subaltern classes (The English translation by Hadi Hussain has omitted these poems).

Unveil your eyes and you will see that in full view of you
Life is creating for itself a world completely new.[160]

Iqbal even went as far as calling for a social and political revolution quite explicitly:

Of the hireling's blood outpoured
Lustrous rubies makes the lord;
Tyrant squire to swell his wealth
Desolates the peasant's tilth.
Revolt, I cry!
Revolt, defy!
Revolt, or die!

The Clerics with strings of Rosaries
Mislead the hearts of the multitude,
Brahman befuddles with his thread
Many a simple Hindu head.
Revolt, I cry!
Revolt, defy!
Revolt, or die!

Prince and Sultan are gamblers,
Loaded are the dice they throw.
They strip their subjects' soul from body
While their subjects are asleep,
Revolt, I cry!
Revolt, defy!
Revolt, or die!
[...]
I have seen into the [crystal] bowls
Furnished by this age for souls;
Such the venom they contain,
Serpents twist and writhe in pain.
Revolt, I cry!
Revolt, defy!
Revolt, or die!

Yet the weak are given at length
Lion's heart and tiger's strength;
In this bubbling lantern, lo!
Haply yet a flame will glow.
Revolt, I cry!
Revolt, defy!
Revolt, or die![161]

160. *Payam-i Mashriq*, 191–92; Translation 103. Translation slightly modified.
161. *Zabur-i Ajam*, 94–96; trans., 86–88. Translation modified.

Thus, in this revolutionary mood, Iqbal asserted that the Qur'an was a "death sentence for the master-man" and a "succor for the destitute and famished slave."[162]

On several occasions Iqbal engaged with the ghost of Marx, as he was wont to do with many Western thinkers, on the question of capitalism. In a poem in *Javidnameh* entitled "Communism and Capitalism," for example, he praised Marx for being a descendent of Abraham, both literally and figuratively, it seems. Yet, he called Marx a prophet without Gabriel whose heart is faithful (*mu'min*) but his mind infidel (*kafir*), and whose religion is founded upon the "equality of the belly," thus deriding the Marxist emphasis on materialism.[163] He concluded the poem by condemning capitalism (*mulukiyat*) because of its materialism as well its exploitation and Marxism for its harms to religion, art and understanding.

In a similar vein, Iqbal expressed nuanced views on the October Revolution in Russia. At one point he called Islam, "Bolshevism with God."[164] Correspondingly, Iqbal praised the Russian revolutionaries for their overthrow of "the bone of imperial rule in this world," and laying down a new scheme for a new world that does away with the oppressive ancien régime. [165] Nevertheless, he vehemently criticized the Bolshevik revolution for its atheism.[166]

The vicissitudes that marked the political dimensions of Iqbal's discourse are undoubtedly related to the depth of his thought and his keen observation of social phenomena. In tune with his general cosmology, revolutionary politics, despite its promises of liberation, was not adequate for Iqbal, and he predicted its failure because of its lack of the Divine/Dionysian element. Yet the cornerstone of his political views consisted of a notion that he shared with a number of Islamists in modern times, namely the idea of non-obedience to non-God. He believed that human bondage is the result of obedience and submission to earthly powers, religious or secular. It is only through submitting to God, and no one but God, that humans can be emancipated. Thus, in a poem that he described as "meaning that the real object of the Prophethood of Muhammad is the formation and foundation of emancipation, equality and brotherhood of mankind," he wrote:

Before the advent of Islam,
Man used to worship *Man*!
Practically he was worthless,
Poor and subordinate!

---

162. *Javidnameh*, 80; trans., 68.
163. *Javidnameh*, 64–65; trans., 56–57.
164. In the context of the debates on a proposed new constitution for India in 1931, Iqbal wrote: "Since Bolshevism plus God is almost identical with Islam, I should not be surprised if, in the course of time, either Islam would devour Russia or Russia Islam. The result will depend, I think, to a considerable extent on the position which is given to the Indian Muslims under the new constitution."
Speeches and Statements of Iqbal, 167.
165. *Javidnameh*, 79; trans., 67.
166. *Pas Che Bayad Kard*, 18. It is interesting to note that, in an apparent cynical mood, Iqbal suggested that exploitation and domination are built into human nature, and no type of social change can do away with it. See the poetic dialogue between "Monsieur Lenin and Kaiser Wilhelm" in *Payam-i Mashriq*, 209–10.

The cruelty and aggression
Of Caesar and Khosrow [Persian Emperor]
Robbed him of everything,
And there were chains
In his hands, feet and neck!

The Soothsayer, the Pope,
The King and the Sultan
They were all Hunters
For a single Deer
[…]
In short, Slavery in every sphere
Of life, degraded his Ego
And all the good Tunes
Within his Flute had died out—

Till Allah sent an Honest Man [Muhammad]
To the People who deserved him,
And thus the Throne
Of the Emperor
Was granted to Slaves.
[…]
He [Muhammad] infused a new Spirit
Into the Body of Man,
And redeemed the Slaves
From their Masters![167]

Iqbal further elaborated on this central theme in his prose writing, attributing to the notion of monotheism (*tawhid*) a new political-ontological dimension: "The new culture [Islam in its inception] finds the foundation of world unity in the principle of 'Tauhid.' Islam, as a polity, is only a practical means of making this principle a living factor in the intellectual and emotional life of mankind. It demands loyalty to God, not to thrones. And since God is the ultimate spiritual basis of all life, loyalty to God virtually amounts to man's loyalty to his own ideal nature [freedom]."[168]

Iqbal found the epitome of emancipation through "non-obedience to non-God," in the Shia Imam, Hussein ibn Ali who, against all odds, fought against the monarchical power of the Ummayids and was slain by the founders of the dynasty in the desert of Karbala in 680. For Iqbal, Hussein's defiance of worldly authority at the cost of his life represented the essence of emancipation through loyalty only to God, which he described in phrases such as: "That Valiant Warrior of Islam, Uprooted Tyranny for Ever," who told the Muslims by practice that a true Muslim cannot be submissive

167. *Rumuz-i Bikhudi,* 102–4; trans., 55–57. Translation modified.
168. *Reconstruction of Religious Thought in Islam*, 147.

to anyone except God.[169] This type of formulation by Iqbal should be seen as an incipient form of republicanism, in which individuals are encouraged to be politically emancipated through non-conformist attitudes toward the secular and clerical authorities without abandoning religion, as he interpreted Islam. On this form of republicanism, Iqbal's thoughts were quite persistent and, in fact, his critique of "Western" notions of republicanism originated in his views that the latter contravened it.

As such, Iqbal had both praise and criticism for republican and modern democratic movements and states in the Islamic world simultaneously. The Republic of Turkey founded by Ataturk served as a prime example of his ambivalent attitude. Thus in *The Reconstruction of Religious Thought*, Iqbal observed that, "the truth is that among the Muslim nations of today, Turkey alone has shaken off its dogmatic slumber, and attained self-consciousness."[170] In the same book, he further argued that Turkish republicanism was in perfect harmony with the Islamic precepts: "Turkey's Ijtihad is that according to the spirit of Islam, the Caliphate or Imamate can be vested in a body of persons, or an elected Assembly [...] Personally I believe the Turkish view perfectly sound. It is hardly necessary to argue this point. The republican form of government is not only thoroughly consistent with the sprit of Islam, but has also become a necessity, in view of the new forces that are set free in the world of Islam."[171] He even condoned issues such as the changing of alphabet to Latin, and recitation of the Qur'an in Turkish in the republican Turkey.[172] But later in his discourse, Iqbal expressed highly critical views on Mustafa Kemal's (Ataturk's) modernity, and by implication republicanism:

> Mustafa Kemal who sang songs of modernization,
> Ordered all traces of the past to be obliterated.
> The Kaba's life cannot be renovated
> by importing new idols from the West.
> The Turk's lyre is empty of any new tune—
> Its new is nothing but the old of the West.
> His breast could afford no new breath.
> His mind could conceive no new world.
> Inevitably he compromised with the existing world
> He melted like wax under its burning impact.
> If you possess the heart of a Muslim,
> Look into your own heart and into the Qur'an.
> A hundred new worlds lie within its verses.[173]

On the question of nationalism, another important hallmark that is often associated with modernity, Iqbal expressed very straightforward views. The Islamic universality

169. *Rumuz-i Bikhudi*, 107–108; trans., 73–76.
170. *Reconstruction of Religious Thought in Islam*, 162.
171. *Reconstruction of Religious Thought in Islam*, 157.
172. *Speeches and Statements of Iqbal*, 135.
173. *Javidnameh*, 66. Translation partly adopted from Fazlur Rahaman, "Muhammad Iqbal and Atatürk's Reforms," *Journal of Near Eastern Studies*, 43, no. 2. (Apr., 1984): 159.

based on shared faith, for him simply precluded the modern notions of a nation-state based on ethnicity, language or other particularistic criteria, as he viewed the notion of the nation-state as a significant source of strife and conflict in modern world.[174] Yet, in a more "realist" mood, Iqbal thought that the nation-state was a political reality that could not be avoided for the time being, but posited that Muslims can and should form a "League of Nations," which "recognizes artificial boundaries and racial distinctions for facility of reference only, and not for restricting the social horizons of its members."[175]

Consistent with his views on modern selfhood and subjectivity and his belief of their inseparability from the sacred, Iqbal posited that in an Islamic state religion cannot be severed from politics, or more accurately, from public affairs. In this regard, Iqbal pronounced rather subtle views that meandered between total separation and complete fusion of religion and state. Thus, while he was not against the separation of mosque and state as such since, for example in Shiism, the "doctrine of the major occultation of the Imam in a sense effected this separation," he believed that, "the Islamic idea of the division of the religious and political functions of the state must not be confounded with the European idea of the separation of Church and state. The former is only a division of functions, as is clear from the gradual creation in the Muslim state of the offices of Shaikh-ul-Islam and Ministers; the latter is based on the metaphysical dualism of spirit and matter."[176]

Yet, Iqbal was very careful that the "metaphysical" unity that he wished to maintain between the body and soul, and its counterpart between religion and state, should not be confused with the political rule by a cleric (and clerical establishment) who considers himself as God's representatives on earth and who, "always screen[s] his despotic rule behind his supposed infallibility."[177] In fact, consistently throughout his discourse, Iqbal expressed critical views on Islamic clerics and their establishments. Despite his deep interest in Islam, and as he interpreted it, in forging a modern subjectivity for Muslims, Iqbal advised his followers not be burdened by "dogma, nor priesthood, nor ritual" in facing the ills of modern society.[178]

Iqbal's distrust of clerics applied also to some Sufi leaders, as he viewed one strand within the Sufi tradition that, in his estimation, promoted anti-subjectivist tendencies resulting in the numbing of the masses and their oblivion. Thus despite his interests and admirations for Iran and the Persian culture in general, Iqbal blamed these for the development of this aspect of Sufism and often complained that Muslim clerics and Sufis, regardless of their location, were corrupted because of this cultural form.[179] Accordingly he made a very sharp distinction between Islam, or his interpretation of it, and the mullah's version:

---

174. See, for example, *Rumuz-i Bikhudi*, 130.
175. *Reconstruction of Religious Thought in Islam*, 159.
176. *Speeches and Statements of Iqbal*, 138
177. *Reconstruction of Religious Thought in Islam*, 154.
178. *Reconstruction of Religious Thought in Islam*, 188.
179. See, for example, *Asrar-i Khudi*, 67; *Rumuz-i Bikhudi*, 149.

The religion of God is more shameful than unbelief,
because the mullah is a believer trading in unfaith;
[...]
At the wily acts of that Koran-trader [the mullah]
I have seen Gabriel himself cry out!
His [mullah's] heart is a stranger to what lies beyond the sky,
for him the Quran is but a fable;
having no share of the wisdom of the Prophet's religion,
his heaven is dark, being without any star.
Short of vision, blind of taste, an idle gossip,
his hairsplitting arguments have fragmented the Community.
Seminary and mullah, before the secrets of the Book,
are as one blind from birth before the light of the sun.
The infidel's religion is the plotting and planning of Holy War;
the mullah's religion is corruption in the Way of God.[180]

This type of aversion to mullahs made Iqbal strongly criticize the Iranian constitution of 1906, because it gave a group of clerics the veto power over the legislation produced by the Majlis. In his diatribe against the mullahs, Iqbal went as far claiming that their "Paradise is wine and houris, page boys [*ghulams*, catamites], eating, and sleeping," very much opposed to his disciplinary prescriptions, as we saw above.[181]

In contrast to some later Islamic thinkers, Iqbal's rather elaborate and convoluted ideas on politics were not matched by his economic views. In earlier phases of the development of his discourse, he emphasized a positive attitude toward modern work ethics. Thus in his *Secrets of the Self*, he showed a near-obsession with time and argued that the slave is idle at day and night, whereas the freeman makes time his slave, which makes him very close to the philosophical foundations of the bourgeois work ethic.[182] As such, early in his discourse Iqbal praised the businessman (*kasib*) as "God's friend (*habib-ullah*)."[183] In a similar vein, and as we saw above, Iqbal's ontology strongly promoted human domination over nature and its utilization for human needs. Yet as he gradually distanced himself from a "materialist" conception, his attitude toward economic activity also changed drastically. Thus, in most of his later discourse, he disparaged the "struggle for existence" in the West as a vile pursuit.[184] The only economic precept that Iqbal reasonably elaborated on and emphasized seems to have been land for all who work on it.[185]

180. *Javidnameh*, 76; trans., 65. Translation modified.
181. *Javidnameh*, 120–21; trans., 93.
182. *Secret of the Self*, 69; trans., 104–5.
183. *Asrar-i Khudi*, 27. In a lecture dated 1908, Iqbal complained that "[o]wing to his indifferent commercial morality, he [the Indian Muslim] fails in economic enterprise." *Islam as an Ethical and a Political Ideal*, 76.
184. See, for example, *Gulshan-i Raz-i Jadid*, 168, See also his *Aramaghan-i Hijaz* (95) where he calls upon the faithful to beware of merchants of modern world whose business is all tantamount to gambling.
185. See, *Javidnameh*, 72; 109.

One area of inquiry that Iqbal discussed, without too much elaboration, interestingly pertained to music, painting and dance. There is no doubt that Iqbal's aesthetics were closely related to his philosophical views on human subjectivity and derived directly from them. Most of his discourse on these issues was articulated in a rather short book of poems entitled "Book of Slaves" (in Persian *Bandegi-nameh*), which dates back to 1927. He started a section on the "Arts of the Slaves" with music which he averred "lacked the fire of life." The song of people who lack selfhood and subjectivity is, according to Iqbal, melancholic, dejected and joyless, reflecting the thralldom of their soul. This type of music is mournful and enervates the people exposed to it. The rhythms of these songs are the rhythms of the death-throes of mankind.[186] In contrast, Iqbal asserted, the music of the free should be agile like a torrent, to sweep away all sorrow from the heart. This type of music is nurtured on pure ecstasy, a fire that is drenched in the heart's blood.[187]

Similarly, in painting the current state of art in Muslim lands is replete with themes and tales of death. Referring to his notion of selfhood and human subjectivity, Iqbal thought that painting, and art in general, that does not reflect and encourage human empowerment is self-alienation. Such an artist:

Like a beggar seeks beauty in Nature,
He is a robber pretending to be destitute.
To seek beauty outside the Self is wrong,
Beauty is within our Selves.
The painter who surrenders to Nature,
Inserts Nature's image and erases the image of the Self.
He does not paint the Self even once,
He does not refurbish our mirror once.
Nature in its varicolored garment,
Is the only thing that his lame canvas can attain.
His picture of today has no vision of tomorrow for us.
[...]
The artist who adds to nature,
Reveals the secrets of the Self to us. [188]

While there is very little doubt that here Iqbal is laying the foundation of a form of human-centered modernist art based on his interpretation of Islamic metaphysics, his views on modern popular forms of Western dance and their "blind imitation" by some Muslims were quite different. He likened the Muslim imitators of these forms of dance to consumers of hashish, not an externalization of any inner joy and lacking a genuine surge of blood in the their veins.[189] His views on dance in general, however, went much deeper. Based on his metaphysical penchant for human empowerment through the

186. *Bandeginameh*, 183–84.
187. *Bandeginameh*, 184.
188. *Bandeginameh*, 186–87.
189. *Armaghan-i Hijaz*, 96.

disciplining of the body, Iqbal propounded the idea that while music is related to the soul and hence to be promoted, dance belongs to the realm of the matter and is therefore to be frowned upon; yet, in this case, not totally dismissed. Thus in a poem entitled "Dance and Music" in his Urdu book, the *Rod of Moses*, he wrote:

> The souls of Satan and Gabriel too
> From verse derive effulgence strong
> For dance and music both provide
> Pathos and rapture [*suz va surur*] for the throng
> A Chinese sage has thus disclosed
> The secrets implied in this art:
> "As if verse is the music's soul
> And dance performs body's part."[190]

Music, Iqbal seems to imply here, is related to the soul and poetry and is thus refined, but dance is related to the body and the masses and is therefore coarse.

Conclusion

In a very significant sense, Iqbal was in pursuit of a modern Muslim identity that can best be described as "authenticity," because, first, it relied to a large extent on local knowledge, even though Iqbal never denied being strongly influenced by modern Western thinkers who were trying to forge an alternative modernity, such as Hegel, Nietzsche and Bergson. Like these European thinkers, Iqbal was attempting to create a modern sense of subjectivity, but at the same time wished to overcome its shortcomings by resorting to categories such as passion and élan. Secondly, in thematizing the notion of Selfhood, Iqbal reversed centuries of denial of the self in Muslim context, not a small feat by any measure. Iqbal was one of the few influential Islamic thinkers who broached one of the indispensable pillars of modernity, namely, the notion of human subjectivity and agency, directly and unequivocally by elaborately discussing the notion of *khudi*. As we saw above, Iqbal endeavored very hard to strike a balance between individual *khudi* and collective *khudi*, albeit later in his life he gravitated more toward a more collective understanding of human subjectivity.

Many Islamic thinkers since the 19th century have attempted to create a variation of the concept of human subjectivity by inevitably resorting to a vicarious concept of human agency and empowerment, which is contingent on God's Agency and Subjectivity. To be sure, Iqbal's concept of human subjectivity is also constructed in this manner, but in his case he partially transcended this contingent notion of human empowerment and made serious efforts to push this notion one step further by arriving at the thresholds of an

190. *The Rod of Moses*, 84.

independent and self-sufficient form of human subjectivity.[191] Yet, at the very same time he attempted to maintain the human subject in close relation with the Divine and the sacred, from which he derived fervor and devotion to remedy the passionless despair of modern world. In a sense his discourse was an attempt to create an abstract, detached and rational modern human individual subject and then reattach it to the universe, the world of passion and emotion, and the collectivity.

This fundamental lynchpin of his discourse was, at times, expressed in utopian visions in which he described in some poems in his *Javidnameh.* In one such poem, Iqbal described a phantasmagorical city that he called Marghadin in which he praised some of the material consequences of human subjectivity, such as tall buildings, while depicting the possibility of a utopian modernity:

> Marghadin and those tall buildings [*imarat-i buland*]—
> what can I say of that noble city?
> Its inhabitants sweet of speech as honey,
> comely their faces, gentle their manners, simple their apparel,
> their thoughts innocent of the burning fever of gain,
> they were intimate with the secrets of the sun's alchemy;
> whoso of them desires silver or gold gathers it from light,
> in the manner of gathering salt from the briny sea.
> The aim of science and art there is service,
> no one weighs work done against gold;
> no one is even acquainted with dinars and dirhams,
> these idols may not enter the sanctuary.
> The demon of the machine has no power over nature,
> the skies are not blackened by smoke;
> the lamp of the hard-toiling farmer is always bright,
> he is secure from the plundering of the landlords,
> his tillage is not a struggle for water,
> his harvest is his own, no other shares in it.
>
> In that world there are no armies, no squadrons,
> none gains his livelihood by killing and murder;
> In Marghadin no pen wins lustre
> from inscribing and disseminating lies;

191. In a poem in his book *Payam-i Mashriq* Iqbal strongly posited a purely humanist notion of the subject:
"I carved an Idol in my own image,
I depicted God in my likeness.
It is impossible for me to pass out of my Self,
I am a worshiper of my Self, no matter in what guise."
Payam-i Mashriq, 68.

in the marketplaces there is no clamour of the workless,
no whining of beggars afflicts the ear.[192]

Thus, what Iqbal aimed for was the invention of an Islamic modernity by forging a Muslim subject whose roots were forcefully grounded in Islam, and by the same token creating an alternative to the actual Western modernity, which he thought was devoid of passion, feeling and care for the other and the world. This was certainly a highly valuable undertaking, even though it was marred by certain streaks of utopian pipe dreaming. One important concern, however, is that in the process of reconciling the subject back to the sphere of passion and the sacred, the subject might become stillborn.

192. *Javidnameh*, 106; trans., 84–85. Translation modified.

Chapter Two

SAYYID ABUL 'ALA MAUDUDI: A THEORIST OF DISIPLINARY PATRIARCHAL STATE

As the founder and the main ideologue of the large and influential Jama'at-e Islami in Pakistan and India, Maududi was both a political activist as well as a theorist of political Islam in the modern world. While it is true that Maududi increasingly gravitated toward politics and political action, especially as his career and age advanced, he nevertheless was deeply engrossed in creating a conceptual framework to advance his political agenda. This chapter focuses on the ideational aspects of Maududi's career, because at the core of his activity stands a cosmology and a theory of an Islamic state that has had far reaching impacts on many Islamist movements around the world.[1]

Maududi began his career as an Islamist activist and thinker in earnest in the early 1930s, when the anti-colonial movement in India was reaching its zenith. At the same time, the Muslim-Hindu conflict and strife were looming large in the minds of Muslim thinkers of his milieu. Furthermore, there is no doubt that many other Islamic thinkers of this time had been exposed to Western colonialism and had begun addressing the issue. Consequently, the notion of power came to occupy a central place in their discourses. And given the historical experience of the Indian subcontinent, with its long history of colonialism, the centrality of the notion of power in Maududi's thought is even more pronounced.

Thus at the core of Madudi's discourse is a complex formulation of power which radiates throughout his conceptual framework of Islamic revival. As we will explore in detail below, Maududi, like many other Islamic thinkers discussed in this volume, posits a notion of human power, which while central to his discourse, is indirect and limited. He considered power to be coterminous with human existence and constitutive of civilization. Without power, human life would be impossible because administration of society necessitates power. Yet the human power that he was advocating is not direct, and it emanates from the power of God. For this reason, humans do not really possess power, but it is vouchsafed to them by God, which makes their hold on power contingent, temporary, limited and subject to being withdrawn at any moment. Nevertheless, this conceptualization of power is essential to Maududi's systematic thought for the establishment of an ideal Islamic society. Yet, although Maududi did not shy away from abstract thinking at times, he was not interested in mere intellectual exercises.

---

1. For an informed discussion of Maududi's political career see: Seyyed Vali Reza Nasr, *Mawdudi and the Making of Islamic Revivalism* (New York: Oxford University Press, 1996).

His thought in general and his discourse on power in particular were closely geared to gaining political power and the eventual establishment of an Islamic state. As such, the architectonics of power in his thought were crystallized in his theories of a Muslim state, which he spent most of his enormous energy and talent trying to bring into existence.

But even though the establishment of an Islamic state was the primary, though long term, goal of Maududi in his intellectual and political endeavors, he also developed important theoretical constructions regarding, for example, human sexuality and gender relations that are essential to his overall conceptual framework and hence politics of state building, as we will see in the following pages.

Sayyid Abul 'Al Maududi was born on September 25, 1903 in Aurangabad in the state of Deccan India (now called Maharashatra).[2] Maududi's father, Ahmad Hasan, born in 1855, was a lawyer by profession and a devout Muslim who had studied at the modernist college of Aligarh, though he left the school before graduating from it. The Maududi family traced their ancestry to a prominent branch of the Chishti Sufis that was founded in the tenth century in Afghanistan. Maududi was also related to the famous 19th century liberal Islamic reformer, Sir Sayyid Ahmad Khan (d. 1898), though Maududi' often criticized the latter in his writings. Maududi received home education at first, studying Urdu, Persian and Arabic religious sciences, as his father deliberately excluded modern learning and Western languages from his curriculum. But at age eleven, Maududi began studying at Furqaniyah school in Aurangabad, which combined a curriculum of traditional Islamic subjects with modern Western subjects. In 1915 when his family moved to Hyderabad, Maududi enrolled at the seminary there, but was unable to stay there long, because of his father's illness, which forced Maududi to go Bhopal to be with his father and earn a living at age 15. In Bhopal, a learned acquaintance encouraged Maududi to embark on a career as a journalist, but it was in 1918 in Bijnur when he actually launched this career, shortly after which he moved to Delhi. In Delhi, Maududi immersed himself in reading both eastern and Western materials, while also improving his English, making Western sources more available to him.

At the same time, Maududi became involved in the independence movement, which was fast brewing in Delhi. This period of Maududi's career is interestingly marked by his Indian nationalist and anti-imperialist sentiments, during which he even wrote a praiseful biography of Gandhi that was never published and which he later denounced. Between 1921 and 1923, Maududi served as the editor of the newspaper *Muslim*, which was run by the Society of Ulema of India. In 1925 Maududi started working for another Islamic newspaper, *Al-jam'iat* in Delhi as its editor, while at the same time pursuing training at the Fathipuri seminary known for its purpose of educating seminarians who could engage the westernized Muslims. It is important to note that Maududi graduated from the seminary and received his clerical certificate (*ijazah*) in 1926 but did not join the ranks of clerics, nor did he advertise his ties to them because, as Vali Nasr points out, he wished to be able to appeal to the educated Muslims of India. As the struggle for independence in India gained momentum, Maududi was alienated from the Indian nationalist cause and

2. Most of the biographical information on Maududi is taken from Vali Nasr, *Mawdudi and the Making of Islamic Revivalism*.

gravitated toward the Islamist political movement. In 1927 he wrote a series of articles defending the notion of *jihad* in Islam, which catapulted him to the attention of fellow Muslims and gradually lead to his career as a Muslim ideologue and a reformer (*mujadid*) of Islam.

While Maududi's career increasingly assumed a political-ideological character, he did not neglect his intellectual development, and in 1931 he was involved in the translation of Mulla Sadra's *Al-Asfar al-arb'ah*, one of the most important philosophical works of Islamic philosophy and was influenced by its proto-humanist message.[3] In 1932 in Hyderabad Maududi bought the journal *Tarjumanul Qura'an* (Qur'anic interpretation) and published mostly his own articles there. Between 1937 and 1939 in Pathankot Punjab, Maududi served as the head of a *darul-Islam*, an ostensibly educational institution funded by an endowment. But in reality, Maududi transformed the endowed institution to serve to disseminate his interpretation of political Islam and used it as the proto-type of his later political party. When Maududi came into conflict with some of the founding members of the endowment, he chose to resign his post and leave Pathankot to settle in Lahore with the supporters he had acquired in the process of establishing the *darul-Islam*. In 1941 Maududi founded the Jama'at-e Islami in Lahore and increasingly gravitated toward the politics of seizing state power and the establishment of an Islamic state in Pakistan. Maududi died on September 22, 1979, having the establishment of a full-fledged Islamic state in the subcontinent elude him.[4]

Power in Monotheism

Reflecting on the causes of the subjugation of Muslim peoples by the West as early as 1934, Maududi declared that as domination is the result of force, subjugation is the logical outcome of weakness and inertia. The nations that are materially strong and spiritually resolute, he argued, rule the bodies and minds of the weaker nations. Sadly, he observed, the Islamic nations of today are experiencing the dual slavery of both physical subjugation and intellectual and moral followership.[5] Influenced by such a traumatic experience of lack of power, Maududi observed that, with the exception of a "monastic civilization," no other civilization, whether Islamic or not, that have a claim to universality and "possess a comprehensive system of administering the worldly affairs, can resist the urge for power," in order that they may change the social life of their people after their own image. "Without the power to enforce" he added, "it is meaningless to believe in or present a doctrine or a way of life." A community of monks has no interest in directing the affairs of the external society. In contrast, a social system such as Islam, "who rises with sole purpose of administering the worldly affairs and reforming humanity at large, cannot help struggling to seize power. For unless one possesses necessary power and

3. See: Vali Nasr, *Maududi and the Making of Islamic Revivalism*, 24.
4. For a good account of Jama'at-e Islami see: Vali Reza Nasr, *The Vanguard of the Islamic Revolution: The Jama'at-i Islami of Pakistan* (Berkeley: University of California Press, 1994). For a somewhat journalistic account of the Jama'at, see: Frederic Grare, *Political Islam in the Indian Subcontinent: The Jamaat-i-Islami* (New Delhi: Manohar, 2001).
5. Syed Abul 'Ala Maududi. *West Versus Islam* (Lahore: Islamic Publications, 1991), 1–2.

authority to enforce one's programme, the proposed system cannot possibly take root in the world of reality." As a matter of fact, Maududi continued, "a civilization in authority alone can force the world to follow its example in the daily routine of life, and accept its lead in the sciences and trends of thought, in arts, literature and morality, in education and character formation, in law and principles of civics, and in all other aspects of life. Thus a civilization without power is rendered helpless and incapacitated."[6] The mission of Islam, Maududi elaborated, was to discipline and regiment all those who have adopted Islamic ideals and formed their life styles in an Islamic manner, "with a view to struggling for power and seizing it by the use of all available means and equipment."[7]

As an astute theorist, or ideologue, Maududi was quite aware that power is an attribute attached to humans and any notion of power entailed the idea of human empowerment or agency. For this purpose, like many of the modern Islamist thinkers, Maududi focused on the Qur'anic notion of humans as the successors of God on earth. By virtue of this very important concept in the Qur'an, Maududi broached the concept of human agency and empowerment that was a part and parcel of his preoccupation with power: "The *khilafat* [successorship] [...] is not the *khilafat* or vicegerency of one individual, one family or one class. All the members of the Muslim world community, individually and collectively are *khalifahs* or vicegerents of God and are equal participants in the task of conducting the affairs of the Islamic state. This is evident from the following verse of Sura Nur (Light): 'Allah hath promised to those among you who believe and work righteous deeds, that He will of surety, grant them in the land inheritance (of power) as he granted it to those before them.'"[8]

Maududi believed that only through faith in Islam could the Muslims acquire power and proposed monotheism as the surest path to it. As such, the real strength of a people, he asserted, lies not primarily in its material resources but in its moral strength and power of character. The Qur'an charges the Muslims to be steadfast in their faith and it "will automatically result in your uplift in the world, and you will be conferred world leadership and caliphate [vicegerency] on the earth." The Qur'an has nowhere required Muslims to build factories, make ships, establish universities and scientific research centers, business concerns and modern financial institutions. These can be built only on the foundation of moral strength that faith in Islam can provide.[9] It is very significant to note the emphasis that Maududi placed on the moral dimension of human empowerment. He maintained that human existence consists of two essential dimensions, one physical and the other moral. What makes humans human in the first place is their moral aspect. "Man's success or failure, advance or decline," he wrote, "depends on both the material and moral factors. Both are necessary, but neither is sufficient. Deeper analysis will however reveal that it is the moral dimension that is more decisive. To acquire material power, employment of physical agencies and control over external causes, is a necessary

6. Syed Abul Maududi, *A Short History of the Revivalist Movement in Islam* (Lahore: Islamic Publications, 1972), 22–23.
7. Maududi, *A Short History of the Revivalist Movement in Islam*, 25.
8. Syed Abul 'Ala Maududi, *Islamic State: Political Writings of Maulana Sayyid Abul 'Ala Maudoodi* (Karachi, Pakistan: Islamic Research Academy, 1986), 11.
9. *West Versus Islam*, 238–45.

condition for success, and so long as man lives in this physical world he cannot ignore this. But the fundamental cause of man's rise or decline and the greatest influence on his destiny is the extent and quality of his moral strength."[10] Furthermore, it is the moral factor in us that determines our will power, our ability to make decisions, ambition, courage and diligence.[11]

However, the human empowerment that Maududi, like many other Islamist thinkers studied in this volume, was seeking was in some very important respects rather different from the subject of the Western Enlightenment.[12] The Westerners, according to Maududi:

> started from atheism and materialism and consequently looked upon the universe as an object without a Creator or Master [...] They found the world of matter at their feet and began to press the forces [of nature] into their service. But they had no idea that they were not the masters or rulers of this world in their own right but the vicegerents of the real Sovereign [...] They denied God and began to worship the self, which, raised to the level of Divine, put them in grave difficulty. And it is the worship of this false and dangerous god that is now leading them, in all fields of thought, to deceptive and dangerous courses.[13]

It is this unrestricted subjectivity of the modern world, in Maududi's reading, that has inflicted the "poison" of selfishness, self-indulgence and ease of life on Western social life. This form of unlimited human empowerment has vitiated the polity with nationalism, racism and the worship of power turning it into a blight for humankind.[14] This form of autonomous and self-subsistent subjectivity is benighted in various ways. Deprived of divine guidance and knowledge, it is inefficient, rendering "man as an autonomous being who is responsible to none."[15] This type of Western agency makes man "himself the sole master of his body and his physical powers. He will therefore use his physical powers and qualities of his head and heart according to his whims and caprices. He will treat all things and all men whom chance places under his power as his chattel and himself feel as their master."[16] In fact, according to Maududi, humans have a natural propensity to dominate others and impose themselves on others as a god:

> The desire for godhood can take root only in man's mind. It is only man's excessive lust for power and desire for exploitation that prompts him to project himself on other people as a god and extract their obedience; force them to bow down before him in reverential awe

10. Syed Abul 'Ala Maudoodi, *The Islamic Movement: Dynamics of Values, Power, and Change* (Leicester: Islamic Foundation, 1984), 94.
11. *The Islamic Movement: Dynamics of Values, Power, and Change*, 95.
12. Of course what Maududi ignored was that the Enlightenment stood on the shoulders of the Protestant Reformation. Without the Reformation disseminating human agency, albeit in a contingent and inchoate fashion, the fully-fledged human subjectivity of the Enlightenment would be inconceivable.
13. *West Versus Islam*, 30–31.
14. *West Versus Islam*, 31.
15. Syed Abul 'Ala Maududi, *Islam and Ignorance* (Lahore: Islamic Publications, 1976), 10–11.
16. *Islam and Ignorance*, 11–12.

> and make them instruments of his self-aggrandizement [...] The pleasure of posing as a god is more enchanting and appealing then than anything else that man has yet been able to discover. Whoever possesses power or wealth or cleverness or any other superior faculty, develops a strong inclination to outstep his natural and proper limits, to extend his area of influence and thrust his godhood upon such of his fellow men as are comparatively feeble, poor, weak-minded or deficient in any manner.[17]

Having posited the notion of human empowerment in close relation to the moral factor, Maududi was keenly cognizant of the close ties between agency and knowledge. For this reason he viewed the modern Western notions of humanist knowledge as quite deficient and problematic. The most prominent aspect of human knowledge, in his view, are that it is severely limited and is in fact not true knowledge. Self-derived human knowledge is restricted, and its judgment can be distorted by sentiments and desires. More significantly, human knowledge, whose source is not divine, is partial and subject to racial and other forms of prejudice and thus precluding universal ethics.[18]

In contrast to this form of absolute agency and autonomy of the humanism of the Enlightenment, Maududi, as we briefly saw above, proposed an Islamic limited and contingent subjectivity and autonomy, "In short, God bestowed upon man a kind of autonomy and appointed him His vicegerent on earth [...] and [a]lthough man enjoys this status, God made it abundantly plain to him that He alone is man's lord and sovereign, even as He is the Lord and Sovereign of the whole universe. Man was told that he was not entitled to consider himself independent."[19] It would be a mistake, however, to consider that by such a formulation, Maududi totally denied human agency. On the next page of the same work, he asserted that from the beginning of creation God had undertaken that, "true guidance would be made available to man throughout the term granted to him and that this guidance would be available in a manner consistent with man's autonomy."[20] In fact, Maududi harshly criticized the Sufi doctrine of "pantheism" for its alleged encouragement of passivity and non-agency:

> This doctrine inculcates the attitude in man that he doubts the result of his existence; he loses all initiative; he considers himself a mere puppet that is made to dance by someone else, or perhaps some external spirit is dancing within it; he forgets himself in the stupor of his illusions; his life is rudderless and has no set course or purpose. The train of his thought is like this; I am only a shadow; no work has been assigned to me; nor can I accomplish anything myself. That All-Pervading Being [pantheistic diety] which casts into shadow through me the entire universe, and which will hold sway from the beginning to the end of the world is the Mover. Every thing is accomplished by that Being alone [...] Why should I act then?"[21]

---

17. Syed Abul 'Ala Maududi, *Political Theory of Islam* (Lahore: Islamic Publications, 1993), 8.
18. Syed Abul 'Ala Maududi, *The Religion of Truth* (Delhi: Markazi Maktaba Jamaat-e-Islami Hind, 1970), 33–34.
19. Syed Abul 'Ala Maududi, *Towards Understanding the Qur'an (vol. 1)* (Leicester: Islamic Foundation, 1988), 9.
20. *Towards Understanding the Qur'an*, 10–11.
21. *Islam and Ignorance*, 21–22.

Thus, with regard to human agency and empowerment, Maududi assumed a *via media* in which the real Subject is the monotheistic God and humans derive a contingent and limited subjectivity from that Divine source.[22] They should use these Divine gifts according to the will and law set down by the Almighty. In contrast to modern doctrines of absolute and pure humanism, Maududi argued, the Islamic doctrine on human empowerment explicated by him, makes for a dynamic and agentive human existence, which at the same time promotes responsibility and ethical behavior:

> [T]his view of life not only transforms an individual into a man of action but also diverts his efforts from the attainment of selfish, sensual or nationalistic ends with a view to achieving lofty aims of justice and morality. It is impossible to find a more dynamic, more productive and a man of more righteous action than the one who entertains the following opinions about himself: "I have not been sent unto the world without any aim; instead God has created me to discharge a duty; the aim of my life is to perform deeds that please God rather than live to please myself or my relations; I shall not be spared until I have rendered full accounts as to how and to what extent did I expend my energy and time.[23]

---

22. Even though Maududi does not explicitly draw on philosophy, Islamic or otherwise, he seems to have strongly believed in a mooring of his discourse on metaphysical foundations. For him the fundamental questions regarding humans and their relations to the universe were essential for formulating his sociopolitical discourse: "Man is surrounded by countless millions of other human beings, animals, plants and minerals and his life is inextricably linked with all these things. Is it possible for you to imagine then that man can adopt a mode of dealing with these things without first forming an opinion about his own self, the nature of things which surround him and the position in which he stands in relation to those things? Is it possible for a person to adopt a way of life without determining: Who am I? What am I? Am I responsible or irresponsible? Am I independent or subordinate to someone? If I stand in a subordinate position who is my superior and if I am responsible, to whom am I accountable? [...] Can a person propose to expend his powers without first deciding the questions: Do these powers belong to me or are they a gift endowed by someone else? Is there someone to call him to account for expending his powers? Is the use of his powers to be regulated by himself or by someone else? [...] All those fundamental problems of life the solution of which is imperative for the active existence of man are metaphysical in nature." (*Islam and Ignorance*, 5–6; 8)
23. *Islam and Ignorance*, 34. One may facilely dismiss these contrasting positions on human agency held simultaneously by Maududi as mere incoherence in thought and feeble reasoning. However, viewed in terms of a dialectical dynamism found in monotheism, in which humans cannot but achieve power through the power of an almighty, all-knowing deity, the enigma of such approaches to achieve human agency may become less perplexing. I have called this approach to human agency, "mediated subjectivity." For a very interesting discussion of a similar phenomenon in the history of the formation of European modernity see Louis Dupre's *A Passage to Modernity* and Charles Taylor's discussion of it in *A Secular State* (795–96). Dupre calls the transitional link between pre-modern and modern conception of human agency the "Baroque" culture, which exhibited a very similar tension between human and divine agency that characterizes the work of a significant number of modern Islamist thinkers. The tensions and conflict found in this paradigm constitute the beginning of modern human agency, which, far from being an incoherence in thought, represent a dynamic culture that could pave the way for full-fledged human subjectivity. See the introduction in this volume.

Mududi held similar views with regard to human reason and rationality. While he did not totally reject human intellectual capacity, he thought that it was limited, and in fact it should be restricted and bound by wisdom derived from divine sources. At various points during his long career as an Islamist thinker and political actor, the proportion between human reason and divine wisdom that he formulated varied, but the significant point is that he posited a form of "mediated" rationality in which human reason derived from God's knowledge and was guided and restricted by it. Thus he wrote, "when your good sense has amply distinguished between the right and the wrong, and you accepted the right and rejected the wrong, the trial of your intellect and common sense and its task of scrutiny and criticism is now over. Now the authority to decide and to command is automatically shifted to Allah instead of human intellect and reason, to the Prophet of Allah and the Guide book of Allah. Now it is not for you to decide but bow before each and every command of Allah and His Holy Prophet. Now the field to apply your mind is the understanding of the implications of the wisdoms of His command, applying it in the minutest details of your practical life."[24] On some other occasions Maududi gave more credit to human reason, but argued that it still needs a divine framework for more efficient and more equitable functioning.[25]

As Maududi vacillated between positing human agency and autonomy, and divine agency and therefore restriction of human autonomy, he also expressed similarly dialectical views on the agency of the individual and her/his autonomy and that of the collectivity. He found fault with Christianity's alleged over-emphasis on individual salvation at the expense of the collectivity.[26] Some of Maududi's hostility toward the individual can be explained as his attempt to attack the secularizing trends that view religion as a personal matter and for the other world—not to be involved in the affairs of the community. In the context of criticizing communism, on the other hand, Maududi strongly supported the individual to the point of saying that "the Islamic point of view attaches real importance to the individual and not to any nation or society. Individual is not meant for society, but the society for the

24. *West versus Islam*, 231.
25. In this regard he wrote, "He [man] is endowed with will and volition. He has to make his choice between different errands. He has to select his course out of a set of alternatives. And this is what distinguishes him from the rest of the creation. This being the situation, man has resolved those manifold problems, his own and of the universe which nature sets for his cogitating mind, but whose solution it does not vouchsafe in unequivocal terms. He needs some system of thought to make this resolve. He needs a scheme and a framework of knowledge in which he may organize and co-ordinate the information which nature proffers to his mind through the promptings of the sense-organs—a body of information that lacks a naturally systematized form." (*The Religion of Truth*, 9) And of course this scheme and framework is provided by the divine source, or what Maududi called "Al-Deen": "There is no denying that reason is a treasure; it has excellent capabilities. Its importance in human affairs is very great. It is, beyond doubt, a great guiding force in our lives and helps and admits and controls us in countless ways. But as far as the question of framing al-Deen is concerned, reason does not lead us much farther [...] taking into consideration the inherent limitations of human reason, would it be proper to depend upon it for providing al-Deen [?]" (*The Religion of Truth*, 23)
26. *West versus Islam*, 82.

individual."[27] This is because it is only the individual, and no collective entity such as a society or a party, who can be held responsible for his or her deeds before God.[28] Ye, what is very important to observe is that the emphasis here is not on the autonomy and the freedom of the individual, but on her or his *responsibility*. On many occasions Maududi attempted to create a balance between the individual and the collectivity, but in general, even when he gave credence to the individual, it was for the sake of acquiring the satisfaction of God and service to the collectivity, not for the individual self: "[In Islam] the relations between the individual and society have been regulated in such a manner that neither the personality of the individual suffers any diminution or corrosion, as it dies in the Communist and Fascist social system nor is the individual allowed to exceed his bounds to such an extent as to become harmful to the community, as happens in the Western democracies. In Islam the purpose of an individual's life is the same as that of the life of the community, namely the execution and enforcement of Divine Law and the acquisition of God's pleasure. Moreover, Islam has, after safeguarding the rights of the individual, imposed upon him certain duties toward the community. In this way requirements of individualism and collectivism have been so well harmonized that the individual is afforded the fullest opportunity to develop his potentialities and is thus enabled to employ his developed faculties in the services of the community at large."[29]

For Maududi, power and empowerment, be it for the individual or the collectivity, was not an abstraction, and he meant to implement the contingent and limited human agency in reality. As such, Maududi called for the formation of a state along the lines that he proposed and agitated to bring about throughout his active life.

The Pastoral/Patriarchal State

One thing that was quite constant in Maududi's thought and political activity was the desire to establish an Islamic state in the subcontinent, and by implication in any Islamic society. As early as 1945, in a concluding address he delivered at the first All India conference of Jama'at-e Islami, Maududi argued that whenever there is corruption, injustice, tyranny and oppression, and wherever there is "poison" that flows in the veins of human culture, economy and politics, the leadership of society is responsible.[30] Conversely, whenever humans advance, it is because of the role of the virtuous people who control the sources of power and manage the affairs of the society. If the God-fearing people hold power and lead the society, it will develop probity, and if it is lead by un-Godly people, the society will drift toward rebellion against divine precepts and toward the exploitation of humans by other humans and toward moral degradation and cultural corruption.[31] Moreover, to bring about moral rectitude in

27. Syed Abul 'Ala Maududi, *Capitalism, Socialism, and Islam* (Kuwait: Islamic Book Publishers, 1977), 56–57.
28. *Capitalism, Socialism, and Islam*, 56–57.
29. *Political Theory of Islam*, 38–39.
30. *The Islamic Movement*, 71.
31. *The Islamic Movement*, 77.

society, nothing short of force exercised by the state would suffice. For these reasons, Maududi argued, the state power should be captured by the Muslims: "It will be impossible to succeed if you want to stop, by means of sermons, the evils of drinking, gambling, bribery, obscene shows, indecent dress, unethical education and such other things [...] Whoever really wants to root out mischief and chaos from God's earth and is genuinely anxious to ameliorate the conditions of God's creation, it is useless for him to work as a preacher and advisor. He should stand up to *finish the government run on wrong principles, snatch power from wrong-doers and establish a government* based on correct principles and following a proper system."[32]

Yet, even a cursory reading of Maududi's writings leaves little doubt that what he had in mind with regard to seizing the state power and creating an Islamic state entailed both a revolutionary as well as a reformist approach. In fact, he attempted to combine revolution and reform. Thus, on the one hand, he portrayed historical Islam in the light of social revolution: "I wish to explain to you concisely that the call of Islam to believe in Allah, the one and the only authority, is not merely a call to accept a religious creed in some conventional sense, as is commonly the call of other religious creeds. It was a call for a real social revolution. The main targets were those privileged classes who had subjugated the common man under the garb of religion as monks and priests, under the cover of politics as monarchs and chiefs, and under the economic cover as capitalists, feudal lords and industrialists, reducing people to mere slaves."[33] However, on the other hand, Maududi immediately qualified this statement by trying to distinguish the Islamist revolution from the communist type of social revolution. The "materialist" revolutionaries often come from oppressed classes or represent their interests and viewpoints. As such, these types of revolutionaries and the revolution they engage in, amount to a vengeful reaction to tyranny, resulting in a class war and a worse despotism that tramples justice and human dignity.[34] Thus although Maududi advocated a social revolution which would upset the relations of domination, he alluded to reform as a vehicle to achieve this goal. When revolutionaries who try their best to establish a social and political system on the basis of revolutionary ideas, "fail in all their novel experiments and are mentally fed up with their own adventures, they retreat to the balanced way of thinking already propounded by reformists."[35] Interestingly, the most important reason for which Maududi opposed a political revolution to achieve his social revolution was that the former could destroy the very social system of an Islamic society:

> Thus any revolutionary move, or moves to be more accurate, if continued for a long time, would shake the very foundations of the existing Muslim society without providing any stable base for the reconstruction of a new social system. It must not, therefore, be ignored that an already weak and fettered nation, if deprived of its exiting social system, shall suffer acute

32. Syed Abu 'Ala Maududi, *Fundamentals of Islam* (Lahore: Islamic Publications, 2000), 246; emphasis added.
33. Syed Abul 'Ala Maududi, *Jihad in Islam* (Lahore: Islamic Publications, 1980), 12.
34. *Jihad in Islam*, 13–14.
35. *West versus Islam*, 178.

degradation and more degeneration. This explains why we are often forced to oppose the revolutionaries rather than the conservatives. Otherwise, so far as general deterioration is concerned, we too agree with them that it must be improved and reformed. We also like to change the state of stagnation forced on Islam into dynamism. But we consider it wrong and unfair to replace Islamic etiquettes with the Western ways of life in the name of dynamism and activity."[36]

The "reformist" approach that Maududi advocated did not mean, however, that he would not wish to export the Islamic revolution and the establishment of the Islamic state beyond the subcontinent. The Qur'an requires, Maududi pointed out, that believers go to the aid of those who are victims of exploitation, discrimination and repression.[37] Given the deep interconnections among human beings, Maududi further argued, and despite the divisions among nations, no state can fully realize its ideological goals unless it expands its ideology to its neighbors. "Hence it is imperative for Muslim missionaries," he continued, "not to rest content with the establishment of an Islamic system of life in a particular piece of land but to extend the suzerainty of Islam to all neighboring lands as far as its resources can carry. It is indispensable not [only] in the interests of its own security but also in the interest of humanity at large."[38]

Sovereignty in Islamic State

More important than the method of bringing about the Islamic state, in Maududi's discourse, was the nature of sovereignty in that state. As we saw before, Maududi posited a close relation between power and knowledge, and the foundations of the state for him were based on the twain. Human knowledge, however, was too defective for him to lay the ground for the construction of the state. Human "opinion," formed by the elite or the masses, is subject to the whimsical nature of human inclinations and desires. It cannot be the foundation of social norms and laws. A state, on this account,

36. *West versus Islam*, 186.

37. *Jihad in Islam*, 20.

38. *Jihad in Islam*, 21. Maududi even went further and suggested that Muslims should spread their influence globally: "The Muslim revolutionaries will have to launch a two-pronged campaign to achieve its [sic] goals. It should propagate its ideology all over the world and extend a general invitation to the people of all countries to embrace the faith and ideology of Islam, which truly guarantees their salvation and welfare. On the other hand, subject to resources and strength, they should subdue and liquidate all those anti-Islamic powers who are usurping the genuine rights of their people and oppressing them by dint of force. This was the policy adopted by the Holy Prophet (peace of Allah be upon him) and the succeeding illustrious Caliphs (May Allah be pleased with them). The country of Arabia where this Islamic revolution started was the first to brought under the suzerainty of Islam. Later on, the Holy Prophet (peace of Allah be upon him) sent invitations to other neighboring States to accept and embrace the faith and ideology of Islam. Whenever the ruling class refused to accept the true faith of Islam and to submit before Allah Almighty, the Prophet (Peace of Allah be upon him) resorted to taking military action against them." (*Jihad in Islam*, 21–22). Of course, Maududi was quick to add, that when Islamic revolutionaries mount attack, they are not after seizing land, but wining the hearts and minds of their opponents. (*Jihad in Islam*, 24)

requires permanent and immutable moral standards to support a civilization, and human fickleness makes such a state impossible.[39] Modern science and its principles of observing the physical world and the knowledge of physical laws, cannot lay the grounds for the foundations of a sophisticated civilization either. At most, modern science can help form a "materialist conception of life" according to which human existence is reduced to its materialistic dimensions and fulfillment of animal desires or inculcation of notions such as survival of the fittest and the legitimacy of dominating the other.[40]

For the above reasons, Maududi proposed the notion of Divine sovereignty, which would presumably eliminate the sovereignty of all the earthly powers in his ideal Islamic state. The fundamental tenet of this theory of state, Maududi declared, was that because the earth and everything in it belongs to God, he is the sole sovereign. No individual, class, tribe, family, nation, or even the entire humanity can claim sovereignty.[41] There is no doubt that the divine sovereignty was absolute in Maududi's view: "in the entire gamut of creation, there is no creature who can rightly claim to possess all attributes of sovereignty [except God]. The Qur'an stresses this very truth when it says repeatedly that sovereignty belongs to God and God alone. He is omnipotent, i.e., He can do whatever He likes; He has to refer to none and render account to none; He is the source and fount of all authority."[42]

Based on these rather abstract theoretical constructions, Maududi directed his attention to the question of who enjoys real political sovereignty. His response again was readily that political sovereignty too belongs to God alone. Yet, in conformity with his ideas about human vicegerency, Maududi considered a role for humans as agents of God's will, implicitly admitting a limited measure of popular sovereignty:

> After this basic constitutional problem of sovereignty, the only problem that remains to be answered is as to who enjoys the political sovereignty in this set up? Unhesitatingly the reply would be that political sovereignty too, as a matter of fact, belongs to God and God alone. Whatever human agency is constituted to enforce the political system of Islam in a state, will not possess real sovereignty in the legal and political sense of the term, because not only does it not possess de jure sovereignty, but also that its powers are limited and circumscribed by the supreme law, which it can neither alter nor interfere with. The true position of this agency [human agency to enforce the political system of the Islamic state] has been described by the Qur'an itself. The term used by the Qur'an for this agency is "*khilafat*," which means that such agency is not sovereign in itself but is the vicegerent of the de jure and de facto sovereign, viz, God Almighty.[43]

39. *West versus Islam*, 56–57.
40. *West versus Islam*, 79–80.
41. Syed Abul 'Ala Maududi, *The Process of Islamic Revolution* (Ichhra, Pakistan: Markazi Maktaba Jama'at-e-Islami, 1955), 14–15.
42. Syed Abul 'Ala Maududi, *First Principles of the Islamic State* (Lahore: Islamic Publications, 1974), 20.
43. *First Principles of the Islamic State*, 24.

State's Pastoral Charge

One of the most important features of the state in Maududi's thought was its edifying charge of the denizens. In contrast to liberal democracy, Maududi often insisted, the Islamic state had the duty of improving the moral and cultural constitution of the society. The idea of an Islamic state, he said, is not a negative but a positive notion. The primary function of the state is not merely maintaining peace and order in society by preventing people from visiting violence on each other or to defend against foreign invasions. The real aim of the Islamic state is to bring about the system of social and economic justice outlined in the Qur'an by propagating those values that support social justice. For these tasks to be accomplished, it is necessary that the state educate people utilizing a combination of its coercive power and public didactics.[44] Maududi's thought on this issue reflects the seemingly inherent conflict in the process of subject formation in modern times. On the one hand, the development of human agency necessitates a coercive pedagogical approach by the state toward society, and on the other hand human agency, even if it is contingent, as in many Islamic discourses discussed in this volume, potentially entails the notion of freedom. Such a dialectical tension is evident in Maududi's attitude toward the state and its relation to society:

> This kind of state cannot keep its functions limited within narrow limits. It is an all-comprehensive state whose activity comprehends all departments of human life. This state tries to transform every aspect of its culture and civilisation in accordance with its ethical viewpoint and its programme for reformation. In the face of its reformatory activities, no person can say: this is my private affair (which you should not touch). In this respect, the Islamic State bears a slight resemblance to the Communist and Fascist states. But as will be seen later on, in spite of this comprehensiveness of the Islamic state, it has nothing of totalitarianism because it does not deprive any citizen of his personal freedom, nor is the Islamic state dictatorship.[45]

It is noteworthy that Maududi justified the pastoral charge of the state by arguing that what distinguishes the Islamic state from other forms of state is its responsibility of educating and teaching people, as well its duty to promulgate the Islamic message to all parts of the world.[46] This is so because, "it has been established by experience that the great mass of the common people are incapable of perceiving their own true interests."[47]

44. *Islamic State*, 15.
45. *Islamic State*, 15. Seeing the close the affinity between a pastoral state and totalitarianism, Maududi attempted to white wash the many features that the two systems have in common by highlighting some of the presumed differences. He wrote, "As against Communism, Islam does not coerce dissidents to accept its ideology. Under Communism no one can live in the Communist state who does not accept its principles and ideology. As soon as the Communists came to power in Russia, they expropriated all non-Communists, killed and exterminated thousands of non-Communists and millions of people were exiled to Siberia to pass their lives in concentration camps. In the Islamic State the non-Muslims enjoy specific rights with which no ruler can tamper." (*Islamic State*, 16)
46. *Islamic State*, 17.
47. *Political Theory of Islam*, 24.

Maududi further explained his pastoral approach toward the state by likening the role of the state to barricades on roads that prevent travelers from falling into the abyss. "Are these barricades," Maududi asked rhetorically, "intended to deprive the wayfarer of his liberty? No, as a matter of fact, they are meant to protect him from destruction; to warn him at every bend of the dangers ahead and to show him the path leading to his destination. That precisely is the purpose of the restrictions (*hudud*) which God has laid down in His revealed Code."[48]

The tensions between didactic restriction and freedom that is exhibited in Maududi's thoughts on the role of the Islamic state took an interesting turn when he incorporated the Qur'anic precept of "enjoining the good and forbidding the evil."[49] Maududi viewed this precept as the embodiment of the empowerment of the faithful to criticize the state and as a form of freedom that protects against totalitarianism that may result from the pastoral nature of the state. Thus he wrote:

> The most important principle which guarantees that the Islamic state would be run and administered on the proper lines is that every individual in an Islamic State has not only the right but also is saddled with the duty of proclaiming the truth whenever he sees that the truth is being side-tracked, that he should support whatever is right and just, and whenever he sees that some wrong is being done and something improper or unlawful is being undertaken, he should prevent and stop from undertaking it [...] According to the Quran, one of the distinguishing qualities of the believer is: "that they enjoin good and forbid evil and observe the limits set by Allah."[50]

Maududi then provided some Hadith that, according to the Prophet, "the highest type of jihad (Holy War) is to speak out truth before a tyrant or tell him to be just and equitable" and "if a people see a tyrant and do not stop him from doing so, it is quite probable that God may send a general punishment upon them."[51]

Ideological State

Closely related to the pastoral characteristic of the state in Maududi's writing, was its moderately utopian quality that operated on the basis of ideology. What guaranteed the health and proper functioning of the state and its officials was not in the first instance a system of checks and balances that would fracture and distribute power to prevent abuse and incompetence, but a moral inculcation of religious values. In every thing that the torchbearers of Islamic revolution and state, say or do, Maududi wrote, "it should be apparent to all who come into contact with them that the ideological state to which these selfless, truthful and God-fearing men of pure character and sacrificing spirit are inviting the world must certainly be a guarantee of social justice and world peace."[52] A state

48. *Political Theory of Islam*, 28.
49. See the Qur'an, 3:104;110 and 9:71, for example.
50. *Islamic State*, 22.
51. *Islamic State*, 23.
52. *The Process of Islamic Revolution*, 23.

system that does not operate on the basis of the faith of the leaders and the populace, in Maududi's view, is doomed to failure. In order to demonstrate this point, he compared the American Prohibition and the Qur'anic injunctions on the consumption of alcohol, arguing that the Islamic order to ban alcohol was instantly obeyed, whereas in America of the early 20th century, even though the Prohibition law was carefully prepared, it was constantly violated and had to be repealed. Then, Maududi concluded that, "It goes to prove that the foundation of a good system of government rests on faith and good conduct. Where these two are lacking, however excellent the laws and constitution are framed on paper, they never succeed in practice."[53]

The internalization of religious values is not only a guarantee of the proper conduct of the populace, but also assures the probity of the state officials, "You can imagine in what excellent condition God's creation will be where the army, police, judiciary, tehsildars [revenue administrators], tax-collectors and all other government functionaries comprise such officers and personnel who are all God-conscious and mindful of being answerable to Him in the Hereafter, where all the rules and regulations of government are formulated on the basis of the guidance vouchsafed by Allah, in which there is not the slightest possibility of injustice and ignorance, and where a timely rectification is done of every evil and evil act and the government is constantly ready to promote virtue and piety with its power and material resources."[54]

Having postulated that religion is the surest guarantor of state officials' integrity, Maududi extrapolated this idea to the population at large, depicting a utopia of morally upright citizenry:

> Then if you reflect a little you will easily understand this point that when this type of government, after functioning for some time, will set aright the detestable habits of the people when it will bar all avenues of illicit earning, lewdness, oppression, indecency and immorality; when after giving a decent burial to the wrong type of education and training, it will reform the ideas of the people through the wholesome system of education and training, and when under its aegis people will get a chance of leading their lives in a clean and chaste atmosphere of justice and fairness, peace and tranquility, good character and pleasing manners; then those eyes, which had been turned blind by suffering for a long time under the supremacy of people who are vicious and heedless of God, will be gradually enabled to perceive and appreciate the Truth.[55]

The State Apparatus

At the core of the Maududi's discourse on the state apparatus was the notion of Shura, or consultation. The Islamic state, being made up of the collective vicegerency of every Muslim, required a mechanism for communication among the faithful according to Maududi. For this reason the Qur'an had mandated consultation in the affairs of

53. Syed Abul 'Ala Maudui, *System of Government under the Holy Prophet* (Lahore: Islamic Publications, 1978), 6.
54. *Fundamentals of Islam*, 251–52.
55. *Fundamentals of Islam*, 252.

the community by mutual consent.[56] But the Qur'an, Maududi added, did not specify any specific form for the institutionalization of the concept of Shura. It could be institutionalized featuring the universal and direct participation of the people, or it could be based on people's elected or selected representatives; the assembly embodying the Shura could be unicameral or bicameral. All these questions are flexible and determined by the people affected in different Muslim societies in space and time.[57] What is essential to the concept of Shura, Maududi insisted, is that all of the Muslims should be able to participate in it, if not directly, indirectly through their representatives. Another crucial stipulation that Maududi made was that "the opinions expressed by the people or their representatives should be free. No pressure should be exercised on them. Similarly, the advice [of the participants in consultation] should be free from the taint of partiality and it should be sincere. Advice given under pressure or temptation means really that no advice has been given."[58]

Closely related to his discussion of the right and the duty on the part of Muslims to "enjoin the good and forbid the evil," Maududi projected the freedom of expressing one's opinion in the Shura back to the Caliphate of the first four Caliphs in Islamic history. The distinctive feature of the rule of the four Righteous Caliphs was that the average Muslim could criticize their government and articulate his views candidly, without fearing any consequences, as the Caliphs "sat in the Shura […] and took part in the discussions of the Shura […] Every person spoke in the Assembly [the Shura] according as his conscious dictated him […] Decisions were taken on the basis of the arguments advanced in favour of certain courses of action and not because of the influence of any person, or because any interests were to be served, or because of any group feeling."[59]

On the actual form of the legislature, Maududi did not make any specific pronouncements. On the spheres and scopes of legislative activities and its power, however, Maududi provided some guidelines for his followers. The sphere of '*Ibadat* or acts of worship, such as obligatory daily prayers, fasting, payment of poor-tax (*zakat*), Hajj and other precepts that regulated human relations to God, all is immutable and no changes are allowed. With regards to *Mu'amilat*, or relations among people, Maududi said, "you should follow what you have been commanded, and you should refrain from doing what you have been forbidden to do," that is following the Shari'ah as handed down from the pre-modern period.[60] In general, in a state in which God is the de jure sovereign, humans cannot undertake any form of legislation that contradicts the Qur'an and the Tradition of the Prophet.[61] The legitimate sphere of legislation for Maududi was in spaces where the Qur'an and Tradition were silent, or when these two sources can be interpreted in more than one way on an issue. Of course these forms of finding and enacting laws could not contravene the spirit of the Qur'an and Tradition, nor could

56. *Islamic State*, 30.
57. *Islamic State*, 31.
58. *Islamic State*, 32.
59. *Islamic State*, 37.
60. *Islamic State*, 47.
61. *First Principles of the Islamic State*, 29.

they ago against the grain of Islamic jurisprudence or Fiqh.[62] Yet, for all new legislation to become law, it has to go through the process of consultation and the consensus of majority vote in the assembly.[63]

With regard to the executive, Maududi remained loyal to his central tenet of Sovereignty of God and vicegerency of humans: "Those who run the government must not become supreme sovereigns but, recognizing God as their sovereign, they must work as His deputies and trustees and must fulfill their responsibilities with the consciousness that ultimately they have to submit an account of their trust to that Monarch who is knower of the seen and unseen [God]."[64] This meant that the state officials, including the executive, are not responsible to the electorate since their accountability lies entirely to the divine.[65] In a nutshell, "In an Islamic state, the real purpose of the Executive is to enforce the directives of God conveyed through the Qur'an and Sunnah [Tradition] and bring about a society ready to accept and adopt these directives for practical applications in its life."[66] On the question of how the head of the state should be determined, Maududi wrote that, "In an Islamic state, the election of its Head depends entirely on the will of the general public, and nobody has the right to impose himself forcibly as their Amir [ruler] [...] The election should take place with the free will of Muslim masses and without any coercive force."[67] Maududi also thought that the power of the head of the Islamic state should be reduced from the period of the Righteous Caliphs, even though for him that period constituted a type of historical precedent and source of political normativity. The first four Caliphs, Maududi wrote, had veto power over their advisory Shura, but since in modern times the conditions and personalities of that period cannot be replicated, the head of the Islamic state cannot enjoy such a power, and the executive should be subordinated to the majority decisions of the legislature.[68]

The same principle of the de jure sovereignty of God, Maududi insisted, applies to the judicial sphere and its operations. When Islam was first established as a state in Medina, the Prophet assumed the role of the judge and dispensed justice in strict accordance with the Law of God. Those who followed the Prophet had no choice but to adjudicate in the same manner.[69] Thus Maududi made the judiciary strictly subjected to the codes of Shari'ah as they had developed in the pre-modern period. On the other hand, he often stressed the separation of the three branches of the state, the executive, legislative and the judiciary, and their independence from one another.[70] As such, in a pamphlet on human rights, he wrote: "In Islam the judiciary is not placed under the control of the executive. It derives its authority directly from the Shari'a and is answerable to God. The judges should be appointed by the government but once a judge has occupied the bench, he will

62. *First Principles of the Islamic State*, 31–32.
63. *Islamic State*, 50.
64. *Fundamentals of Islam*, 248.
65. *The Process of Islamic Revolution*, 15.
66. *First Principles of the Islamic State*, 32.
67. *First Principles of the Islamic State*, 48–49.
68. *First Principles of the Islamic State*, 38–42.
69. *First Principles of the Islamic State*, 33–35.
70. *First Principles of the Islamic State*, 35–36.

have to administer justice among the people according to the law of God in an impartial manner, and the organs and functionaries of the government will not be outside his legal jurisdiction, so that even the highest executive authority of the government is liable to be called upon to appear in a court of law as a plaintiff or defendant like any other citizen of the state."[71] In some of his writing, Maududi implicitly approved of the applications of the penal codes of the Shari'ah, such as cutting the hands of thieves and stoning of those engaged in adultery. In general, Maududi approved of the content and precedent of not only the Shari'ah codes, but also of its procedures, such as the notion that in Islam all justice is done publicly, and there should not be any secret trials.[72]

Citizenship in the Islamic State

Maududi's writings on the Islamic state included considerable discussions regarding the denizens of such a state. He consistently upheld the right of the Muslim populace to vote and participation in elections. The partial and contingent agency that the notion of vicegerency to God implied, carried the right to vote in elections: "In the Islamic state every adult, man or woman, is eligible to vote because he or she is the vicegerent of Allah. His or her vicegerency has not been conditioned by any educational or monetary qualifications. Only faith and good works has been required of him."[73] Yet, Maududi limited the legal qualifications of running for office only to men, by referring to the Qur'an that "'Men are in charge women' [4:34] and the Prophet declares: 'Verily, that nation would not prosper which hands over the reins of its government to a woman.'"[74] As we saw before, Maududi made the election of the Head of the state by the Muslims a requirement for his state theory. And, he invoked the early history of the Righteous Caliphs for this purpose. The first four successors to the prophet, Maududi argued, were all selected by the consent of the nascent Muslim community, and this signified that the head of the modern Islamic state should be determined by the vote of the majority. The candidates for office in general also, Maududi warned, should be appointed to office by earning the trust of the Muslims.[75] Even though, historically, there was no specific way of ascertaining this trust as the means of entering an office, Maududi suggested that the modern system of election found in liberal democracies was permissible, "provided that it is not tarred with those corrupt practices which render democracy a sheer farce."[76]

71. Syed Abul 'Ala Maududi, *Human Rights in Islam* (Leicester: Islamic Foundation, 1976), 12.
72. *System of Government under the Holy Prophet*, 8.
73. *Islamic State*, 12.
74. *First Principles of the Islamic State*, 60.
75. Again, here he invoked the historical precedent by arguing that the companions of the prophet (*sahabah*) had earned the support of the Muslim population to function as the de facto assembly of consultation at the time of the prophet. (*The First Principles of the Islamic State*, 51–53)
76. *First Principles of the Islamic State*, 55. One of these "corrupt practices" in Maududi's estimation was electioneering: "Islam detests the notion that the voters should be fed and feasted and taken around in motor-cars and that the candidate who beats others at the game of lying cheating and squandering money should win the game. These accursed methods are characteristic of a Godless democracy." (*Political Theory of Islam*, 43)

Maududi also believed that the citizens of the Islamic state must enjoy certain civil rights. But these rights were first and foremost grounded in the citizens' obligation to be obedient and loyal to the Islamic state and work for its welfare, prosperity and betterment.[77] Once these were granted, based on the Qur'an or precedent in the classical period of Islam, Maududi upheld certain freedoms and rights, such as the right to privacy, the right to protest against government tyranny, freedom of association and formation of parties and organizations. The freedom of association and organizing parties should, however, be exercised to propagate virtue and never to spread "evil and mischief."[78] Thus according to Maududi, freedoms of opinion and belief and of expression are to be upheld and in modern times these rights cannot be enjoyed with the freedom of the press.[79] Freedom of consciousness must be respected, since the Qur'an has laid down the injunction that there is no compulsion in matters of faith [2:256]. Invoking this Qur'anic principle, Maududi argued, no one can force a non-Muslim to convert.[80] Based on purported precedent during the Caliphate of 'Umar, Maududi declared that no one in Islam can be imprisoned without due course of justice, and the accused has the right to defend himself.[81]

Maududi also stipulated some more "positive" rights, such as the right for social mobility in the Islamic state. In a utopian tenor, he wrote, "Every Individual, Muslim or non-Muslim, in an Islamic state will be allowed to make as much progress as he can, in accordance with his physical, mental and moral powers, without any impediment being placed in his way."[82] Free education at least up to university in this state, Maududi, proposed, should provide the means of social mobility for the talented from all walks of life.[83]

Maududi grounded his theory of an Islamic state on the notion of universal equality of Muslims before the law.[84] On the issues of non-Muslims in the Islamic state, however, his ideas were more convoluted. Maududi maintained that Islamic criminal law for Muslims and Non-Muslims would be the same. For example, the blood of a non-Muslim living in the Islamic state (*dhimmi*) is as good as a Muslim, and if a non-Muslim is killed by a Muslim, the punishment would be the same as if a Muslim had been killed. But in personal status affairs, such as marriage and divorce, the non-Muslims would follow their own laws and traditions.[85] In other spheres, however, Maududi prescribed significant restrictions on the rights of non-Muslims. Because the Islamic state can be run and its

77. *First Principles of the Islamic State*, 71–72.
78. *Human Rights in Islam*, 32.
79. *Islamic Sate*, 10.
80. *Human Rights in Islam*, 32–33. Maududi upheld the death penalty for apostasy from Islam, arguing that Islam is not a religion in the western sense of being a mere belief, but an allegiance to a political and social order, rejection of which is tantamount to treason and sedition. See Maududi's *Punishment of the Apostate according to Islamic Law*, 44–50.
81. *First principle of the Islamic State*, 69; *Islamic State*, 41
82. *Islamic State*, 12.
83. *Islamic State*, 24.
84. *Islamic State*, 54.
85. *Islamic State*, 60–62.

affairs "managed only by those who believe in its principles [...] it can employ non-Muslims in the Government, but it cannot place them in a position where they hold effective power and direct the policies of the Government."[86] Neither can non-Muslims serve in the military for the same issue of not believing in the state ideology.[87]

The state that Maududi was envisioning also included some of the features of a welfare state, "As far as economic life is concerned, it is the duty of the Islamic state and society to remove and abolish poverty as much as it its duty to eradicate atheism, materialism and disbelief. The Holy Prophet once said: 'Poverty leads to *kufr* (disbelief)' and he used to pray, 'Allah, save me both from poverty and disbelief.'"[88] Very much in conformity with its pastoral nature, the state in Maududi's imagination was charged with Guardianship of the needy and overseeing their material welfare. If the income of the Muslim treasury (*Bayt al-Mal*), does not "suffice to look after the economic needs of the poor, the Sultan (ruler) can force the rich to look after their needs."[89] But the Islamic system, Maududi was quick to add, is different from a Western welfare state, "in so far as it provides economic security to the people as a matter of right and not because it is afraid of mass protests and public agitation."[90]

Political Economy of the Pastoral State

Again in close conformity with his core idea of the limited agency of humans, Maududi conferred some economic liberties and self-oriented rights to the individual, but at the same time restricted them. He wrote, "Islam recognizes the right to private property and permits every man to make his outmost efforts to acquire property. But it also has laid stress on the concept of Amanah (trusteeship), which means that property really belongs to God, and man holds it in trust from God so that he cannot acquire or spend property, except by fair and lawful means and on fair and lawful objects and purposes."[91] At the practical level, Maududi staunchly supported the notion of private property, especially in the context of criticizing Marxism and communism, "the right of ownership of means of production is not an innovation brought into being by the bourgeois Capitalists, but such ownership has been the foundation through the ages on which all cultural and economic structures have been laid."[92] Marxists, Maududi continued, invented a brand new philosophy of history to demonstrate that, in the beginning of civilization, the right of individual ownership was unknown, and the

86. *Islamic State*, 58.
87. *Islamic State*, 63.
88. *Islamic State*, 26.
89. *Islamic State*, 27–28.
90. *Islamic State*, 29.
91. *Islamic State*, 26. Trusteeship in the Qur'an is a concept closely related to human's vicegerency and has similar connotations in terms of contingent human agency. See the Qur'an, 33: 72, "Lo! We offered the trust unto the heavens and the earth and the hills, but they shrank from bearing it and were afraid of it. And man assumed it. Lo! He hath proved a tyrant and a fool."
92. *Capitalism, Socialism and Islam*, 25.

ruling classes established it later to serve their interests.[93] The shortsightedness of the communists, Maududi observed, was their denial of such a thing as "human nature," which has an "inherent craving for personal gains," and it is this innate appetite for profit which is responsible for the constant desire for the revival of the old order of individual proprietary rights in communist societies. [94]

Maududi's visceral reaction against communism and other sorts of ideology that have some collectivist components, such as Fascism, was so strong that when discussing the principles of political economy he was much more on the side of tenet of Western capitalism than the general outline of his discourse otherwise seems to allow. Thus, he wrote that the foremost Islamic economic principle is the one that "attaches real importance to the individual and not to any party, nation or society. Individual is not meant for society, but the society for the individual. No party, nation or society in its entirety [i.e., as a collectivity] is accountable before God, rather every individual singly and in his personal capacity is answerable to Him for his deeds. And on this personal responsibility and accountability depends the entire moral value of mankind."[95]

On the other hand, Maududi severely criticized the capitalist system for giving free reign to the individual to pursue his interest at any cost and without much consideration for anyone or anything else, "the concept of personal freedom on which was raised the superstructure of capitalism provided the individual with an open and unconditional license to earn wealth by all means, fair or foul. The new ethics taught him that every means by which wealth could be amassed was lawful and fair, no matter whether the prosperity of one individual led to the ruin of many. Thus, the new-emerging social order favoured the individual's interest in every way against those of society, and the latter was provided without any safeguard against the former's greed and avarice."[96]

What Maududi, like many other Islamist thinkers in the twentieth century, aimed at was a form of restricted capitalism in which the essential right of private property was respected but on the theoretical level it was contingent and impermanent as human agency was contingent, and on a practical level, it was subject to certain significant limitations. He even went as far as declaring that "individual proprietary rights and craving for personal gain" were, "really useful and essential for collective interest, provided they were not unlimited as in an uncontrolled economy and were kept within proper bounds."[97] Based on these observations, especially the evils of a Soviet type economy, Maududi

93. *Capitalism, Socialism and Islam*, 25.
94. *Capitalism, Socialism and Islam*, 37.
95. *Capitalism, Socialism and Islam*, 38.
96. Syed Abul 'Ala Maududi, *Purdah and the Status of Women in Islam* (Lahore: Islamic Publications, 1979), 38.
97. *Capitalism, Socialism and Islam*, 40. In the same spirit, Maududi was prepared to denounce a planned economy. "Where there is planning [in economic matters] there must be control on speech and thought as well; no discussion, differences of opinion, criticism, explanation or stock-taking will be allowed. In fact, barring a few select brains, the whole nation will be deprived of freedom of thought [...] A few individuals of the nation may live as men and the rest as cattle, nay, the intimate parts of a machine [which] is too heavy a cost for the satisfaction that every one is assured of his share of daily sustenance." (*Capitalism, Socialism and Islam*, 45)

came to the conclusion that capitalism is the natural form for human society, but it has to be reformed and modified. He wrote that the tenets of capitalism:

> are the true principles of human economy, provided they are shorn of exaggerations incorporated with them by the bourgeoisie of the West because of their selfishness and extremist nature. Again, it will be appreciated that the sources of evil enumerated therein [with regard to modern Western capitalism] are really responsible for all the evils, and if removed, human economy can very smoothly run on its natural principles, without the evils of capitalism cropping up therein and resorting to artificial remedies. This is exactly the modus operandi adopted by Islam. It converts "uncontrolled economy" into free economy, and limits this freedom in the same way as it curtails this freedom in the cultural, social and other spheres of human society. And along with it closes all avenues by which the characteristics, effects and consequences of oppressive capitalism can enter the free economy.[98]

Theo-democracy

Perhaps the most succinct way of describing the sociopolitical state system that Maududi was trying to implement is described by the use of the neologism "Theo-democracy," which Maududi himself had coined. This term seems to have been used by Maududi to distinguish his notion of an Islamic state from both modern liberal democracy as well as theocracy. He defined a theocracy as a type of state in which a body of clerics claim to represent God and interpret divine law and words to promulgate laws by themselves and force it on the populace. Maududi argued that the Islamic state that he envisioned was fundamentally different from this type of state. In a theocracy, real power and management of the affairs of society is in the hands of a small elite of mostly clerics with absolute authority, whose opinions are deemed to be equivalent to law and beyond criticism and accountability.[99] But in an Islamic state, "there is no such permanent body of priests or religious leaders. Every individual Muslim is in direct communication with God and does not need the intermediary of holy men or priests. The teachings of Islam are available to every Muslim and, according to Islam, it is the duty of every Muslim to acquire a modicum of religious knowledge. Those who conduct and manage the affairs of the Islamic State are answerable to God as well as to the people. The people in authority in an Islamic state are only required to be men of knowledge and piety, and it is open to everyone to acquire knowledge and develop a pious character."[100]

---

98. *Capitalism, Socialism and Islam*, 60.
99. *Islamic State*, 64.
100. *Islamic State*, 64. Maududi thought Islam's anti-passivity that distinguishes it from Christianity, further precludes the development of a theocracy: "There is another important difference between Islam and theocracy. The fundamental concept of theocracy is that this life is a punishment for our original sin and this punishment must be born by everyone with outmost patience. The consequence of this outlook is that the struggle to reform the state and protest against its wrong polices becomes an undesirable thing. Man becomes submissive and resigned to his fate. On the contrary Islam says that man is the vicegerent of God. He has been blessed with innumerable gifts which make for happiness in this life." (*Islamic State*, 66)

In contrast to theocracy as defined and described above and a liberal democracy, Maududi's Theo-democracy was a state that, in close conformity to his notion of human vicegerency, the real power lies with God, but people have some sovereignty:

> The entire Muslim population runs the state in accordance with the Book of God and practice of His of Prophet. If I were permitted to coin a new term, I would describe this system of government as a "Theo-democracy," that is to say a divine democratic government, because under it Muslims have been given a limited popular sovereignty under the suzerainty of God.[101]

As I have been suggesting, at the core of Maududi's discourse is a notion of human subjectivity, which is contingent upon God's subjectivity who is the real subject. I have called this form of indirect human empowerment as "mediated subjectivity," in which humans' power and agency derives from that of the divine and is dependent upon it. This core notion in Maududi, and most other Islamist thinkers in the twentieth century, is what gives humans a limited power, and in political terms limited sovereignty. As such the idea of the human individual that Maududi entertained was a proto-agent who vicariously carried the burdens and benefits of this limited subjectivity. For such a human to be formed in reality, Maududi had designed a program of discipline that was essential to the construction of his ideal Islamic state.

Disciplining the (Vicarious) Agent

A pastoral state is disciplining by nature. The very didactic approach that is, as we saw above, essential to Maududi's discourse, entails the disciplining of the proto-agent that he was attempting to forge for the creation of the Islamic state.

Islamic civilization, Maududi argued, started to decline when its upper classes began a life of comfort and ease. Here Maududi invoked the Qur'anic notion of *itraf* to make his point. The Arabic root *tarifa*, from which *itraf* is derived, means to live in opulence and luxury, with negative connotations of a life of ease, emasculation and corruption.[102] After the era of the Righteous Caliphs, the well-off classes in the Islamic civilization started ignoring the requirements of Allah and followed the path of Satan, liberalizing the commandments of

---

Maududi also insisted that the role of Ulema in the running of a modern Islamic state would be relatively minor because their expertise would be consulted only if some law is deemed to impinge on the domain of the Shari'ah or contradict basic principles and values of Islam. (*Islamic State*, 66)

101. *Political Theory of Islam*, 22. In terms of the procedures of formal democracy, Maududi insisted, Theo-democracy was not different from secular democracy; the difference lied in the grounding of the two systems: "In Western Secular Democracy, the Government is established or changed by the exercise of the will of the common voters. Our Democracy envisions the same; but the difference lies in the fact that whereas in the Western system, the democratic state enjoys the right of absolute authority, in our democracy the *khalifat* is bound to keep within the limits prescribed by the Divine Code." (*First Principles of the Islamic State*, 26)

102. The Qur'an repeatedly warns of the devastating consequences of a life of ease, where a term related to *itraf* is used in the context of the warning. See 11:116; 17:16; 21:13; 23:33; 23:64; 34:34; 43:23 and 56:45.

the Shari'ah to adopt a life of license. This process, Maududi contended, has reached a new zenith since the 19th century when the Muslim upper classes, at least in the subcontinent, took up the life-style of Europeans and abandoned themselves in a life of luxury, and by doing so causing the disempowerment of the Muslims even further.[103]

Maududi set out to reverse this process, and for this reason he often praised discipline:

> You cannot find even a solitary example of any nation in history attaining power and prestige through easy going, lotus eating and gain seeking, if you are not ready to lean any lessons form Islamic history. No nation could attain respect and prestige in the world without observing some principles and discipline, without taking pains and suffering want and hardship for a sacred cause and without the spirit to sacrifice its ambitions and its own interests. This discipline, this commitment to principles and sacrifice of luxuries and comforts and benefits could be noticed in one form or the other in the progressing nations.[104]

The most important factor in the lack of discipline, Maududi pointed out, was the succumbing to excessive temptations of the flesh. "The greatest factors to misguide men," he maintained, "are his own corporeal urges. It is quite impossible for one to become a slave of God while he submits himself to his corporeal urges. He will constantly be looking out as to which work will fetch him money, which undertaking will bring fame and honour, which pursuit will give him pleasure, and what will provide him with comfort and ease."[105]

Maududi's interest in discipline and its connection to the control of human corporeal urges in turn led him to embark upon rather elaborate speculations on human sexuality. First, he believed that sexual urges in humans are higher and greater than those of animals, because among humans, while a portion of the libido provides the energy needed for procreation, a large part of it is utilized establishing close human bonds necessary for the construction of community life and civilization. "The more one thinks the more will one be convinced that nature intends to make the human race, unlike other species, a civilized race used to community life. That is why the heart of man has been infused with an unusual urge for sexual love and attachment, which demands not only physical union and mating but also an enduring and sincere spiritual fellowship. That is why man has been endowed with sexual inclination in a degree greater than what is required for the

103. *West versus Islam*, 190–94.

104. *West versus Islam*, 264. Maududi made a point of conveying the idea that discipline and power are closely related, as he continued his thoughts on discipline: "Islam puts it in one way while other progressing nations put it in some other forms. Visit any of the people, you will have to follow their rules and regulations and bear the rigours of their discipline. Anywhere you go, you will be requested to follow a set of principles and to offer sacrifice for some objectives and principles. If you are fond of easy going and relaxation and lack stamina to endure any rigour and bitterness, then you can be free from the bondage of Islam and go any where, but you will get no position of respect anywhere, neither shall you find any source of strength." (*West versus Islam*, 264–65) It is interesting that by "progressing nations" Maududi most probably had Western nations in mind and although he is very critical of their life of luxury in their late modernity, he praises their discipline.

105. *Fundamentals of Islam*, 51

purpose of mating."[106] History has shown, Maududi further argued, that the people and nations who have indulged in pleasures of the flesh have always been doomed, as their literature, art, religion and intellectual pursuits abounded in "sensational themes."[107]

Nature, Maududi contended, has devised some mechanism to curb the excessive sexual urges—such as women's "charm and sweetness of manner" or children's charm to soften men's aggressive libido—but they are hardly adequate. It is only monotheistic religion that can induce discipline and regulate runaway human sexual urges. Referring to Abrahamic religions, Maududi wrote, "it was the social discipline brought by them that gave birth to the family system whose grip makes mere boys and girls co-operate with each other and understand their responsibility as husband and wife, otherwise the demands of their animal nature would be too vigorous to be prevented from indulging in free sexual gratification by the mere sense of moral responsibility without any external discipline."[108]

Based on these premises, Maududi prescribed certain mechanisms that already existed in many Islamic societies to discipline the body and regulate human sexuality in the service of forging the Islamic proto-agent. Most important of these mechanisms was the institution of sexual segregation, known by the term Purdah. For Maududi, the very social discipline that is necessary for the construction of his Islamic proto-agent hinges upon keeping men and women apart: "Thus the objective of Islam is to establish a social order that segregates the spheres of activity of the male and the female, discourages and controls the free intermingling of the sexes and curbs all such factors as are likely to *upset and jeopardize the social discipline.*"[109] In the same vein, it is not surprising that Maududi believed that the very foundation of Islamic civilization was located in the proper segregation of men and women. He argued that the institution of Purdah may seem unimportant to some, but it constitutes the very lynchpin of Islamic social order:

---

106. *Purdah and the State of Women in Islam*, 85

107. *Purdah and the State of Women in Islam*, 88. It is for this reason, Maududi claimed, that Islam has frowned upon certain aspects of art, "From the earliest times, the picture has served as the greatest vehicle for spreading immortality and lewdness in the world. Wine, music, dancing, indecent literature and statute have always been [and] are now more than ever before, the most potent instigators of adultery and fornication." (Syed Abul 'Ala Maudoodi, *Correspondence between Maulana Maudoodi and Maryam Jameela* (Lahore: Mohammad Yusuf Khan, 1969), 57.) It is important to note here that Maududi also warned against the other extreme, that is asceticism and complete denunciation of sexual urges: "Similar will be the fate of the civilization which follows the other extreme. Just as dissipation of sexual energy is harmful, so is that tendency to curb and suppress it unduly. The civilization that leads man into retirement, towards celibacy and monasticism, fights against nature. But nature has never been defeated by any opponent; it has rather crushed its opponents. Pure monasticism can never become the basis of a civilization [...] it is possible to create a civilization with a non-sexual atmosphere by inculcating monastic ideas in the minds [of the people] and by educating the people to look upon the sexual relation as something base, despicable and filthy, keeping away from which may be a criterion of morality and curbing which by all possible means an act of piety. But curbing the sexual urge is in fact curbing humanity itself." (*Purdah and the State of Women in Islam*, 89)

108. *Purdah and the State of Women in Islam*, 92–93.

109. *Purdah and the State of Women in Islam*, 23; emphasis added.

> If one has in mind only a pillar of the whole structure of a building, one cannot help wondering why the pillar has been erected at all. One will find it devoid of any wisdom, any sense. It will never occur to one who suitably and proportionally has the engineer devise it to give support to the building, how the building will be affected in case it is demolished. Exactly similar is the case of Purdah. When it is considered apart from the Social System in which it has been provided like a pillar in a building to fulfill a particular need, it will appear devoid of all sense of wisdom, and nobody will realize why the two sexes of the human race have been segregated. Therefore, it is absolutely essential that in order to understand the wisdom of the erection of the pillar, the whole building for which it has been provided should be carefully examined.[110]

Derived from Persian, Purdah literally means a curtain, symbolizing the near total separation of men and women. But as in many other types of segregation the two segregated populations are not equal, one is confined while the other is at large. For Maududi segregation meant not only the covering of women's bodies, but a general exclusion of women from the public sphere. Thus he meticulously articulated a system of segregation that started with the body, particularly women's bodies, and extended it to include the mind. Maududi interpreted Qur'an, particularly verse 59 of chapter 33, in such a way that it would be preferable if even women's faces were covered.[111] The voice of a woman should not be heard by an unrelated man either: "The voice is another agent of the evil spirit. There are countless mischiefs which are caused and spread by the voice. A man and a woman may apparently be absorbed in innocent talk, but the hidden motive of heart is at work: it is rendering the voice more and more sweet, and the accent and the words more and more appealing."[112]

In close conformity with above formulations, Maududi demanded that the most appropriate place for women was the house. Islam does not allow distinction between

110. *Purdah and the State of Women in Islam*, 213.

111. *Purdah and the State of Women in Islam*, 191–98.

112. *Purdah and the State of Women in Islam*, 164. Even the perfume of a woman, Maududi asserted, should not be spread to unrelated men. (*Purdah and the State of Women in Islam*, 165) In fact Maududi placed a considerable amount of emphasis on "non-physical" aspects of segregation: "In the eyes of law, adultery implies physical union only, but from the moral point of view every evil inclination towards a member of the opposite sex outside marriage amounts to adultery. Thus enjoying the beauty of the other woman with the eyes, relishing the sweetness of her voice with the ears, drawing pleasure of the tongue by conversing with her, and turning of the feet over and over again to visit her street, are all the preliminaries of adultery, nay, adultery itself. Law cannot have jurisdiction over such an act, for it springs from the hidden motives of man." (*Purdah and the State of Women in Islam*, 162) Apparently Maududi was quite lax with respect to how purdah applied to his wife. Vali Nasr writes: "From before her marriage, Mahmudah Begum [Maududi's wife] was quite liberated and modern in her ways. Early on, she rode a bicycle around Delhi and did not observe purdah. Ironically, Mawdudi had complained of the absence of purdah, which he witnessed during the very trip in which he got married, as one of the reasons for dismay at Islam's future prospects. Mawdudi clearly loved his strong-willed, liberal, and independent-minded wife, however, and allowed her greater latitude than he did Muslims in general. The standards that prevailed in his household were very different from the standards he required of others, including Jama'at members." (*Mawdudi and the Making of Islamic Revivalism*, 34)

men and women, in so far as acquiring knowledge is concerned. But, "from the Islamic point of view, the right sort of education for women is that which prepares her to become a good wife, good mother and good housekeeper. Her sphere of activity is the home."[113] Even insofar as essential Islamic duties, such as congregational prayer, are concerned, it is best if women offer their prayers at home in seclusion.[114] "Men are free to undertake a journey at will," declared Maududi, "but a woman, whether she is married, unmarried or a widow, cannot travel unless she is accompanied by a *mahram* [a close male relative]."[115]

Maududi seemed to have felt a necessity for justifying his misogynistic views. For this reason he was willing to exert his utmost effort to prove that women's free behavior would lead to destruction of civilization, and to demonstrate the inherent inferiority of women. Very much in agreement with his philosophy of history, Maududi thought that civilization has a tendency to lead to laxness in controlling women, which in turn leads to the undermining of the family that undergirds civilization,

> History testifies that when a community shakes off barbarism and advances toward civilization, its women follow its men as maids and bondwomen. Initially the community gains momentum from the store of energies that accrue from the wild life the desert, but at a later stage of development it begins to realize that it cannot go any further by keeping half of its population in a state of bondage. Thus, when the community finds the pace of advancement being retarded, the feeling of necessity compels it to enable the neglected half also to keep pace with the advanced half. But it does not rest content with making amends only, it bestows freedom upon the fair sex with result that the latter's excessive freedom deals a fatal blow at the family which is the very basis of civilization.[116]

113. *Purdah and the State of Women in Islam*, 152.
114. *Purdah and the State of Women in Islam*, 202.
115. *Purdah and the State of Women in Islam*, 147. Though in dire circumstance women may have to work outside the home to earn a living, Maududi allowed it as the last resort, in case men are disabled, for example.
116. *Purdah and the State of Women in Islam*, 2. Maududi identified women's economic power and the allure of their sexuality as two essential factors in decline of a civilization. In regard to Roman civilization and it decline, for example, he wrote: "With the advancement on the road to civilization, the Roman concept about the position of the woman underwent a serious change [...] Marriage was reduced to a civil contract which was held at the sweet will of the partners, which rendered the responsibilities of married life very light. Moreover, the woman was given full proprietary rights over inherited and other property and the law made her free of the authority of the father and husband. Thus the Roman women not only became economically independent, but gradually a good portion of the national wealth also slipped into their control. They lent money to their husbands at high rates of interest with result that husbands of wealthy wives virtually became their slaves [...] [When] the checks on public morality became weak, the fold of sexual licentiousness, nudity and promiscuity burst upon Rome. Theaters became the scene of moral perversion and nude performance; dwelling places were decorated with nude and immoral painting; and prostitution became so widespread and popular [...] naked women competed in race contests. Males and females took bath together in public baths [...] When the Romans became so overwhelmed by animal passions, their glory completely faded away leaving not even a trace behind it. (*Purdah and the State of Women in Islam*, 7–9)

In a similar vein, Maududi tried to justify his scheme for the seclusion of women on biological grounds. "From the time that sex formation of the foetus starts," Maududi wrote, "the physiological structures of the two sexes begin to develop differently. The female physical system is evolved in order to bear and bring up children."[117] He also marshaled a litany of evidence from Western scientific literature of the early twentieth century, from difficulties in menstruation to pregnancy and childbirth, to demonstrate women's unfitness to hold positions of power, or even making a simple living, in society.[118] More important, however, was Maududi's philosophical views of the differences between men and women which were connected to his reading of gender biology. Not surprisingly, he viewed men as subjects and agents and women as objects and passive, "And since in the sexual life man has been made active and woman passive, she has been endowed with those very qualities alone which help prepare her for the passive role in life only. That is why she is tender and plastic instead of rough and rigid. That is why she is soft and pliable, submissive and impressionable, yielding and timid by nature. With these qualities she cannot be expected to function successfully in these spheres of life which demand firmness and authority, resistance and cold-temperedness, and which require the exercise of unbiased, objective judgment and strong will-power."[119] Maududi then unabashedly declared the superiority of active men to women who are by nature passive, thus sealing the subject-object relationship between men and women:

> "Activity" in itself is naturally superior to "passivity" and femininity. This superiority is not due to any merit in masculinity against any demerit in femininity. It is rather due to the

117. *Purdah and the State of Women in Islam,* 114. At times Maududi's writings strongly implied that the sole purpose of women in life is procreation: "It appears as if the entire machinery of the woman's body is directed to serve the needs of the race [...] Soon after the conception has taken place her entire psycho-physical being undergoes a remarkable change. Now the interests of the child reign supreme over every organ of her body [...] By the time she reaches old age all beauty, freshness, charm depart from her. Her vibrant youthfulness, charming looks, and bewitching form all leave her. In fact it is the beginning of all sorts of bodily ailments and psychological depression and apathy that actually culminates in death. This abundantly shows that the best period for a woman's life is the one when she is most suited for the procreation of her race and when she is left to live just for herself, that is the worst and most difficult time she has to brace." (*Purdah and the State of Women in Islam,* 90–91)
118. *Purdah and the State of Women in Islam,* 114–20.
119. *Purdah and the State of Women in Islam,* 120. Interestingly, Maududi used men's alleged natural subjectivity and women's objectivity as the model for subject-object relationship in general that presumably operates in the universe: "Now let us consider the nature of the sex-relationship. This relationship itself implies that one partner in the pair should be active and the other receptive and passive; one prompt to influence and the other ready to be influenced, one prepared to act and the other willing to be acted upon. This relationship between the active functioning and the passive functioning, influencing and being influenced, acting and being acted upon, is the sex relation between the partners of a pair. This is the basic relation which gives rise to all other relations functioning and operating in the world. All that exists in this world has been created in pairs and the real and basic relationship between the members of each pair is the sex-relationship, the relationship signifying "activity" and "passivity," though it has assumed different forms in different strata of the Creation." (*Purdah and the State of Women in Islam,* 132)

> fact of possessing natural qualities of dominance, power and authority. A thing that acts upon something else is able to do so on account of its being dominant, more powerful and impressive. On the other hand, the thing that submits and yields, behaves so simply because it is by nature passive, weaker and inclined to be impressed and influenced. Just as the existence of both the active and the passive partner is necessary for the act to occur, so its is also necessary that the active partner should be dominant and able to produce the desired effect, and the passive partner yielding and inclined to be receptive. For if both partners are equally powerful and neither is dominant, there will be no question of submission and the act will not take place at all.[120]

The socio-legal consequences of such theorization on Maududi's part were that he confirmed the principles of patriarchy evermore strongly by recognizing men as the sole bearer of authority in the family and by extension the society. He likened the family to an army which necessarily needs a leader and asserted that such a leader could only be a man.[121]

We should always bear in mind, however, that Maududi's misogynistic views were closely linked to his obsession with discipline, to forge the male proto-agent of his ideal state, as we saw briefly above. For this reason, he dwelled extensively on the idea of discipline and its roots in Islamic ethos and notions of temperance in the teachings of Islam. As such Maududi often juxtaposed instances from military training and acts of discipline intrinsic in some Islamic rituals such as daily prayer and fasting. The military, Maududi often remarked, offered the best example of the need for discipline and sustained training. Men have to be ever vigilant in Islam, just as in the army, to fight against the forces of evil and strive to build the kingdom of God (i.e., Maududi's utopian state) upon earth:

> Islam is not a matter of mere precept but is very much a practical religion which embraces all of one's life activity. To accept Islam is to enter the service of God, a service which entails perpetual duty in which there is no let-up, no casual or other leave, and no holidays. It does not require much stretching of the imagination to visualize the degree of discipline and quality of training required, and the stringency of the tests, which must be imposed for keeping it in constant state of readiness. How can merely oral acknowledgement of Creed suffice for this? [...] It is with the objective of instilling this kind of sense of duty and of discipline that the five daily prayers have been made an obligatory act.[122]

And the *adhan*, or the call to prayer, corresponded for Maududi to the bugle in the military that summons the disciplined solders to practice their agency on the world.[123] Similarly, fasting, observed Maududi, "is a special intensive month-long course, which imposes a rigid and relentless discipline for a continuous period of 20 or 30 days in order to strengthen the effects of Prayer whenever they have been rather light."[124] In this regard Maududi provided

120. *Purdah and the State of Women in Islam*, 134.
121. *Purdah and the State of Women in Islam*, 122.
122. Syed Abul 'Ala Maududi. *Worship in Islam* (Karachi: Islamic Research Academy, 1977), 18–19.
123. *Worship in Islam*, 19.
124. *Worship in Islam*, 73.

a somewhat new interpretation of a central concept in Islam. Normally the concept of *taqwa* is understood analogously to the idea of piety, but Maududi interpreted it in a manner that stood in proximity to the notion of temperance and self-control, which in fact is closer to the etymology of the term *taqwa* in Arabic. Thus Maududi believed that some of the most important characteristics of a modern agency (e.g., perseverance, fortitude, goal-oriented attitude) on the one hand, and the characteristics of his proto-agency, such as trust in God, on the other hand, could only be formed on the basis of Islamic disciplinary power of temperance (*taqwa*) as manifested in fasting:

> [Q]ualities which Islam needs in its adherents are: perseverance so that they dedicate their entire lives to an apparently fruitless effort for the sake of a high and sublime objective; steadfastness so that they are not lured away by the conveniences and comforts and delights and enjoyment of wrong paths; fortitude so that no matter what the set-backs, hardships, dangers, calamites and reverses, there is no faltering of effort; single-mindedness so that they disregard all temporary and expedient considerations and march steadily towards their goal; and an abiding trust in God so that they suffer no doubt as to the far-reaching but time-consuming outcome of their efforts aimed at serving and establishing Truth, even though there may be no sign of such result making their appearance in this world during their own life-time. It is such persons who can be depended upon and the task of which Islam wants its party to accomplish needs only those who have dependable and reliable character based on all the qualities enumerated above. This is the kind of men *taqwa* produces, and there can be no better programme than fasting for the training of those who have in them the seed of *taqwa* and for developing it to the full.[125]

Another very important characteristic of the modern agent is the development of willpower and, Maududi believed, *taqwa*, as he defined the concept, is instrumental in strengthening the willpower. Referring to the impact of fasting on the person in the past tense he wrote: "he had full sense of duty and of responsibility; acted as his own censor and entirely on his own kept his mind and self under full control so that the moment any thought of or desire for committing a breach of the regulations took birth in the innermost recesses of his heart, and well before it could manifest itself in practice, he stifled it forthwith by the exercise of his will-power. In other words, he did not need any external pressure for keeping within the law."[126] In fact what Maududi was trying to achieve was very close to the idea of the human mind controlling the inner nature and the body, which is the most important step toward the creation of a modern subject. Not surprisingly, he thought this essential task should be accomplished through the disciplinary power of fasting:

> Of all the things in the universe which God has made subservient to us, it is the human body which is the most useful and most efficacious. All the natural desires it possesses are directly related to its primary needs, which it is our duty to fulfill. It has a right to expect us to keep it in comfort, to provide it with nourishment, to satisfy its urge for the preservation of the species and not allow it to go to waste or overuse. But, when all is said and done, this particular

125. *Worship in Islam*, 92.
126. *Worship in Islam*, 95.

> animal has been created within us for service to us and to our own goal in life, and not the other way round [...] One of the most important objects of Fasting is to confer on man that very kind of control over this animal which we have just mentioned. The three powerful urges [hunger, thirst and sex] which it possess and which it seeks to employ to compel us to give it our obedience [—] it is those very urges and weapons which the Ramazan fast trains us to control, and after putting the bit in the mouth, hands over its reins to that self in us which has pledged its belief in God and has resolved to follow the path prescribed by Him. How helpless does the animal [within us] become! From morning till evening it keeps begging for food or drink and we turn a deaf ear to all its entreaties.[127]

We should also not lose sight of the fact that, for Maududi, this type of discipline was necessary for acquiring power in this world to act upon it. "A person who has never been accustomed to controlling his desires, who has always submitted tamely to any demand of his base self and for whom each and very urge of his animal nature has meant an irresistible command," he wrote, "can never achieve anything worthwhile in the world." In order to "accomplish great things a person should at least have so much of self-control that he might keep his physical desires within proper bounds and be able to employ the mental and the physical faculties which God has bestowed on him in a rational manner. This is why fasting on other days than in Ramazan has been declared as an approved act so that one's will-power keeps getting reinforced."[128] Of course Maududi was quick to add that the power of the self-control that Islam prescribes does not allow humans to be autonomous of God, and not being subservient to him and his injunctions.[129]

Secularity within Religiosity

As we saw above, Maududi's discourse displays a striking degree of concern with mundane questions in general. For this reason it is not surprising to find specifically secular themes and trends in his thought also. Thus Maududi showed a specific distaste for magical trends in Islam. He complained that the Qur'an, which had been the beacon of knowledge and fountainhead of power for Muslims for centuries, had been reduced to a mere object of veneration and formal respect.[130] Similarly he chastised the Ulema for being engrossed in futile theological and metaphysical debates, such as "whether the Prophet had knowledge of the Unseen or not," or whether God could tell a lie, or what are the merits of visiting graves of "saints," or the merits of saying Amen in a loud voice. These and many other questions like them, only dissipate the energy of the faithful, detracting them from the great struggle they face over right and wrong, vice and virtue taking place all around the world.[131] In a similar spirit Maududi blamed all those, "who have deflected the attention of the Muslims from their real mission

127. *Worship in Islam*, 102–3.
128. *Worship in Islam*, 105.
129. *Worship in Islam*, 106.
130. *West versus Islam*, 36.
131. *West versus Islam*, 76.

to superstitions and talismans, incantations and supererogatory offerings of shortcuts to salvation and welfare, to solutions of all problems, removal of all difficulties and achievement of all aims and objectives without any struggle and labour and through the favour of some late divine."[132]

There is very little doubt that Maududi's stance against magic was closely related to his notion of human empowerment through the Divine and the proto-agent that he was pursuing. Magic and superstition, in Maududi's estimation, annul the possibility of human empowerment that was the main aim of the Qur'an. Referring to Muslims, Maududi wrote, "The Quran was sent to them that they would read it, understand it and act upon it, and with its help would establish on God's earth a government which will function according to the law of God. The Quran came to grant them dignity and power. It came to make them a genuine vicegerent of God on the earth. And History testifies that when they acted according to its directions its power making them Imam and leader of the world. But now for them its utility is confined to keeping it in the house in order to drive away *jinns*, to inscribe the verses on paper and hang it round the neck or wash it in water and drink it, and read the contents unintelligibly to get some blessing."[133] Maududi even extended his anti-magic approach to the main rituals in Islam if they are treated as mere physical acts: "You think that standing toward Qibla [direction of prayer toward Mecca] with folded hands, bowing with your hands resting on the knees, prostrating with hands placed on the ground and uttering a few stereotyped words—only such few actions and movements are by themselves 'Ibadat [acts of worship]. You think that to be hungry and thirsty from morning till evening every day from the first of Ramadan till the appearance of Shawwal moon [end of Ramadan] is called 'Ibadat. You think that a verbal recital of some parts of Surahs [chapters] of the Quran is called 'Ibadat. You think that a visit to Mecca and circumambulation of K'aba is 'Ibadat."[134]

132. *Jihad in Islam*, 29. It is important to note that the reason why Maududi was so vehemently against magic was that it detracts from the real source of power, which in his scheme lies with the Divine from which humans derive their power. Superstition, in this view, destroys the source of power and consequently its recipient: "Addressing a prayer to a saint confined to his grave hundreds or even thousands of miles away, clearly indicates that I believe him—though dead—to be possessed of the power to listen to a prayer at such a distance or to otherwise be aware of things so far off, or if one may use the appropriate Arabic words, to be both *samee* [all-hearing] and *baseer* [all-seeing]." (Syed Abul 'Ala Maududi, *Four Basic Qur'anic Terms* (Lahore: Islamic Publications, 1979), 14) In sharp contrast to Hussein Nasr who, as we will see in a later chapter, wishes to "magicalize" Islam, Maududi grounded his denunciation of magic in the Qur'an. Referring to the Qur'an 4:51, in which notions of *jibit* and *taghut*, meaning idols and false deities (with connotations of magic and thaumaturgy), are broached, Maududi wrote: "The word *jibet* is a comprehensive term for all myths and superstitions, embracing such superstitious things as magic, the art of occult, black magic, necromancy, witchcraft, soothsaying, divination, the belief in talismans or lucky stones or unlucky colours or numbers or a natural phenomenon, etc., or in the influence of the heavenly bodies on human affairs [...] So when the Jews and Christians committed the two errors [believing in *jibet* and *taghut*] [...] the result of the first was that different kinds of superstitious beliefs took hold of their minds [...]" (*Four Basic Qur'anic Terms*, 64)

133. *Fundamentals of Islam*, 17.

134. *Fundamentals of Islam*, 97.

This type of attitude on the part of Maududi led him to take up a radically practical approach toward religion. He believed that the real cause of the decline in Islamic civilization and the deterioration of its culture lied in the "rupture between religion and practical life," and the only way to revitalize the Islamic world and restore its power was to "re-establish the liaison and contact between religion and day to day practical life."[135] As we saw above, Maududi redefined daily prayer and fasting largely in terms of their utility for development and disciplining the proto-agent. He also had had another utility for some of the essential requirements of Islam, namely their functionality in forging and maintaining social solidarity in Muslim ranks. In this tumultuous world in which the Muslims are besieged by the forces of evil, Islamic solidarity is essential for strength and "*salah* [prayer] is the greatest instrument to build up this strength."[136] In the same vein, Maududi accentuated the this-worldly benefits of the Hajj and its positive impacts on the wellbeing of the Muslim community at large.[137] In this respect Maududi went as far as implicitly equating worship with action in this world:

> In short, the renunciation of the world, taking up one's abode in some remote or secluded spot and repeating Allah's name even with the utmost concentration and fear of Him in heart, is not *'ibdah* [worship] as He wants it. Rather it is the full involvement in the affairs [of] the world of which He has created us to be a part, and over it made us His vicegerent, and the shouldering of all responsibilities of life and conducting ourselves strictly in accordance with His law while doing all this, which is *'ibadah* in its real sense. The way to remember God, that is, to perform *zikr* [remembrance of God] is not to go on repeating His name in parrot-like fashion but, rather, to fully participate in those affairs and activities which are likely to make one forget God, and yet never forget Him.[138]

But, of course, he immediately added that this form of agency is not unbounded and that the human control over the earth and its riches is not permitted in absolute terms, but only as contingent vicegerency of God, who is the real owner of the universe.[139]

Maududi's pragmatic approach to religion had very important implications for the political sphere. Just like some other Islamist ideologues studied in this volume, at the core

135. *West versus Islam*, 274.

136. *Fundamentals of Islam*, 107.

137. *Fundamentals of Islam*, 219–37. Interestingly, Maududi thought that the idea of life after death possessed a great utility for social order, namely guaranteeing moral behavior in this world: "A little reflection should help us to see that the question of life after death is not merely a philosophical question; it is deeply and intimately related to our everyday life. In fact our moral attitude depends entirely upon this question. If a person is of the view that the life of this world is the only life and that there is no life of any kind after that, he must develop a particular type of moral attitude. A racially different kind of attitude and approach is bound to result if he believes that this life is to be followed by another where one will have to render account of all one's acts in this world, and that one's ultimate fate in the Hereafter will depend upon one's conduct in worldly life." (Syed Abul 'Ala Maududi, *Life after Death* (Lahore: Islamic Publications, 1968), 3–4)

138. *Worship in Islam*, 7–8.

139. *Worship in Islam*, 8.

of Maududi's concept of contingent human agency was that no human being is fit to rule other humans, because sovereignty belongs to God only: "Man has not been created to be a servant and slave of anybody else nor is there anyone else except that real Master who is capable of giving reward and punishment […] This means that Allah has sent His messenger with the true Din [religion] for the purpose that should end the sovereignty of all false gods and make man so emancipated that he should become servant of none except that of the Lord of the universe no matter what hue and cry the unbelievers and polytheists may raise against it because of their ignorance."[140] "The real objective of Islam," he stated in later pages of the same book, "is to remove the lordship of man over man and to establish the government of One God."[141] Accordingly, Maududi often rejected monarchy, oligarchy, aristocracy, and theocracy.

The idea of humans not submitting to any other entity except that of God is a contradictory but potentially emancipatory phenomenon. While in Maududi and other Islamist ideologues this notion is very often burdened by obedience to religious precepts and restrictions, in the political sphere, it has the *potential* of preparing a population for self-rule and republicanism by rebuffing the domination of monarchs, and other ruling elite. It is true that Maududi and other Islamists wished to achieve this goal by empowering the small revolutionary (or in the case of Maududi a reformist-revolutionary) elite, but in the long term this experience of conditional and inchoate autonomy may contain the possibility of giving rise to the spirit of republicanism and self-rule among the populace. For this reason I would call this phenomenon "proto-republicanism." This type of conceptualization of power has the potential, but not inevitability, of engendering a political culture of self-rule and popular sovereignty, even though its current advocates vehemently reject the idea of sovereignty of the people.[142] In this connection it is very important to note that Maududi, for the most part, maintained an anti-clerical stance. Although he stated that in his Islamic state the expertise of the Ulema would be used to ensure conformity of new laws with the Islamic law, Maududi otherwise castigated the Islamic clerics for their intransigence towards new ideas and exigencies that the modern world has placed before Muslims and thought the Ulema were responsible for the domination of Muslims by the Westerners.[143]

140. *Fundamentals of Islam*, 82.

141. *Fundamental of Islam*, 243.

142. It is very easy to conflate an analysis of the potentiality of historical transformation with a "teleological" approach. While no one can assert that what I identify as proto-republicanism, constituting the core of the political theory of some of the Islamists considered in this volume, would develop into a full-fledged popular sovereignty, it is reasonable to assume that the historical foundations of the mass desire for self-rule could be laid through the mechanism of Islamists' rejection of submission to non-God as discussed here. I sometimes use the prefix "proto" in describing some of the intellectual, social and political phenomena in Muslim societies, judiciously. These societies are experiencing deep-seated transformations which require the term proto before certain words to capture these changes.

143. *West versus Islam*, 40–42.

Conclusion

For Maududi, as we saw above, the category of power and human's relations to it, is central. This is true for many of the Islamist thinkers discussed in this book. But for Maududi's ideology, it occupied an even more prominent position, no doubt because of his first hand experience with colonialism and the struggle as a minority in non-Muslim context before the foundation of Pakistan and after that as the leader of a political party seeking state power. Maududi was keenly aware that for the achievement of power, and formation of the state, the members of society (in his case men) had to go through the process of empowerment and subject formation. But the subject he was attempting to forge was only a partial agent whose subjectivity was very much contingent upon the Agency of God, which accordingly could be negated or at least severely limited at times. Nevertheless, the formation of this male proto-subject necessitated a regimen of harsh discipline that Maududi incorporated in his discourse. To be sure most of the Islamist theorists in the twentieth century had articulated similar ideas. What makes Maududi's thought stand out is the meticulous and systematic elaboration in the expression of these ideas. This characteristic of Maududi's thought was especially true with regard to his linking of discipline, religious tenets and regulation of human sexuality. For most of the other Islamists, the links between the formation of proto-agent, discipline, religious principles and human sexuality is there, but it is more or less implicitly articulated. In Maududi's discourse, however, this theoretical concatenation is quite explicit and elaborate. He was perhaps unique in elaborately theorizing on human sexuality from a contemporary Islamic perspective.

By linking the disciplining of the proto-subject, through the control of human sexuality, to seclusion of women, Maududi also shed much needed light on the status that he considered for women in his ideal Islamic state. This is particularly important because what other contemporary Islamists practiced, i.e., seclusion of women and tight control of their sexuality, but did not articulate well, Maududi articulated and provided a theoretical grounding for it. In this way Maududi explicated, beyond merely his own ideology, the contemporary Islamist obsession with the control of women and how it leads to their subordination.

Chapter Three

AN ISLAMIC TOTALITY IN THE IDEOLOGY OF SAYYID QUTB

"Totality" has indeed enjoyed a privileged place in the discourse of Western culture. Resonating with affirmative connotations, it has generally been associated with other positively charged words, such as coherence, order, fulfillment, harmony, plentitude, meaningfulness, consensus and community. And concomitantly, it has been contrasted with such negatively valenced concepts as alienation, fragmentation, disorder, conflict, contradiction, serialization, atomization and estrangement. Although it has not entirely escaped censure—Albert Camus' linkage of it with totalitarianism in the Rebel is a striking example—it has normally been imbued with what Lovejoy called "metaphysical pathos" the power to arouse a positive mood on the part of its users by the congeniality of its subtle associations.[1]

There is a general tendency among most versions of radical Islamic ideology to portray themselves as a complete system of life for all of humans regardless of time and space. Among these, the discourse of Sayyid Qutb is one of the most influential and comprehensive, attempting to create a Neo-Islamic civilization to compete with, and eventually replace, not only modern authoritarian states in the Muslim lands, but also the modern welfare state of liberal democracies as well as the now-defunct communist systems.

There is no doubt that Qutb's influence on other Islamic thinkers and revolutionaries has been quite significant. The impact of his thought on Islamic movements is not confined to the Muslim Brotherhood in Egypt, as the influence of his ideology in other Muslim countries has been studied by a few scholars so far.[2] This chapter attempts to present a close examination and evaluation of Qutb's discourse as a model of a comprehensive socio-political system as he propounded it throughout his career as an Islamist. Qutb's methodical thought aimed at creating a viable design of a utopian substitute for late modern societies. In this pursuit, he mainly relied on his interpretation of the Qur'an and Hadith directly, effectively circumventing centuries worth of Islamic jurisprudence, theology, philosophy and Sufi thought. The very fact that he skirted these traditional mediums for the interpretation of Islamic holy texts itself indicates that in

1. Martin Jay, *Marxism and Totality*, 21.
2. For Qutb's role in the Egyptian Muslim Brotherhood see: Richard P Mitchell, *The Society of Muslim Brothers*. On Qutb's general influence on Islamic movements see: Yvonne Y. Haddad, "Sayyid Qub: Ideologue of Islamic Revival," in *Voices of Resurgent Islam*, ed. John L. Espositio, For Qubt's impact on Iranian Islamic architects of the 1979 revolutions, see: Vanessa Martin, *Creating an Islamic State: Khomeini and the Making of a New Iran.*

his interpretation of the Qur'an and Hadith he was ironically as much influenced by modern socioeconomic discourses and their intellectual methods as well substance, as he tried to refute them. In this sense his interpretation of Islamic holy texts is not traditional at all. In fact, as this chapter argues, Qutb's attempt to introduce an Islamic alternative as a totality is very much in conformity with 19th and 20th century Western attempts to overcome the alienating features of modern society.

In this chapter I will first present Qutb's ontological views on human beings and their connections with the universe through their ties to the monotheistic deity, as he understood these notions. Through his interpretation of the Qur'an, Qutb presented a dynamic view of human beings that he claimed the Islamic "concept" necessitated, and linked this dynamism to God. Based on this fundamental view of human existence, Qutb projected an Islamic utopia in which various aspects human reality are harmonized with one another and with the rest of life.

Subsequently, I will analyze Qutb's scheme for a political system. It is well known that Qutb shunned a blueprint for his political system, unlike, for example, his Iranian counterpart Ayatollah Khomeini. Yet, Qutb devoted a good portion of his discourse to a discussion of the political dimensions of his proposed system. Similarly, Qutb's views on economical questions are mostly confined to a broad-brush treatment, but they contain highly significant issues that bear significantly on his overall attempts in erecting his ideology. Before we start though, a brief biographical sketch of Qutb is in order.

Sayyid Qutb was born in 1906 in Musha, a village in Asyut Province in Upper Egypt. His family of small landowning farmers was pious and educated in Islamic tradition and, during Qutb's youth, experienced financial misfortune. Nevertheless, Qutb was sent to Cairo when he was 13 to receive his secondary education. In 1929 he attended Dar al-Ulum which featured a curriculum combined of traditional Islamic learning and modern education. In 1933, he graduated from the institution with a teacher's degree and worked for the ministry of education for six years. Apparently, from early on in Cairo he was involved in the Wafd party, which advocated parliamentary and anti-colonial nationalist politics. Early in his career, he was influenced by secular thinkers such as Mahmud al-'Aqqad (d. 1964), Taha Hussein (d. 1973) and Tawfiq al-Hakim (d. 1987) and engaged in literary activities and criticism, publishing poetry and two novels, including an apparently autobiographical love novel. In 1948 Qutb wrote his highly influential Islamic work, *Social Justice in Islam*, which was published in 1949 in Cairo. He spent two years, from 1948 to 1950, in the United States, where his Islamic tendencies were reportedly strengthened. Upon return from the United States and his visits to Switzerland, England and Italy, he formally joined the Association of Muslim Brothers, with which he had been in contact as a sympathizer since the 1930s. Qutb quickly became a leading ideologue of the Brothers, which was founded by another schoolteacher, Hassan al-Banna, in 1928. With the advent of the Nasserite revolution in 1952, Qutb at first supported the revolution and the Free Officers reportedly sought his input in political affairs of Egypt. But soon, in 1954, when the Muslim Brothers fell out with the Free Officers, Qutb and some of his fellow Brothers were arrested. He spent most of the rest of his life in prison, where he wrote copiously and revised some of his earlier works. He was briefly released from prison in 1964, only to be executed in 1966, accused of conspiring to overthrow Nasser's regime.[3]

Human Soul and the Source of Creativity

In his earlier and less Islamist-oriented writings of the 1930s, when Qutb was interested in literary pursuits, he viewed the human "soul" as the source of poetic creativity, which can be construed as something akin to the notion of human subjectivity and agency.[4] Later, during his Islamist career, however, the idea of the human soul, not as a direct source of creativity and agency, but as a vehicle of these, was reincarnated in his discourse. In one of the more theoretical works of his fully-fledged Islamist period, Qutb positively viewed Muhammad Iqbal's (d.1938) attempts to construct Muslims' "personality" (*khudi*) as a way of entrance into the modern world.[5] The annihilation of the self, the passivity of mystic ways, "which negate human endeavor and participation in worldly activity," Qutb concurred with Iqbal, was detrimental to the cause of Islamic revival.[6] Iqbal, in Qutb's view, however, went too far in glorifying the human "self" which made him interpret the Qur'an in ways that were contrary to its intentions.[7]

Nevertheless, at the core of Qutb's discourse lies a concept of human selfhood, as he insisted that one of the foundations upon which Islam builds social justice is "absolute liberation of the inward soul (*taharrur wijdānī*)"[8]. The very foundation of social justice, in this view, is based on a "feeling within the soul that the individual deserves and that the community needs it [inward liberation]."[9] External legislation, Qutb contended, will not lead the individual to claim the inward liberation until the individual *feels* he or she has a right to it and in practice can maintain the inward liberation.[10] The very foundation of Islam, according to Qubt, was to liberate the "human soul [*wijdān*] from service to anyone other than God and from submission to anyone other than God".[11] In fact, according to Qutb, Islam:

3. The biographical information on Qutb is taken from William E. Shepard, *Sayyid Qutb and Islamic Activism: A Translation and Critical Analysis of Social Justice in Islam* (Leiden: Brill, 1996), and Oliver Carre, *Mysticism and Politics: A Critical Reading of Fi Zilal al-Qur'an by Sayyid Qutb* (Leiden: Brill, 2003). See also: Shahrough Akhavi, "Qutb, Sayyid," in *Oxford Encyclopaedia of the Modern Islamic World* (New York: Oxford University Press, 1995), v. 3: 4000–4004; J.J.G. Jansen, "Sayyid Kutb," *Encyclopedia of Islam II.*
4. Shepard, xxx
5. On Iqbal's conceptualization of human subjectivity, or what he called *khudi* ("selfhood"), see chapter one in this volume
6. Sayid Qutb, *The Islamic Concept and its Characteristics* (American Trust Publications, 1991), 14–15.
7. *Islamic Concept and its Characteristics*, 15.
8. *Sayyid Qutb and Islamic Activism. A Translation and Critical Analysis of Social Justice in Islam*, 40. Hereafter, I refer to this book as "*Social Justice in Islam*," which corresponds to the original Arabic title.
9. *Social Justice in Islam*, 41.
10. *Social Justice in Islam*, 41.
11. *Social Justice in Islam*, 43.

> seeks to rouse the greatest powers in human nature and through them to push for the clear and complete liberation of the soul, since without complete liberation it cannot resist the factors making for weakness, submissiveness and servility and will not demand its share in social justice, nor will it endure the burdens of justice when justice is given to it. This liberation is one of the cornerstones in the construction of justice in Islam; indeed it is the first pillar upon which the others stand.[12]

This passage leaves very little doubt that what Qutb is referring to here as human "soul" is very closely akin to the concept of human subjectivity and agency.

Empowering of the Soul through Discipline

An essential condition for the triumph of human soul, which as we just saw constitutes one of the foundations of Islamic revival for Qutb, is its emancipation from instinctual forces: "[T]he human soul may be liberated from servitude to sacred institutions, from fear of death, harm, poverty or degradation, and from all external considerations and social values and yet remain enslaved to itself, to its pleasures and passions, its ambitions and desires, so that it is bound by inner shackles when it has escaped from outer ones".[13] This strong disciplinary attitude toward liberation of the soul from the carnal self led Qutb to claim that the "battle" against one's desires is tantamount to a battle against Satan and on a par with actual fighting in the battlefield on behalf of Islam.[14]

In fact Qutb, very similar to Maududi as we saw in chapter two, often discussed certain Islamic rites in terms of disciplinary measures that were meant to strengthen the soul: "the obligation of fasting is meant to elevate the soul above the insistent demands of its nature for a period of time, so that its will can be strengthened and gain mastery, so man may rise above himself as he rises above his [carnal] needs."[15] Thus, in an unusually unequivocal statement, Qutb made a close association between the worship of God, control of animalistic desires and the "supremacy of the humanity of man over material things," as the groundwork of Islamic civilization.[16] As is evident from this account, Qutb's was invoking a form of endowing human "soul" with power, which is closely related to monotheistic divinity and the disciplining of the instinctual forces within human self. In a different passage he made an even more explicit connection between the idea of human empowerment and human interaction with God:

12. *Social Justice in Islam*, 56.
13. *Social Justice in Islam*, 53.
14. *Milestones*, 129.
15. *Social Justice in Islam*, 54.
16. *Milestones*, 196. In another very explicit passage on the emancipatory effects of discipline, Qutb wrote: "When we take the ethical aspects which appear to be bonds and fetters, we find them in reality to be aspects of movement, liberation and vitality. Let us take, for example, self-restraint from indulgence of forbidden sexual passion. It appears to be a bond and an obstacle. But in reality it represents a liberation from slavery to these passions, release from servitude to them, and the *exaltation of human will*, so that the indulgence of these passions may be chosen within the bounds of decency laid down by Islam, and within the sphere of legitimate enjoyment decreed by God." (*This Religion of Islam*, 28; emphasis added)

> The primary objective of the Islamic concept is to inform people about their Lord, and to inform them of Allah's Person, of His glorious attributes, and of what pertains to Him alone as distinct from what pertains to His creation. It also informs them concerning His relationship with the universe and with people, and with all the worlds and all the peoples of the earth. The Qur'an speaks about all these matters at great length and in such a vivid and forceful fashion as to make the Person of God interact with the human soul in a living, active, and concrete relationship, surrounding it from all sides. The human soul remains linked with Him never forgetting His presence and *deriving inspiration and power from Him.*[17]

Ideology and Empowerment

Although Human life is short, and human existence is a mere speck in the universe, Qutb argued, we nevertheless have within our reach the ability to contact the "eternal source of power," to understand the way the universe works and to harmonize our lives with it. This source of power allows us to "initiate events and affect other beings [...] manipulate the present, and plan for the future [...] [and] control matter and events".[18] All these, however, can be achieved only through what Qutb called a "concept" (*taswir*), which roughly corresponds to a form of ideology. The Islamic ideology or concept was a crucial element in his discourse that was the central theme of one his major books entitled *The Islamic Concept and its Characteristics.* Only when men have a clear "concept" and certainty in their ideology, their souls acquire an unshakeable foundation upon which a solid system of morals, manners, laws and a corresponding firm organization of society, economy and politics, may be built.[19]

It was the Islamic belief as a "concept" that allowed the liberation of the human inner soul from the thought, life and the conceptual prison of the Pre-Islamic cultures.[20] The spirit of Islam, a notion that Qutb seems to have used interchangeably with the "concept", is responsible for "acts of heroism" and the "geniuses" that appeared in the history of Islamic civilization. In fact, "the measure of the greatness of every individual genius is its aptitude to receive that cosmic emanation [spirit of Islam], and it is not surprising that the highest greatness is that of the prophethood of Muhammad ibn 'Abdallah (SAW) since it was what received and contained the whole emanation".[21] This spirit, in Qutbs estimation, was manifested in the conquering of Persian kings and Caesars by a small group of Arabs in a very short period of time.[22] It is the same spirit that instills the "man in the street" with the confidence to resist the power and domination of oppressive rulers.[23]

The emphasis on notions such as "spirit," and "concept" and their close links to the idea of human empowerment makes it clear that the main thrust of Qubt's arguments here revolves around the idea of human subjectivity. However, as in the case of many

17. *Islamic Concept and its Characteristics*, 91–92; emphasis added.
18. *Islam and Universal Peace*, 1.
19. *Islamic Concept and its Characteristics*, 34.
20. *Islamic Concept and its Characteristics*, 35.
21. *Social Justice in Islam*, 184.
22. *Social Justice in Islam*, 184.
23. *Social Justice in Islam*, 185.

other Islamic thinkers of modern times, the human subjectivity that Qutb promulgates is not self-sufficient and is contingent upon the Subject, the God of monotheism:

> The inclination of man to change the existing conditions of his environment in order to improve it is also a permanent reality. This desire is in the depth of his nature and is product of his position as the deputy of Allah on earth because this responsibility requires the control and development of earthly resources. The expression of this desire however, varies according to time and place [...] Man, as a species, is the noblest of all creatures on earth, because he is the deputy of Allah on earth, in the sense that to him belongs the control and management of this earth and whatever it contains, and because there is no material value on earth that can be raised higher than the value of man or for which man can be sacrificed.[24]

This conditional approach to human subjectivity at times makes Qutb espouse a form of humanism that is surprising. Yet, this form of humanism and human empowerment is more often quite curtailed in most of the reset of his discourse. Thus, on the one hand, Qutb seems to adopt an unabashed form of humanism, "Man is the most cherished of God on this earth, the fundamental creature therein, the vicegerent over its potentialities. Whatever is on earth lies at his disposal, or so it should be. Humanism is the ultimate scale by which his development or his backwardness should be measured, while his spiritual happiness is the measurement of the fitness of the elements of his civilization to his nature".[25] Moreover, belief in the monotheistic God, in Qutb's view, is conductive to the self-same identity of human beings, which is essential in making decisions in life. The belief in the oneness of God disciplines the mind and the heart so that the believer knows who he is and what the purpose of his life is.[26] Qutb even went as far as hinting that every Muslim can potentially interpret and *implement* the Sharia for her/himself.[27]

On the other hand, Qutb's discourse significantly limits human capacity and free will: "There is a balance between the domain of free Divine Will, and the domain of limited wills of human beings. This is the famous dilemma that has appeared, in one form or another, among all religions, all philosophies, and all mythologies [...] At a deeper level we see that the very existence of man, his freedom of choice and his power to do things, and his movements and his acts are all according to the all-encompassing Divine Will."[28]

Submission as Empowerment

One of the central statements in Qutb's discourse is the paradoxical notion that by submitting to God, humans acquire liberation. However, from Qutb's point of view, the central notion of human empowerment through God contains no paradox. "When the inward soul," Qutb reasoned, "is liberated from the feeling of servitude and submission to any of God's servants and is filled with the feeling that it is in complete contact with

24. *Islamic Concept and its Characteristics*, 68–69.
25. *Islam the Religion of the Future*, 49.
26. *Islamic Concept and its Characteristics*, 195–96.
27. *Social Justice*, 12.
28. *Islamic Concept and its Characteristics*, 116.

God, then it does not fear for its life, or any fear for its livelihood, or any fear for its reputation. These are harmful feelings that diminish the individual's sense of himself and may lead him to accept and to surrender much of his honor and many of his rights."[29] By surrendering to Allah, Qutb declared, man is born. In the secular systems, where sovereignty and the power of legislation belong to humans, some humans are enslaved by others. But it is only in Islam in which all people without exception are liberated from such slavery because they worship God alone.[30] According to Qutb, human legislation, by which he meant something larger than the mere passage of laws and something closer to the wielding of power in general, reflects the narrow interests, prejudices and whims of special groups, whereas the divine legislation is universal and not prejudiced to any particularity.[31] Throughout human history, Qutb believed, the call toward God has had one purpose: to bring "*islam*" (submission) to them, that is bringing "human beings into submission to God, to free them from servitude to other human beings so that they may devote themselves to the One True God, to deliver them from the clutches of human lordship and man-made laws, value systems and traditions so that they will acknowledge the sovereignty and authority of the One True God and follow His law in all spheres of life."[32] As a result, Qutb argued, Islam does away with the tyrannical forces of not only class, but also race:

> After annihilating the tyrannical force [of rule by other than God], whether it be in a political or racial from, or in the form of class distinction within the same race, Islam establishes a new social, economic and political system, in which the concept of freedom of man is applied in practice [...] Islam is a declaration of the freedom of man from servitude to other men. Thus it strives from the beginning to abolish all those systems and governments which are based on the rule of man over man and the servitude of one human being to another.[33]

The antithesis of this emancipation through submission to God for Qutb was epitomized in what he called "*Jahiliyya*." He used the notion of *Jahliyya*, which in traditional Islamic sources referred to the "ignorance" of pre-Islamic paganism in the Arabian peninsula, to convey the idea that all societies regardless of historical time, which denied the sole sovereignty of God by allowing the sovereignty of some over others, were the negation of Islam.[34]

The limits that Qutb's notion of liberation through submission to God posed on human subjectivity, however, was not in any way a deterrent toward a form of human

29. *Social Justice*, 46
30. *Islamic Concept and its Characteristics*, 200.
31. *This Religion of Islam*, 18.
32. *Milestones*, 166. In this regard Qutb relates the story of a certain Shaykh Hasn al-Adawi who, "remembered his religion and forgot about worldly benefits, and kept in mind that there was no glory except to God. He entered [the Sultan's court] with his head high [rather than bowing before the Sultan], as men who have faith in God should." (*Social Justice in Islam*, 209).
33. *Milestones*, 109.
34. For further analysis of the very important notion of *Jahiliyya* in Qutb's political ideology see, for example, Leonard Binder's chapter on Qutb in, *Islamic Liberalism: A Critique of Development of Ideologies* (Chicago, University of Chicago Press, 1988).

action and agency that fitted well in his overall scheme of human empowerment through God. In fact, it seems as if Qutb's notion of agency as more or less pure action was a mirror image of his idea of contingent subjectivity.[35]

Dynamism as Agency

Qutb's ideology was very much geared to action. For this reason, throughout his discourse, one finds a lopsided anti-intellectual element. He had no use for philosophy and philosophers, including those of Ibn Sina and al-Farabi, or Ibn Rushd whose philosophies "are nothing but a shadow of Greek philosophy."[36] He also condemned theological debates that arose during the early centuries after Islam as metaphysical speculation, which just gave cerebral pleasure to those who engaged in it.[37] According to Qutb, the philosophers and theologians (*mutikalimun*), "abandoned the Islamic concept and its own pure and independent format, which suits its nature so perfectly since both concept and format address the total nature of man with all his faculties and concerns, and not merely his intellect in cold logical terms." [38]

While Qubt dismissed philosophy, he was very much in favor of literature because it "has the strongest influence in creating the inward emotional (*wijdani*) idea of life and in giving the human soul a particular character."[39] And within literature, Qutb favored poetry over prose, as, for example, he described Iqbal's prose as "difficult, terse, as well as dry," and his poetry as, "alive, dynamic and vibrant".[40] This emphasis on dynamism led Qutb to

35. While the notions of human subjectivity and agency are very close, as they denote autonomy, consciousness, volition and action, there can be a distinction between them in that the first three may be regarded constitutive of subjectivity, and the last term, action, belonging to the sphere of agency. It is true that in reality these spheres are not separated, yet the distinction between the two in this particular context is a useful analytical tool, given that in his discourse Qutb placed much more emphasis on action by humans than self-subsisting autonomy.
36. *Social Justice in Islam*, 25; 333.
37. *Islamic Concept and its Characteristics*, 6.
38. *Islamic Concept and its Characteristics*, 8. It is not accidental that throughout his book *al-Taswir al-Fani fil-Qur'an*, he insisted that impact of the Qur'an is due to its pictorial nature, which primarily impresses the senses not the intellect.
39. *Social Justice in Islam*, 308. Qutb had the following to say about the connection between literature and action in his ideology: "The Islamic view does not believe that man plays a negative role on this earth or an insignificant role in renewing and raising life. Therefore the literature or art that issues from the Islamic conception of life does not speak to human beings of their weakness, deficiency and decline, nor does it fill their feelings and lives with visions of sweet sensuality or with cravings that create only anxiety, uncertainty, envy and negativity. It speaks rather to humans of the desire for mastery and freedom and fills their lives and feelings with goals for humanity that renew and raise life whether in the inward consciousness of the individual or actual life of the community (*Social Justice in Islam*, 310)."
40. *Islamic Concept and its Characteristics*, 15. The prominence of the more expressive aspects of knowledge in Qutb's ideology did not deter him from emphasizing the importance of modern natural sciences: "We proclaim that the Islamic concept leaves a vast field of activity for human reason and scientific experimentation. It does not put any obstacles in front of reason for doing research and for engaging in contemplation in order to discover the universe and its workings.

place much emphasis on action in his thought. Thus, the mission of Islam for him was to change its entire surroundings and context and, for this to happen, action was necessary:

> The Qura'an was struggling against the entire human environment as it was. It was addressing itself to the whole of humanity, which was drowned under the vast ocean of corruption. The style of theology would have been useless for it because, although Islamic belief is a belief, its main program is in the practical sphere of life; it does not remain circumscribed in theoretical discussions and the speculation of theology."[41]

As we saw above, the source of human subjectivity is by no means human in Qutb's view. But this does not mean that the agency that follows this notion of human subjectivity does not belong to the human realm. "The fact that the Islamic conception did not originate in human thought," Qutb argued, "does not mean that it is outside the domain of human intellect [...] Its divine origin, however, does imply that it is the task of human thought to receive it, grasp its significance, and adapt to it, *and then translate it into action*".[42] In fact, for Islam to be viable, it is essential that it takes the form of a "living soul," an active organization, and a practical movement.[43]

Interestingly, when it came to the idea of action, Qutb gave a considerable amount of credibility to the role of the individual as the carrier of human agency. While it is clear that Allah wills what he wills, and all changes in the universe are a result of Allah's commands, Allah's "decree operates among a people [...] through the will of individual members and through their actions within their own selves. 'Verily Allah does not change the condition of a people unless they change what is in their selves' [Qur'an 13:11]."[44]

Yet, Qutb's emphasis on the notion of individual agency here should not lead us to think that this form of agency would automatically lead to the idea of individual freedom.[45] As we will see more elaborately below, Qutb sternly condemned modern capitalism, which he associated with usury and individual freedom.[46] As such, Qutb allowed individuals just enough freedom to hold them responsible for their actions and hence liable for punishment and deserving reward.[47] On the other hand, this type of

---

Indeed, the Islamic concept encourages and inspires it to engage in such research. Again, it does not stop scientific experimentation, but counts it as a necessary function of man's role as Allah's deputy on earth. We appreciate the great blessing and favor of Allah upon us in giving us this concept and keeping it secure from human interpretation and interference" (*Islamic Concept and its Characteristics*, 64–65).

41. *Milestones*, 65.
42. *Islamic Concept and its Characteristics*, 43; emphasis added.
43. *Milestones*, 69.
44. *Islamic Concept and its Characteristics*, 118.
45. To be sure, the ability to act upon the world by the individual strongly implies the idea of individual freedom. But, like many other contemporary thinkers, Qutb's idea of individual freedom was quite restricted in comparison to liberal-democratic tradition. For an analysis of contemporary Shi'a thinkers on the notion of individual freedom, see chapter seven in this volume.
46. *Milestones* 260–61.
47. *Islamic Concept and its Characteristics*, 119.

reasoning allowed Qutb to explain away an important philosophical dilemma, namely, the question of the existence of evil given the omniscience and omnipotence of God. The limited capacity for free individual will that Qutb posited allowed him to account for the existence of evil, which is embedded in human action, without any harm to God's role in humans' evil-doings.[48]

Thus the notion of human agency as an instrument of God's will was central to Qutb's ideology. He pointed out that the Marxist ideology, because of its materialist approach toward the notion of action, denies human agency.[49] In fact he called what he considered to be a cosmic plan for human agency a "divinely ordained path" that is realized by human effort and described it as "the greatest truth of the faith."[50] As such, praxis occupied a very central position in Qutb's ideology. In Christianity, Qutb argued, "The soul is pure while the physical body is impure, and a person is supposed to sublimate the soul from the lowly physical body [...] Surely Islam [in contrast] is a practical religion, a religion for this life, for action, for work, production, and progress, and a religion in accordance with man's nature and his role in life assigned by Allah."[51]

It is significant to observe that in his more systematic approach to the notion of human agency, Qutb preferred to use the term "dynamism" (*al-ijabiyah*) instead of agency (*fa'yillah*). It seems the reason for this preference was that agency denotes more of a human origin, whereas dynamism connotes a divine will that materializes in human action. Thus in his important "theoretical" book, *The Islamic Concept and its Characteristics*, he wrote, "The fifth great characteristic of the Islamic concept is 'dynamism.' Dynamism is expressed in the active and ongoing relationship of Allah Most High with His creation, with the universe, life and men. And dynamism is also expressed in the activities of man himself in his own sphere".[52] The Qur'an, Qutb contented, is full of descriptions of the dynamic and positive relationships of God with humans and this, together with the notion of Allah's oneness constitutes the foundation of Islam's cosmology. In Islam, "Allah is active and participatory and not like the gods of Aristotle or Plotinus, which are passive and self-centered."[53] In this way Qutb indeed conveyed a very forceful view of Islam:

48. *Islamic Concept and its Characteristics*, 120–24.
49. *Islam, the Religion of the Future*, 45.
50. *This Religion of Islam*, 13.
51. *Islamic Concept and its Characteristics*, 181. In a related vein, Qutb considered "luxury" as a source of corruption of human soul, leading to passivity and hence responsible for the affliction of nations. (*This Religion of Islam*, 10) Qutb went as far as considering action qua struggle against oneself and the Other as essential for the development of the individual: "This struggle is necessary on the part of the individual for he struggles against himself while struggling against other people, and thereby horizons are opened to him in the faith which would never be opened to him if he were to sit immobile and at rest [...] His soul, his feelings, his imagination, his habits, his nature, his reactions and responses—all are brought to a point of development which he could not have attained without this hard and bitter experience." (*This Religion of Islam*, 9) Throughout his discourse Qutb proposed that this form of agency and the struggle associate with it be directed at the "system of Jahiliyya" of modern nation-states to bring about the Islamic utopia that he was outlining.
52. *Islamic Concept and its Characteristics*, 148.
53. *Islamic Concept and its Characteristics*, 154

> Thus the Islamic concept keeps the mind of the Muslim restless, always calling him to action from the depth of his consciousness, telling him to get up and go out and actualize this concept in the real world. It refines his sensibilities in order to bring the entire power of his belief and will to bear upon the reconstruction of a society so that the Islamic faith may be realized in the lives of the people.[54]

This type of contingent agency in Qutb led him to posit a form of human rights that is, to be sure, rudimentary, but nevertheless foundational. He maintained that poor people have a claim over the possession of rich people. In fact, the oppressed people have not only a right to demand their rights but an obligation to do so. For this purpose Qutb invoked the Qur'anic verse (4:97) that:

> [T]he angels will say, 'In what circumstances were you?' They will say, 'We were oppressed (*mustada'fin*) on the earth.' The angels will say, 'But was not God's earth wide, so that you might have emigrated in it?' Such men, their refuge will be Gehenna—an evil homecoming!" It rouses them to fight for their rights, "Whoever is killed seeking to right a wrong done to him is a martyr [Hadith reported by al-Nasa'i].[55]

At times, Qutb was bold enough to posit a strong form of human subjectivity, but only with regard to the objective world. Islam, according to him, has "declared the complete freedom of thought vis-à-vis the material world, its laws, energies and potentialities. It gave the green light to the mind to meditate and innovate as widely as it could, exploring the vast universe where man acts as viceregent of his God."[56] However, when it came to the social sphere Qutb was much more reluctant to grant such a capacity to humans, "We forget that this mind can work only upon material things, because it is fitted to understand the laws of matter and its comprehension penetrates through only the matter. When we apply the mind to 'the world of man' it comes to be at a loss, acting in an immense wilderness because it is not intrinsically adapted to comprehend the tremendousness of the human reality."[57] Thus it is not surprising that Qutb attempted to develop a social system in which the subject was very much submerged in a totality that he prescribed as an Islamic utopia.

---

54. *Islamic Concept and its Characteristics*, 155. This view of human agency had a developmentalist component that would have made the proponents of developmental theory very happy: "It is the very nature of the Islamic concept to encourage and urge human being to do something positive and productive, because according to the Islamic concept man is an active agent and not a passive recipient on this earth. To begin with, he is the deputy of Allah on earth, and he has been made the deputy in order to actualize the way prescribed by Allah, which is to *initiate, build, and to change and to make developments in the land in reliance on the natural forces that Allah has created to be of use to human beings in their work.*" (*Islamic Concept and its Characteristics*, 158; emphasis added)
55. *Social Justice in Islam*, 16.
56. *Islam, the Religion of the Future*, 75.
57. *Islam, the Religion of the Future*, 74. This attitude explains the general tendency among many Islamic thinkers who adopt modern natural science easily but not modern social sciences and humanities.

Islam as a Totality

What makes the Islamic path unique, declared Qutb, is that "this religion is an indivisible whole." Its worship, social relations, its laws and moral guidance together constitute an integrated totality in which devotional rituals are not divorced in their nature or their goals from the political and social affairs of the community.[58] This wholeness in Qutb's cosmology is not confined to these spheres alone, as "man is a unity composed of desires aspiring to heaven and inclinations cleaving to earth. There is no split between heaven and earth in the nature of universe, and no separation between the world and the afterlife or between behavior and worship or between creed and Shari'ah in the nature of this religion."[59] By subjecting all to the unified authority of God, Islam came to offer a perfect harmonious depiction of the universe without any distortions or confusions and conflicts. It came to unify all forces and powers in the cosmos and to blend together all tendencies, thus recognizing an integrated unity in the universe, life and human affairs.[60] True to his anti-philosophical tendency, Qutb derided Plato for distinguishing between Intellect and Matter and Plotinus for the notion of hierarchy of being.[61] He even attempted to reconcile human "spirit" and the body:

> When Islam exalts the spirit and condemns lust, it does not mean that man must suppress his desires or waste their energy. It simply means that man should be his body's master and not its slave. He should exercise his will and not blindly succumb to his instincts. Man's will distinguishes him from animals. God says: "While those who reject God will enjoy this world and eat as cattle eat; and fire will be their abode" [Qur'an LVII:12]. Once man is in control of himself, he responds to his bodily requirements and enjoys the bounties of life within the limits set for them by God [...] The Islamic society excludes Freudian social neuroses which result from the unhealthy suppression of the individual's ego [sic] and desires for the "benefit" of the community. Islam eliminates the causes of these neurotic diseases by recognizing that human desires and impulses are neither filthy nor abject. Moreover, it allows the individual to legitimately satisfy these impulses as long as they are gratified in a manner which does not degrade the person or incite licentious behavior in the community.[62]

In his attempts at integration, Qutb posited that it is only in Islam that humans are concerned with this world and the hereafter simultaneously.[63] He also criticized the

58. *Social Justice in Islam*, 8.
59. *Social Justice in Islam*, 31.
60. *Social Justice in Islam*, 31.
61. *Islamic Concept and its Characteristics*, 140–41.
62. *Islam and Universal Peace*, 19–20. Qutb's attempt to avoid the repression of human impulses should be taken with a grain of salt. A few pages later he writes: "As long as a person is capable of reproduction, his sexual urges are too powerful for him to completely subdue under the circumstances existing in Western society. Aware of the implications of sexual arousal, Islam commands that all observe propriety and chastity by averting the eyes. In addition it prohibits the wearing of alluring apparel in public, and restricts male-female free mixing. It aims at tranquilising the human conscience and establishing peace in the family." (*Islam and Universal Peace*, 33.)
63. *Islamic Concept and its Characteristics*, 105.

distinction that some Muslim scholars made between the acts of worship (*'ibadat*) and human interactions (*mu'amalat*) because the division is against the idea of totality in Islam. As a result of this distinction Muslims came to believe that they could be true Muslims if they performed their acts of worship while in human affairs they could follow non-Islamic systems. This is an immense error because Islam cannot be divided, and anyone who commits such acts of division is a rebel against the religion of Islam.[64]

Another aspect of Qutb's attempt at creating a totality involved the claim that in order to satisfy human personality, a belief system should have some elements of knowledge and some elements of "mystery," without being contradictory.[65] Of all the creatures, only humans have the ability to fathom the magnificence of God, which is partly intuited and partly acquired by understanding, as the "human person finds a balance between the great unknown and the great known by believing in the one and enjoying the other."[66] As such, Qutb attempted to reconcile human reason and revelation. Islam, Qutb stated, considers Revelation (*wahy*) as the true source of knowledge because it is not contaminated by falsehood and human particularistic desires. Yet, at the same time, human reason is not abolished, and human abilities of observation and sensory perception are not nullified. The one difference between human knowledge and revelation is that the former is subject to error and further verification, but revelation is true without any doubt.[67] The reason why, in Western modernity, science and religion came into conflict, Qutb maintained, was that the Church's suppression of free scientific inquiry led to a rebellion against the Church and thereby religion in general, which caused the rebellious scientists to denounce religion, along with the Church. This, in Qutb's view, was a uniquely Western experience that does not apply to the case of Muslims.[68]

In some parts of his discourse Qutb arrived at a purported reconciliation of the subject and the object that reflects his interests in totality very clearly. Thus in *Social Justice in Islam* he wrote:

> Because existence is a unity whose parts are integrated, harmonious in its character, organization and orientation, by virtue of issuing directly from one comprehensive and absolute Will, it is suited for and conducive to the existence of life in general and the existence of man—the highest form of life—in particular. Thus the universe is not an enemy to man, nor is "nature"—in the expression of the contemporary Jahiliyya [i.e., modern world] an adversary that man struggles with and conquers, but part of God's creation. It is a friend, whose tendencies do not differ from those of life and man. It is not the task of living things to struggle with nature, when they have arisen from its bosom. They and it are both part of the one existence that issues from the one Will. Thus man lives in a friendly environment among things that are his friends.[69]

64. *Islamic Concept and its Characteristics*, 106.
65. *Islamic Concept and its Characteristics*, 109–10.
66. *Islamic Concept and its Characteristics*, 112.
67. *Islamic Concept and its Characteristics*, 134.
68. *Islam, the Religion of the Future*, 39–41.
69. *Social Justice in Islam*, 27. What Qutb says here regarding humans and nature is in spite of what he quotes in the next page, that the Qur'an (67:15) states that God made the earth submissive to humans. (*Social Justice in Islam*, 28.)

In a similar vein and finding fault with the idea of the opposition between the self and the object that he attributed to Fichte, Qutb asked, "Why should the existence of Not-self contradict the existence of the Self? Why cannot there be things and objects as well as minds?"[70] Ontologically, Qutb believed that humans by their very nature cannot live in the world as "a detached, free-floating particle of dust." They must be related to the world by formulating a worldview regarding their place in the larger scheme of things.[71]

Reconciling Men and Women

Since Islam considers the family the nucleus of society, Qutb argued, the reconciliation between men and women is also essential. To begin with, the marriage contract in Islam requires the free consent of both parties and no woman should be married without her consent.[72] In order to achieve this "reconciliation," however, Qubt assigned specific roles to men and women that he believed complemented each other and thereby guaranteed the "harmony" between the wife and the husband.[73] Thus the woman has to "look after the husband and rear the children," because a woman under the pressure of making a living cannot provide a tranquil and joyful atmosphere in the home. "Homes of the working mothers are similar to hostels, always lacking that devoted feminine touch which characterizes a real home and which nobody but a wife can create for her children."[74] As such, Qubt simply reproduced the patriarchal divisions that, in his estimation, provided peace in the family. In fact, the alleged peace in the family that Qubt envisioned was indeed based on hierarchy, which he denounced at the surface, but which was constitutive of his worldview at a deeper level:

> There must be one captain to every ship. In family life likewise there must be a leader who assumes the responsibility and brings about order and discipline. In Islamic logic, the choice of this leader is simple, as we have to choose between the wife who is naturally adapted to the task of motherhood and the man who is responsible for the support of the family. Leadership is assigned here to the man for this reason and because he is the more fit owing to his natural role in life.[75]

From the purported harmony in the family, Qutb extrapolated the idea of harmony in society at large. Modern societies, in Qutb's view, are based on antagonism and conflict among individuals, which render their relationships to their government those of suppression and coercion. Society in Islam, in contrast, operates on principles of compassionate and cooperative relationships. In Western societies, in which materialism and the individual interests constitute the basis of law, the rise of class struggle is

70. *Islamic Concept and its Characteristics*, 62.
71. *Islamic Concept and its Characteristics*, 18.
72. *Islam and Universal Peace*, 30.
73. *Islam and Universal Peace*, 30.
74. *Islam and Universal Peace*, 30.
75. *Islam and Universal Peace*, 31. On women in Qutb's ideology see, Shehadeh Lamia Rustum, "Women in the discourse of Sayyid Qutb," *Arab Studies Quarterly*, vol. 22, no. 3 (2000): 45–55.

inevitable.[76] But in an Islamic society where laws are enjoined by God and not by "self-ordained law makers," materialism and class conflict will not arise.[77] Islam's universal and harmonious cosmology replaces social conflict and struggle with social solidarity by connecting human life to its creator and avoiding purely materialistic goals, even though material activity is considered worship in Islam.[78] Thus in Qutb's utopian discourse, the principle of social organization is very different from modern capitalist societies: "Life in the view of Islam is mutual love and respect, cooperation and solidarity [...] This, too, is the view of Christianity, but it is not based on clearly stipulated legislation or upon well defined well known facts.[79]

However, Qutb was quick to add that Islam could not ignore the self-interests of the individual:

> When Islam derives its systems and its legislation, as well as its exhortation and its guidance, it does not ignore that natural self love nor forget that profound natural greed. Rather it treats selfishness and greed with guidance and legislation and it imposes on man only what he can bear. At the same time it does not ignore the needs and interests of the community or the goals of the higher life in the individual and community throughout the ages and generations.[80]

In fact here too Qutb attempts to weld together the interests of the individual and that of the collectivity. If it is wrong that the "desires" of the individual ride roughshod over the community, it is also wrong for the collectivity to domineer over the individual initiative, because this is not only detrimental to the individual but also deprives society from fruits of the individuals' full capacities.[81] Yet, Qutb accorded a "higher interest" to the collectivity which must limit the freedom of the individual as it is in the interest of the individual to be restricted in freedom so that "he does not get carried away by his instincts, desires and pleasures to the point of destruction, and also so that his freedom does not clash with the freedom of others," leading to continual wrangling, turning freedom into a torment and arresting the development of society in the interests of myopic individualism.[82] Islam, Qubt contended, has granted the individual "freedom in its most attractive forms and

76. *Islam and Universal Peace*, 45.
77. *Islam and Universal Peace*, 45.
78. *Social Justice in Islam*, 350.
79. *Social Justice in Islam*, 34. It is rather rare for Qutb to praise any aspect of actual Muslim societies after the period of the Righteous Caliphs that ended with the death of Ali in 661. Yet, interestingly, he had the following to say about what he believed to be the cooperative character of Muslim societies: "I have seen many [Muslim] societies that continue to live an excellent life of independence, solidarity and cooperation based on charity, continuing to be closer to the good society envisaged by the founder of the Islamic mission than tens of millions who have been dazzled by the materialistic Western civilization, living for themselves even at the cost of destroying their communities and preferring to gratify their selfish desires rather than to be charitable toward their families, much less their neighbors." (*Social Justice in Islam*, 219)
80. *Social Justice in Islam*, 35.
81. *Social Justice in Islam*, 35.
82. *Social Justice in Islam*, 68.

human equality in its most precise meaning," but it does not tolerate chaos, because the collectivity has priority, and as a result Islam establishes the "principle of responsibility over against individual freedom [...]"[83] Furthermore, "Every individual is obligated to watch out for the interests of the community as if he were appointed to be its guardian, for life is a vast ship and its passengers are all responsible for its safety, and one may not make a hole in his section in the name of individual freedom."[84]

In this way Qutb envisioned a socio-political system based on primary Islamic scriptures (Qur'an and Hadith) that constituted a comprehensive totality covering every aspect of human existence and after-existence:

> Islam is a system for practical human life in all its aspects. This is a system that entails the ideological ideal—the convincing concept which expounds the nature of the universe and determines the position of man in this universe as well as his ultimate objectives therein. It includes the doctrines and practical organizations, which emanate from and depend upon this ideological ideal, and make of it a reality reflected upon the everyday life of human beings. For instance, these doctrines and organizations include the ethical foundation and its sustaining power, the political system together with its form and characteristics, the social order and its bases and values, the economic doctrine with its philosophy and institutions, and the international organism with its interrelations. In fact this Islamic system is so comprehensive, interdependent and interwoven that it covers all aspects of human life and various genuine needs of man as well as his different activities.[85]

Politics of Totality

In conformity with his overall scheme, the linchpin of Qutb's political vision consists of the view that sovereignty belongs to God and to God alone. The theory of government in Islam, he wrote, is based on the testimony that there is no god but Allah, which means that sovereignty (*hakimiyah*) in human affairs belongs to God only. God's sovereignty in human situations is exercised through directly controlling human affairs by His will and determination (*qadar*), as well as by establishing the principles of social life, duties, relationships and mutual obligation which is contained in His Sharia and Program (*minhaj*).[86] However, this does not mean that Qutb was trying to build a hierocracy. Referring to Qura'n 4:59, Qutb said that "obedience to one in authority is derived from obedience to God and the Apostle, because the one who holds authority in Islam is not obeyed for his own sake, but is obeyed only because he submits to the authority of God and recognizes His Sovereignty and then carries out the Shari'ah of God and His apostle [...]"[87] It is incumbent on the people to obey a leader who executes the law of God, but

83. *Social Justice in Islam*, 68–69.
84. *Social Justice in Islam*, 75. In a fashion very much reminiscent of Durkheim's analysis of crime, Qutb considered sexual "transgressions" such as adultery and fornication as crimes against the collectivity and prescribed the "*hadd*" (non-discretionary) punishments for them, including lapidation for adultery. (*Social Justice in Islam*, 80–81)
85. *Islam the Religion of the Future*, 5.
86. *Social Justice in Islam*, 111–12.
87. *Social Justice in Islam*, 113.

if he abandons the Sharia, he is not be followed and obeyed. A distinction must be made between a ruler that enforces the laws of Islam and one who attempts to derive personal authority through religion.[88]

Immediately after these pronouncements, Qutb made a statement that is quite remarkable: "The ruler has no religious authority that he receives directly from heaven, as was the case with some rulers of ancient times in the kind of government called 'theocracy,' but *becomes a ruler only by the absolutely free choice of Muslims.* They are not bound by any choice made by his predecessor, nor is the position inherited within a family."[89] Here Qutb seems to be proposing an important element of republicanism without fully engaging in it. To support this claim on the grounds of precedent in Islam, Qutb pointed to the selection of the successors to the prophet by the oath of allegiance, which shows that the authentic principle of government in Islam is "the unfettered choice of Muslims," and the only criteria that gives legitimacy to the government.[90] The fact that Ali, the cousin and son in law of the prophet, did not become the immediate successor of the prophet had the merit that it did not create the institution of hereditary leadership, which is farthest from the principles and spirit of Islam. In fact, Qutb argued, the establishment of the Umayyid kingship through inheritance stabbed the heart of Islam and its political system.[91]

Similarly, Qutb seems to have been very much against any form of clerical rule: "The way to establish God's rule on earth is not that some consecrated people—the priests—be given the authority to rule, as was the case with rule of the Church, nor that some spokesmen of God become rulers, as is the case in a 'theocracy.' To establish God's rule means that His laws be enforced and that the final decision in all affairs be according to these laws."[92] In reality, Qutb pronounced, in Islam there is no official clergy. As such, Islamic government is not carried out by any specific official body.[93]

As we saw above, this type of "proto-republicanism" in Qutb's discourse, for the most part, but not entirely, does not allow legislation by mortals. Yet, Qutb made a case for consultation among Muslims, "Government in Islam is based, after the acceptance of the sole divinity and sovereignty of God, on justice on the part of rulers, obedience on the part of the ruled, and consultation between the rulers and the ruled."[94] Since there is no precedent system of consultation in Islam, Qutb argued, the institution for consultation can take different forms depending on existing circumstances and needs of the society.[95] It is imaginable that such an institution could be in the shape of a "consultative assembly" with elected representatives, as it has appeared at least nominally in some Islamic societies. In Qutb's writings, however, it is not clear what the exact function of such institution would be, since as far he is concerned most of the laws and moral precepts for

88. *Social Justice in Islam*, 114.
89. *Social Justice in Islam*, 114; emphasis added.
90. *Social Justice in Islam*, 223.
91. *Social Justice in Islam*, 223–26.
92. *Milestones*, 104.
93. *Social Justice in Islam*, 115.
94. *Social Justice in Islam*, 112.
95. *Social Justice in Islam*, 116.

the organization and running of the Muslim community are already available in the text (*nass*) of the Qur'an and the Tradition of the prophet.

One sphere that Qutb allowed for *ijtihad* (a form of legal casuistry or more accurately "law finding") was when there is a lack of authoritative text (*nass*) from the two primary sources of Islam, the Qur'an and Hadith. In *Social Justice in Islam* which belongs to the middle period of his career, Qutb argued that such a capacity belongs to the Islamic leader, the imam, who in looking after the welfare (*masalih, mursalah*) of the community, may "make as many new decrees as he finds new problems in order to carry out God's statements."[96] Here, however, it is not clear whether the ruler is an individual or an assembly. In *Islam and the Universal Peace*, on the other hand, Qutb is more explicit on this issue:

> The Islamic political system can be explained as rule through consultation. The Qur'an describes Muslims as those "who (conduct) their affairs by mutual consultation (Q. XLII.159) and commands: "consult them in affairs of moment." (Q. III.159). Mutual consultation is necessary for good government, though there is no specific system of consultation prescribed in Islamic jurisprudence. Modes of consulting opinions depend upon different circumstances arising in each age and environment. Since consultation implies that Muslims must participate in decisions concerning their political life, they ought to have no reason to be dissatisfied about matters in which their opinions were sought."[97]

But in the *Milestones*, which is a later work, he is even more vague regarding who might be the person or persons in charge of *ijtihad*. As long as it is in conformity with the "well-defined principles, which are consistent with God's religion and not merely following one's opinions or desires," *ijtihad* is valid.[98]

In what may be interpreted as a mechanism for preventing his totality turning into totalitarianism, Qutb, in a relatively rare moment in his discourse, addressed the question of citizens' rights to criticize the government. He wrote that the leader may not, "strip people of all their possessions and leave them poor, or take control of their whole livelihood so that he can abase them and make them his slaves, thus depriving them of the ability to carry out their obligation to speak freely in advising him, to keep an alert watch over his actions, and to change whatever is objectionable whatever its source." Individuals cannot enjoy this freedom unless they possess private sources of income over which the leader or the imam and his agents should not have control. "The neck of slaves," he added "must bow to the one who owns their source of income!"[99]

In accordance with his totalizing vision, Qutb thought that a government of God's law and of human choice could hold the citizens together: "A government based on free choice, popular consensus and the application of laws prescribed by God is bound to promote confidence in its citizens. There would be few complaints, no motives for revolt

96. *Social Justice in Islam*, 119.
97. *Islam and the Universal Peace*, 54.
98. *Milestones*, 157.
99. *Social Justice in Islam*, 119–20.

because the society would be legislating according to the teachings of Islam."[100] As such, Qutb believed that his system would guarantee social harmony and solidarity, and the Islamic utopia he was projecting would not face the class and other conflicts that modern Western societies have faced:

> All coeds of law, ancient or modern, are deficient while the Islamic legislation alone is complete. Here, one need not suspect that the laws are prejudiced toward an individual or a class of people. In the Islamic concept, God is the Supreme Legislator and He has no reason for favouring an individual or a class as all belong to Him equally. Consequently, class consciousness simply does not exit within the doctrine or laws of an Islamic society. All the individuals have equal rights and obligations, and all are equal before the law. There are no class conflicts nor is there preferential treatment. There is no class system in Islam and so there is no class discontent when the Islamic laws are fully implemented in the political and economic spheres. Nor is there resentment caused by crime and injustice, except perhaps from those few who can never be content."[101]

In his vision for the political institutions of his totality, Qutb did not engage in much detail and presented mostly an outline. But when it came to his views on the economic principles of his dream he was more forthcoming.

The Economic Philosophy of Totality

Qutb posited the right to private property, quite forcefully—or it may just seem so. Islam, he contended, established the right of the individual to ownership of property, and in fact makes it the basis of its economic system. It protects this right against theft, looting, fraud and arbitrary confiscation.[102] Islam also allows the right to free disposal of property by sale, rental, pawning, gift and bequest as well as the right of reasonable usage. "There is no ambiguity in the establishment of this clear and unequivocal right in Islam and there is likewise no ambiguity in its being the basic principle of Islamic life and the basic principle of Islamic economy."[103] The harsh penalty against theft, in Qutb's view, is the best proof of the respect for the right to private property and ownership. The emphasis that Islam places on this right, Qutb reasoned, stems from the fact that it is a just reward for one's effort.[104] Private property is in conformity with human nature and agrees with "the genuine tendencies of the human soul" which form the basis of social order in an Islamic society. This is so because the individual has a "natural love for good things [...] [and a] natural love for his posterity and desires to pass on to them the result of his labor."[105] Furthermore, private property gives self-respect, honor and independence to the Individual, which is crucial for the development of the individual subject. Private

100. *Islam and Universal Peace*, 54.
101. *Islam and the Universal Peace*, 69.
102. *Social Justice in Islam*, 125.
103. *Social Justice in Islam*, 125.
104. *Social Justice in Islam*, 125.
105. *Social Justice in Islam*, 127.

property also promotes the welfare of the community by encouraging the individual to endeavor for the advancement of life.[106]

Here also Qutb attempted to reconcile the interests of the individual with that of the community in the institution of private property. Somewhat reminiscent of Adam Smith, he thought that there is no harm in allowing the individual's egoistic "natural tendencies" some free rein so that he will expend his fullest energy in productive activity; but, it is also the community that will profit from his effort and labor.[107] Yet, underlying Qutb's rhetoric, there is a deeper priority of the community over the individual in the principles of his political economy:

> The first principle established by Islam—alongside the right of private ownership—is that the individual is virtually the community's agent in relation to his property and that his tenure of it is more like employment than ownership, and that ownership in general is fundamentally the right of the community and that the community has this as a delegation (*mustakhlafah fihi*) from God, who is the only true owner of anything. [...] In the noble Qur'an it says: "Believe in God and his Apostle, and expend of that unto which He has made you stewards (*mustakhlafin fihi*)". The text of the verse does not require a deep interpretation (*ta'wil*) to yield the meaning that we have found in it, and that is that the property in the hands of humans is the property of God and that they are stewards (*khulafa*) of it, *not the original owners*."[108]

The most forceful element in Qutb's economic philosophy that bears significantly on the importance of the self-interest in social relations was his position against what he called "usury." Based on his writings, it seems that he considered any type of interest on money borrowed simply as illegitimate.[109] He believed that the introduction of any interest on loans would result in "eliminating the moral factor from life and expelling

106. *Social Justice in Islam*, 126.
107. *Social Justice in Islam*, 127.
108. *Social Justice in Islam*, 129; emphasis added. Qutb expressed the same idea somewhat differently and is worth quoting: "So we will content ourselves with saying that the basic principles of this system [economic system] can be summarized as follows: 1- It is based on the principle of 'conditional stewardship (*istikhlaf mashrut*)' God is the creator and owner of everything in the world, whether food or sustenance for wealth, and He has appointed the human race as His steward (*istikhlaf*) on earth on the condition that he manages this property in accordance with God's Shari'ah. Any departure from this condition means he has nullified his right to manage God's property and has failed his covenant of stewardship (*istikhlaf*)." (*Social Justice in Islam*, 177)
109. For example in *Social Justice in Islam* (p. 145) he wrote, "Usury is a forbidden means [...] 'O believers, devour not usury, doubled and redoubled, and fear your God; haply so you will prosper.' The prohibition here is not merely of doubling and redoubling, as if a low rate were permitted." And on p. 151 he wrote: "It doesn't matter whether the debt is for consumption or production in Islamic practices. If it is for consumption, that is, for the debtor's expenditure upon necessities, it is not permissible to burden him with returning more than he borrowed, it is sufficient that he return the principle when he can. If it is for production, the basic point is that the effort he expends is what brings the profit, not the money he borrows—except by way of sharing—based on bearing both profit and loss. Therefore usury is forbidden in all cases, and lending to the borrower for his needs is a duty in all cases."

the spirit of cooperation and charity from the people's hearts, that spirit which Islam made the basis of society and the pillar of cooperation among people."[110] Here it is crucial to observe that the principle of social organization for Qutb was a purported mutual "love," which is the opposite of the principle of organization of modern capitalist society, which is the mutual self-interests of the individuals. For this reason he vehemently opposed an economic system that allowed any form of interest on money: "An individual with character and conscience does not consume usury, nor does love and neighborliness remain when usury spreads in a community. The one who gives me a *dinar* in order to demand two in return is my enemy and I cannot feel friendship or love toward him. Cooperation is one of the bases of Islamic society; usury destroys it and weakens its foundations. Thus Islam detests it."[111]

Based on this fundamental principle of economic philosophy, which dovetails with the general logic of his totality, Qutb proposed a *zakat*-welfare system that would undergird the social policies of his community.[112] *Zakat*, he wrote, is the very foundation of a society marked by mutual responsibility and solidarity, as the opposite of the system of usury.[113] The truth of *zakat*, he continued, has disappeared from the memory of those wretched generations after the early period of Islam that have never tasted the lofty form of humanity that lived under its system. Being born under the materialistic system of usury, they have only seen the "miserliness, the brawling, the wrangling, and selfish individualism which rule the soul of men and make it so that money passes to those who need it only in the despicable form of usury!"[114]

Conclusion

Qutb was an ideologue of an Islamic movement that was hostile to both the West and its capitalist system and the Soviet system. As such, his was an attempt to create an ideology that challenged both of these systems. This is not to say that he did not borrow from the two. In fact, his attempt to create a totality is very much indebted to the Marxian attempt to create a communist utopia. Yet, this does not mean that Qutb's ideology was disingenuous because it rejected Marxism, socialism and communism, while being heavily indebted to them. At the political level, Qutb's ideology was a reaction to Western imperialism as well as Soviet encroachments. But, in its general contours, it attempted to create a "modernity" from Islamic sources. It was an attempt to create a modernity because it broached the notion of human subjectivity and agency, notwithstanding its severe shortcomings in this attempt. The subjectivity that appears in his discourse is contingent, inchoate, and hostile to the individual as its carrier. In fact, Qutb reduced human subjectivity to mere agency (and contingent agency, to boot), thereby circumventing and precluding further development of human moral autonomy.

110. *Social Justice in Islam*, 264.
111. *Social Justice in Islam*, 147.
112. *Zakat* is the obligatory tax paid by Muslims for the benefit of the poor and other classes of recipients.
113. *Social Justice in Islam*, 167.
114. *Social Justice in Islam*, 167.

Yet, what makes his ideology even less amenable toward acceptance of modernity is his attempt to submerge this very embryonic subjectivity in a totality that is central in his discourse. In the West, the attempt to create a totality has been the result of the overdevelopment of the subject and the desire to be tame and reconciled with society and nature. In Qutb's case, the human self is in its embryonic stage and has a long journey to reach maturity. As a result, compared to the discourses of his Iranian counterparts, for example, Qutb's discourse is less open to an internal dynamism that could bring about a more developed individual self, which is the foundation of the modern world and modern citizenship rights.[115]

This is not to completely deny the potential for such development in Qotb's legacy. By rejecting any authority except that of God, Islamist ideologies such as Qutb's may in effect pave the way for the emergence of a proto-republicanism. This has been one of the key mechanisms behind the political developments in the history of Protestantism, with regard to which we can observe close parallels in the contemporary Islamic movements and ideologies.[116] The difficult question is how long these processes will take to bring these Islamic movements that are inspired by Qutb and others like him to parity with the rest of the modern world, and what types of conflicts the clash between the two sides will engender. In the age of Globalization, with an increasing emphasis on individualism, consumerism and the desire for instant gratification, conflicts with totalistic ideologies, relying on collectivity and ascetic discipline, seem only inevitable.

---

115. For an analysis of the development of subjectivity in the discourses of Iranian Islamic thinkers see: Farzin Vahdat, *God and Juggernaut: Iran's Intellectual Encounter with Modernity* (Syracuse: Syracuse University Press, 2002).

116. Michael Walzer observed very similar processes in Calvinism paving the way for republicanism: "It is a commonplace of political history that despotism often plays an important part in clearing the way for democracy. A despot destroys the structure of intermediate powers and makes possible a politics based in individual interests. He overcomes the feudal baronage, breaks down the highly developed system of clan and tribal loyalties, attacks regional separatism and local privilege. He imposes uniformity and a kind of rough equality: he levels the political universe. Something of this same role is played the by the Calvinist God; his very existence endangers the medieval hierarchy of orders and powers. He destroys the intermediate power of the angels, of the Blessed Virgin and the saints, of the pope, the bishops, and finally even the king. This God, this arbitrary and willful, omnipotent and universal tyrant, shaped and dominated the Puritan conscience. But if he required an obedience so precise and total as to be without precedent in the history of tyranny, he also freed men for all sorts of alternative jurisdictions and authorities." (*The Revolution of the Saints: A Study in the Origins of Radical Politics* (New York: Atheneum, 1974), 151–52) The following excerpt from Calvin's *Institutes of the Christian Religion* (p, 551) speaks to this point, albeit in convoluted fashion: "But in the obedience which we have shown to be due to the authority of governors, it is always necessary to make one exception, and that is entitled to our first attention—that it do not seduce us from obedience to him, to whose will the desires of all kings ought to be subject, to whose decrees all their commands ought to yield, to whose majesty all scepters ought to submit [...] if they command any thing against him, it ought not to have the least attention; nor, in this case, ought we to pay any regard to all that dignity attached to magistrates."

Chapter Four

FATIMA MERNISSI: WOMEN, ISLAM, MODERNITY AND DEMOCRACY

One of the most essential criteria for choosing the thinkers analyzed in this book has been their influence in the Muslim world. Some of these thinkers have been academics whose discourse has had major impacts outside the academic setting. Others have had some affinity with the academic world, but their influence has been far beyond the rather limited university audience. Fatima Merniss is by training and profession an academic whose discourse enjoys rather broad currency in academic settings in the Muslim world and outside. Most importantly, she addresses gender issues in the Muslim world elaborately and deeply, drawing on a complex theoretical and philosophical approach. Moreover, Mernissi's impact in the Muslim world is not just confined to academia, because in many of her writings, especially of more recent vintage, her idiom is quite non-academic and accessible. From the very beginning of her career, Mernissi's focus has been on gender relations in Muslim societies and Islamic cultures. From early on Mernissi observed that the most urgent problem that Muslim societies had to solve was that of the relation between women and Islam. To solve this problem, she has advocated the agentification of women, continually criticized the notion and practice of veiling and gender-based segregation, and insisted on desegregation of women and men in Muslim societies.

A few scholars who have analyzed Mernissi's discourse usually refer to two phases in her writing. The first phase started with her dissertation, completed in 1973 and continued with *Beyond the Veil* (1987) and *Women in the Muslim Unconscious* (1984), which she published under a pseudonym. In this period, Mernissi drew on Freudian, Marxian and Marcusian theories to radically criticize, in a rather essentialzing manner, gender relations in Islam and Muslim societies. In her so-called second phase that begins with *The Veil and the Male Elite* (1988), Mernissi changed the tone of her writings to address the same issues. Yet, her agenda of women's empowerment, criticism of veiling and support for unveiling and desegregation remains in full force, albeit she treats them in a more nuanced and subtle fashion. For these reasons, making a sharp division in Mernissi's discourse in terms of phases is ultimately inaccurate. Yet for the sake of clarity I have complied with dividing Mernissi's work into two phases.

Fatima Mernissi was born in 1940 to a well-to-do landowning (*fellah*) family in Fez Morocco.[1] Mernissi spent her childhood in a traditional domestic harem consisting of extended family and, she claims, designed to protect women from outside men and

1. Fatima Mernissi, *Dreams of Trespass: Tales of a Harem Childhood Reading* (Addison-Wesley, 1994), 89.

the public sphere in general. As a child she attended Qur'anic schools. Mernissi studied political science at the University of Mohammed V in Rabat, and later studied at the Sorbonne on a scholarship. After that she attended Brandies University in Waltham, Massachusetts and received her PhD from the sociology department in 1973. Upon completing her doctorate, Mernissi returned to Morocco, where she has been serving as a professor of sociology at University Mohammed V.

Phase I: Vitriolic Attack on Muslim Social Order

The early phase in Mernissi's career can be characterized as a vitriolic critique, sometimes bordering on assault, of many aspects of Islamic culture and Muslim social order.[2] In her dissertation, Mernissi argued that the establishment of Islam in the seventh century Arabian Peninsula was achieved as a result of a profound transformation in the social order that was in turn based on a change in the family structure of the Arab community. According to Mernissi, "The link in the Muslim mind between sexuality and the Sharia has shaped the legal and ideological history of the Muslim family structure and consequently of the relations between the sexes."[3] Moreover, in Mernissi's view, this history is assumed to be transcendental and unchangeable because it is perceived as divine.[4] Most importantly, the new social order created by the advent of Islam, in Mernissi's analysis, was based on patriarchy, which deprived women of many of their previous freedoms and advantages: "The new social structure of Islam, which constituted a revolution in the mores of pre-Islamic Arabia, was based on male dominance. Polygamy, repudiation, the prohibition of *zina* [illicit sex], and the guarantees of paternity were all designed to foster the transition form a family based on some degree of female self-determination to family based on male control. The Prophet saw the establishment of the male-dominated Muslim family as crucial to the establishment of Islam. He bitterly fought existing sexual practices where marital unions for men and women alike were unstable and lax."[5] The thwarting of women's freedoms, Mernissi maintained, included "all practices in which the sexual self-determination of women was asserted," while Muslim marriage provided absolute male authority the stamp of sacred sanction.[6] Mernissi focuses on sexuality as the core component of the oppression of women in Islamic cultures. Thus according to her, by prohibiting *zina*, or fornication and adultery, which were prevalent and licit in the pre-Islamic period, Islam denied women their sexual freedom.

In order to fully demonstrate the impact of the advent of Islam on women's sexuality, Mernissi attempts to reconstruct the socio-sexual conditions of Arabia before Islam, the Jahilliyah (ignorance) period. She elaborately discusses different types of sexual union

2. Mernissi herself described her early writings in the 1970s as "vitriolic." Fatima Mernissi, *Women's Rebellion and Islamic Memory* (Zed Books, 1996), 3.
3. Fatima Mernissi, *The Effects of Modernization on the Male-Female Dynamics in A Muslim Society: Morocco* (Dissertation, Brandeis University (Sociology Department), 1973), 22.
4. *The Effects of Modernization on the Male-Female Dynamics in a Muslim Society,* 22.
5. Fatima Mernissi, *Beyond the Veil: Male-Female Dynamics in Modern Muslim Society* (Indiana University Press, 1987), 64.
6. *Beyond the Veil,* 66–67.

during the Jahilliyah period, which can be identified under two broad categories: the *sadica* marriage, which was matrilineal, and the *ba'al* or "dominion" type of marriage, which was patrilineal.[7] To demonstrate the prevalence of the matrilineal type of union, Mernissi argues that, "The Prophet's great-grandfather, Hashim, contracted a matrilineal marriage. The offspring of the union, the Prophet's grandfather, Abd Al Muttalib, was raised by his mother. "The Prophet's own father, Abdallah, contracted a matrilineal marriage with Amina Bint Wahb"[8] In the matrilineal union the women had a right of self-determination in choosing and repudiating their husbands. In fact, Mernissi points out that the Prophet himself was solicited in marriage *by* women several times and also was rejected by many.[9] Moreover, Mernissi avers, "The general picture that emerges from Bukhari's [d. 870] description [of four types of marriage before Islam wherein women were much more in control] is a system characterized by coexistence of a variety of marriages, or rather sexual union. In three of the four kinds of marriage, biological paternity seems unimportant, and the concept of female chastity is therefore absent [...] Two of the marriages were polyandrous, the woman having as many 'husbands' as she desired."[10] As far as Mernissi is concerned, the most significant aspect of the pre-Islamic sexual mores was that women's sexuality was not tied to the concept of legitimacy. In many cases children belonged to their mother's tribe. Most importantly, "Women had *sexual freedom* to enter into and break off unions with more than one man, either simultaneously or successively. A woman could either reserve herself to one man at a time, on a more or less temporary basis, as in *mut'a* marriage, or she could be visited by many husbands at different times whenever their nomadic tribe or trade caravan came through the woman's town or camping ground."[11]

During her radical phase Mernissi insisted that the advent of Islam drastically changed the social order of Arabian society by transforming the socio-sexual structure of that community, of course to the detriment of women's autonomy in general and their sexual freedom in particular. The result was a powerful and unified society at the expense of women's autonomy:

> That its [Islam's] institutions were appreciated is shown by its success in connecting both communal and self-serving tendencies and channeling these otherwise contradictory trends into the most cohesive social order Arabia has ever known. The communal tendencies were channeled into warfare for *Pax Islamica*, and self-serving tendencies were mainly vented in the institution of the family, which allowed new allegiances and new ways to transfer private possession of goods while simultaneously providing tight controls over women's sexual freedom.[12]

The new social order, Mernissi maintained during her earlier writings, was a guarantee for paternity and transfer of wealth from father to son, which relied on polygyny, the

---

7. *The Effects of Modernization on the Male-Female Dynamics in A Muslim Society*, 114.
8. *The Effects of Modernization on the Male-Female Dynamics in a Muslim Society*, 117–18.
9. *Beyond the Veil*, 50–52.
10. *Beyond the Veil*, 76–77.
11. *Beyond the Veil*, 78.
12. *Beyond the Veil*, 80.

male right to divorce at will, and the banning of female promiscuity. According to her, the new social structure of Islam constituted a revolution in the mores of per-Islamic Arabia, transforming it to a civilization that was based on male dominance. As we saw above, polygyny, men's ability to divorce women at will, the prohibition of *zina*, and the guarantees of paternity were all intended to promote the transformation of the Arabian family form one allowing a measure of women's autonomy to a family based on male dominance. In this social order, Mernissi argues, the potentially intimate relations between a heterosexual couple is interrupted by rituals to create an emotional distance between the two with the goal of reducing their embrace to that of a purely reproductive act.[13] Another aspect of the Islamic social order that was founded in Arabia of the seventh century was the fostering of a fear of women. According to Mernissi in her early phase, the Islamic civilization has held two opposite types of views of women's sexuality simultaneously:

> Muslim society is characterized by a contradiction between what can be called "an explicit theory" and "an implicit theory" of female sexuality, and therefore a double theory of sexual dynamics. The explicit theory is the prevailing contemporary belief that men are aggressive in their interactions with women, and women are passive. The implicit theory, driven far further into the Muslim unconscious, is epitomized in Imam Ghazali's classic work. He sees civilization as struggling to contain women's destructive, all-absorbing power. Women must be controlled to prevent men from being distracted from their social and religious duties. Society can survive only by creating institutions that foster male dominance through sexual segregation and polygamy for believers.[14]

In Mernissi's interpretation, the "implicit theory of women's sexuality," which is articulated most effectively by Abu Hamid al-Ghazali (d. 1111), one of the most influential thinkers of all times in the Muslim world, holds that women act like the hunter and men as their passive victims. As such, Ghazali identified the power of women, which works through deception, cunning and intrigue (Ar. *Kayd*) as the most destructive and threatening in the Muslim social order.[15] Here Mernissi makes a very interesting and significant distinction between the sources of misogyny in the Western and Islamic civilizations. In contrast to what is commonly assumed, Mernissi observes, there is no theory of inherent inferiority of women. Whereas in the Judeo-Christian civilization, one of the major sources of misogyny can be traced back the notion of the inherent inferiority of women, in Islamic civilization there is no such assumption. In the West there is hatred of women based upon the assumption of their inferiority. In the Muslim unconscious there is *fear* of their destructive power that leads to their segregation and legal subordination within the family: "In Western culture, sexual inequality is based on belief in women's biological inferiority. This explains some aspects of Western women's liberation movements, such as that they are almost always led by women, that their effect is often very superficial, and that they have not yet succeeded in significantly changing

13. *The Effects of Modernization on the Male-Female Dynamics in A Muslim Society*, 217.
14. *Beyond the Veil*, 32.
15. *Beyond the Veil*, 33.

the male-female dynamics in that culture. In Islam there is no such belief in female inferiority. On the contrary, the whole system is based on the assumption that women are powerful and dangerous beings. All sexual institutions (polygamy, repudiation, sexual segregation, etc.) can be perceived as a strategy for containing their power."[16] The chaos and disorder that women and their untamed sexuality can create are the source of fear in Islamic social order. In order to capture this fear, Mernissi uses the Arabic term *fitna* and notions related to it. The term *fitna* in Arabic is originally associated with placing precious metals in fire for the purpose of purification. *Fitna* also means the chaos, disorder and the social trepidation that they create in the community. As Mernissi has observed, "*Fitna* also means a beautiful woman—the connotation of a femme fatale who makes men lose their self-control [...]"[17] Thus, according to Mernissi, fear of *fitna* and chaos in Muslim culture constitutes the foundation of misogyny in Islamic culture.

Islamic Ontology and its Hierarchy

In Mernissi's early analysis, one of the consequences of the transition from the pre-Islamic tribal system to the much larger community of *Umma* was the "birth" of the male individual. Paraphrasing a passage in Montgomery Watt's *Muhammad in Medina*, Mernissi wrote, "But the *Umma* [the larger Islamic Community] created a mechanism which was to steer the tribes' bellicosity, usually invested in warfare, in a new direction—the holy war. The old allegiance to the tribe was replaced by an allegiance entirely different in both form and content. The form is the *Umma*, where the *basic unit is not the tribe, but the individual.* The tie is not kinship but a more refined concept, an abstract link, communion in the same religious belief."[18] The creation of the *Umma* was made possible by the absorption of male individualistic tendencies in the family structure. And one of the

16. *Beyond the Veil,* 19.

17. *Beyond the Veil,* 31. It is quite interesting that Mernissi adopted the pseudonym Fatna A. Sabbah, for the book that is attributed to her, *Women in the Muslim Unconscious* (Fatna is an alternative transliteration of Fitna). Further developing the contrast between the sources of misogyny in the Western and Islamic civilizations, Mernissi has observed that, "Different social orders have integrated the tensions between religion and sexuality in different ways. In the Western Christian experience sexuality itself was attacked, degraded as animality and condemned as anti-civilization. The individual was split into two antithetical selves: the spirit and the flesh, the ego and the id. The triumph of civilization implied the triumph of soul over flesh, of ego over id, the controlled over the uncontrolled, of spirit over sex. Islam took a substantially different path. What is attacked and debased is not sexuality but women, as the embodiment of destruction, the symbol of disorder. The woman is *fitna*, the epitome of the uncontrollable, a living representative of the dangers of sexuality and its rampant disruptive potential." *Beyond the Veil*, 44.

18. *The Effects of Modernization on the Male-Female Dynamics in A Muslim Society*, 129. Emphasis added. Mernissi made the same point in *Beyond the Veil* (p. 80), which in many ways parallels her dissertation: "But the *umma* steered the tribes' bellicosity, usually invested in tribal feuding, in a new direction—the holy war. The old allegiance to the tribe was replaced by an allegiance entirely different in both form and content. The new form is the *umma* and the basic unit is not the tribe, but the individual. The bond between individuals is not kinship but a more abstract concept, communion in the same religious belief."

mechanisms for this absorption "was the concept of fatherhood and legitimacy, which allowed full expression to the believers' individualistic wishes and needs."[19] As such, Mernissi posits that the advent of Islamic social order gave birth to the male Muslim individual subject. Yet, she strongly believes that this subjectivity for even the male was not authentic because God is considered to be the only real subject. In Islam, according to Mernissi, humans do not possess subjectivity and agency because the believer owes everything to the Deity. The believer cannot acquire material or immaterial wealth except through the intermediary of God's will. Human labor does not generate food, shelter or wealth: "In the Muslim universe human work is not the creator of wealth. One acquires wealth by submission to him who possesses that wealth: God. Access to wealth and opulence is assured through allegiance to the possessor, the provider, the almighty, the proprietor."[20] In Mernissi's reading, the monotheistic God monopolizes all there is to be possessed, leaving nothing for the human subject:

> The divine monopoly of everything that exists introduces an element that renders any idea of exchange in the relationship impossible. As a matter of fact, one of the parties, the human being, figures among the possessions of the other. The divine being owns the believer. The relationship of possession wipes out the possibility of exchange. In order for there to be exchange, there must be two wills that confront each other at the start and negotiate a relationship and fix its terms. So in the sacred universe, which is a coherent and logical universe par excellence, the being possessed has no will."[21]

Worship as one of the pillars of monotheistic religions, Mernissi argues, is an exercise in the denial of the creative, intellectual, and volitive capacities of the human subject. The subject cannot surrender her selfhood in worship to another:

> The worship that God demands of man requires him to excise from himself his capacity to formulate conceptions, create alternatives, produce changes, and question relationships and the system underlying them. Worship, which is an affective capacity, the impulse of love toward another, inevitably implies the paralysis of another capacity—that of will, of the exercise of liberty. Love, as the divine conceives, demands, and imposes it, is an exercise in self-mutilation and a design for the worshipper to kill in himself every day any impulses toward liberty, any impulses to change the status quo, the plan of the loved one. Any manifestation of the will of the lover, the worshipper, can only be a weakening of the loved one, God.[22]

---

19. *The Effects of Modernization on the Male-Female Dynamics in a Muslim Society*, 130.
20. Fatna A. Sabbah/Fatima Mernissi, *Women in the Muslim Unconscious*, 79–80. Even though Mernissi has not publically acknowledged, or denied, that she indeed is the author of *Women in the Muslim Unconscious*, there are many good reasons to believe Fatna A. Sabbah is her pseudonym in this work. The topics addressed in *Women in the Muslim Unconscious*, the writing style, and contextual references in the book all carry the hallmarks of Mernissi's other works. Other scholars who have written extensively on Mernissi also believe Mernissi is the author of *Women in the Muslim Unconscious*. See, for example, Raja Rhouni, *Secular and Islamic Feminist Critiques in the Work of Fatima Mernissi*, 40, 59, 82.
21. *Women in the Muslim Unconscious*, 82.
22. *Women in the Muslim Unconscious*, 89.

The one way love, Mernissi argues, that exists between humans and God is assured to lead to reification as a being deprived of volition, freedom and imagination to envision different alternatives and bring about change "has much more in common with a thing than a human" being.[23] In fact, in Mernissi's view, the Subjectivity of God completely annihilates human subjectivity:

> The relationship of love between the divine and the human is inscribed in a precise relationship to time and space. It is a relationship in which one of the parties, the divine being, has complete mastery of time and space, the two components of action and thus of power, and the other party, the human being is fatally bereft of it. The master of time and space, the manifestation of divine power, is at the same time the incarnation of human impotence. The two parties, the divine and the human, are bound together in a relationship of inversion in which the affirmation of the one signifies the weakening of the other, in which the triumph of the one inevitably signifies the defeat of the other. This inversion-linkage, which freezes the two elements in a hierarchized relationship of inequality and conflict, is the key schema that animates all the elements of creation and programs of their interaction. This inversion-linkage is the code that programs the interaction of elements from the time they enter into a relationship with each other, and this relationship is always predetermined.[24]

This ontological view by Mernissi leads her to posit that women's agency is even more radically denied in Muslim culture. The master-slave linkage between God and male believers provides a paradigm that also applies to the relationship between men and women in a Muslim context. Nowhere in the Qur'an, Mernissi writes, "do we have direct access to the point of view of the weak one, the servant, the slave, the believer whose submission God demands." The only access to the servant is through the master. This paradigm is essential for understanding the relationship between women and men as it has been fashioned in Muslim civilization. In fact, "the relationship between the sexes is nothing but a reflection and incarnation of the fundamental relationship between God, the Master, and his slave, the believer. One of the givens of the relationship between the sexes, as Islam has designed and effected it, is that this relationship is shaped according to the desire of the master, the husband."[25]

Reification: Women and Men

As we saw above, Mernissi posits an absolute negation of women's subjectivity in the Islamic world and much of her early discourse is devoted to flesh out and elaborate on the mechanisms that lead to women's (and men's) reification. Mernissi identifies Ghazali as one of the most influential Muslim thinkers who has left an indelible impact

23. *Women in the Muslim Unconscious,* 93.
24. *Women in the Muslim Unconscious,* 66. The view that God's Subjectivity denies human subjectivity, as expressed by Mernissi, is indeed close to Islamic Foundationalists and diametrically opposed to liberal Muslim theologians such as Mohammad Mojtahed Shabestari, who is discussed in this volume. Also compare Mernissi's analysis to my notion of mediated subjectivity in this volume.
25. *Women in the Muslim Unconscious,* 81.

on Islamic culture since the 11th century. Mernissi holds Ghazali responsible for creating and establishing "silence, immobility, and obedience" as the key criteria of female beauty in the Muslim society. Ghazali, Mernissi believes, was also responsible for the seclusion of women in Muslim culture, as he advised that the ideal woman "must remain in her private quarters and never neglect her spindle. She must not make frequent trips to the balcony nor spend her time gazing down from there. Let her exchange but few words with her neighbors and not go to visit them."[26]

Reification of women, Mernissi argues, is very much rooted in the Islamic tradition's reduction of them to the sphere of materiality. Mernissi makes a distinction between what she calls "Orthodox Islam" and "Erotic Islam." The first refers to the official and mainstream discourse of Sunni tradition that relies on theology and jurisprudence. By the "Erotic discourse" she means the views on human sexuality expressed by some mainstream and some non-mainstream thinkers, obviously all men. In the erotic discourse, "The omnisexual woman is woman-as-body, exclusively physical. Her other dimensions, especially the psychological, economic, and engendering dimensions, are not reduced or marginalized; they are nonexistent. Their absence is symbolized by two attributes much prized in this woman-as matter—silence and immobility."[27] In the Erotic discourse, according to Mernissi, the woman is reduced to her sexual organs which define her entire being and behavior, called *al-faraj* in Arabic, meaning a slit, opening or passage.[28] In this discourse, "the eclipsing of the psychic dimension of this creature [the Muslim woman], the annihilation of the ego is carried out by the simple omnipresence of the physical dimension."[29] In fact Mernissi argues that in this discourse the woman is reduced to animality.[30] This discourse, Mernissi argues, reduces women to nature and crass sexuality, "she stands in opposition to culture, to patriarchal, hierarchized, and hierarchizing Islam. By listening to the muscles that throb between her legs, the woman erodes the social hierarchy, opens her vagina to the large phalluses of men of low estate, whom the social order places at the bottom of the social scale, thus effecting a reversal of values."[31] Islam, Mernissi argues, bestows "spirituality" to the materiality, but with regards to women, it denies them the spiritual dimension.[32]

Women's reification has a purpose, according to Mernissi: subjectification of men. "In the orthodox discourse," writes Mernissi "while the mobile, animate man acts vertically in a space that he controls through his will, woman is deprived of will. Horizontal and immobile, she offers herself up to the force that animates the universe, the male force. It is in and by the sexual act that the principle of domination is carried out, that the hierarchical principle, which is the patriarchal universe, is created and maintained. This hierarchy, the domination of man over woman, is only established at the price of the reification of women."[33] Very

26. *Women in the Muslim Unconscious*, 3.
27. *Women in the Muslim Unconscious*, 25.
28. *Women in the Muslim Unconscious*, 24.
29. *Women in the Muslim Unconscious*, 25.
30. *Women in the Muslim Unconscious*, 26.
31. *Women in the Muslim Unconscious*, 36.
32. *Women in the Muslim Unconscious*, 63–64.
33. *Women in the Muslim Unconscious*, 44. Mernissi makes a similar point in one of her later writings: "The concept of honour and virginity locate the prestige of a man between the legs of a

much following the spirit of Hegel's master/slave dialectic, Mernissi believes that for power, i.e., domination, to operate, it is necessary that one party loses her subjectivity: "The reification of woman is a necessary condition for patriarchal domination."[34] The notion of being the property and possession of someone is only possible if the person being possessed is deprived of her will and the capacity for counter-power. A fully conscious, volitive human being cannot be the possession of another human.[35] The reification of women, Mernissi insists in her early writing, has it roots in some of the Qur'anic verses:

> In Verse 14 of Surah III women are put in the category of possessions that tempt men on earth, just like gold, money, horses and lands. The unilateral character of the sexual act is clearly stated in the Verse 223 of Surah II: "Your women are a tilth for you (to cultivate) so go to your tilth as ye will." In this surah, the human being is man. Woman is a category whose human dimension is ambiguous. Woman is defined in terms of her function, her relationship to man. As an entity, she is land, she is real estate, she is inert.[36]

Having posited that women's subjectivity is sacrificed to build men's subjectivity, Mernissi takes a step further and attempts to demonstrate that even men are reified in monotheism. Ultimately, young Mernissi argues, in Islam the male believer is not much different from the woman, because his subjectivity is annihilated vis-à-vis the Divine Subject. Quoting her own alias, she writes:

> [T]he [male] believer is fashioned in the image of woman, deprived of speech and will and committed to obedience to another (God). The female condition and the male condition are not different in the end to which they are directed, but in the pole around which they orbit. The lives of beings of the male sex revolve around the divine will. The lives of beings of the female sex revolve around the will of believers of the male sex. And in both cases the human element, in terms of multiple, unforeseeable potentialities, must be liquidated in order to bring about the triumph of the sacred, the triumph of the divine, the non-human.[37]

---

woman. It is not by subjugating nature or by conquering mountains and rivers that a man secures his status, but by controlling the movements of women related to him by blood or by marriage, and by forbidding them any contact with male strangers." Fatima Mernissi, *Women's Rebellion and Islamic Memory* (Zed Books, 1996), 34.

34. *Women in the Muslim Unconscious*, 45.
35. *Women in the Muslim Unconscious*, 45.
36. *Women in the Muslim Unconscious*, 44. It is interesting that Mernissi points out that in the Erotic Discourse, women are perceived to be the subject and men reified: "In the omnisexual sphere it is man who is inert, and woman who is active. To use the terminology of the hunt, so dear to Al-Akkad, one of the most eloquent theoreticians of modern Muslim patriarchy, she is the pursuer, he is the prey. The power relationship is still there, but the roles are reversed; it is the woman who has a project, and that project is orgasm, in which she invests her will and energy. The man becomes merely an instrument to be pursued [...] It is the voracious-vagina-crack woman who is the subject, the force that dominates the scene. Man is the sought-for object; he is reduced solely to what is useful: his phallus, described in great detail." *Women in the Muslim Unconscious*, 45.
37. Fatima Mernissi, *Women's Rebellion and Islamic Memory* (Zed Books, 1996), 109.

The obedience, silence, and immobility that constitute the ideal of women's beauty in Islam, according to Mernissi, equally apply to men, who ultimately suffer from the same inertia and passivity. Men, in this reading, just like women, are created to worship the monotheistic Deity and any manifestation of agency by them is forbidden as "innovation":

> The [male] believer must dedicate his life to obeying and worshipping God and abiding by his will. The believer comes into a world organized and programmed beforehand by divine power, and God explicitly requires him to be passive. Any manifestation of will by the believer, any attempt to change the existing order, to create alternatives is *bida'*, innovation, and this is errant behavior. The source of the orthodox discourse is the Koran, which is the discourse of the superior one, God. The voice of the believer cannot make itself heard without destabilizing the equilibrium of the system and preventing the order. Man must invest his energy, not in attempts to express himself, but in attempts to decipher the discourse of the almighty. This is the objective of religious science. The *fuqahas* [sic] and imams devote themselves to the task essential to the lives of individuals and the *umma*: interpreting the will of the other and abiding by it. The believer is fulfilled not by expressing himself, but by making his own the expression of the other, the superior one, God.[38]

Thus, in Mernissi's rather simplistic reading of Islamic ontology, while the subjectivity of women is negated vis-à-vis that of men, the subjectivity of both, men and women, is negated vis-à-vis the Divine, "The lives of beings of the male sex revolve around the divine will. The lives of beings of the female sex revolve around the will of believers of the male sex. And in both cases the human element, in terms of multiple unforeseeable potentialities, must be liquidated in order to bring about the triumph of the sacred, the triumph of the divine."[39]

Interestingly, Mernissi traces the foundations of male reification on earth to the eschatological paradigm of the Islamic belief system. In the Muslim conception of paradise, Mernissi argues, men are reduced to digestive and genital apparatuses who merely enjoy food and sex without any form of agency, volition or creativity:

> The male believer is an automaton. He is a being reduced to a digestive tube and a genital apparatus—a genital apparatus, moreover, deprived of its creative function, for the houri [heavenly woman] is a virgin. The genitality of the believer is stripped of its capacity for giving life, for projecting itself into the future. Paradise, with its food and its houri, is programmed for a consumer-believer deprived of the creative dimension. The believer is fulfilled in Paradise by renouncing all the potentialities that define a human being, all possibilities of making choices not programmed by an external will. The purpose of the believer is to fit himself into the plan organized, conceived, and programmed by another will. The purpose of the believer is to reduce himself to a consumer and annihilate within himself his creative potential, for to create within the paradisal context would be to disturb the order and destroy the plan. The believer is passive: He digests, makes love to houri deprived of a uterus (for she is a virgin), and relaxes. Like the houri, he forms an integral part of a system where he exists as a thing deprived of will.[40]

38. *Women in the Muslim Unconscious*, 118.
39. *Women in the Muslim Unconscious,* 118.
40. *Women in the Muslim Unconscious,* 96–97. In her later writings, as we will see, Mernissi almost completely reverses herself by claiming that Islam bestows power and subjectivity to its

Desire, Reason and Domination of Women

In her later book, *Beyond the Veil*, which also belongs to her early phase, Mernissi further develops her analysis of the "Muslim system" that constitutes the familial and social structure of Islamic societies. As in her earlier works, she posits that the men-women relations comprise an essential component of the social structure in the Muslim world. In this "system," what is feared most is the full development of love between a woman and a man in its different dimensions such as sexual, emotional and intellectual.[41] As a psychic energy that should be solely invested in the monotheistic deity, love and desire constitute, according to Mernissi, a serious threat to the structure of Muslim society. Mernissi again refers to Ghazali as the most brilliant medieval Muslim thinker who recognized and in fact promoted such a view. For Ghazali, commitment to God is the most essential duty of men. On the other hand, Ghazali recognized that the tension of sexual excitement in men has to be satisfied in the most economic fashion possible. Yet, "Any psychic investment by him [the man] in sexual relations would be a very serious danger, for it would reverse the divine order, which demands that woman be inferior to man and be fixed at the level of a fetish, the merely physical."[42] In contrast to Christianity, the Muslim civilization never totally suppressed men's sexual satisfaction. In fact, "The Muslim theory of sublimation is entirely different from the Western Christian tradition as represented by Freudian psychoanalytic theory. Freud viewed civilization as a war against sexuality. Civilization is sexual energy "turned aside from its sexual goal and diverted towards other ends, no longer sexual and socially more valuable. The Muslim theory views civilization as the outcome of satisfied sexual energy. Work is the result not of sexual frustration but of a contented and harmoniously lived sexuality."[43] However, what Islam suppressed, Mernissi maintained, is genuine love and desire and all that belongs to this category.

Mernissi attempted to provide an insight into the mechanism by which Islam allegedly suppresses desire and sensuality on the one hand, and promotes "reason" on the other. For her the monotheistic God is, among other things, a projection of men's wish for subjectivity and power, or what she calls "self-fertilization." Male yearning for subjectivity

---

adherents: "The secret of Islam's sweeping resurgence today is that it gives men at birth an inherited right to claim world hegemony as a horizon and guiding dream. It gives, of course, also many other, more constraining limits and hierarchies. But the ability of Islam to equip its members to see the entire universe as their playground is stunning to anyone who takes the time to go through the classical religious literature[...] How can a 'medieval religion,' ask Western students raised in a secular culture, be so alive, so challenging to the effects of time, so renewable in energy? How can it be meaningful to educated youth? We'll soon see that one of the characteristics of fundamentalism is the attraction Islam has for high achievers among young people today. In Cairo, Lahore, Jakarta, and Casablanca, Islam makes sense because it speaks about *power and self-empowerment*." (Fatima Mernissi, *Beyond the Veil: Male-Female Dynamics in Modern Muslim Society* (Indiana University Press, 1987), x–xvi; emphasis added.)

41. Fatima Mernissi, *Beyond the Veil: Male-Female Dynamics in Modern Muslim Society* (Indiana University Press, 1987), 8.
42. *Women in the Muslim Unconscious*, 118.
43. *Beyond the Veil*, 44.

that is projected onto God precludes any other form of desire and love. Furthermore, this attitude leads the Islamic civilization to emphasize the opposite of desire, namely, reason:

> One can only understand the fundamentally misogynistic attitude of the sacred by placing it within the power struggle that God, the abstract body, and woman, the concrete body, wage every day. The sacred can be interpreted ultimately as a homosexual experience. It is the attempt of the male principle at self-fertilization, if one regards the monotheistic God as a projection of earthly man. The sacred is, among other things, the fertilization of earthly man by the male principle erected into a divine (that is, abstract) body. It is this that produces the fundamental conflict between heterosexual union and the sacred, which in Islam is focalized around the conflict between reason and desire. Since it cannot prevent heterosexual union on earth without destroying the human race, the sacred will try to drain it of its human dimension, the affective dimension. Islam integrates sexuality by lopping off its human dimension, desire.[44]

As such, Mernissi believes that there is a fundamental conflict between desire and reason in Muslim societies. Reflecting a Marcusian approach, she wrote:

> The Conflict between Reason and Desire in the Muslim Order, or the Decapitation of Eros: Islam is the religion of reason. It is organized around the concept of the believer as a reasonable being capable of understanding and deciphering signs (*al-ayat*). To be Muslim is first of all to understand God's signs, to decipher the *ayat* [...] Muslims are people who understand signs. In the Koran, understanding means using one's reason. Orthographically, the Arabic words for to understand and reason are indistinguishable. This centering of Islam on reason (*'aql*) leads to defining under the broad rubric of "desire" (*shahwa*) everything that risks deflecting the believer's attention from his focal point, God, who is only accessible in and through the constant exercise of reasoning. In order to illustrate this fundamental conflict of Muslim civilization, which opposes civilization not to sexuality but to desire (which is only a component of sexuality), we must skim through the treaties on love and/or women. We must look at some examples of the discourse of chivalry in our Muslim culture.[45]

Thus, in a rather one-dimensional fashion, Mernissi creates a binary opposition between reason and desire. Once reason is considered the key faculty of human existence, and the foundation of religion and order, she maintains, desire will emerge as the "negative pole of the universe, the incarnation of the forces of disorder." Desire will be viewed as the opposite of the divine will.[46] Reason in Islamic civilization, Mernissi states, is regarded as the instrument of divine worship as it is presumed that reason is the most effective instrument for the believer to disarm Satan. Satan allies with women to defeat the male believer, but reason is the surest safeguard to protect the believer. Women's beauty plays a large part in this scenario also. In fact women's beauty is the manifestation

---

44. *Women in the Muslim Unconscious*, 109.
45. *Women in the Muslim Unconscious*, 110. Given the influence of Marcuse on the left in general and the fact that Mernissi did her doctoral program at Brandeis University where he had taught between 1958 and 1965, the Marcusian influence on her work at this time seems quite natural.
46. *Women in the Muslim Unconscious*, 111.

of the devil, because it provokes desire. Mernissi argues, "This identification of the desire/devil/woman triad is very clear in [Muslim] religious literature."[47] Based on these observations, young Mernissi states that, in Islam, reason is the mechanism by which religion controls desire and subjugates women:

> From this comes the necessity to control woman, to neutralize her as much as possible, for she is the unique concrete incarnation of desire. The devil, like God, has no physical existence. Mastering women means mastering desire. Subjugating women means the triumph of reason, the divine will, and order. Marriage, according to Ghazzali, is slavery (*riqq*). The supremacy of man over women means the supremacy of reason over unreason.[48]

Mernissi's romantic moment takes her to a rather extreme position in which she blames volition and discernment, the very elements whose denial she claimed caused women's reification, for the suppression of desire: "Will (*al-'azm*) and discernment (*al-ra'i*), which are aspects of reason, work together in the struggle against desire (*al-hawa*): 'If reason governs, desire surrenders (*salamahu al-hawa*) and becomes its servant and slave. And if desire governs, reason becomes its prisoner. It submits to it.'"[49] The alleged structural misogyny that is imbedded in Islam, Mernissi claims, is the result of the attempt to suppress desire.

> And it is the necessity to subjugate woman as the incarnation of desire, the necessity for the believer to dominate and master her that explains the fundamentally misogynistic attitude of Islam, which is very plain in legal Islam and especially in the Sahihs [authenticated reports of the Traditions attributed to the Prophet]. Misogyny—contempt for women and discrimination against them—is a structural characteristic and a pivotal axis of the Muslim order.[50]

---

47. *Women in the Muslim Unconscious,* 112.
48. *Women in the Muslim Unconscious,* 113. It is important to note that from very early in her career, Mernissi maintained that Islam does not consider women to be *inherently* inferior: "Paradoxically, and contrary to what is commonly assumed, Islam does not advance the thesis of women's inherent inferiority. Quite the contrary, it affirms the potential equality between the sexes. The existing inequality does not rest on an ideological or biological theory of women's inferiority, but is the outcome of specific social institutions designed to restrain her power: namely, segregation and legal subordination in the family structure." *Beyond the Veil,* 19.
49. *Women in the Muslim Unconscious,* 112.
50. *Women in the Muslim Unconscious,* 113. Mernissi expressed very similar views in the later phase of her discourse. Reminiscing about her childhood in her semi-autobiographical book, she wrote: "I decided then and there that if I ever led a battle for women's liberation, I definitely would not forget about sensuality. As Aunt Habiba said, 'Whey rebel and change the world if you can't get what's missing in your life? And what is most definitely missing in our lives is love and lust. Why organize a revolution if the new world is going to be an emotional desert?'" Fatima Mernissi, *Dreams of Trespass: Tales of a Harem Childhood* (Addison-Wesley, 1994), 133. However, in *Beyond the Veil* (27), she has articulated rather different views on human sexuality and by connotation "desire" in Islam: "The Christian concept of the individual as tragically torn between two poles—good and evil, flesh and spirit, instinct and reason—is very different from the Muslim concept. Islam has a more sophisticated theory of the instincts, more akin to the Freudian concept of the libido. It views the raw instincts as energy. The energy of instincts

The segregation and veiling of women, in Mernissi's analysis, is also closely related to the destructive power of desire that is associated with being a woman. As such, the woman must be under the authority of men, i.e., their fathers, brothers, or husbands. Because the woman is considered to be the source of destructive desire, she must be kept under spatial confinement and excluded from non-family affairs.[51]

Phase II: Nuanced Analysis of Islam

Sometime in the middle of her career, Mernissi changed her approach to analyzing Islam and the Muslim cultures.[52] Mernissi explains the reasons behind this transformation quite explicitly: "If you want other people to stop being monsters who attack you as soon as you open your mouth to say something interesting and unique (of course!), you have to begin by giving up the boxer's posture. It took me years to understand that. I began by writing articles that were vitriolic. That was in the 1970s in the now defunct monthly magazine *Lamalif*, administered and published, come hell or high water, by Zakia Daoud from Casablanca."[53] This new approach has allowed Mernissi to view even her nemesis, that is fundamentalist political Islam, as potentially capable of producing a discourse that is in tune with feminist aspirations. Thus she acknowledges that there could be women within some Islamic fundamentalist movements who are engaged in reinterpretation of the Islamic heritage and whose work in this field is necessary for the construction of a

---

is pure in the sense that it has no connotation of good or bad. The question of good and bad arises only when the social destiny of men is considered. The individual cannot survive except within a social order. Any social order has a set of laws. The set of laws decides which uses of the instincts are good or bad. It is the use made of the instincts, not the instincts themselves, that is beneficial or harmful to the social order."

51. *Beyond the Veil*, 18–19.
52. It would be a mistake, however, to assume that the two "phases" constitute an abrupt break from each other. Significant elements of one phase are strongly present in the other. For example, as early as her dissertation, Mernissi emphasized that at its core, Islam does not consider women inferior by *essence*:
"Indeed, it was not difficult for the male-initiated and male-led Feminist movement to affirm the need for woman's emancipation, since traditional Islam recognized equality of potential and the democratic glorification of the human individual, regardless of sex, race and status, is the kernel of the Muslim message. What was, and is still, at stake is not an ideology of female inferiority but institutions which have insured that women's status remains one of subjugation, namely, family law which is based on male authority and sexual inequality." Mernissi, *The Effects of Modernization on the Male-Female Dynamics in A Muslim Society*, 3.
53. Fatima Mernissi, *Women's Rebellion and Islamic Memory* (Zed Books, 1996), 3. On the same page Mernissi continues, "Then, one day, I came to the conclusion that I really had to find a different method. What if I accentuated the positive, the things that were right, that gave hope, instead of getting bogged down in all that was wrong? Perhaps I would help myself—and others too—to see how you could wade on through the mire, and perhaps how you could avoid it—possibly even how you could learn to fly. And, anyway, what was there to lose from imagining a better world? What was there to lose from imagining a better world? This shift opened up to me incredible doors of friendship and comradeship and brought me harsh but constructive criticism and so much emotion, so many dreams and hopes reciprocated by readers of both sexes, giving me the boldness I needed to continue my explorations."

Muslim modernity. More importantly, she observes, "Our liberation will come through a rereading of our past and a reappropriation of all that has structured our civilization. The mosque and the Koran belong to women as much as do heavenly bodies. We have a right to all of that, to all its riches for constructing our modern identity."[54]

In her later writings, Mernissi is also centrally concerned with identifying the root causes of women's inferior status in Muslim societies. These causes, Mernissi argues, can be traced back to some type of vested interest in stunting women's subjectivity. In her book *The Veil and the Male Elite*, she compares Islam and the Judeo-Christian traditions with regards to women and asserts that, because Islam is no more repressive than the Western tradition, there must be a vested interest in obstructing the rights of women in Islamic cultures. This interest, according to her, must be based on profit, or more exactly "how and where a businessman who profitably exploits women (whether the head of a multinational or a local bazaar entrepreneur), finds a source in which he can dip his spurious rationale to give it a glow of authenticity?"[55] The delving into the causes of the thwarting of women's subjectivity in Mernissi's later discourse takes an even more historical dimension. To identify different types of vested interest that entailed the "violation of women's rights it is necessary to go back into the shadows of the past."[56]

In her historical search for the causes of the frustration of women's subjectivity, Mernissi rather drastically revises her own account of the formative events of early Islamic history. Thus, on the verge of a newly found nativism, she wrote:

> The vast and inspiring records of Muslim history so brilliantly completed for us by scholars such as Ibn Hisham, Ibn Hajar, Ibn Sa'ad, and Tabari, speak to the contrary. We Muslim women can walk into the modern world with pride, knowing that the quest for dignity, democracy, and human rights, for full participation in the political and social affairs of our country, stems from no imported Western values, but is a true part of the Muslim tradition. Of this I am certain, after reading the works of those scholars mentioned above and many others. They give me evidence to feel proud of my Muslim past, and to feel justified in valuing the best gifts of modern civilization: human rights and the satisfaction of full citizenship.[57]

---

54. Fatima Mernissi, *Islam and Democracy: Fear of the Modern World* (Addision-Wesley, 1992), 160–61. It seems that the "paradoxical," or more accurately dialectical, process of emergence of a feminist discourse from Islamist women in Iran, has had some influence on Mernissi: "Reducing women fundamentalists to obedient bystanders is to badly misunderstand the dynamics of the religious protest movement. We have seen the importance of the concepts like *huqq* (right) and *'adl* (justice). Even if at the beginning women recruits were there to be manipulated, in many Muslim countries today—for instance, Iran and Algeria—we see the emergence of a virulent feminist leadership within the fundamentalist parties. We don't have to fall victim to stereotyping. We must remain vigilant and keep open, analytical minds, as have the Iranian sociologist Nayereh Tohidi and the whole group of women experts who recently attended the conference "Identity, Politics, and Women." Their conclusion was that even within the ranks of the fundamentalists, feminist challenge is emerging and causing surprises." *Islam and Democracy*, 160–61
55. Fatima Mernissi, *The Veil and the Male Elite: A Feminist Interpretation of Women's Rights in Islam* (Perseus Books, 1991), vii.
56. *The Veil and the Male Elite*, vii.
57. *The Veil and the Male Elite*, viii.

Very much in contrast to what she wrote earlier, Mernissi now believes that the advent of Islam and actions of the Prophet empowered and emancipated women of the earliest Islamic era, which by implication should serve as a model for our time. There is much historical evidence, Mernissi claims, to demonstrate that women in the Prophet's Medina liberated themselves from bondage and violence and participated equally with men to create their history: "Women fled aristocratic tribal Mecca by the thousands to enter Medina, the Prophet's city in the seventh century, because Islam promised equality and dignity for all, for men and women, masters and servants. Every woman who came to Medina when the Prophet was the political leader of Muslims could gain access to full citizenship, the status of *sahabi*, Companion of the Prophet."[58] In fact the Prophet's era, Mernissi claims, was a paradigmatic time for Islamic democracy. Islam was sent from the heaven to encourage people to achieve higher cultural goals and achieve equality for all in the midst of various conflicts that afflicted the Arab society of that time. But most significantly, "For those first Muslims democracy [that Islam brought] was nothing unusual; it was their meat and drink and their wonderful dream, waking or sleeping."[59]

Beyond the paradigmatic period of the Prophet's life, history and historical memory, Mernissi proclaims, have been distorted because of the political, economic and patriarchal interests, and she sets herself the task of correcting them. One of the earliest forms of distortion was in regard to Hadith, or the sacred account of the Prophet's actions and sayings. The manipulation of the Hadith, Mernissi observes, took place because the political system in Islam after the death of the Prophet was elitist and did now allow the populace to participate in the process of choosing the head of the state.[60] The panorama of manipulation of sacred texts by and for the powerful, "gives us an idea of the magnitude of the political and economic stakes that presided over, and still preside over, the manipulation of the sacred text, since that Monday of the year AD 632 when the Prophet, who had succeeded in creating a community that was both democratic and powerful, lay forgotten and unburied."[61]

---

58. *The Veil and the Male Elite,* viii.

59. *The Veil and the Male Elite,* ix. Mernissi describes the "democratic" features of the paradigmatic period: "At Basra in year 36 the dilemma that confronted a Muslim—whether to obey an unjust caliph or to take up arms against him—was not just being posed in the circles of the ruling elite. The mosques were veritable plenary assemblies where the leaders came to discuss with the people they governed the decisions to be taken in the conflict between A'isha and Ali, and it must be pointed out (after reading the minutes of those meetings) that the people spoke up and demanded to be informed about what was going on." Ibid. 55.

60. *The Veil and the Male Elite,* 46.

61. *The Veil and the Male Elite,* 48. One of the examples of Hadith manufacturing to which Mernissi refers is the set of misogynistic Hadiths by Abu Hurayra (d. 681) to the effect that the Prophet is supposed to have said that three causes of interruption of prayer were dogs, donkeys and women. Mernissi refutes the authenticity of the Hadith by arguing that "Since [in Islam] the whole earth is a mosque, aligning woman with dogs and asses, as does the Hadith of Abu Hurayra, and labeling her a disturbance, amounts to saying that there is a fundamental contradiction between her essence and that of the divine. By lumping her in with two familiar animals the author of the Hadith inevitably makes her a being who belongs to the animal kingdom." *The Veil and the Male Elite,* 69–70.

One of the central questions that preoccupies Mernissi throughout her discourse is the veiling of women and their segregation and physical confinement in Islamic history. Mernissi attempts to question these institutions and show that they contradict the democratic and pro-women spirit of early Islam. Mernissi attempts to explain the imposition of the *hijab* (veiling) and segregation through a series of interrelated events in the early history of Islam. The difficult political, military and social circumstances in which the Prophet was caught forced him to decree veiling that, according to Mernissi, was contradicting the emancipatory message and mission of Islam. It was the difficult period after the defeat of Uhud battle in year three of migration to Medina as well the psychological and physical wounds of the Battle of the Trench in year five, that the political opposition to the Prophet took the shape of mostly indirect attacks by the so-called Hypocrites (Munafiqun), who would use slander, rumor-mongering and other insidious tactics such as following and harassing the wives of the Prophet in the streets of Medina. As such, "Demoralized by his military difficulties, the Prophet was defenseless against such tactics, which led him to doubt his wives and to accept the famous *hijab* [rule]."[62] In fact Mernissi suggests that the Prophet did not order the veiling, but it was 'Umar, the second Caliph, who is responsible for it: "...the *hijab*, which is presented to us as emanating from the Prophet's will, was insisted upon by 'Umar Ibn al- Khattab, the spokesman of male resistance to women's demands. Muhammad only yielded on this point when the community was in the middle of a military disaster and when economic and political crises were tearing Medina apart."[63] A minor incident, Mernissi argues, also prompted the Prophet to agree to the institution of sexual segregation. After an evening meal at the Prophet's house, some quests delayed their departure longer than they should, which provoked a response as fundamental as dividing the space in the Muslim world into two spheres, the private sphere of the household to which women were largely confined and the public sphere that was to become nearly exclusively for men.[64] In conclusion, Mernissi declares that veiling opposes the spirit of Islam and that its imposition represents the triumph of its insidious internal enemy, the Hypocrites: "In the struggle between Muhammad's dream of a society in which women could move freely around the city (because the social control would be the Muslim faith that disciplines desire), and the customs of the Hypocrites who only thought of a woman as an object of envy and violence, it was this latter vision that would carry the day. The veil represents the triumph of the Hypocrites."[65]

To be sure, Mernissi attributed a very significant role to *hijab* in negating women's subjectivity. The hijab epitomized the very opposite of what the Prophet wished to institute. The hijab was "the incarnation of the absence of internal control; it was the veiling of the *sovereign will*, which is the source of good judgment and order in a society. 'Umar who had never reflected about the principle of the individual that the new religion

62. *The Veil and the Male Elite*, 105–6.

63. *The Veil and the Male Elite*, 114.

64. *The Veil and the Male Elite*, 110. Mernissi's response to this event is worth reading: "One can only be astonished at the disproportion between the incident and the response, since the Prophet could have simply asked people to no longer come uninvited to his dwelling."

65. *The Veil and the Male Elite*, 187.

emphasized, could not understand this. To him, the only way of reestablishing order was to put up barriers and to hide women, who were objects of envy."[66] In the contemporary period, Mernissi argues, the veil, plays a very anti-democratic part also, by preventing women from participating in the public sphere and thus making them invisible.[67] In fact Mernissi condemns veiling in the strongest terms comparing it to "terrorism":

> The veiling of women as a political ideal and terrorism are but strange, dream-like sex-distorted mirror images of the same fierce garroting of citizen's voices and the pitiless choking of their desire for self-expression. They are mirror images of the same mutilation of self-expression, but while the veil concerns women, terrorism is primarily a man's affair. The enforcement of the veil as a state religion-justified policy by Muslim oil leaders as different in their backgrounds as Imam Khomeini and the King of Saudi Arabia in the 1980s was not so much a sex-targeted, religion-inspired, spirituality-inclined endeavor, as many believed it to be. The 1980s' oil-rich statesman's incredibly aggressive veil obsession was not in fact an offensive targeted at women, it was an assault on democratic process, and an attack on civil society's burgeoning hopes.[68]

Mernissi makes a connection between the *hijab* of women and the "veiling" or insulation of the political power and rulers in the Islamic history. As if connecting the idea that the personal is also political, she seems to suggest that the isolation of women and the anti-democratic insularity of political power and those who rule, from the underlying populace are two sides of the same coin. Soon after the death of the Prophet and the era of the so-called Rightly Guided Caliphs (Abu Bakr, Umar, Uthman and Ali), the caliphs insulated themselves from the *umma* and abandoned the assembly-like feature of the Prophet's mosque. They erected a *hijab*, or barrier between themselves and people who they ruled and governed: "The institution of the *hijab,* that is, a curtain in the sense of a barrier that separates the sovereign from the people and impedes their access to him—which was considered by the Prophet and the first four caliphs as a grave failure in duty by the leader—was very quickly adopted in political practice."[69] Mernissi even

66. Ibid. 185. Emphasis added. On page 176 of the same book Mernissi wrote: "what is involved in the ritual of the veil is the annihilation of the free will of beings who are physically present, of women who are here and who look at you with wide-open, alert eyes."
67. *Women's Rebellion and Islamic Memory*, viii. There is no doubt that Mernissi's proposal that the veil in general, and historically speaking, has functioned to confine women to the private sphere. However, there are instances in the contemporary period where veiling has had the unintended consequence of actually allowing vast numbers of women, especially those of the lower-middle class to enter the public sphere. The forced veiling in Iran after the Revolution of 1979 is a case in point. The forced rules of veiling by the Islamist regime in Iran, which brutally targeted women of the middle and upper-middle classes, had the unintended consequence of allowing, and in fact to some degree encouraging, women of the more traditional and religious backgrounds to enter the job-market and, very significantly, attend the rapidly expanding universities in that country, which transformed them into the "Muslim feminists" that Mernissi mentioned above.
68. *Women's Rebellion and Islamic Memory,* xi.
69. Fatima Mernissi, *The Forgotten Queens of Islam* (University of Minnesota Press, 1991), 79. Mernissi continues: "The name of the official responsible for controlling access to the sovereign

speculates that had the "political veil" not seized the Islamic civilization, democratic practices would have emerged from within Muslim institutions such as the mosque. "One can imagine," she wrote "the transformation of the *masjid*, the mosque, into a popular assembly with the expansion of the *umma* and the growth in the number of Muslims. We might have seen the birth in the heart of Islam of a democratic practice founded on a neighbourhood mosque/local assembly since mosques are found everywhere where there is a community of Muslims and someone to lead them. The Prophet left everything in place for moving in that direction. A parliament could have been created without arguing about it as a satanic Western importation."[70]

Women's Status Revised

In her so-called second phase, Mernissi represents the status of women in the early Islamic civilization in a different light compared to the earlier phase of her discourse. The advent of Islam, Mernissi argues, opened new horizons for women's subjectivity. One of the most important aspects of these new horizons was the financial status that Islam designated for women. Most notably, "Not only would a woman no longer be 'inherited' like camels and palm trees, but she would herself inherit. She would enter into competition with men for the sharing of fortunes."[71] In fact, according to Mernissi in her later phase, Islam bestowed subjectivity to both men and women. In the pre-Islamic period, "A wife, at a time of inheritance, seemed to be nothing but an object to be claimed by male heirs, whether they belonged to the clan of the dead man or to her own clan. The new laws [of Islam] threw all this into question. Islam affirmed the idea of the *individual as a subject*, a free will always present in the world, a sovereign consciousness that cannot disappear as long as the person lives."[72] Thus by recognizing certain rights for women such as the rights to inheritance, Mernissi suggests, early Islam created laws that could potentially confirm women's subjectivity.

However, from the very beginning men opposed these concepts and the laws based on them. The Companions of the Prophet were the first to reject the new concepts and laws, adhering to the pre-Islamic norms and values. They raised objections to the new laws, pressuring the prophet to change them. However, the Prophet was not persuaded and maintained his position, which came from God. As a last recourse, these men resorted to interpreting the holy texts in their own interest, neutralizing the laws in favor of women.[73] But in the end the heavens yielded to the wishes of the patriarchy;

---

was coined from the same linguistic root as *hijab;* he was called *al-hajib,* literally, the one who veils the caliph. The *hajib* was the one who acts as a buffer; he received the applicants for an audience in place of the caliph and decided who should be received and who sent away." While the two institutions, veiling of women and the insularity of rules, are etymologically related in Arabic, the pair may not be a good conceptual instantiation of the "personal is political."

70. *The Forgotten Queens of Islam,* 80.
71. *The Veil and the Male Elite,* 119–20.
72. *The Veil and the Male Elite,* 121. Emphasis added.
73. *The Veil and the Male Elite,* 121–25.

> After Umm Salama's [a female companion of the Prophet] success and the verses affirming women's equality and especially their right to inheritance, a critical period followed. Other verses came, which temporized on the principle of equality of the sexes and reaffirmed male supremacy, without, however, nullifying the dispositions in favor of women. This created an ambiguity in the Koran that would be exploited by governing elites right up until the present day. In fact, women's triumph was of very short duration. Not only did Heaven no longer respond to their pleas, but every time they formulated a new demand, revelations did not, as before, come to their rescue."[74]

The ambivalence that the later-phase Mernissi finds in Islam with regards to women in general leads her to posit a similar ambivalence with regards to women's subjectivity in Islam in particular. Her answer is again complex. In the pre-Islamic period, since a woman could be inherited or be reduced to slavery, her free will was subject to negation.[75] The Prophet of Islam, Mernissi argues, introduced a system that supported human subjectivity including that of women,

> "The Islam of Muhammad banished the idea of supervision, of a police system of control. This explains the absence of clergy in Islam and the encouraging of all Muslims to get involved in understanding the written word. Individual responsibility came into play to balance the weight of aristocratic [i.e., from above and by the elite] control, finally making it ineffective in an *umma* of believers whose behavior followed precise, internalized rules. Recognizing in women an inalienable will fitted into this scheme of making everyone individually responsible."[76]

However, according to Mernissi in historical reality this potential for women's subjectivity was never realized in the Muslim civilization. A woman who has an independent will and exerts it is called a "*nashiz*" in Arabic, which is a derogatory term for a disobedient woman: "A *nashiz* is a woman who declares herself to be an individual, and no longer just a being who aligns herself with the will of someone else. And *nushuz* [disobedience] is obviously synonymous with *fitna,* disorder. The definition of citizenship in the Universal Declaration of Human Rights is a synonym for *nushuz,* because it involves the emergence of the will of the individual, whatever the sex, as sovereign on the political scene."[77]

---

74. *The Veil and the Male Elite,* 129. Historically speaking, Mernissi argues, the religious leaders applied the negative aspects of Islam towards women: "The imams, who devote their lives to explaining the divine will, could have developed an egalitarian Islam based on the verse that Umm Salama obtained from Heaven (sura 33, verse 35), which established the principle of equality between the sexes. But instead of citing that verse, they brandished verse 34 of the sura on women, which is a verse in flagrant contradiction to the one we will henceforth call Umm Salama's verse, doubly so, since it introduces access to wealth as a factor in establishing social hierarchies, a very disputed question in the Islamic community: 'Men are in charge of women, because Allah hath made the one of them to excel the other, and because they spend their property (for the support of women)'." Ibid. 154.
75. *The Veil and the Male Elite,* 148.
76. *The Veil and the Male Elite,* 186.
77. *The Forgotten Queens of Islam*, 177.

The factual disempowerment of women in the history of Islam, in Mernissi's analysis, has a very significant institutional dimension. The most important political institution in Islamic history, that of the Caliphate, Mernissi observes, has been closed to women. Mernissi makes a significant distinction between Caliph and Sultan in the Muslim world. Whereas the institution of the Sultanate has been sometimes, albeit rarely, open to women, the Caliphate has never been open to women, neither on theoretical nor on practical grounds. The legitimacy of the Caliphate, Mernissi argues, has been much more effective because it carries with it the Divine mandate. "Not just anyone can claim to be a caliph; access to this privilege is subject to strict criteria. By contrast, titles like *sultan*, the linguistic origin of which is *salata* (dominate), and *malik* (king), which has the same connotation of raw power not tempered by religion, are available to anybody. And that is why women can carry them; they do not imply or signify any divine mission. But women could never lay claim to the title of caliph. *The secret of the exclusion of women lies in the criteria of eligibility to be a caliph.*"[78] As a result, Mernissi claims, Islamic history displays a constant resistance by the upholders of the orthodoxy toward any woman who vied for power, especially divinely approved power, as a severe violation of Islamic rules and ethos.[79] This resistance has plagued Muslim women to this day, when women such as Benazir Bhutto could never receive the ideological support of legitimacy that men could:

> Islam is crystal-clear about principles. So if one acknowledges *a priori* that women effectively have no power, then one cannot directly transmit any divine mission to them. And Islam's essential institution, the caliphate, leaves no doubt about this exclusion of women from politics. If Benazir Bhutto's enemies had taken their stand on the level of principles and had specified that they were only speaking about the function of caliph, inaccessible to a woman, they would have been unassailable.[80]

The only channel open to women to become prominent and "powerful" in the Muslim world, Mernissi maintains, was through the institution of *jariya* or courtesanship. The *jariya* (pl. *jawari*), or beautiful female slaves who were purchased by the rich and the powerful, could gain positions of power in Islamic civilization; yet, by its very nature the "power" that it could entail was quite fleeting. Historically speaking, Mernissi distinguishes between three periods in the development of the concept of women's empowerment in Islam. The first period, that of the Prophet, witnessed women becoming pre-eminent in the political scene, as Companions of Muhammad. The second period, a few generations after the death of the companions, was one in which aristocratic Arab women became prominent as the wives and mothers of princes and Caliphs. The third period, starting with the Abbasids (750 1250) and which continues to this day, is characterized by the institution of *jawari*, the courtesans of the court who would represent the only type of women "empowerment."[81]

78. *The Forgotten Queens of Islam* 12. Emphasis added.
79. *The Forgotten Queens of Islam* 29–30
80. *The Forgotten Queens of Islam* 33–34.
81. Fatima Mernissi, *Women's Rebellion and Islamic Memory* (Zed Books, 1996), 81. Mernissi observes that the terrestrial *jawari* model has a celestial parallel in the form of *houri*, the virgin

Humanism and Democracy

In the later phase of her discourse, Mernissi pays even more attention to modern humanistic values, of course with some caveats. In this phase Mernissi places even more emphasis on the centrality of the individual in any scheme of modernity in the Muslim world:

> The assertion that the individual and his freedom are not the sole property of the West is at the heart of our tradition, but it has been submerged in incessant bloodbaths. The West, with its insistence on democracy seems to us eminently *gharib*, foreign, because it is a mirror of what frightens us, the wound that fifteen centuries have not succeeded in binding: the fact that personal opinion always brings violence. Under the terrror of the sword, political despotism has obliged Muslims to defer discussion about responsibility, freedom to think, and the impossibility of blind obedience. That was called the closing of the gates of *ijtihad*, "private initiative."[82]

In fact, Mernissi claims that the germs of individuality have always existed in the Muslim world, but never had a chance to thrive: "Who wants to remember? Who wants to disinter the bodies of the past and look back into that distant gloomy dawn when the cry for individuality and dignity was stifled in blood? How are we to flee from the wound within oursleves that we thought scarred over and long forgotten? If we had a true understanding of our past, we would feel less alienated by the West and its democracy. Does the *gharb* [the West] frighten the ruling despots, and the mini-despots who deram of replacing them, because it obliges them to plunge into that extraordinary quest for the Arab's truncated individuality?"[83] Very significantly, Mernissi associates women's disobidence, which as *nushuz* she identifies as one of the most severe threats to Islamic sense of community, with individualism. She suggests that women's disobedince is so much dreaded among the Muslims because it invokes the feared notion of individualism: "Muslim societies resist women's claim to changing their status, and they repress feminist trends which are actually evident all over the Muslim world, condemning them as Western imports, not simply because these societies fear women, but because they fear

---

promised to the pious male believers in the afterlife: "it is the coincidences, the continuities, and the similarities between the sacred models and the historical and imaginary model which are fascinating. For it must not be forgotten that the sacred writings also present an image of women as the source of pleasure through the model of the houri. This model strongly calls to mind the characteristics of the *jariya*. The houri, the female creature in paradise, is supposed to be offered as a reward to believers who have merited access to heaven by their good works on earth." Ibid. 71.

82. *Islam and Democracy*, 19.
83. *Islam and Democracy*, 20. Mernissi invokes the tenth century mystic, Hallaj, who proclaimed "I am the Truth," as evidence of the seeds of individual sovereignty in Islamic history: "The West, which constantly talks about democracy via its satellites and media networks, is frightening to some because it awakens the memory of forgotten greats of the past who are never celebrated by today's leaders. They were the defenders of that little thing, so fragile, so vulnerable, called *karama*, "dignity." There was Hallaj, the Sufi who insisted that the human being is the depository of *haqq*, "truth," and that each person reflects divine beauty and as a result is necessarily sovereign." Ibid.

individualism."[84] Yet Mernissi's understanding of modern individuality is quite different from that of the Enlightenment. She in fact grounds individuality not in "reason" but in the body and sexuality: "Women were veiled not only because their invisibility made it possible to forget difference and create the fiction that the *umma* was unified because it was homogeneous, but above all in order to make people forget what the Arabs of the jahiliyya knew only too well: it is the body and its unconqureable sexuality that is the irreducible fortress of soverign individuality."[85]

Nevertheless, Mernissi, at least at times, praises the legacy of the Enlightenment and excoriates those in the Muslim world who opposed it. Since the early period in Islamic history, a coalition between the statesmen and jurisconsults (*fuqaha*) opposed and condemened independent opinon (*ra'y*), novelty (*ihdath*) and innovation (*ibda'*) as alien and blaspehmous. In the modern period the stifling of Western rationalist tradition by the same powerblock further eroded the possibilty of the development of the hallmarks of modernity. "With complete impunity, the Muslim leaders would battle the Muslim intellectuals who tried to explain and spread the philosophy of the Enlightenment."[86] Just like the Mu'tazilites of early Islamic centuries, the modern intellectuals and enlighteners were harassed, persecuted and condemned in the Muslim world. "The Mu'tazila were the traitors who imported Greek ideas; the modern intellectuals are called servants of the West. Twentieth-century humanism, celebrated elsewhere as the triumph of creativity and the flowering of the individual, is forbidden to us on the pretext that it is foreign. Obscurantism is proposed as the ideal of the future, and one to defend."[87] In fact, in one concise paragraph Mernissi delineates a connection between democracy, secular humanism, humanistic ideas, individuality, civil society and tolerance and their paucity in the Muslim world, which in her view arises from the resistence to colonialism:

> Arabs do not so much have a fear of democracy as suffer from a lack of access to the most important advances of recent centuries, especially tolerance as principle and practice. By this I mean the secular humanism that has allowed the flowering of civil society in the West. Humanistic ideas—freedom of thought, the sovereignty of the individual, the right to freedom of action, tolerance—were propagated in the West through secular schools. With a few rare

---

84. *Women's Rebellion and Islamic Memory*, 109–10.

85. *Islam and Democracy*, 127. In another passage, Mernissi grounds individual subjectivity in "desire" and "passion": "Like the other monotheistic religions, Islam promises peace at the price of sacrifice the sacrifice of desire, *huwa*. *Rahma*, peace in the community, can exist only if the individual renounces his *ahwa* (plural of *hawa*), which are considered the source of dissention and war. The *jahiliyya* saw the unbridled reign of *hawa*, individual desires and passions. *Rahma* in exchange for freedom is the social contract that the new religion proposed to the citizens of Mecca. Renouncing freedom of thought and subordinating oneself to the group is the pact that will lead to peace; *salam* will be instituted if the individual agrees to sacrifice his individualism. *Hawa* means both "desire" and "passion," but it can also signify "personal opinion." It is the unbridled individual interest of a person who forgets the existence of others in thinking only of his own advantage. Desire, which is individual by definition, is the opposite of *rahma*, which is an intense sensitivity for the other, for all the others, for the group." Ibid. 109.

86. *Islam and Democracy*, 40–41.

87. *Islam and Democracy*, 40–41.

> exceptions (notably Turkey), the modern Muslim state has never called itself secular, and has never committed itself to teaching individual initiative. On the contrary, individualism always held a rather ambiguous place among the "reformers" of the nineteenth century nationalist movement. This movement, focused on the struggle against colonization and therefore viscerally anti-Western, was obliged to root itself more deeply than ever in Islam. Facing the militaristic, imperialistic West, Muslim nationalists were forced to take shelter in their past and erect it as a rampart—cultural *hudud* to exorcise colonial violence.[88]

Thus, while as we saw above, Mernissi grounds individual subjectivity in the "body" and sexuality, she is quite emphatic about the centrality of reason and the latter's undergirding of democracy. Delving into Islamic history, Mernissi identifies two trends that opposed and challenged the despotic rule of the Muslim caliphs and other rulers. One was based on the rebellion of the Kharijites in late seventh century, and the other was grounded in the rationalist approach of the Mu'tazilites. Unlike the Kharijites, who preached and practiced violence against despotism, the Mu'tazilites "held that the thinking individual could serve as a barrier against arbitrary rule."[89] In fact:

> The Mu'tazila moved the problem to the philosophical level, asking, What is the purpose of our existence on earth, and to what use should we put *'aql*, that marvelous gift from heaven? If God has created us intelligent, it is to carry out a plan. The rationalist opposition replaced the murder of the imam with the triumph of reason as the barrier against despotism. To achieve the ideal of the well-governed community, all the faithful must be enlisted as the bearers of God's most precious gift, the ability of the individual to think and analyze. By introducing reason into the political theater, the Mu'tazila forced Islam to imagine new relationships between ruler and ruled, giving all the faithful an active part to play alongside the palace.[90]

Democracy, Mernissi proclaims, is like a "sovereign boat that floats on the river of time," that forces us to recognize the pivotal role of reason (*'aql*) and individual judgment (*ra'y*). Since the beginning of their history, Mernissi further claims, Muslims have had to "solve the question that has remained an enigma up until the present: to obey or to reason, to believe or to think?"[91] Thus, in her Enlightenment moment, the next logical step for Mernissi is to posit a link between individual subjectivity and modern scientific spirit:

> Above all else, colonial governments were brutal and culturally limited. The nationalist governments that supplanted them were just as brutal and just as hostile to the flowering of the scientific spirit and inidividual initiative. This produced a virtual cutoff of the the Third World from the advances of humansim in the last centuries in both its aspects: the scientific aspect (promoting the use of government resources to invest in scientific research and encourage freedom to explore and invent), and the political aspect (establishing representative democracy, with citizen's exercise of the right to vote and to participate in political decision making).[92]

88. *Islam and Democracy*, 42.
89. *Islam and Democracy*, 32.
90. *Islam and Democracy*, 32.
91. *Islam and Democracy*, 18–19.
92. *Islam and Democracy*, 46. Mernissi further (44) chastises the Arab states for stifling the scientific spirit and democracy: "Among the nine largest purchasers of arms in the world in 1983, four were Arab

Generally speaking, Mernissi has advocated modern Western democracy, which has some echoes in her second phase. Yet, in her second phase also she has discussed the obstacles that impede the acceptance of democracy in Muslim lands. Patriarchy is the first obstacle. Thus she states, "Societies that have defined the identity of a man by his virile ability to control and veil women do not seem ready to relinquish such a definition of self, nor are they ready to enjoy democracy."[93] More fundamentally, however, Mernissi argues that monotheism and Islam are opposed to freedom of conscience, which is the foundation of democracy. She states that the most appropriate term for translating the notion of freedom in Universal Declaration of Human Rights which refers to freedom of thought, conscience and religion including freedom to change one's religion, in the Arabic language is *shirk*. In the Islamic context, *shirk* can be best translated as "polytheism," which Islam vehemently rejects and which Mernissi believes is essential for modern democracy: "It is in that brief Article 18 [of the Universal Declaration of Human Rights] and the concept of *shirk* that the conflict between Islam and democracy lies as a philosophical debate, a fundamental debate that was blocked for fifteen centuries, supported by the power of the palaces."[94]

With regards to the other institution related to Western modernity, i.e., capitalism, Mernissi has expressed complex views. In general, Mernissi is not concerned with economic issues too much. Discussing the complexities of individual subjectivity, she observes that women's asserting the demands for their rights represents a challenge to the notion of community, which is primary in the Muslim context. Yet, in the modern world, there is another quarter from which individualism poses a challenge to the status quo, namely capitalism:

> That other quarter is capitalism, which is based upon the profitability of individualistic innovation. Capitalism is seen as ferociously aggressive and fiercely individualistic. Arab countries have also become dumping grounds for the goods of the capitalist world: Western arms, films and consumer goods constitute a virtual invasion. Ironically, innovation—the freedom to doubt—is precisely what makes scientific inquiry and the Western ideology of capitalism so strong and successful! And innovation is what makes women's rebellion so subversive from within.[95]

Even though Mernissi does not seem to analyze the complex relations between individual subjectivity and democracy on the one hand and capitalism on the other, she does recognize and deeply delves into the connection between human agency and subjectivity and democracy, as we saw above.

---

states: Iraq, Saudi Arabia, Libya and Egypt What the officials of these states ignore is that the age of fetishism is over, and importing military hardware increases dependence. Power comes from the cultivation of the scientific spirit and participatory democracy. Despite its incredible investment in 'King Khalid Military City,' as the Americans call it, a megaproject that cost $6 billion, the Saudi regime was incapable of defending itself when the Gulf War broke out, and the recourse to American help became inevitable. The Gulf War exposed the extent of the military dependence of not just Saudi Arabia but all the Arab States."

93. *The Forgotten Queens of Islam*, 31.

94. *Islam and Democracy*, 87.

95. *Women's Rebellion and Islamic Memory*, 119.

Conclusion

Fatima Mernissi is one of the few individuals who have addressed issues such as women, Islam, democracy and modernity in terms of their complex relations to each other in the past few decades. She has accomplished this task with seemingly undiminishable enthusiasm, depth, complexity, as well as contradiction. Mernissi's discourse is usually divided into two phases, even though in substance there are more continuities than disruptions between these phases. Utilizing Marxian, Freudian and to some extent Critical Theory, especially the Marcusian approach, Mernissi has analyzed the structure of Muslim society, particularly in its formative period, to understand key problematics such as the position of women, individual subjectivity for both women and men, the fundamentals of democracy, and the prospects for modernity in the Muslim world. There is no doubt that in pursuing these interests she has essentialized many aspects of Islam and the Muslim cultures around the world; yet the insights that her discourse have generated are quite significant and of heuristic value, to say the least. One of the most important aspects of Mernissi's work is that she has explored women's, and in fact human, sexuality in general, and in relation to Islamic cultures in particular, in such depth and to an extent that seems to be unprecedented. In this regard, Mernissi has produced a very complex, though sometimes theoretically incongruent, account of the roots and contemporary realities of misogyny in the Muslim world, while prescribing remedies for improvement. Her work has created a theoretical platform from which significant future works on women in the Islamic world could be launched.

Chapter Five

MEHDI HAERI YAZDI AND THE DISCOURSE OF MODERNITY[1]

The thought of Mehdi Haeri Yazdi can potentially occupy a very significant place in the current debates on modernity and Islam in Iran. His expertise in Islamic philosophy and other Islamic fields of learning as well as his formal training in modern Western philosophical traditions enabled Haeri to explore the fundamental issues of modernity and Islam deeply.

A relative paucity of the ideological and polemical elements usually involved in a discussion of modernity and Islam characterizes Haeri's discourse. This can be attributed not only to the high level of abstraction in which he engaged with the philosophical aspects of the question of Islam and modernity, but also to his personal sensibility, which seems to have disposed him toward an elitist attitude in his writing that made him deliberately shun writing for a larger public, which is in sharp contrast to other contemporary Islamic thinkers in Iran. For this reason, his thought, the promulgation of which spanned some three decades, may seem inaccessible even to experts and as a result has not received the attention that it deserves. In this chapter I intend to present his work to a wider audience and bring out the significance of his thought as it regards the issues of modernity and Islam in Iran and possibly other Islamic societies.

For this reason, I propose that the best way to analyze Haeri's thought on modernity is to view his discourse along three different dimensions or levels of analysis. The first dimension, and the deepest level, is his discussion of ontology or more accurately theontology. At this level, which is the most abstract and comprises a large portion of his discourse, Haeri deals with questions such as existence—that is, God's and humans' locations in this vast and esoteric expanse. The second level is what may be called his philosophy of ethics or practical reason, in which he discussed the philosophical principles governing human action and ethics. The third, least abstract dimension is a discussion of political and social issues that Haeri derived from the two previous dimensions.

The main thesis of this chapter suggests that at the first level, the theontological dimension, Haeri posited the notion of subjectivity primarily for the Being and the Divine, and human subjectivity assumed a secondary and derivative status. Yet even at this level, he did not totally deny human subjectivity, though he relegated it to an epiphenomenal position. Thus Haeri left a space in his theontology for the development of human subjectivity, and therefore for its sociological and political ramifications. Secondly, in the two other dimensions, his discussions of the ethical/practical sphere

1. An earlier version of this chapter appeared as "Mehdi Yazdi and the Discourse of Modernity" in *Iran between Tradition and Modernity*, edited by Ramin Jahanbegloo.

and the political realm, this space for human subjectivity expanded as he built an ethical/practical discourse and socio-political vision based on a rather developed notion of human subjectivity. As a result, in Haeri's discourse as a whole, we can observe an attempt to reconcile Islam and modernity in that both Divine Subjectivity and human subjectivity exist side by side, albeit in different dimensions and at different levels. Later in his career, Haeri elaborated and expanded the notion of human subjectivity and arrived at the idea of modern universal citizenship in the socio-political realm without damaging or interfering with the notion of Divine Sovereignty and Subjectivity.[2]

Theontology and Modernity

Mehdi Haeri Yazdi was born in 1923 in Qom. His father was the renowned Ayatollah Abdul Karim Haeri Yazdi, who transformed Qom into the major center of Shia studies inside Iran. Mehdi studied Islamic jurisprudence, theology and most significantly Islamic philosophy with his father and other prominent Shia scholars in Qom and other places in Iran and received his ordination as an Ayatollah. He also earned a doctorate from University of Tehran in the field of theology. During this period, Haeri developed an intense interest in Western philosophy and spent many years in the United States and Canada, which led to a doctorate in analytical philosophy from University of Toronto in 1979. After that, he returned to Iran to teach Islamic philosophy at the University of Tehran. He died in the summer of 1999 at the age of 76.[3]

Philosophical Inquires

Early in his career, Haeri embarked upon a notion of human subjectivity that was grounded in his philosophical inquires. Philosophy for him was a vehicle to learn the truth and the secrets of creation, insofar as human capacity allows, and thereby achieve a likeness of the Divine.[4] In fact, like many other Islamic thinkers in Iran, Haeri attributed divine qualities to the *Logos*-possessing humans. Thus, in one of his earlier books called *Ilm-i Kulli* (Universal Knowledge) published in the late 1950s, Haeri wrote:

> Man's sacred self, just like a heavenly being, is clear from any abomination and pollution of matter in its origins. Man's power, knowledge, volition, life, vision and auditory ability are the manifestations of the holy essence of the Divine. The powerful God has created

2. Haeri articulated the last aspect of his thought, his more direct socio-political views, in a relatively accessible book, entitled *Hekmat va hukumat* (Philosophy and Government), that he wrote in the last years of his life. This book, which was published not in Iran but in Europe by Iranian expatriates, has been used by some scholars, notably religious thinkers in the country, to deconstruct the notion of the Guardianship of the Jurist (*Velayat-e Faqih*) and envision an Islamic polity that is more compatible with modernity and democracy. See for example, Muhsin Kadivar, *Nazariyeha-ye Dulat dar Fiqh-e Shieh* (Theories of State in Shia Jurisprudence).
3. Most of the biographical information presented here is taken from Masoud Razavi, ed. *Afaq-e Faslafeh: Az Aql-e Nab ta Hekmat-e Ahkam* (Horizons of Philosophy: From Pure Reason to Philosophy of Law).
4. *Ilm-i Kulli* (Universal Knowledge). (Tehran: Intesharat-e Ḥekmat, 1970), 1.

for this celestial being a dominion like His own in which man can be a willful agent and an absolute ruler. Man is in likeness to the transcendent God [...] and like God, man in his [own] dominion is in the position of command and creativity.[5]

In Haeri's early thought, the ability to act, which in humans is combined with consciousness and volition, is the source of agency that leads to power.[6] This agency in humans, according to Haeri, is mediated through our faculty of representation whereby we create pictures of the external objects in our minds, which in turn become the ground for our actions and the power of agency. Moreover, these representations are under our willful control because they are formed by the creative capacity of our minds.[7]

Following Ibn Sina (Also translated Avicenna, d. 1037), Haeri believed that the "perfection" of the self is possible most directly via the study of philosophy. Paraphrasing Ibn Sina, Haeri asserted that "speculative" philosophy is the active agency through which the self, insofar as *intellectus in actu* (*'aql bil fi'l*) is realized, achieves perfection.[8] The transformation of humans from the realm of materiality to the sphere of intellect is achieved as a result of philosophical development. This transformative power of philosophy, in Haeri's reading of Mulla Sadra (d.1640), is the goal of and the ultimate desire of humans seeking perfection and release from entanglement in matter.[9] The high status that Haeri attributed to philosophy led him to view philosophy as constitutive of human authenticity. This understanding is a far cry from a conservative Islamic notion of authenticity. Thus he wrote:

Inasmuch as the truth of philosophy in general is but the knowledge of existence and beings and understanding of reality, it is clear and necessary that this particular form of human knowledge is directly related to the reality and essence of man himself. This is because understanding reality is either necessary, or alternatively, it is the distinguishing feature [differentia, *fasl*] of humans from other animals. Accordingly, we must admit that philosophy is not only the human mode of thinking, it is also what constitutes our essence and our real boundary [separating us from other beings]. [...] The question of "What is philosophy?" is identical to the question of "What is man?" [...] Because man possesses a distinguishing feature such as *Logos* [...] his [essence] is the same as philosophy.[10]

5. *Ilm-i Kulli*, 23.
6. *Ilm-i Kulli*, 91.
7. *Ilm-i Kulli*, 95–96.
8. Haeri Yazdi, Mehdi. *Kavoshha-ye 'Aql-e Nazari* (*Investigations of Pure Reason*). (Tehran: Amir Kabir, 1982), 32.
9. *Kavoshha-ye 'Aql-e Nazari*, 32–33.
10. *Kavoshha-ye 'Aql-e Nazari*, 35–36. Haeri makes no bones about the fact he considered only a few elite individuals capable of pursuing philosophy. He forbade (*haram*) the teaching of philosophy to the "majority of people" because, he thought, they do not possess the vision and the discerning required for the intricate issues involved in philosophy. See *Kavoshha-ye 'Aql-e Nazari*, 34.

Philosophy and Being

In spite of the central role that Haeri considered for philosophy in human affairs and the pivotal place of human existence for philosophy, he believed that the essential question of Being lies at the core of philosophical inquiry. The philosophical tradition, especially metaphysics and ontology, he maintained, was primarily concerned with Being and this Being has constituted the predicate in philosophical propositions such as "God exists," "reason exists," "self exists" and "matter exists."[11] Moreover, following Mulla Sadra, Haeri believed that Being and God are not different, and that modern European philosophers are at fault for denying the Being and God as predicates in logical judgments. Haeri criticized Immanuel Kant in particular for arguing that Being is not a real predicate and simply a copula that merely connects the subject and the predicate in a proposition.[12]

Based on these premises, Haeri argued that primacy and authenticity should be given to the Being. Invoking Ibn Sina and more importantly Mulla Sadra, Haeri argued that since the knowledge of all essences is dependent upon Being and the knowledge of Being depends upon itself, the realization of everything is possible only through Being, and the realization of Being is not possible except through itself. Since Being does not need anything else to be realized, it is in the position of primacy and authenticity. Just as an object is white because of its whiteness and whiteness is not white because of anything else, in the same way the Being is self-realizing and "in its authenticity [*isalat*] and existence is self-made and needs no agent for its realization and has not acquired

11. *Kavoshha-ye 'Aql-e Nazari*, 28.

12. *Kavoshha-ye 'Aql-e Nazari*, 107–15. In his argument against Being as a real predicate and thereby negation of the primacy of Existence, Kant wrote: "'*Being*' is obviously not a real predicate; that is it is not a concept of something which could be added to the concept of a thing. It is merely the positing of a thing, or of certain determinations, as existing in themselves. Logically, it is merely the copula of a judgment. The proposition, 'God is omnipotent,' contains two concepts, each of which has its object—God and omnipotence. The small word 'is' adds no new predicate, but only serves to posit the predicate *in its relation* to the subject. If, now, we take the subject (God) with all its predicates (among which is omnipotence), and say 'God is' or 'There is a God,' we attach no new predicate to the concept of God, but only posit the subject in itself with all its predicates, and indeed posit it as being an object that stands in relation to my concept. The content of both must be one and the same; nothing can have been added to the concept, which expresses merely what is possible, by my thinking its object (through the expression 'it is') as given absolutely." Immanuel Kant, *Critique of Pure Reason*, trans. Norman Kemp Smith (New York: St. Martin's Press, 1965) 506–507. In this very important passage, Kant criticizes the traditional ontological assumption that the predicate in a logical proposition constitutes the proof of Being. As a result, Kant argues, the notion of predication cannot be attributed to the Most Perfect Being. Haeri took issue with these arguments and tried to counter them. Haeri's most significant counterargument claimed that Kant attempted to reduce all existential propositions to synthetic ones and as a result ignored the analytic type of judgments in regard to the questions of Being and reduced the Being to mere copula. This approach, Haeri insisted, is very much opposed to the Islamic philosophical tradition that regards Existential propositions to belong to the analytic type, therefore holding the Being as predicate. See *Kavoshha-ye 'Aql-e Nazari*, 107–15. There is little doubt that Haeri's knowledge of Islamic thought was more comprehensive than his knowledge of Kant as well as that of Hume.

this authenticity from elsewhere."[13] The corollary of this argument is, obviously, the primacy of Existence over Essence, which Haeri considered the truth of philosophical Existentialism.[14] The upshot of this argument was that only the Being, and in fact the Supreme Being, is a self-subsistence reality and all other beings derive their existence and status from it.[15]

In this scheme one can easily ascertain the secondary and derivative position that human beings are allotted. In this regard Haeri chastised the Western Existentialist philosophers, naming Jean-Paul Sartre in particular, because while they profess the precedence of Existence in relation to essence, they ultimately give authenticity (*isalat*) to essence and the related notions of the human mind and subjectivity over Existence.[16]

These formulations constituted Haeri's early views on theontology according to which, while the primacy belongs to the Being (God), human subjectivity is not totally denied (as I tried to demonstrate above). However, Haeri's more mature metaphysical and theontological views were framed in a grander scheme to which he devoted much time and energy.

Mapping the Universe: The Pyramid of Existence

The discussion of the notion of the "Pyramid of Existence" constituted a part of Haeri's doctoral dissertation that he completed at the University of Toronto in 1979. Haeri analogized the entire system of existence to a pyramid at the apex of which is the Supreme Being, and other beings receive their existence from this Supreme Being. The point of analogy between the vast expanse of Existence and the pyramid, Haeri argued, is that while the apex of the pyramid is indivisible and, from the point of the lower echelons, invisible, it also encompasses all other points of the pyramid. In a similar manner, he further argued that the Concealed Divinity is the only One fully in possession of self-subsistence and independence and yet other beings receive their existence and subsistence from that Being.[17] Haeri posited that God is pure existence and self-subsistence (*wujud bil dhat*) at the apex of the pyramid and that beings are self-subsistent and self-supporting in no other point of the pyramid. However, other points in the pyramid, that is other beings

13. *Kavoshha-ye 'Aql-e Nazari*, 77.
14. For a lucid discussion of the pair notions of existence and essence in Islamic philosophy and in the philosophy of Mulla Sadra—as well as Mulla Sadra's philosophy in general—see Fazlur Rahman, *The Philosophy of Mulla Sadra* (Albany: State University of New York, 1975). For Mulla Sadra's philosophy see also James Morris, *The Wisdom of the Throne: An Introduction to the Philosophy of Mulla Sadra* (Princeton: Princeton University Press, 1981); and Hossein Nasr, *Islamic Life and Thought* (London: George Allen and Unwin, 1981).
15. *Kavoshha-ye 'Aql-e Nazari*, 99.
16. *Kavoshha-ye 'Aql-e Nazari*, 90–91.
17. *Heram-e Hasti: Tahlili az Mabadi-e Hasti Shenasi-e Taṭbiqi* (Pyramid of Existence: An Analysis of the Foundations of Comparative Ontology). Tehran: Mu'assesehe Muṭale'at va Tahqiq-e Farhangi, 1983, 75.

except the Supreme Being, do receive the substance that Haeri called "existence" and that makes their being possible as a blessing issuing from the apex.[18]

Haeri borrowed a set of conceptual terms from Mulla Sadra to articulate the same idea, which illuminates the core of his theontological and cosmological views. According to Mulla Sadra's thesis, in Haeri's rendition, the Supreme or Necessary Being is pure existence and humans, animals and other celestial and terrestrial beings all share the same substance of existence, but to varying degrees that correspond to the positions that they occupy on the pyramid. As we reach the bottom of the pyramid, we encounter the matter that contains the least degree of that substance: namely, existence. Haeri called this phenomenon, after Mulla Sadra, the Unicity of Being in Differentiation (*wahdat wujud tashkiki*), or just the principle of *tashkik*, which can be translated as "existential variance."[19] He elaborately discussed these theontological issues in *Heram-e Hasti* (*Pyramid of Existence*). In that book, Haeri wrote:

> I want to explain the category of [existential] differentiation [*tashkik*] and propose the notion of Unicity of Being in Differentiation for the reality of existence: an existence which the universe, God, humans and all beings, have in common. This means that all [beings] are the [different] stages [*maratib*] and determinations of this Undivided Being. All beings are the manifestations and stations [*marahil*] of this Undivided Being; God in this Existence, the universe, and humans in the universe all share the sameness of One Being. There is nothing more than one determined Undivided Being and we call that the Unicity of Being. [...] Based on the principle of Differentiation, this Being, while a determined real Unicity, contains the very plurality of stages and [different] manifestations. This type of plurality which is predominant in the reality of Being harbors no contradiction toward the Unicity of Being.[20]

It seems that what Haeri is suggesting in this highly abstract passage is that all beings in the universe are but from One source, and yet there are differences in the intensity of the substance of existence that these beings possess, which counts for plurality of beings, and yet there is no contradiction in all of this. He provided the example of a weak and a strong light. What is common between, as well as what differentiates, strong and weak lights, is the light itself. The reality of the light is the same, and what differs is the weakness and strength of the light.[21] This brings Haeri to the closely related notion of "unity in difference and difference in unity," which he also adopted from Mulla Sadra. In accordance with

18. *Heram-e Hasti*, 195. While in Persian or Arabic there cannot be any distinction between "Existence" and "existence," Haeri uses the term *wujud* in slightly different senses. By rendering *wujud* as "Existence," I intend to convey his understanding of the entire system of Being. In other contexts, Haeri uses *wujud* slightly differently, that is as the "substance" that constitutes the being of all beings no matter at what level of hierarchy.
19. In his book on Mulla Sadra's philosophy, Fazlur Rahman has translated *tashikik* as "ambiguity." However, in order to avoid any misunderstanding about the connotations that ambiguity may carry, Haeri has insisted that *tashkik* should be understood as differentiation and variance with regard to existence. For this reason I have translated *tashkik* in this context as differentiation or variance.
20. *Heram-e Hasti*, 134–35.
21. *Heram-e Hasti*, 134.

the tenor of this concept, Haeri maintained that in ordinary logic wherever we think of plurality, there is no unity, but in the logic of *tashkik*, what is the basis of differentiation is also the basis of unity.[22] This is the same as Mulla Sadra's solution to the same problem, in which the notion of "unity in multiplicity and multiplicity in unity" constitutes a major achievement of Mulla Sadra, in contrast to the non-philosophical and unsophisticated approach of Muhi al-Din Ibn 'Arabi (1165–1240) to the idea of unicity of being.[23]

From this grand scheme, Haeri deduced the status of humans in terms of contingence, in contrast to the necessity of Being. He argued that possibility or contingence (*imkan*), as opposed to the necessity of Being, characterizes the imperfection and weakness of humans' existence. Human existence is marred by existential weakness, essential dependence and lack of self-sufficiency and self-subsistence.[24] In this context, Haeri used another Sadraian concept to describe the relation of all contingent beings, including that of humans, to the Being—an idea that may be translated as "[existential] poverty" (*faqr*) of all contingent beings. As such, in the last pages of the *Pyramid of Existence*, Haeri wrote:

> The entire truth of the phenomenal world is nothing, save a "from" [*az*]. However, since this "from" has an existence, its [existence] is nothing but a shadowy and dependent being. It is not authentic. [...] The truth of the entire phenomenal world is that whatever is [except the Being itself], is nothing but dependence. [...] Therefore when you say "I," this "I" is false. [...] There is no "I" or "you," because you cannot know your own essence independently. You may achieve this [i.e., self-knowledge] if you assume your absolute dependence on the Origin. In that case you do not exist anymore; whatever that exists is Him or is "from" Him. The attribution of being can only be applied to the Origin and this is the [meaning of the] "existential poverty" of contingent entities as opposed to the Substantial Necessity [of the Being].[25]

In a related vein, Haeri argued that human status is that of (epi)phenomenon in relation to the Being. Accordingly, he argued, in Islamic philosophy one cannot speak of human subjectivity—one cannot say "I." When one says "I did this or that," or "I went," this is a falsity, because we are not in possession of an independent personality. We might entertain the idea of having an independent personality, but we are an absolute (epi)phenomenon, "a very weak manifestation of an infinite source of being."[26] In sum, Haeri's theontological formulations can be thought of in terms of a pyramid at the vertex of which is the Supreme Being, and other beings receive their existence from this Supreme Being. As we descend from the peak to the base of this pyramid, the intensity of the substance that he calls "existence" is reduced at the lower levels and rungs, but the substance itself is not totally lost. Thus humans and animals and other celestial and

22. *Heram-e Hasti*, 134.
23. *Heram-e Hasti*, 101.
24. *Kavoshha-ye 'Aql-e 'Amali: Falsafeh-ye Akhlaq* (Investigations of Practical Reason: Philosophy of Ethics). (Tehran, Mu'asseseh ye Mutale'at va Tahqiqat-e Farhangi, 1982), 92.
25. *Heram-e Hasti*, 299–302.
26. *Metafizik: Majmu'eh-ye Maqalat-e Falsafi-Manteqi* (Metaphysics: A Collection of Philosophical and Logical Essays). (Tehran: Nehzat-e Zanan-e Musalman, 1982), 36.

terrestrial beings all share the same substance of existence, but to varying degrees and as we reach the bottom of the pyramid we encounter matter that contains the least degree of that substance. As we saw, in this scheme, the Being or Existence is primordial and human status is secondary, derivative, and epiphenomenal with significant implications for negation of human subjectivity. Yet, in this formulation, it is wrong to assume that human subjectivity is totally denied, and in a dialectical fashion human status is, as we will see below, to a significant degree redeemed.

Dialectics of Redeeming Human Subjectivity

It is a peculiar characteristic of the annihilation of the potential subject in Being that the subject may in the end acquire at least some of the attributes of the Being. In elaborating the notion of "existential poverty," Haeri explained that "poverty" in this context is different from our ordinary understanding of the notion. In the everyday usage, the term "poverty" (*faqr*) means that as a human one may lack a certain "perfection" (*kamal*). But in the existential relation of humans to God, depicted in terms of "poverty," the meaning of poverty is different. Here "poverty" denotes, "the derivative [i.e., the human] is identical to the Origin." The need and dependence associated with this notion of poverty mean existential proximity (*nazdiki wujudi*) to and ontological connection (*irtibat ontolozhic*) with the Origin. Here poverty and dependence are desirable and not despicable.[27]

The idea that as humans we are a "possibility" or a contingency does not mean that we do not have any existence and are absolute "nothingness" (*ma'dum mutlaq*). In fact, in an important passage Haeri thought of annihilation in terms of "finding of the self," or in other words, the very foundation of human subjectivity. Using the trope of a genitive case (*idafah*), in which belonging and dependence are the essential properties of what is appended to the source and reflecting human relation to the Being, Haeri wrote:

> According to Plotinus, if no genitive relation is postulated between us and that Transcendent Existence, then we would be absolute nothingness. That means that we do not exist even in imagination. [...] The truth of the "appendage" [*mudaf*] is annihilation in the "genitive source" [*mudafun 'alayh*]. [...] In my interpretation, the significance of annihilation lies in the *finding of the self*, [*khvishtan yabi*]; and this means that to anyone who realizes his own truth, this truth is nothing but significance.[28]

In this type of argument we can easily recognize the versatility inherent in the notion of *tashkik* and its utility in postulating a type of mediated subjectivity for humans while reserving the real subjectivity for the Being and God.[29] The notion of multiplicity permitted a differentiation between the Supreme Being and all other celestial and terrestrial entities. On the other hand, the idea of unity makes possible the elevation of the human to the proximity of the Divine. Emphasizing the notion of unity at the

27. *Heram-e Hasti*, 299–300.
28. *Heram-e Hasti*, 54. Emphasis in original.
29. For the notion of "mediated subjectivity," see the Introduction in this volume.

expense of differentiation and plurality, Haeri broached the assumption of human unity with the Divine:

> The meaning of unicity [*tawhid*] that is in the Qur'an and in Islam, is that we achieve this unicity and the truth of oneness [...] In fact there is no differentiation in Existence, there is no plurality in the universe. Plurality is an accidental [*'aradi*] affair [...] All the plurality we see in the universe is imaginary [...] [In our attempt to] explore the Islamic ontology of unicity, from a philosophical [as opposed to mystical or *Irfani*] point of view, we would solve all of our problems if we understood unicity in this sense. This implies that even human societies are based on this ontology of uncity [*ontolozhi tawhidi*]. The very meaning of the human society is rooted in the unicity of existence, viz., we are unified [*yeganeh*] with our God and not separate [from Him].[30]

This form of mediated subjectivity was even applicable to the notion of necessity and contingence. While the Transcendent is the real Necessary Being, we mortals also possess necessity, but it is mediated through that of the Divine. "The fact the you are attending the class," Haeri once told his students, "is because you thought you need to be here. This thought has created your free decision to be here and [therefore] you are a necessary [and not contingent] being here, like the Transcendent Truth [*Haq Ta'la*]. However, your necessity is through-the-Other [i.e., mediated subjectivity] and the only Essentially Necessary Being [*Wajib-ul Wujub bil-Dhat*] is Him. But, in regard to the principle of necessity, your being is equal to that of Transcendent Creator [*Bari Ta'ala*] in [being] necessary."[31]

30. *Metafizik*, 37–38.

31. *Aql-e 'Amali*, 195. In addition to the theontological system presented here, Haeri developed a parallel scheme in his book, written in English, *The Principles of Epistemology in Islamic Philosophy: Knowledge by Presence* (New York: State University of New York Press, 1992). In this book, which may be thought of as an application of epistemological approach to his theontological views, Haeri delineated the dialectical relation between human knowledge, and therefore subjectivity, and what he called "presence," an epistemological code for the "order" of Being. In the light of the analysis presented here, the following passage, which is worth quoting at length, may shed light on what otherwise might seem an esoteric book by Haeri: "This inquiry will begin with an examination of knowledge by presence. On the basis of this knowledge, we will also try to establish the truth of the performative self-identity [subject of knowledge] in the human being. Then we will turn to its most important implication, which is the philosophical solution, the paradox of mystical unity of the self with the One, and the One with the self. The analysis of the nature of knowledge by presence will then be extended: first, to specify the connotation of the concept of knowledge by presence as identical with the concept of unqualified meaning of the being of the self-identity of human nature; and second, to bring to light its radical implication, which is the rational explanation of mystical experience. Hence, mystical unity taken as another form of knowledge by presence is expressed through the notion of the annihilation (*fana*), and the annihilation of annihilation (*fana al-fana*), which results in unity with the absolute truth of Being. However, heuristic exigencies, as well as the attempt to relate mysticism to philosophy, have led this study to view the mystical annihilation and absorption as forms of knowledge by presence, yet depicted as two separate notions, interrelated in a unitary simplex, where God and the self [subject] are existentially united. While this unitary consciousness signifies an absolute oneness in truth, intellectual reflection on it yields a material equivalence between God

One of the spin-offs of this type of cosmology in Haeri's discourse was a parallel type of relationship between the universal and the individual, with very significant ramifications, as we will see later, for the relations between the individual in society and society itself as the universal. In the same book in which he most elaborately laid out his theontological views, *Pyramid of Existence*, Haeri also devoted a considerable amount of attention to questions of the universal and the individual. In his discussion of the notion of "physical universal" (*kulli tabi'i*) in the tradition of Islamic philosophy, Haeri argued that the same dialectical relation that obtains between differentiation and unity in the notion of *tashkik* applies to the relation between the individual and the universal. In other words, while the universal and the individual are two different entities, they share the same basic substance. The beneficiary in this formulation is the

---

and the self. In that case it can be inferred that the formal equation of mysticism is: 'God-in-self = self-in-God'" (3). In this epistemological equivalent to his theontological inquiries, Haeri articulated the secondary and epiphenomenal status of humans in the notion of "knowledge by presence," whereby human qua "knowledge" is fused in the Being qua "presence": "In this prime example of presence-knowledge [i.e., the case of immediate self-knowledge that is not based on representation], the meaning of knowledge becomes absolutely equivalent with the very "being" of the self, such that within the territory of 'I-ness,' to know is to exist and to exist is to know. This is the meaning of self-objectivity of knowledge by presence" (81). This view is the opposite of what Suhrawadi, according to Haeri's interpretation, seems to have posited with regard to human subjectivity: "Basing himself on the grounds that whatever one knows of oneself by virtue of presence must count as the sole reality of one's self, he [Suhrawardi] believes that it follows that the existence of the performative 'I-ness' [i.e., the acting subject] is absolutely pure, and that the purity of the 'I-ness' in existence is nothing but its 'independence' from being in another. Since in the scope of this knowledge nothing can be found in an act other than the 'I-ness' of the self, the objective reality of the self must be in conformity with a mode of being that does not exist in another. This kind of existential independence counts for substantiality [i.e., the self-sufficiency of the human subject]" (91). This type of pure human subjectivity, Haeri suggested, is opposed to the notion of knowledge by presence, where the "dualism between the subject and the object, or 'I-ness' and 'It-ness' " is eliminated. However, just like his theontological views, Haeri postulated redemptive escape for the subject. In a chapter on "Mystical Unity" in *The Principle of Epistemology in Islamic Philosophy*, he wrote: "we can legitimately say that the self, as a substitute instance of emanation, enjoys knowledge of God by the presence of absorption. We can legitimately say that the self is known by God through knowledge by presence of illumination. Because of the identity of these two senses of presence in reality [emanation and absorption], they are also identical in their proportionate degrees of presence. That is to say, to the same degree that God has presence by illumination in the reality of the self, the self also, to the same degree, enjoys its presence in God in the sense of absorption. Thus, in that particular stage of being, God and the self are identical" (146). The precise mechanism that Haeri proposed for this redemption was the notion of the "annihilation of annihilation" (*fana al-fana*): "The ultimate degree of annihilation is a 'double' annihilation which in Sufi language is called '*fana al-fana*' meaning 'annihilation of annihilation.' In correspondence with the logical double negation, double annihilation implies the completely positive state of unitary consciousness, called in Sufi terminology *baqa'*, meaning the unity of continuity with the One. Just as double negation logically implies affirmation, so also double annihilation arrives existentially at the complete unity with the reality of the Principle. This is what the self is in itself, which is its ever-presence in God and God's ever-presence in the self. This is the meaning of unitary consciousness" (158).

individual, since here all the "perfection" that belongs to the universal is also given to the individual. Based on these observations, Haeri concluded that a) the individual in society has sanctity and is not a mere appendage or instrument, and b) all individuals, by virtue of being human, and nothing else, have equal and universal rights that we recognize as human rights.[32]

All in all, we might think of human status in Haeri's cosmology as basically secondary, derived and epiphenomenal, which would be very much in conformity with the principles of mediated subjectivity. Yet, we must keep in mind that here human subjectivity is not denied, and despite its secondary status, it is given a space that Haeri develops at other levels of his discourse and in spheres outside his theontology.

Philosophy of Ethics

Haeri's discourse on the philosophy of ethics and what he called "normative ethics," while closely related to his theontological reflections, gave considerably more free rein to human subjectivity that, as we will see shortly, had significant implications in the socio-political sphere. In this endeavor, Haeri stayed away from the theomorphic approach to human subjectivity and utilized his training in Anglo-American analytical philosophy to adopt what may be called an epistemological approach. In other words, instead of addressing human subjectivity in terms of approximation to God and appropriation of his attributes, Haeri broached human subjectivity in terms of the knowing subject and in the context of the process of achieving knowledge. In this regard, Haeri consistently considered knowledge, that is human knowledge, to be made of the same material as, and qualified to belong to, the order of Being (Divine realm). He therefore deemed a lofty status for knowledge.[33] In a related vein, as we saw before, Haeri believed that philosophy and philosophical inquiry, undergirding human intellectual and moral action, constituted the authentic essence of being human. In order to give substance to these views, Haeri, in his discussions of ethical philosophy, posited a dual scheme of subjectivity, one belonging to the Divine and the other belonging to humans.

Dual Structure of Subjectivity

Haeri argued that the creative capacity of human mind is closely associated with free will, and that by virtue of this free will, humans are capable of producing their own norms and values while free from any external interference, even from God. In fact, based on these premises, Haeri constructed a dual structure of sovereignty and subjectivity, one for God and one for humans. In his book on practical reason, entitled *Investigations of Practical Reason* (*Kavoshha-ye 'Aql-e 'Amali*), Haeri argued that as God is the creator of nature and the universe, in the realm of norms and values, humans are sovereign:

32. *Herum-e Hasti*, 215–20.

33. On the high status (belonging to the order of Being) that Haeri attributed to knowledge, see, for example, *Koavoshha-ye 'Aql-e Nazari*, 120–48.

> [On] the meaning of God's successor[:] In virtue of his [free] will and [sense of] responsibility, man is the lord and creator of deeds and actions that take place in the realm of norms and values. And like the Creator of Existence who created the entire universe and the "azure dome" of Being from nothingness, man also is the maker and creator of his various deeds and actions and [responsible for] the transformations of his own world. If we accept the principle of man's sovereignty over his internal and external worlds, [then] the deeds and consequences of his free will can be considered as equally real as the objective realities of the natural world and the universe that have come into being as a result of God's will.[34]

In this passage, we can see that in Haeri's view, as God is the creator of nature and the material universe, in a similar fashion humans enjoy sovereignty and subjectivity in the realm of ethical norms and values. The term that he often used to convey this approach to the construction of norms and values was the Perso-Arabic term *maqdurat.* This term may be translated as the objects over which one has power. Since Haeri believed that norms and practical/moral values are created by humans, he often referred to them as *maqdurat.* He argued that as humans possess, at a very micro-level, a will similar to that of the God of creation, their will is manifested in their own creation of *maqdurat* as principally moral/practical norms and values. As humans, Haeri believed, we are also "the lord of the 'created world' of our actions. [...] That means that we possess a volition similar to that of God and if we want we can give order to our *maqdurat* or make them disorderly. The difference is that our will is not applicable to the entire universe and is confined to our *maqdurat* within the parameter of our power."[35]

On Haeri's part, this view was in turn grounded in his approach to the fields of, on the one hand, pure or speculative reason, and on the other hand, practical reason. While he posited that with regard to pure reason human subjectivity is limited, in the sphere of practical reason we are very much sovereign. He wrote:

> Because in principle the realities of the world are of two kinds, this type of duality has permeated the human mode of thought also, dividing the acquiring of knowledge into two categories. [On the one hand], speculative philosophy [qua knowledge] is applied to those objective realities that are beyond [the domain of] our will and [sphere of] freedom. [...] Practical philosophy applies to other realities in life that are under our control. To be sure, al-Farabi and Ibn Sina as well as other Islamic thinkers [...] defined the [notion] of practical philosophy in such a way that the [domain of practical philosophy and] ethics applies to *maqdurat*, while our knowledge in speculative philosophy is confined to non-*maqdurat* [i.e., material objects in the universe]. However, we should add here [...] that there is no difference between practical philosophy and speculative philosophy with regard to acquiring knowledge and thinking about the realities of existence. Both types of philosophy explore the objective realities and real entities [...] the only difference is that some of these realities are under the power and control [that is, they are in the domain of practical philosophy] of humans and

34. *Kavoshha-ye 'Aql-e 'Amali*, 54.
35. *Kavoshha-ye 'Aql-e 'Amali*, 85. The more humans have control and subjectivity over the sphere of norms and values that they have created, Haeri believed, the more they can act with decisiveness and determination. This is desirable from the viewpoint of practical ethics because indecisiveness and "moderation" are not of value here (*Kavoshha-ye 'Aql-e 'Amali*, 11).

some of them are without their control. [...] Otherwise, there is no substantial difference in our mode of acquiring knowledge and manner of thought.[36]

This attempt to bring together the two domains of practical and speculative philosophy, as we will see below, had its roots in Haeri's attempt to resolve one of the most profound gaps that has been the crucial division in the history of modernity in the West, namely the schism between speculative reason and practical reason, between science and moral/practical spheres or between "is" and "ought."

Is and Ought: Haeri on Hume and Kant

At many points in his discourse, but especially in his book *Kavoshha-ye 'Aql-e 'Amali* (Investigations of Practical Reason), Haeri referred to, and attempted to overcome, the chasm that David Hume (1711–1776) applied to the spheres of "is" and "ought" or facts and norms.[37] Taking Hume to task for hemming in the issues, Haeri broached the idea of the relationship between moral propositions and factual judgments in the broader context of human mental capacity and modes of acquiring knowledge.

Haeri's stratagem in addressing these issues was to appeal to the creativity of human mind in forging moral values and norms and its manifestation in free will, a phenomenon that, in Haeri's view, is also closely related to our capacity to acquire knowledge about nature. Haeri argued that the same mental capacity by humans that makes possible the acquiring of knowledge is also at work in the creation of practical norms and values. As a result, he insisted that the separation of the *is* and *ought* and the gulf that some Western positivistic approaches since Hume have presumed between, on the one hand, speculative reason that has to do with the acquiring of knowledge about nature, and on the other hand, practical reason that deals with moral/practical issues, was unwarranted. He wrote:

---

36. *Kavoshha-ye 'Aql-e 'Amali*, 85–86.

37. In a well-known passage on the impossibility of deriving moral injunctions and "oughts" from descriptive statements, Hume wrote, "In every system of morality, which I have hitherto met with, I have always remark'd, that the author proceeds for some time in the ordinary way of reasoning, and establishes the being of a God, or makes observations concerning human affairs; when all of a sudden I am surpriz'd to find, that instead of the usual copulations of propositions, *is* and *is not*, I meet with no proposition that is not connected with an *ought*, or an *ought not*. This change is imperceptible; but is, however, of the last consequence. For as this *ought*, or *ought not*, expresses some new relation or affirmation, 'tis necessary that it shou'd be observ'd and explain'd; and at the same time that a reason shou'd be given, for what seems altogether inconceivable, how this new relation can be a deduction from others, which are entirely different from it." David Hume, *A Treatise of Human Nature*, David Fate Norton and Mary J. Norton, eds. (Oxford: Oxford University Press, 2000), 302. Haeri transcribed this passage in *Discoveries of Practical Reason* in English and provided a translation for it that became the basis of his discussion of Hume. See Haeri, *Kavoshha-ye 'Agl-e 'Amali*, 14–16. For contemporary Western analysis of Hume's position on these issues see, for example, Lewis White Beck, *Essays on Kant and Hume* (New Haven: Yale University Press, 1978) and David Fate Norton, ed., *The Cambridge Companion to Hume* (New York: Cambridge University Press, 1993). On one of the latest important attempts to fill the gap between facts and norms from a critical theory perspective, see Jürgen Habermas, *Between Facts and Norms: Contributions to a Discourse Theory of Law and Democracy* (Cambridge, MA: MIT Press, 1996).

> The meaning of practical philosophy is that one gains knowledge over one's acts; one is the "efficient cause" [*'illat fa'ili*] over one's actions, because one is created to possess knowledge and [have] freedom over one's actions. [...] The more you have knowledge over things and the more you comprehend your relations to the [world] of being and the source of being through speculative philosophy, the better and more wisely you can act and reconstruct the world around you. As a result, practical philosophy is in reality a branch of speculative philosophy, except that it is the type of knowledge that its object is the acts and the *maqdurat* of the subject of knowing.[38]

Furthermore, Haeri argued, the closely related faculties of free will and the capacity to know lie at the core of being human, and the two are inseparable.[39] As a result, Haeri paid much attention to role of the free will in human affairs. It is thanks to free will that humans can bring about changes in the world of facts and transform the realm of "is." Because "humans possess freedom," Haeri wrote, "and have free volition, they can change the being of things or create them from nothingness. Man has the complete freedom to create things or make changes in their being."[40] Based on these premises, Haeri concluded that "the gist of our argument and the source of the troubles in [pitting] the facts against [moral] injunctions, [lies in ignoring the] question of [free] will. In our opinion, all the intellectual disorder and incongruous discourses that have created a gap between facts and [moral] imperatives [*bayasti-ha*] [...] stems from the reality that the questions of necessity [*jabr*] and free will have not been properly analyzed and discerned."[41] In fact, Haeri believed that there is an undisrupted "interlink" that connects metaphysics, which is concerned with issues of the Being, to the realm of science, which deals with facts of nature and continues to the practical/moral sphere. In other words, according to Haeri, in Islamic philosophy there is a concatenation that begins with the Being and leads to the "is," and from there connects to "what ought to be," and there are no breaks in the links in this chain. In this respect, he wrote: "[it is] due to the fact that both 'is' and 'ought' derive from the core of Absolute Being that philosophy is divided into speculative and practical philosophy or rationality. However, both branches of philosophy revolve around the realities of Being, and there are no differences between these two branches of philosophy. The baffling gap that Hume promulgates between 'is' and 'ought' is entirely invalid and unacceptable in Islamic philosophy."[42]

Even though Haeri believed that these questions were elaborately discussed and answered in Islamic philosophy, he sought further answers to these questions in Kant's analytical philosophy.[43] He thought that we could also see the connection between the

38. *Kavoshha-ye 'Aql-e 'Amali*, 9.
39. *Kavoshha-ye 'Aql-e 'Amali*, 51.
40. *Kavoshha-ye 'Aql-e 'Amali*, 168.
41. *Kavoshha-ye 'Aql-e 'Amali*, 170.
42. *Kavoshha-ye 'Aql-e 'Amali*, 94. See also 65.
43. A significant part of Kant's system was in response to Hume's type of skepticism about human intellectual capacity. And it is in Kant's discussion of predications and specially the notion of "synthetic a priori" that Haeri finds the space to posit human subjectivity qua the capacity to know and act. Kant's discussions of predications and synthetic a priori in the analytic part of his philosophy were in response these types of questions. Kant demonstrated that we can achieve new knowledge with certainty and he called this "synthetic a priori." In

evaluative judgments and the realm of being, or the 'is' in the Kantian system. Haeri thought of freedom in the Kantian sense as a category belonging to the realm of being, with deep metaphysical roots. He also thought that freedom is the most important link that connects the *is* and the *ought*. Using his own philosophical language that considered the *is* as a category belonging to the realm of being, Haeri wrote:

> In our opinion Kant wishes to retort to Hume that we can deduce the evaluative propositions such as "ought" and "ought not," from our [categories] of "being" [i.e., the "is"]. One of these [categories] of being is freedom, that is free will [*ikhtyar*], and [by that we] mean the noumenon of freedom. This is the being-in-itself [*wujud fi dhatihi*] of freedom, not the phenomenon of freedom. [...] These are the [categories] of being that can deliver to us the evaluative propositions, since if we do not have freedom, these moral propositions have no meaning at all.[44]

In this passage, we can recognize the pivotal role that the notion of human free will and freedom in general play at this level of analysis in Haeri's discourse. As such, Haeri considered the free human volition as the foundation of ethical norms. Without free human will, the notion of human responsibility and commitment would be impossible. It is the free volition, Haeri argued, that creates responsibility.[45] In this sense, it is human reason alone that determines what is good and what is evil. The determination of good and evil by reason (*'aql*), itself grounded in free human volition, is therefore even outside the sphere of religion. The determination of good and evil by religion, Haeri thought, runs into logical contradiction, because perception of good and evil has an a priori character in humans and in this sense is outside the sphere of religious ordinances.[46]

The most important conclusion that Haeri derived from his discussion of human free will was the idea that free volition lies at the very the foundation of the edifice of society and politics. As he put it:

> In all the three branches of ethics [*ilm al-akhlaq*], i.e., the cultivation of morals [*tahdhib akhlaq*], household management [*tadbir-i manzil*] and politics [*siyasat mudun*], the foundation is the human will.[47] If there were no volition, you could not regenerate and cultivate your self and your

---

Kant's philosophical system, it is implied that this synthetic a priori knowledge or judgment is possible only because of the creative faculty of the human mind and its capacity to think about novel phenomena. In this regard Haeri elaborately discussed the issues involved in predicates (*mahmulat*) and different forms of judgments in Ibn Sina and Mulla Sadra. He found similarities between Sadra's discussions of predicates and those of Kant, but he acknowledged Kant's innovative understanding of synthetic a priori judgments. However, Haeri finds fault with Kant's rejection of the notion of God in the existential argument for God's existence. For Haeri's discussions on different types of predicates in Kant and Islamic philosophers see, for example, *Kavoshha-ye 'Aql-e 'Amali*, 145. See also Haeri's discussion of Kant in his *Metafisik*, 75–100. On Hume and Kant and the notion of synthetic a priori in relation to human mental creativity, see, for example, James B. Wilber and Harold J. Allen, *The Worlds of Hume and Kant* (Buffalo: Prometheus Books, 1982) 105–06.

44. *Metafizik*, 91.
45. *Kavoshha-ye 'Aql-e 'Amali*, 50–51.
46. *Kavoshha-ye 'Aql-e 'Amali*, 215–20.
47. *Tadbir-i manzil* is a translation of the Greek term for "economy."

> character. If you did not possess volition, you could not organize your household management or economy on the basis of natural or mathematical order. If you did not have a will, you could not harmonize your relations with your city, your household, the country [you live in], or with other countries in the world. [This is so] because the foundation of all these three branches [of ethics] is the will, the autonomy of the will, and in fact the decisiveness of the will.[48]

Haeri's crucial emphasis on the role of free human volition in his views on the philosophy of ethics should be considered the climax in his development of human subjectivity in his discourse. It is in the last stage of his discourse, his thought on the social and political spheres, that this development yields very concrete results in establishing universal human subjectivity and its materialization in rights of citizenship.

Politics

The third dimension of Haeri's discourse is comprised of his political and social visions, which were based on the conceptualization of human subjectivity in the ethical sphere discussed above. Haeri's most explicit and concrete views on politics and social issues were articulated in his last book, *Philosophy and Government*, which was published outside Iran in 1995 due to censorship. However, even before this book, Haeri had laid some of the groundwork for the discussion of political and social issues in his earlier works. One important fundamental idea was the notion of the individual as the carrier of human subjectivity. Throughout his intellectual career, Haeri consistently recognized the significance of the individual in modern society. He criticized the political philosophies of Jean-Jacques Rousseau and Marxism, for example, for giving the individual short shrift and giving the priority to the collective.[49] In his view, Marxism and the communist and even socialist regimes treat the individual as a mere instrument bereft of any rights of membership in society as an individual. "Ontologically," individuals in these societies, Haeri contended, "enjoy no [rights of] membership, but are reduced to instrumentality. As such, they have no human rights. An instrument is an instrument. It [the individual as an instrument] is not an end in itself. […] The rights that belong to society do not apply to it. […] It has no rights; right to life, dignity. […] Its blood and life has no sanctity unless it is an instrument for the benefit of the collectivity."[50] Interestingly, Haeri also criticized Western democracies for reducing individuals to numbers and statistical facts.[51]

This view of the individual and the collectivity was also based on some of Haeri's philosophical reflections. The individual as a microcosm of the universal, Haeri maintained, is a "complete" and autonomous entity and therefore shares all the rights and privileges that belong to the universal. As the individual human being carries all the privileges of the human species, so the individual member in society has all the rights and the autonomy

48. *Kavoshha-ye 'Aql-e 'Amali*, 112.
49. For Haeri's critique of Rousseau's prioritizing the collectivity over the individual, see, for example, *Hekmat va Hukumat* (Philosophy and the State). London: Shadi, 1995, 85–87, 90–95.
50. *Metafizik*, 42–43.
51. *Heram-e Hasti*, 219.

that one can consider for the collectivity.[52] Based on these views, Haeri firmly believed in individual and social freedoms such as the freedom of thought and even of religion in a politically pluralist system for both the Muslims and non-Muslims in an ideal state.[53]

Despite his persistent emphasis on the individual and the sanctity of her or his rights, Haeri thought that since individuals live in societies and among collectivities, there should be some type of equilibrium between the individual and the collectivity. Moreover, even though he firmly believed that responsibility presupposes freedom of the individual, Haeri was critical of the "arbitrariness" and "whimsicality" that might be associated with individuality.[54] For these reasons, he believed that the "truth" of the individual is only realizable in the society and the collectivity, and conversely, the reality of the collectivity can only materialize in that of each member of the society.[55]

In his *Philosophy and Government*, Haeri developed a theoretical framework that, based on a view of the concept of "natural rights," attempted to ground the reconciling of the individual and the collectivity. In fact it is in this scheme that, as we will see below, he developed a notion that is in close parallel to the notion of intersubjectivity, or more accurately universalization of subjectivity, as opposed to mere subjectivity.

Natural Anthropology of Proprietorship

In *Philosophy and Government* Haeri introduced a form of natural anthropology that laid the theoretical foundations of his political views in this last major work before his death. Based on the Islamic endorsement of private property, Haeri accorded the individual sovereignty

52. *Hekmat va Hukumat*, 88–89.

53. *Hekmat va Hukumat*, 117. Despite his theoretical sophistication and professing of universal human rights, Haeri held very negative views of the Baha'is and falsely accused them of committing crimes against Muslims, which vitiates the possibility of human rights for them in Iran. See *Khaterat-e Mehdi Haeri Yazdi* (Memoirs of Mehdi Haeri Yazdi), (Cambridge, MA: Center for Middle Eastern Studies, Harvard University, 2001), 56–57.

54. *Kavoshha-ye 'Aql 'Amali*, 80–81. In this context, it must be noted that Haeri, like many contemporary Islamic theorists in Iran and elsewhere, was very much in favor of suppressing the "inner" nature and the domination of the spirit over the "instincts." The domination of nature, whether it is the outer nature or the inner nature, has characterized the Western journey toward subjectivity, with certain dire consequences that appear in the full-fledged modern period in the West. Here we can see a very close parallel between the Islamic and Western paths to modernity. Thus, in *Hekmat va Hukumat* (15), describing the stage of rationality and humanism, Haeri wrote: "All the acts of volition that issue from the human individuals must naturally be accompanied by rationality and responsibility. For this reason, the deeds and acts of the individual must be under the supervision of his practical reason that has separated him from other beings in creation. […] It is in this respect that the meaning of human freedom, which is a rational and intellectual freedom, is differentiated from the absolute freedom that is synonymous with barbarity. The point is that even the natural animal inclinations and impulses that exist in the natural being and life of humans [ ] must come under the command and rule of his superior nature which is his faculty of thought and intellect. […] Therefore, all the inclinations and impulses in the natural and animal existence of man must be guided by his superior power and conquered by his human faculty and reason."

55. *Kavoshha-ye 'Aql-e 'Amali*, 174.

and subjectivity over his or her property, which as an act of appropriation of nature is indispensable for one's subsistence. He called this "private proprietorship" (*malekiyat-e khususi*).[56] Since we live in a social space, this private proprietorship, Haeri maintained, must be disseminated and universalized. He used a *fiqhi* notion and the corresponding terminology, *malikiyat khusisi musha'* to convey this concept, which can be translated as "universal individual proprietorship," or, for short, universal proprietorship.[57] What he emphasized very often in this book was that the notion of universal proprietorship must not be conflated with a collective notion of proprietorship where the individuality of proprietors is obliterated in the amorphous totality of the collectivity.[58]

In fact what Haeri has in mind here seems to be a notion of human subjectivity based on "natural rights" and its universalization, which is very close to the idea of intersubjectivity, the promise of the modern world, and the foundation of a just polity. Thus Haeri believed that government in the Islamic tradition is based on the idea of proprietorship. This type of proprietorship is not based on positive law or conceptual constructs because it is an ownership grounded in nature. The right to property in general is derived from the exclusive ownership of an object by the human subject that totally dominates the object. The right to property by humans in their environment is one of the natural and original rights that is not subject to legislation or construction. This exclusive relation is called "private proprietorship" (*malekiyat khususi*). Private proprietorship is realized in two ways: one is particular and the other *musha'*. What he meant by *musha'* was the universalization and 'inter-penetration' of private proprietorships and not a collective ownership. This type of *musha'* property is the foundation of a free and open social space in which the multitude of humans have of necessity chosen to live inter-subjectively as in a city or a nation-state. This is the meaning of the Islamic and human principle, "People are dominant over their properties" (Hadith, attributed to the Prophet).[59]

In positing the notion of human subjectivity in these terms, Haeri rightly invested the individual as the primary carrier of subjectivity. In contrast to someone like Ali Shariati, who considered human subjectivity as the privilege of the collectivity, Haeri has repeatedly endowed the individual as the beneficiary of modern subjectivity. In *Philosophy and Government*, Haeri wrote:

56. *Hekmat va Hukumat*, 96–97.

57. *Hekmat va Hukumat*, 97–98.

58. *Hekmat va Hukumat*, 104–105, 109. In this respect, in rather sweeping generalization, Haeri wrote: "The difference between, on the one hand, the society that Rousseau and all other Western sociologists have envisioned, and the society that we are now designing based upon the universal individual proprietorship, on the other hand, will be clear. The society of Rousseau and the sociologists [...] is derived from social contract and establishment of an all-inclusive union coinciding totally to the collectivity. [...] [However, in the society based upon the natural universal individual proprietorship], every single one of the citizens consistently enjoys an autonomous individual identity in all aspects of her or his natural or rational existence and nothing except death can encroach upon her or his individuality and autonomy" (*Hekmat va Hukumat*, 111).

59. *Hekmat va Hukumat*, 108–9.

> In the most glorious Qur'an as well as in the religious rules and requirements and in Islamic ethics, whenever humans in general, or as Muslims, or the faithful, are addressed, whether [they are called upon] as individuals or as collectivities, the real addressee is the individual. Because in the same way that individuals are autonomous due to essence of being human, so are they absolutely independent in their ethical responsibilities and religious duties. Even if such terms as tribe and community (*ummat*) and the like have been used [in the Qur'an and other religious sources], the reference is to the individual in the community not their sum total. A collective unit is nothing but an imaginary and abstract phenomenon, and it is not reasonable to charge an unreal entity [i.e., the collectivity] with responsibility. It is only the real and autonomous individual who must accept the burden of human responsibilities and discharge them.[60]

This type of privilege and responsibility that Haeri attributed to the individual, to be disseminated and universlaized among the citizenry, constituted the foundation of the nation and nationalism in the modern sense for him.[61] In this sense, the construction of national identity and sovereignty that is often based on religion, race or even language, Haeri implicitly rejected. In its stead, the autonomy and independence of the individual subject and its dissemination and universalization constituted for Haeri the foundations of a democratic state.

Once he established the autonomy of the individual as the basis of citizenship in the community, Haeri pointed out the absurdity of the notion of the Guardianship of the Jurist (*velayat-e faqih*), which has been the ideological mainstay of the Islamic Republic. Guardianship, according to Haeri, is only for the minors and invalids, not for autonomous individuals who can claim the rights of citizenship. Elaborating on this theme in the last parts of *Philosophy and Government*, Haeri delivered devastating blows to the notion of the Guardianship of the Jurist and pointed out the central contradiction that this notion and institution has contained ever since its conceptualization and implementation.[62]

Although he avoided any attempt to articulate a blueprint for a democratic polity for good reasons, Haeri did propose the principle of representation or *vekalat* as the principle of organization in a democratic society that should replace the notion and institution of Guardianship of the Jurist, which, of course, entails a full parliamentary system and the provisions for the free election of public officials who are unconditionally accountable to their constituencies.

60. *Hekmat va Hukumat*, 159.
61. *Hekmat va Hukumat*, 119.
62. *Hekmat va Hukumat*, 177, 216–17, 219.

Chapter Six

POSTREVOLUTIONARY ISLAMIC MODERNITY IN IRAN: THE INTERSUBJECTIVE HERMENEUTICS OF MOHAMAD MOJTAHED SHABESTARI[1]

Postrevolutionary Islamic thought in Iran is very much characterized by a hermeneutic approach. However, the hermeneutics involved in this thought are of a different nature from those of its predecessors, that is the Islamic revolutionary discourses of the 1960s and '70s. The contemporary Islamic discourse in Iran is no longer engaged primarily in direct interpretation of Qur'anic verses, and much less so of the Tradition (Hadith). The chief reason for this turn of events, it seems, is the peculiar nature of sociopolitical developments in Iran, particularly the advent of the Islamic Revolution and its complex relations with the forces of the modern world. The Islamic revolutionary discourse of the previous generation undoubtedly advanced serious challenges to the discourse of modernity. Yet, in its own discourse, the Islamic thought of the revolutionary era was itself very much affected by the discourse of modernity, mostly at the philosophical and theoretical levels. Thus, many of the figures who contributed to the Islamic thought of the 1960s and '70s were in one way or another involved in the interpretation of the Qur'an, and to a lesser extent the Tradition, in light of what they considered to be the essential elements of modernity. Ali Shariati (1933–1977), Ayatollah Mahmud Taleqani (1911–1979), Mehdi Bazargan (1907–1995) and Ayatollah Morteza Motahhari (1920–1979) were the most prominent of those who were more or less directly involved in their discourses in reinterpreting Qur'anic verses, in light of what each believed to be the crucial aspects of the modern civilization.[2] In contrast, the post-revolutionary Islamic discourses, and especially those articulated by Mohamad Mojtahed Shabestari and Abdulkarim Sorush, have, by and large, refrained from interpreting the Qur'anic text directly. It would appear that the post-revolutionary conditions have led to different sets of interests and preoccupations among contemporary Islamic thinkers in Iran.

---

1. This chapter is republished with permission from an entry in *Modern Muslim Intellectuals and the Qur'an*, edited by Suha Taji-Farouki (Oxford: Oxford University Press in association with the Institute of Ismaili Studies, 2004)
2. For the ideas of such figures representative of the Islamic revolutionary discourses, see: Hamid Dabashi, *Theology of Discontent: The Ideological Foundation of Islamic Revolution in Iran* (New York: New York University Press, 1993), and Houchang Chehabi, *Iranian Politics and Religious Modernism: The Liberation Movement of Iran under the Shah and Khomeini* (Ithaca: Cornell University Press, 1990).

The main reason for this shift from a Qur'anic exegetic approach to that of a hermeneutics that is not primarily based on the Qur'an lies in the peculiar nature of the Islamic revolutionary paradigm of the previous generation. The logic of the revolutionary discourse of the founders of the Islamic state could not have developed any further because of the particular fashion in which the metaphysics of the Qur'anic text was interpreted to construct a notion of human subjectivity and agency which could not proceed any further, in the context of a deeply religious society. I term "mediated subjectivity" for the paradigm that emerged in the process of reinterpreting Islamic thought in light of modern concepts: it is the result specifically of the interpretation of the Qur'an in light of modern conceptions. Because of the contradictory nature of this paradigm and the conundrums it has engendered, post-revolutionary modernist Islamic thought has largely stayed clear of direct reinterpretation of the Qur'an and the Hadith. Instead it has focused on an alternative hermeneutic approach, which I analyze in the discourse of Mohammad Mojtahed Shabestari in this chapter.

Hermeneutics of Intersubjectivity

Shabestari was a professor of theology at Tehran University until 2006, when he was forced by the government to retire. He was born in Shabestar, a district of Tabriz, in 1936 and received a traditional seminary education at Qom, where he lived from 1950 to 1968.[3] From 1970 until the Revolution of 1979, he was the director of the Islamic Center at Hamburg, West Germany. He is fluent in German and well versed in the German theological and philosophical tradition of scholarship. In Qom, Shabestari served on the editorial board of the *Makatb-e Islam*, a Shii journal, which addressed many of the social and political issues of the 1960s and 1970s. He contributed frequently to this journal, and after the revolution he published his own journal called *Andishe-ye Islami* in Tehran. Shabestari was elected to the first Islamic Consultative Assembly after the revolution from his native Shabestar, but since then he has devoted most of his time to teaching and writing.

Unlike Sorush, who has totally eschewed the theomorphic approach to human subjectivity, Shabestari has upheld the metaphysical assumptions of his predecessors, Islamic revolutionary thinkers of the 1960s and '70s in Iran, more or less intact.[4] He maintains that "the Qur'an recognizes the human as the ruler on earth, its developer, employer of other living forms and creators of civilization and culture."[5] In fact, Shabestari

3. Most of the biographic data for Shabestari is taken from Hasan Yusefi Eshkvari, *Nougarai Dini* (Religious modernity) (Tehran: Qasideh, 1998), 160.
4. Sorush has warned against the desire on the part of humans to achieve the status of divinity as the first step toward corruption and evil. See Abdulkarim Sorush, *Hekmat va Ma'ishat* (Philosophy and life) (Tehran: Serat, 1984), 62. He has also criticized the notion of humans as a "becoming-toward-perfection." Faulting the expectation of moral perfection by citizens, Sorush has blamed the Islamic government for setting unrealistically high moral standards for Iranians. See Abdolkarim Sorush, *Tafarruj-e Sun'* (Promenading creation) (Tehran: Entesharat-e Sorush, 1987), 263.
5. Mohamad Mojtahed Shabestari, *Hermenutik, Ketab va Sunnat: Farayand-e Tafsir-e Vahy* (Hermeneutics, the Book and the Sunna: process of interpreting revelation) (Tehran: Tarh-e Naw, 1996), 56.

has posited a form of "journey toward subjectivity" that characterized the discourses of his revolutionary predecessors Shariati, Khomeini and Motahhari. Referring to existential conditions such as "history," "language," "society" and the "[human] body" as four sources of human unfreedom, Shabestari has called for a migration from a "self" caught in these "prisons" toward divinity:

> Islam is a "total (re)orientation," and when there is a reorientation, there is an emerging from the "self," a migration from the self, a travel from the self to the Other [God]. It is our self from which we must migrate, the self which constitutes the dimensions of human identity; the historical self, social self and the linguistic self. Humans are limited by four "dimensions" in which they normally live: history, society, body and language. The role of Divine revelation is to open another horizon and, without negating the four [existential] dimensions, to make them transparent, traversing the human toward God. To be certain, this transcendence is always accompanied by dust and is never completely transparent.[6]

Shabestari also paraphrases Allamah Tabatabai (1903–81) to the effect that the idea of prophethood finds its meaning in its role of guiding humans in a movement from nature toward the "metaphysical" realm and perfection.[7] Very much reminiscent of his intellectual parents in the two decades prior the Islamic Revolution, Shabestari broaches the notion of human subjectivity in terms of humans as God's vicegerents on earth. He writes:

> Both Islam and Christianity consider man a being whose essence is superior to matter. He is the noblest being and God's successor [*khalifah*] on earth. He is in possession of a God-seeking, free, and independent nature, and carries God's trust. He is responsible for himself and the universe, dominant over nature, the earth and heavens; he is inspired [by knowledge] of good and evil [...] his capacity to know and act are limitless.[8]

However, compared to his revolutionary forerunners, Shabestari places less emphasis on a theomorphic approach to human subjectivity. Just like Sorush, and alarmed by the excessive revolutionary zeal that such approaches inspired during the early phases of the revolutionary period, Shabestari has warned against notions of humans becoming God-like (*khoda- guneh shodan*) in the process of historical development.[9] In addition to the concern about the excessive zeal that can result from a theomorphic approach to human subjectivity, there is also another crucial factor involved. The logic of theomorphic subjectivity, albeit deeply rooted in an Islamic metaphysics, can not further develop in a strongly religious society like Iran, since it inevitably would come into conflict with other, more entrenched, aspects of religiosity and notions of Divine Sovereignty.

6. Mohamad Mojtahed Shabestari, *Iman va Azadi* (Faith and freedom) (Tehran: Tarh-e Naw, 1997), 120.
7. *Iman va Azadi*, 95. For a discussion of Tabatabai's work see, Hamid Dabashi, *Theology of Discontent*, 273–323.
8. *Iman va* Azadi, 114.
9. Mohamad Mojtahed Shabestari, "Fetrat-e Khoda Jouy-e Ensan dar Qur'an" (The God-seeking nature of man in the Qur'an), *Andishe-ye Eslami* 1, no. 9 (1979): 6.

A Hermeneutic Approach to Subjectivity

Because of the impossibility and undesirability of further extending the logic of theomorphic subjectivity, it seems that Shabestari's discourse has taken an epistemological detour. As early as 1979, and possibly before, Shabestari had insisted that our understanding of revelation must be viewed in terms of a hermeneutic exercise, and that this understanding is not a fixed category.[10] It is, however, his very important book *Hermenutik, Ketab va Sunnat: Farayand-e Tafsir-e Vahy* (Hermeneutics, the Book and the Tradition: process of interpreting revelation), published in 1996, that provides the hallmark of Shabestari's mature work. In this book he has posited the act of "interpretation" as a form of agency that can easily be elevated to the position of subject in the hermeneutic process. In this process, the text cannot but be the object to the subjectivity of the hermeneutic interpretation: "Every text is a hidden reality that has to be revealed through interpretation. The meaning of the text is produced in the act of interpretation. In reality, the text comes to speak by means of interpretation, and pours out what it contains inside."[11]

Arguably, it is the silence of the text that leads to the agent and subject of interpretation. This subjectivity of the interpreter vis-à-vis the text is valid even in regard to revelation.[12] As Shabestari has put it:

> Verses [of the Qur'an] do not speak by themselves. It is the interpreter [*mufaser*] who raises a question first, and then seeks its meaning by interpreting different verses. Wherefrom does the interpreter derive his basic assumptions? His question contains basic assumptions that are not derived from the Qur'an itself, but from various [human] sources of knowledge.[13]

Shabestari's hermeneutic approach is also marked by other unmistakable characteristics of modern subjectivity. He has argued that interpretation is possible only as a result of a critical attitude. First, as he has argued, the very belief in the necessity of interpretation for the text is grounded in the critical attitude,[14] associated, one may add, with the modern subject. Second, the interpretive act involves volition and intention on the part of the interpreter, characteristic attributes of the modern subject. As Shabestari has described it, "every interpretation of the text" involves a volitional act that is "derived from interpreters' interests and is implemented in order to achieve a goal."[15]

---

10. Mohamd Mojtahed Shabestari, "Fetrat-e Khoda Jouy-e Ensan dar Qur'an" (The God-seeking nature of man in the Qur'an), *Andishe-ye Eslami* 1, no. 7, (1979): 7–9.
11. Shabestari, *Hermenutik*, 15.
12. It is the interpreter's task to understand the revelation-in-itself. See *Hemenutik*, 128.
13. *Hermenutik*, 36. Shabestari has described his understanding of hermeneutics along a Kantian epistemological approach, in that for him the data of revelation constitutes a noumenal ground as the "revelation-in-itself" (*wahy fi nafsi*), from which the subject may derive phenomenal understandings.
14. *Hermenutik*, 15
15. *Hermenutik*, 22.

Delving into the Mu'tazalites' linguistic theories, Shabestari has argued for the "conventional" [*muvaze'he*; Ar. *Muwadi'ah*] character of signifiers, and the intentionality of the speech acts.[16] The intentionality in the Mu'tazalites' semiotics secures a place for agency, since the subject of speech attaches the signifier to the signified only by intention:

> In the view of the Mu'tazalites, the first condition for [establishing] signification is *muvaze'he* and pre-agreed human conventions to determine the relation between the signifiers and the signified. The second condition is the knowledge of the circumstances, attributes and intentions of the speaker. In his oeuvre, al-Qadi 'Abd al-Jabbar emphasizes the conditions of the speaker, his attributes and his *intentions*.[17]

One of the radical corollaries of Shabestari's hermeneutic approach is the idea that knowing God is impossible without a body of human-based knowledge. Knowing God and his prophets in all ages has not been possible, except through human knowledge and the episteme of the specific period. In every period the intellectual foundations utilized by everyone who engages in understanding and interpreting God or the prophets are derived from the human sources of knowledge available in that period. These bodies of knowledge, whether philosophical or experimental, are the only means that make human conceptualization and acknowledgment of God and the Prophet possible. Society can only survive with these mundane and human sources of knowledge, and religious thought can only receive nourishment from these sources. Moreover, these types of knowledge are subject to change, since human history changes.[18] Even the *ijtihads*, or efforts in Islamic jurisprudence (*fiqh*) to derive religious injunctions from the Qur'an and the Sunna that are based on certain preconceptions and accepted conventions, are all grounded in human knowledge.[19]

This approach has inevitably led Shabestari to make a distinction between what is eternal and fixed and what is subject to change in religion.[20] As I will analyze more elaborately below, Shabestari believes that specific precepts and rules, for the most part, belong to the realm of "change," and only general and broad principles fall into the fixed and eternal category. With regard to the political sphere and the issue of the state and its forms and institutions, for example, Shabestari maintains that there are no given preferences, and all that is emphasized in Islam is the principle of justice.[21] The Qur'an does not consider it within its purview to determine the form of the state and methods of ruling. Rather, the proper task of revelation is to establish the fundamental values involved in governing.[22] In fact, Shabestari has alluded that he concurs with some Islamic theologians and jurisconsults (*fuqaha*) that the general and principal purposes established by the Prophet and the Sharia may be confined

16. *Hermenutik*, 104.
17. *Hermenutik*, 105; emphasis added.
18. *Hermenutik*, 33.
19. *Hermenutik*, 36–37.
20. *Hermenutik*, 40.
21. *Hermenutik*, 56–57.
22. *Hermenutik*, 56–57.

to the following: "The protection of persons [*nufus*], intellects [*'uqul*], lineages [*ansab*], properties, and religion."[23]

Another implication of Shabestari's hermeneutic approach is the need for new bodies of knowledge and human sciences to inform the preconceived notions that Muslim scholars bring to their intellectual activities and understanding of the world. The new branches of knowledge are necessary, because without them it is not feasible to distinguish between the fixed and eternal principles and the rules and precepts that are subject to change.[24] The contemporary jurisconsults need to be conversant with modern human sciences and philosophical approaches in order to be able to renew their preconceptions and areas of interest. Sciences such as modern anthropology, philosophy, sociology, history, economics, political science, and psychology are necessary to inform the foundational assumptions in *fiqh*. Traditional philosophy is not adequate in achieving the task. The fact that the Shi'i seminaries have neglected the modern human sciences is the reason why, "today, we do not have a proper philosophy of law, neither a philosophy of ethics and politics, nor a philosophy of economics."[25]

The subtle confirmation of human subjectivity through a hermeneutic approach and its corollaries constitutes only one dimension of Shabestari's mature discourse. The full extent of his thought is evident in his attempt at reconciling the two disparate terms of the Islamic intellectual paradigm that he has inherited *nolens volens*.

Reconciling Divine and Human Subjectivity

Shabestari believes that human knowledge can never penetrate the depth of Divine Existence; yet, this fact does not mean that human knowledge is to be denied vis-à-vis the Ultimate Truth. In fact, according to Shabestari's somewhat pantheistic argument, the Infinite Truth (God) cannot negate the "finite truth," (humans) even though the former subsumes the latter and is in a position of transcendence. Therefore, one must be cautious "not to set God against the human and make Him deny human existence."[26] Here again, the conceptual framework that Shabestari draws on consists also of a hermeneutic approach that postulates a dialogue between the two sides of a message, the sender and the receiver—in this case the divine message or revelation—crucial in the understanding of the message. According to Shabestari, every message is addressed to a specific receiver and the meaning of the message transpires in the interplay between both the sender and the receiver of the message.[27] Thus, in understanding Divine revelation, both sides of the message, God and human, are equally crucial entities.

In a closely related vein, Shabestari has criticized those who claim that *fiqh* can provide the answer for all problems that the Muslim community encounters in modernity. This

23. *Hermenutik*, 58.
24. *Hermenutik*, 47.
25. *Hermenutik*, 48–49.
26. *Iman va Azadi*, 112.
27. *Hermenutik*, 69.

means the denial of the ability of human knowledge to organize society, and sets religion against reason. Advocates of such views believe that "unless the human is denied, no space would be created for God, and until reason is rejected, there cannot be revelation."[28] Then, in a footnote, Shabestari explains that those who hold such views always consider the relation between God and humankind in terms of opposition and domination from above, while in Islamic mystical tradition (*'irfan*), this relation is nothing but "love."[29] This means that the Islamic revelation should not be pitted against human achievements in civilization and culture. As Shabestari has put it:

> In sum, the Qur'an had declared that it did not come to nullify human culture and civilization. On the contrary, it came to give a new impetus to the existing [human achievements] in the direction of Monotheism [*tawhid*]. In the early centuries of Islam, a group of fanatic and benighted people appeared who, by denying the entire human knowledge and heritage, claimed all principles and procedures in life must only be derived from the exoteric [*zaher*] dimensions of the Book and the Sunna. But the Muslims did not submit to this shortsightedness, and the dignity of human sciences and knowledge was preserved. Had this not happened, there would not be a trace of Islamic culture and civilization today.[30]

There should be no doubt that Shabestari's positing of human subjectivity and steering clear of any friction with the Divine Subjectivity is secured by first surrendering to God's Sovereignty. As such, Shabestari invoked a central doctrinal concept in the Islamic faith, *tawhid*, which has different layers of meaning, but here can be translated as Divine Unity and profession of the oneness of God. He defined this concept in terms of negation of divinity or sovereignty for all beings except God, and sincere submission to the will of God and surrendering to His law, while living with His love.[31] Yet, Shabestari argues, this will not lead to the negation of human subjectivity: "This view of *tawhid* is a type of relation between God and man. When this relation is 'lively' (*zendeh*) and 'limpid' (*zulal*), man experiences God [...] neither God is negated nor man. In a relation based on pure *tawhid*, God's sovereignty is not competing with man, but gives him meaning and solidifies him."[32]

We can easily distinguish the traces of mediated subjectivity at the core of Shabestari's discourse here. However, what distinguishes Shabestari's discourse is that he tries to avoid the contradictory vacillation of simultaneously positing and negating human subjectivity that characterized the thought of his revolutionary predecessors. In fact, the upshot of Shabestari's discussion of the God-human relation here is not the negation of human subjectivity. Shabestari has proposed a dialectical scheme in which humans gain consciousness in a perpetual dialogical interaction between Divine revelation and human reason. The outcome of this dialogical relation between the human and the Divine is

28. *Hermenutik*, 52.
29. *Hermenutik*, 52.
30. *Hermenutik*, 57.
31. *Hermenutik*, 182.
32. *Hermenutik*, 182.

the confirmation of the human. Describing the early human consciousness as "meager capital," Shabestari wrote:

> The story of [our] understanding of God's word is that of a timeless, wrangling [*jedal amiz*], passionate, and two-sided conversation between man and God. With his meager capital, man [first] turns to God's word and receives a ray [of light] from His word. Man makes sense of what he has received from God's word with his own interpretations. These interpretations [...] are given an acceptable form through critique by philosophy and science. This will be man's capital in the next phase, and constitutes his assumptions and predispositions in this phase. A second time man turns to God's word with this [new] capital, and there would be another ray of light [...] This dialogue between man and God, the most incredible story in the universe, continues endlessly. This is how the interpretation of revelation is achieved and there is no end to it. Thus, under these circumstances, as man is never negated vis-à-vis God, he will always remain one party in the dialogue and the addressee of God's revelation.[33]

As mentioned earlier, following other Islamic thinkers before him, including Shariati, Khomeini and Motahhari, Shabestari also employs the notion of a journey from our foundation in matter and nature to a "spiritual" sphere beyond nature, a process that I have designated as a journey toward subjectivity. Among the previous Islamic thinkers, this journey usually does not culminate in human subjectivity and the modern self-consciousness of the individual, since at the end the "traveler" is annihilated in God. The usual metaphor that these previous thinkers advanced was that of "the drop and the ocean," wherein the drop disappears in the ocean at the end of the process of its theomorphic journey.[34] In Shabestari's ontology, however, not only is this outcome avoided, the result of the movement toward the Absolute is the affirmation of the human. Shabestari has expressed this crucial ontological difference with his predecessors clearly:

> The question is that if man qua a fluid, regenerating and self-transcending, but finite, being of intellect, finds himself at the threshold of the Absolute Universal Essence, and experiences himself as a drop of the Ocean, would the Absolute negate the human or affirm [*qawam*] him? If the Absolute negates the finite, then God is against human freedom. If the Absolute affirms the finite, then God makes man into man [i.e., subject]. With deep philosophical reflection it becomes apparent that God does not limit and negate man; He does not confine or eliminate man. God is the Absolute Universal Essence through whom man becomes man.[35]

In fact, the outcome of this journey in Shabestari's account is freedom and especially freedom of consciousness and thought, a sine qua non for modern subjectivity. The human subject's most important characteristic, which is the product of this journey, is that of freedom of consciousness. Shabestari, arguing in an existentialist fashion, believes that freedom of subjectivity is the necessary result of human contingency and finitude,

---

33. *Hermenutik*, 238.
34. See *God and Juggernaut*, chapter 4.
35. *Iman va Azadi*, 26.

a finitude that is in contrast to attributes of the Absolute. Yet this contingency does not negate freedom and consciousness, but is the very essence of freedom itself.[36] In some instances, Shabestari takes his position on human freedom to some rather unexpected levels. The radical freedom of volition that Shabestari has posited seems to belong to the type of the will that wills itself, i.e., human volition liberated from any force, external or internal, an autonomous self-foundational will who knows no numen other than itself.[37] Similarly, Shabestari has declared freedom as the "authentic identity of humans," and the meaning of authentic human existence as freedom under all circumstances.[38]

I and Thou

Despite, or perhaps because of, such radical ontological ventures, Shabestari's notion of subjectivity is, in its larger context, contained by the notion of a "subject-subject" scheme that is informed by his hermeneutic and existentialist approaches. The "philosophy of subject," that of unbridled subjectivity in the modern world, has been criticized as the "dark" side of modernity, from various points of view. Briefly, this critique is in reference to the ontological foundation of modernity that grounds itself in a subject-object relation, where the unbridled freedom of the subject is not delimited by another subject, but a relation of domination that prevails between the subject and the object.[39]

Drawing on his erudition of European, and specifically German, hermeneutic theology, Shabestari has proposed an "I and Thou" design in a subject-subject paradigm. The archetypal sides of the I and Thou relation in Shabestari's discourse are of course none other than the human and the Deity. Yet, the principle actor seems to be the human in this relation. We humans, Shabestari argues, are capable of two types of action. There is action that takes place in reference to objects, and there is action that is directed toward another person as a consciousness.[40] It is only the second type of action that can bring about freedom. We cannot establish an interaction between objects and ourselves. When we direct our volition at an object, our will encounters a barrier and rebounds.[41] But it is different in the case of action directed toward another consciousness. The encounter between one person as a consciousness and another also as a consciousness is the only means of guaranteeing freedom for, and the integrity of, both sides.[42] This logic, Shabestari maintains, is true especially in the relation between God and humans,

36. *Iman va Azadi*, 24.
37. *Iman va Azadi*, 33.
38. *Iman va Azadi*, 33. The radical nature of Shabestari's thought on this subject is underscored when one compares other understandings of "authenticity" in terms of essentialized notions such as religion, tradition, ethnicity, etc.
39. For a discussion of discourse theory on this issue see, for example, Jürgen, Habermas, "Communicative Versus Subject-Centered Reason," in *Rethinking the Subject. An Anthology of Contemporary European Thought*, ed James Faubion, (Boulder: Westview Press, 1955).
40. *Iman va Azadi*, 34.
41. *Iman va Azadi*, 34.
42. *Iman va Azadi*, 35–36.

where the notion of I and Thou guarantees the highest form of freedom for humans.[43] There is little doubt that Shabestari is dwelling on an intersubjective paradigm here. Yet, owing to his relatively parsimonious treatment of the individual as the carrier of human subjectivity, his notion of intersubjectivity lacks much needed concreteness.

Faith as Choosing: Individual as the Carrier of Subjectivity?

To be sure, throughout Shabestari's discourse, one can detect an implicit recognition of the individual as the carrier of human subjectivity. However, this implicit recognition by Shabestari rarely becomes explicit in his writings. It is a cardinal principle in Islam, Shabestari argues, that every Muslim should obtain a rigorous "conception" [*tasawur*] of God, the Prophet, the Resurrection [*ma'ad*] and the creed [*din*] by herself or himself, without imitating even the highest religious authority.[44] Here the crucial role of the individual subject in making decisions with regard to such solemn tasks needs very little elaboration.

Yet, in Shabestari's thought, like that of some other contemporary Islamic thinkers in Iran, any notion of the individual qua subject is closely intertwined with that of "faith."[45] What makes the subtextual acknowledgment of the individual prevalent in Shabestari's discourse is the grounding of faith in the ability, and in fact the requirement, of the individual, who comes to believe in the creed, to choose freely. Without the ability to choose freely, faith has no meaning. As Shabestari has put it:

> Faith is an act of choosing, a fateful act. The question is when a human being is facing a dilemma and chooses the type of lifestyle he wants to live by, what path should he take? [...] The ideal society for faith and the faithful [to flourish] is one in which [the condition for making] this choice is most widely available [...] The truth of faith is a free act of conscious choice. All of our mystics [*'urafa*] have urged the forsaking of imitated faith and adoption of conscious faith.[46]

Similarly, Shabestari has grounded his understanding of the notion of faith firmly in freedom of thought and free human will. In his book, *Iman va Azadi* (Faith and Freedom), Shabestari's attempt at reconciling the two conflicting terms in the paradigm of mediated subjectivity is manifested in his effort to harmonize the two categories of faith and freedom. As such, he has presented four approaches toward the concept of faith in Islamic tradition. According to the first approach, what he refers to as the Ash'arite doctrine, the truth of

43. *Iman va Azadi*, 36–37.

44. *Hermenutik*, 92–93.

45. Sorush, for example, considers freedom of the individual as pivotal for any conception of faith: "The faith of each individual is the exclusive experience and the 'private property' of that individual. Each of us finds faith as an individual, as we die as an individual. There may be collective rituals but there is no collective faith." Abdulkarim Sorush, "Modara va Modiriyat-e Mo'menan: Sokhani dar Nesbat-e Din va Demokrasi" (Conciliation and administration of the faithful: a discussion of the relation between religion and democracy), *Kiyan* 4, no. 21 (Sep-Oct 1994): 7.

46. *Hermenutik*, 184–85.

faith is the profession of belief in God and the prophets as well as Divine decrees based on sincere feelings.[47] In the second approach, espoused by the Mu'tazilites, the essence of faith is comprised of "action based on responsibility." In this formulation, faith stems from innate human rationality that makes us capable of distinguishing between good and evil, and accordingly charges us with duty and responsibility. The faithful person is one who acts in accordance with this sense of responsibility, and the mere acknowledgment of the prophets is an inadequate measure of faith.[48]

The third approach is that of the Islamic philosophers, for whom the truth of faith is expressed as "gnosis" [*ma'rifat*] and philosophical knowledge of the "realities in the sphere of being." According to the proponents of this view, faith consists of human evolution toward a state of contemplative perfection.[49] Finally, Islamic mystics have interpreted faith as "embracing' [*iqbal*] God and turning away from non-God."[50]

What all these conceptualizations of faith have in common, Shabestari argues, is that they are inseparable from freedom of thought and human free will. The profession of belief as the criterion of faith is only possible through human will, and the latter in its essence belongs to the category of freedom. Since the profession of belief is contingent upon knowledge and "rational attestation," it cannot be possible without liberation of reason from imitation and unfreedom.[51] The same is true of the Mu'tazalites' view of faith as grounded in the notion of "natural responsibility." This responsibility only can be recognized through reason and realized through action. Action that is the principle foundation of faith, in this view, is in turn the result of human volition, which is again free in its essence.[52]

An analysis of the third conceptualization of faith as "philosophical knowledge," Shabestari maintains, demonstrates that this type of knowledge, like other types of knowledge, cannot be possible except through free thought.[53] The mystic's interpretation of faith as "embracing of God," is possible only if thought is capable of critically transcending itself and liberating itself from any form of dogmatism. Without such a thorough critical attitude, thought cannot be directed toward the embracing of God, while the precondition for a critical attitude is freedom of thought and free human volition.[54]

Throughout *Iman va Azadi*, Shabestari's principal aim seems to be the positing of a close link between different interpretations of "faith" and human freedom, especially freedom of consciousness and free will, in his effort to reconcile modern subjectivity and religion. Yet, he rarely makes any explicit references to the individual as the carrier of modern subjectivity. Only in one passing reference in the entire book does he suggest that a collective notion of faith is a vague idea, and that it is only individuals who can undergo

47. *Iman va Azadi*, 12–13.
48. *Iman va Azadi*, 13–14.
49. *Iman va Azadi*, 16.
50. *Iman va Azadi*, 19.
51. *Iman va Azadi*, 21.
52. *Iman va Azadi*, 21.
53. *Iman va Azadi*, 22.
54. *Iman va Azadi*, 22.

a religious experience.[55] The rest of Shabestari's discourse seems to be silent on any explicit discussion of the individual as the carrier and beneficiary of human subjectivity. Perhaps one of the factors contributing to this phenomenon has to do with Shabestari's familiarity with some of the discontents of modernity, a familiarity which is first and foremost informed, not by an "Islamic" critique of modernity, but by "Western" critiques of the modern world, expressed in the 20th century by some Western philosophers and theologians.

Modernity and Its Discontents

Shabestari thinks that one of the most significant achievements of modernity is the abandoning of dogmatism. Before Muslims encountered modernity, and willingly or unwillingly adopted its epistemological tenets, he argues, Islamic theology and cosmology in general were primarily and obsessively concerned with the question of truth about God, prophecy, and the future of humans in this world and the next. The intellectual atmosphere in which this type of inquiry and pursuit of truth were conducted was one of dogmatism and the search for absolute facts that could corroborate the preconceived notions about religious beliefs.[56] In such an atmosphere "certitude" was considered the measure for correspondence to truth as well as the salvation of the believers.[57] In our modern era, however, the intellectual and epistemological atmosphere has changed. In this new milieu, the philosophical and epistemic dogmatism has been rejected and the certitude of the bygone era is proved fruitless, and as a result, a form of "non-dogmatism" pervades in all fields.[58]

The positive consequence of this process, Shabestari seems to suggest, is the prevalence of a critical attitude with regard to all types and facets of knowledge. In the centuries since modernity has taken root, humans have taken a detached attitude toward the mind and its activities, resulting in self-consciousness and a ubiquitous critical approach.[59] As a result, modern humans find themselves in a position that requires constant evaluation, rethinking, and above all constant movement, without having a determined and demarcated goal and destination in view. In such a world, humans always quest after something and always "face a problem." Yet, people seek moorings in this world, since all that is solid is constantly deconstructed. This is a world without a definitive "conception," and meaning and humans lack a definitive conception of themselves.[60] Shabestari suggests that the proper task for modern theology is to address these issues and provide some possible solution to the loss of meaning and "conception," which is a byproduct of the loss of permanence.

55. *Iman va Azadi,* 124.
56. *Hermenutik,* 171–72.
57. *Hermenutik,* 171–72.
58. *Hermenutik,* 172.
59. *Hermenutik,* 172.
60. *Hermenutik,* 173. For a by now classical discussion of loss of all permanence and fixity in modernity, see: Marshal Berman, *All that is Solid Melts into Air: The Experience of Modernity* (New York: Penguin Books, 1988).

Parallel to the loss of meaning and "conception," Shabestari argues, is the emergence of a "perplexed self" (*man-e sargardan*, borrowing the notion from Muhammad Iqbal), which has visited the Westerners in modernity because they have abandoned their permanent principles.[61] The Muslims, Shabestari advises, should not be afflicted by a "perplexed self," and therefore they should not abandon their principles. On the other hand, the rejection and prevention of change in life that caused Muslims' misfortune in the past centuries is neither possible nor desirable. Therefore, the only solution is preserving both by trying to create a synthesis between what is permanent and what is changeable, a principal goal in Shabestari's discourse.[62]

Shabestari also has criticized the negative side of human subjectivity, that is, domination and its sociopolitical consequences. He is rightly cognizant of the darker side of modern subjectivity and its devastating effects, afflicting the victim of the Western subject manifested in such phenomena as colonialism and imperialism, as well as some of the consequences of modern subjectivity affecting the Western subject more directly, e.g., domination of humans by technology and consumerism. As Shabestari has put it:

> If we ask what is the most prevalent and ubiquitous manner of thought and action of the majority of people in Western societies—the motor of their society—the answer that emerges would be along the following lines: "empowering of man and making him dominant over the process of everyday life by utilizing the three weapons of science, technology and wealth" [...] Cardinal evils such as domination of life by machines, old and new colonialism, severe scientific, technological, and even cultural dependence of the countries that are kept underdeveloped on the West [...] endangering of human life by nuclear weapons, reducing the meaning of life for the masses to consumerism, the appearance of nihilism and philosophies of nullibicity and other evils of this kind are the consequences of this manner of thought and action.[63]

What Shabestari has described as reification by modern technology (utilizing the term "*mashinism*," a transliteration from French), seems to be in close parallel to the humanist critiques of the oppressive aspect of modern subjectivity articulated by more than one current of thought in the West in the 20th century. He has admonished Iranians and other Muslims to be aware of the problems involved in the transfer of technology and to act with prudence to achieve a technology that is in "conformity with humans."[64] Yet, Shabestari is quick to point out that the modern West cannot be reduced to this reifying aspect. Moreover, there is a growing opposition to this phenomenon in the West itself, and the quest for new, as well as old, forms of spirituality remains strong there. Modernity, Shabestari argues, is inevitable and no country, Muslim or otherwise, can

61. *Hermenutik*, 203.
62. *Hermenutik*, 203.
63. *Iman va Azadi*, 149–50.
64. *Iman va Azadi*, 155. Interestingly, here Shabestari has exempted modern natural sciences from the reifying effect, and considers them neutral in nature.

escape adjusting itself to its different aspects.[65] In fact, in the past 150 years the Islamic countries, including Iran, have chosen the modern life-style. The remaining question is how to cope with the darker sides of modernity. Religion can lend its support to ameliorate the crises of meaning, disempowerment, and perplexity that accompany the process of modernization.[66] It can do so by facilitating the creation of a religious art and literature to provide spiritual nourishment for a society in the process of modernization.[67] Shabestari, however, does not hesitate to emphasize here that the spiritual support religion can provide in the process of modernization is totally different from the management of society, political or otherwise, through religion.

Shabestari's discourse can be characterized primarily as sociophilosophical; yet, the sociopolitical aspect of his thought, albeit very subtle and lacking overt polemical and contentious attributes, closely reflects the first aspect and deserves some examination in itself.

Politics of Intersubjective Hermeneutics

In *Hermenutik, Ketab va Sunnat,* Shabestari has discussed three types of positions with regard to the encounter of religion and modernity among contemporary religious thinkers in Iran. According to the first approach, Shabestari contends, it is human civilization that needs to adapt itself to the Qur'an and Sunna. In this context, Shabestari has likened civilization and religion to a garment and body. In the view of the proponents of the first approach, according to Shabestari, the body representing civilization needs to be tailored to fit the garment of religion. Religion in this view is the criterion of a healthy civilization, and as such all civilizations and forms of social organization at all times must conform to its dimensions.[68]

Among the proponents of the second approach, the consensus is that only the general values undergirding government and society are fixed, while the form of state is not. When civilization undergoes change, the political institutions of a Muslim society must assume new forms also.[69] These institutions should be organized in such a way as to secure the maximum possibility for the observance of religious requirements in society. This type of state, however, is the product of Muslims' excogitation and as such is not the institutionalization of the Sharia itself. It is not uncriticizable, since it is a human institution and unsacred.[70]

The third group believes that the Qur'an and Sunna do not articulate even general values undergirding the political institutions and the state, which are fixed and permanent. According to this point of view, Shabestari argues, the normative principles in the Qur'an and Sunna address the "ethics of the individual" only. This is the doctrine that advocates

65. Mohamad Mojtahed Shabestari, "Qarat-e Rasmi az Din" (Official reading of religion), *Rah-e Naw*, no. 19, *Shahrivar* 7, no. 1377 (August 29, 1998): 19.
66. Qarat-e Rasmi az Din, 20.
67. Qarat-e Rasmi az Din, 20.
68. *Hermenutik,* 63–64.
69. *Hermenutik,* 64–65.
70. *Hermenutik,* 64–65.

the separation between politics and religion. The people, in this view, choose not only the type of state organization that fits their needs, they also determine their sociopolitical norms and values by themselves.[71]

Shabestari has rejected the first and the third positions and opted for the second. He rejects the third position because in his view, the complete severance of politics from normative religious principles is untenable among a religious population. It is the second position that is most conducive to reconciliation between religiosity on the one hand, and change and modernity on the other. Shabestari seems to endeavor to ensure that, in this reconciliation, human freedom is not sacrificed. Reflecting Ali Shariati's critique of institutionalized religion, Shabestari has maintained that when religion is institutionalized, the peril of it negating the human looms large. Shabestari has explained the reason for this phenomenon in his own dialectical-dialogical formulation that views the mutual integrity of God and human as preconditions of each other:

> When religion is institutionalized, the danger appears that man is negated by the institution. Why? Because when religion is institutionalized, God's "absoluteness" is denied. With the institutionalization of religion, God is confined [...] within the enclosure of Church or Mosque. God thus is eclipsed, and when He is eclipsed, man no longer finds himself before an absolute God, but before a God that is confined and reified. Under these circumstances man is negated, and when man is negated God is experienced as anti-freedom.[72]

In a radical departure from a religious thinker like Khomeini, who considered the act of legislation by humans blasphemous, Shabestari has alluded, albeit rather subtly, to the possibility of legislation by mortals. In this scheme God's legislation is primarily the enactment of general, but eternal, value systems. God is first and foremost the fountainhead of the ethical principles, which leaves space for human decisions such as "framing" laws.[73] In this way the possibility of change in Divinely inspired laws and regulation are not ruled out, while the Divine values themselves do not change. This important premise leads Shabestari to the conclusion that laws themselves are not sacred, even though they might have been legislated in conformity with the general religious values in the first place. The range that Shabestari has allowed for human legislation is considerably large and covers areas that usually are not considered open to change. These areas include legal relations in the family, social relations, politics, the state and its institutionalization, judicial matters, the punishments and legal sanctions as well as contracts in general.[74] In this context Shabestari obliquely criticized the lack of the possibility for women to divorce their husbands in many of the countries that profess to be Islamic. He has referred to the example provided by Iqbal of some Muslim women in Punjab resorting to apostasy to be able to divorce.[75]

71. *Hermenutik*, 66.
72. *Iman va Azadi*, 29.
73. *Hermenutik*, 78.
74. *Iman va Azadi*, 87–88.
75. *Hermenutik*, 207–8.

In a society in which this type of attempt at reconciliation between religion and modernity constitutes the organizational principle, Shabestari suggests, critical attitude and the concept of critique are of central importance. In this type of society, even external critiques of religion, for example those of Marx and Feuerbach, not only are tolerated, but they can help the faithful refine their conceptions of religion and thus achieve purer forms of religiosity.[76] In this type of society, if books against religion are not published and critique of religion is not allowed, faith loses it main characteristic and no longer would be a conscious act of choosing.[77] Furthermore, "in the society of the faithful there are no 'red lines' to demarcate the limits of critique. The critics must have all the space to engage in critique without any red lines."[78]

Shabestari has credited development of modernity with the process of transforming despotic polities in the past few centuries. The cultural-political transformation that has characterized modernity is conducive to a "reflexivity" and detached attitude toward the "self," which led to a desire for political change that aimed at overthrowing despotic regimes. In this way, issues such as freedom and political participation, equality, and human rights were thematized in the modern period.[79] In a similar vein, Shabestari argues, in order for a society of the faithful to be viable in the modern industrial world, there must exist institutional guarantees for freedom, since in "totalitarian and despotic societies the seeds of faith," which as we saw before he equates with a conscious act of choosing, "would rot."[80]

Consequently, in what seems to be an oblique critique of the concept of Guardianship of the Jurist (*velayat-e faqih*), Shabestari has argued that Islam neither recognizes nor recommends any single form of polity.[81] Instead, given the definition of faith that Shabestari has provided, the form of polity in which faith can flourish is none other than one in which, in addition to the institutional guarantees of freedom, there is also distribution of power, provision for checks and balances, and a mechanism for peaceful transition of power.[82] Such a polity, Shabestari argues, is only possible in a society in which a parliamentary system works hand in hand with a "well-operating" judiciary and a "healthy," sustainable economy.[83] In this regard, Shabestari has denied that only the *ulema* and Islamic experts are capable of determining whether the polity is compatible with Islam; it is the right of non-expert citizens to participate in the political affairs of the country.[84]

What seems to be of most significance among Shabestari's political views is that he considers the state and political institutions to be civil, as opposed to religious, in

76. *Hermenutik,* 186.
77. *Hermenutik,* 186.
78. *Hermenutik,* 187.
79. *Hermenutik,* 210.
80. *Iman va Azadi,* 8.
81. *Iman va Azadi,* 74–75.
82. *Iman va Azadi,* 79.
83. *Iman va Azadi,* 132. Shabestari does not elaborate on what he means by a "well-operating" judiciary and a "healthy," sustainable economy.
84. *Iman va Azadi,* 75–76.

nature. As marriage and divorce are two civil institutions, and the application of religious measures to them does not strip them of their civil identity, the same is true of the state and political institutions. The fact that religious criteria may be applied to these institutions does not mean that they are not civil by nature. Shabestari even has used the term *'urfi*, which can be translated as "secular," to describe the state in this context.[85]

Conclusion

From a theoretical perspective, Shabestari's discourse in general may best be viewed as an attempt to reconcile the contradictions that Islamic revolutionary discourse engendered in the 1960s and 1970s. As such, Shabestari's discourse is embedded in the paradigm of mediated subjectivity. While Shabestari's thought is a valuable attempt to overcome the contradictions of this paradigm, it is not totally immune from relapsing, albeit very infrequently, into the types of contradictions it tries to heal. For example, while he has advocated political and social freedoms of various types, he has expressed conservative views with regard to personal matters, i.e., the affairs of private life regulated by the Sharia, at least in one occasion in his relatively recent writings.[86] Similarly, it may be argued, while Shabestari attempts to drastically reduce the contradictions of religious modernity in Iran, he has not directly tackled the largest of these contradictions, that is the concept and the institution of Guardianship of the Jurist (*velayat-e faqih*).

Yet, the most significant achievement of Shabestari's discourse seems to lie in a hermeneutic construction of intersubjectivity in terms of which the discourse of religious modernity in Iran can be advanced. Because of the perceived or real contradiction that the paradigm of mediated subjectivity has engendered between human and divine subjectivity and sovereignty, this paradigm could not have developed further, together with a hermeneutic that involved a direct exegesis of the Qur'an. The result has been the development of a hermeneutic that represents the expansion of the subjectivist elements in mediated subjectivity, without emphasizing the theomorphic approach that characterized the thought of the revolutionary predecessors. The further development of the logic of the theomorphic approach could have confronted the process of modernity with serious problems in a profoundly religious society, because human subjectivity could easily be perceived as challenging the divine subjectivity and sovereignty. The subtle detour that Shabistari has taken toward a hermeneutic approach to subjectivity saves him from this possibility. Another significant characteristic of this approach is that it relies upon the principle of intersubjectivity. Shabestari's approach constructs a hermeneutics in which the human assumes a position of subjectivity by treating the text as the "object" of his subjectivity. However, because the text, sacred or otherwise, always presupposes an author who is a subject, the relationship that exists between two sides of the hermeneutical process is not that of subject-object, but that of subject-subject. The I and Thou principle that Shabestari has introduced into his discourse is very much a model for a religious notion of intersubjectivity. It may serve to deter the positivist form

85. *Iman va Azadi*, 68.
86. *Hermenutik*, 81.

of modernity, based on a subject-object relationship, from dominating the process of modernity in Iran once again.[87]

---

87. Since this chapter was originally written, Shabestari's thought has further evolved, which necessitates additional discussion of his more recent work. In an article, entitled "The Prophetic Reading of the Word" (Qara'at-e Nabavi az Jahan; http://www.taravat.ir/index.php?option=com_content&task=view&id=1397&Itemid=1. Visited on April 8, 2008.) that was published in the journal *Madreseh* and caused its closing in 2007 by the government, Shabestari has outlined some controversial views regarding the nature of Muhammad's prophecy, and based on that, some contentious remarks on the essence of the Qur'an. By examining the text of the Qur'an as a historical document, Shabestari argues, we will find that the claim of Muhammad as a human being is that, although the words that he recites as revelation to invite people to embrace it are his own words, they have a divine source. By thus distinguishing the source from the word itself, Shabestari seems to be attempting to create a larger space for freer interpretations of the Qur'an. Muhammad did not claim, according to Shabestari, that he would initiate the utterance of the divine words; rather Muhammad's experience was that he was selected and "instigated" (*mab'uth*) to utter meaningful words, which are in reality the "symbols" (*nemud*) of God. Treating the Qur'anic verses as historical documents, Shabestari believes, one could not argue that these verses, in their meaning and wording, came directly from God, and Muhammad just recited them, as for example an intoner (*qari*) of the Qur'an has no role in shaping the meanings and words of the Qur'an and merely chants them. Muhammad was not a mere "sound conduit" (*kanal-e souti*) to convey the sounds that he heard. Had the prophet been a mere sound conduit, his word would not be understood by the people, and the Islamic civilization could not be built upon that word. In order to justify this position, Shabestari proceeds to a linguistic analysis, according to which all human languages must meet five criteria that are linked to each other: the speaker, the listener, the context, the linguistic community and the content of the language. If one of these criteria is missing, human language cannot take place. All of these links of language involve humans, and if the human element is eliminated from any of them, human language becomes impossible. The speaker as the first link in the generation of language cannot be like a parrot or a megaphone. Therefore the speaker as a human being, in this case Muhammad, is essential in the formation of language. From a Qur'anic point of view, Shabestari contends, *wahy* (divine inspiration, revelation) is God's conversation with the Prophet that causes the "instigation" in Muhammad, which in turn results in the prophet's utterances. As such, the Qur'anic verses are the products of *wahy* and not the *wahy* itself. The Qur'anic verses are thus simultaneously attributable to the Prophet, who formulates these words, and to God. In Shabestari's new approach, in the Qur'an God does not provide Muhammad with factual statements or verifiable/falsifiable truth claims about the universe. All that is provided is an "outlook" or "perspective" (Shabestari uses the German term *blick* and the Persian term *negaah*) to interpret the world: "The Qur'an, (i.e., the verses in the noble book), is a 'reading,' or an interpretive understanding of the world by the prophet." Shabestari insists on translating the units of the Qur'anic text known as *ayas*, not as signs (Persian, *neshan*) but as "symbols" (Persian *nemoud*), implying that *ayas* should be considered as the phenomena in the world, which are rooted in the noumena. But since we have no access to the noumenal world, we can only deal with the phenomena, which are of necessity material for interpretation. These postulations enable Shabestari to declare the holy text even more open to interpretation than before. Thus for Shabestari, the legal injunctions found in the Qur'an are not universal and can be reinterpreted differently across time and space: "The legal injunctions of the Qur'an are based on an interpretive understanding of the social realities and relations of the Hijaz [of the 7th century]. The purpose of those injunctions was to interpret social realties in a manner that would be in agreement with God's will. Those injunctions were never meant to serve as rulings for all societies and all times."

Chapter Seven

RELIGIOUS MODERNITY IN IRAN: DILEMMAS OF ISLAMIC DEMOCRACY IN THE DISCOURSE OF MOHAMMAD KHATAMI[1]

During the first few years after the election of Mohammad Khatami to the Presidency of the Islamic Republic in 1997, pro-democracy groups and individuals experienced an episode of euphoria and enthusiasm, which soon turned into despair and apathy. As early as the first term of his tenure, Khatami's promises of freedom, civil society and the rule of law were frustrated and blocked from being implemented by the conservative groups within Iran's ruling establishment. Khatami himself proved unwilling to take necessary risks to implement his project of civil society, and his inactions and capitulations resulted in further frustration of many, but not all, of his promises. This chapter attempts to analyze the failures, achievements and some of the possible political ramifications of the presidency of Mohammad Khatami by focusing on his discourse in the context of the intellectual trajectory of the Islamic thought from the revolutionary period to the postrevolutionary reformist phase.[2]

The case of Khatami is of particular interest, because he is not only an intellectual, but also a political practitioner who served two terms as the president of the republic. To be sure, his intellectual caliber is not on the same level as that of Soroush and Shabestari; yet, because of his direct involvement in the political fray at the highest level of electoral politics in Iran his discourse and its practical ramifications, as well as the outcome of his political maneuverings, are very much significant.

1. "Religious Modernity in Iran: Dilemmas of Islamic Democracy in the Discourse of Mohammad Khatami" is reprinted from *Comparative Studies of South Asia, Africa and the Middle East*, volume 25:3.
2. For informative analyses of the political conditions under Khatami see: Ramin Jahanbegloo, "The Deadlock in Iran: Pressures, from Below," *Journal of Democracy* 14, no. 1 (January 2003); Ali Gheissar and Vali Nasr, "Iran's Democracy Debate," *Middle East Policy* XI, no. 2 (Summer 2004); Said Amir Arjomand "Civil Society and the Rule OF Law in the Constitutional Politics of Iran under Khatami," *Social Research*, Vol. 67 Issue 2 (Summer 2000): 283–302; and Ahmad Sadri, "The Varieties of Religious Reform: Public Intelligentsia in Iran," *International Journal of Politics, Culture, and Society*, Vol.15, No.2 (Winter 2001).

Khatami: The Philosopher President

Seyyid Mohammad Khatami was born in Ardakan in the central province of Yazd in 1943. He is the son of Ayatollah Ruhollah Khatami who founded the seminary in Ardakan. Khatami finished his primary and secondary schools in Ardakan and then attended Qom Seminary in 1961. It is noteworthy that before finishing his seminary studies he received a bachelor's degree in philosophy from the secular University of Isfahan, a relatively rare experience among the Shii clergy at the time. In 1969 Khatami entered another secular institution of higher education, the University of Tehran, from which he earned a master's degree. Later he returned to Qom seminary to attend philosophical classes of some renowned religious scholars such as Ayatollah Motahhari. Khatami was a political activist in the Islamic movement before and during the revolution of 1979. After the revolution he replaced Ayatollah Beheshti as the head of Hamburg Islamic Center in West Germany for a short period of time.

Khatami was elected to represent the people of Ardakan and the nearby Meibod in the first session of the Islamic Majlis in 1980, and in 1981 Ayatollah Khomeini appointed him as the head of the influential *Kayhan* newspaper. In 1982, he became the minister of culture and Islamic guidance. During the 1980–88 war with Iraq, he served in different capacities, including deputy and head of the Joint Command of the Armed Forces and chairman of the War Propaganda Headquarters. In 1989 Khatami became the minister of Culture and Islamic Guidance during the presidency of Hashemi Rafsanjani, but after three years, under pressure from conservative forces, he chose to resign his post rather than stay and fight.[3]

Khatami's Cosmology: Humanism with a Caveat

At the center of Khatami's cosmology is a conceptualization of humans as endowed with certain attributes fundamental to monotheistic ontology. In his address at the General Assembly of United Nations in New York in 1999, he referred to humans as having been created by "God's hand" and in His "image." The "hand of God," he added, has proffered to humans, "history, freedom [*ikhtiyar*] and the ability to choose, and 'God's image' has bestowed upon them culture, and spirituality," while "God's Spirit" has endowed them with "life and vitality."[4] Humans, in this view, because they are God's successors or vicegerents on earth (*khalifatullah fi al-ardh*) possess power and consciousness.[5] However, these essential attributes are contingent upon those of God, and humans never

3. The biographical data on Khatami is taken from the following: http://www.president.ir/farsi/khatami/bio (November 5, 2004).
4. Mohammad Khatami, *Hezareh Goftogu va Tafahom: Gozareshe-e Safar-e Mohammad Khatami be Sazman-e Melal-e Motahed* (The Millennium of Dialogue and Understanding: The Report of Mohammad Khatami's Trip to the United Nations), (Tehran: Nashr-e Resanesh, 1999), 51.
5. Khatami has invoked the notion of humans as God's vicegerents on earth in the context of respecting the dignity and human rights of prisoners and people accused of crimes. See, Mohammad Khatami, *Gozideh Sokhanraniha-ye Rai'is Jomhur dar bareh-ye Tose'h-ye Siyasi, Tose'eh Eqtesadi va Amniyat* (A selection of President's speeches on political and economic development, and security), (Tehran: Tarh-e Nou, 2000), 270.

possess them directly. It is only through God's will that humans possess volition and can determine their own destiny: "In contrast to other animals, man possesses will. That means that *willed by God Almighty*, man himself can affect his own destiny."[6]

This type of cosmology leads Khatami, like many of his predecessors among the Shii modernists, to emphasize human reason, which to him is inseparable from the idea of "justice". In the Shii tradition, Khatami argues in the manner of the Mu'tazilites, justice has occupied a central place. Shiism, both in the realm of individual action and that of social relations, believes in justice. As soon as we posit justice, we should also posit reason.[7] God, Khatami maintains, congratulates Himself because after He created man's body, He conferred reason upon him.[8] Very much in accordance with a prevalent tendency in the Islamic tradition, Khatami's emphasis on reason and consciousness is accompanied by a disciplinary attitude toward the body and what he calls "appetites" (*hawa-yi nafs*). Islam, says Khatmi, forbids the domination of the appetites and desires over the self. "Piety (*taqwa*), means preventing the supremacy of desire and anger over the person." The month of Ramadan is the month to "construct the self." Ramadan is the month of *taqwa* because God has "designated *taqwa* as the goal of fasting and *taqwa* means [gaining] control over the [corporeal] self; what our Glorious Prophet has named the Greatest Jihad [*Jihad Akbar*]."[9]

Thus, Khatami's cosmology allows him to posit a notion of empowered humanity, which is very much located in the paradigm of mediated subjectivity. Yet, as we will explore in more detail below, compared to his revolutionary predecessors, his vacillations on subjectivity and negation of empowered humans is more restrained, even though his discourse suffers from other types of contradictions. Based on this formulation, Khatami, invoking the 14th century Persian poet Hafez, asserts that the self can "overset the firmament, if it doesn't revolve to one's content."[10] And, it is not surprising that, in a less poetic mood, Khatami considers mountain climbing the most satisfying athletic activity:

> Among the sports, mountain climbing has a symbolic aspect also. The mountains are the symbols of the hubris, firmness and resistance of the earth and life. Taming this symbol of resistance [of the universe to human will] is indicative of the peak of vitality, power, honor and nobility of man. Those who step on the high peaks of the mountains are the outstanding specimens of human resolution and demonstrate that man is most powerful compared to all other beings and can overstep all the loftiest symbols of the power of the natural world. As a religious and monotheistic people, we believe that human power should be at the service of humanity. That means that human determination and power should be utilized in the service of God.[11]

---

6. Mohammad Khatami, *Islam, Rohaniyat va Enqelab-e Islami* [Islam, the clergy, and Islamic Revolution], (Tehran: Tarh-e Nou, 2000), 35. Emphasis added.
7. *Islam, Rohaniyat va Enqelab-e Islami*, 48.
8. Mohammad Khatami, *Zanan va Javanan* (Women and the Youth) (Tehran: Tarh-e Nou, 2000), 148.
9. *Islam, Rohaniyat va Enqelab-e Islami,* 123.
10. *Hezareh Goftogu va Tafahom,* 52.
11. *Zanan va Javanan,* 184.

As this passage reveals, Khatami's cosmology directs him to posit a notion of human subjectivity which is contingent upon Divine Subjectivity and is purported to be in the service of other humans and in the path of God.

History, in Khatami's view, however, has not realized this ontological potential in Islamic lands. Universal human empowerment has been stunted in the Islamic East because of what Khatami views to be the predominance of "tyranny."

Philosophy of History: Tyranny

After his resignation as the minister of Islamic Culture and Guidance and before being elected the President of the Islamic Republic, Khatami found an intellectual refuge by delving into the study of Western and Eastern traditions of political thought. During these years he was appointed the head of Iran's National Library, and for five years he seems to have engaged in a study of political thought in the West and the Middle East. The result was two books, one entitled *From the World of the City to World-City: A Study of Political Thought in the West*; and another book was entitled *Religion and Thought in the Snare of Autocracy: A Study in the Political Thought of Muslims during the Ascent and Descent of Islamic Civilization.*[12]

In the former book, Khatami first traces the development of Western political thought from Plato and Aristotle, through the Stoics and the Epicureans, and then to Cicero. He also treats the issue of political thought in Christianity in subsequent parts of the book. He maintains that in Europe, Christianity had little impact on political thought because Christianity was a "guest" in a land that had already very much developed its political culture and legal tradition owing to its Greek and Roman foundations.[13] Moreover, from Saint Augustine, to Saint Thomas Aquinas and to the present, in the Christian world the emphasis has always been on a duality between this world and the next.[14] Christianity has always relegated the affairs of this world to worldly forces, and as such it has not really developed a Sharia or a religious law, because it mostly sanctioned and appropriated the Roman law.[15] Because politics has been separated from the domination of the clerics in the West and society has enjoyed a parallel system of powers in Christendom, Khatami argues, there has always been space for the discussion of politics and the possibility, at least in the realm of political thought, of elimination of many instances of despotism.[16] Furthermore, because the Church was focused on theology and matters of dogma, in contradistinction to legal and political matters, it developed an extreme intolerance toward most discussions of theological issues and dogma, whereas it was relatively charitable toward political debates:

12. The titles of the two books in Persian are, *Az Donya-ye Shahr ta Shahr-e Donya: Seyri dar Andisheh-e Siyasi Gharb*; and, *Ai'in va Andisheh dr Dam-e Khodkamegi: Seyri dar Andisheh-ye Siyasi Moslamanan dar faraz va forud-e tamadon-e Islami.*
13. Mohmmad Khatami, *Az Donya-ye Shahr ta Shahr-e Donya: Seyri dar Andisheh-e Siyasi Gharb* (From the World of the City to World-City: A Study of Political Thought in the West) (Tehran: Nashr-e Ney, 1999), 120.
14. *Az Donya-ye Shahr ta Shahr-e Donya*, 122.
15. *Az Donya-ye Shahr ta Shahr-e Donya*, 129.
16. *Az Donya-ye Shahr ta Shahr-e Donya*, 133.

> [As theological] theory degenerates in Christendom, the sphere of "praxis" [*'amal*] becomes the cauldron of ideas. [Theological] theory becomes sacred and praxis is construed as secular and human. In the realm of [theological] theory whatever is against the Church, is [deemed to be] against God; yet, anybody can comment on "praxis," because it is a human affair [...] But in this part of the world [i.e., in the Islamic world], "praxis" becomes sacred and the field of inquiry into the sphere of [theological] theory opens up (or becomes more open) and for this reason [the realm of] politics [and political thought] remains closed, while [non-political] philosophy and other theoretical sciences expand.[17]

In his book on the political thought in the Islamic world, Khatami's focus is on what he describes as the sclerosis of political discourse in the Muslim world and what he proposes to be its correlate, the predominance of tyranny. He divides the history of Islamic civilization into three periods. The first period consists of the forty years from the founding of the Islamic polity in Medina by the Prophet to the end of the era of the Righteous Caliphs (621–661). This is the only period in which the Muslim community had any hope for liberation.[18] The second period started from the end of the Righteous Caliphs' era, that is, with the Umayyads (661–750) and the Abbasids (750–1258), and continued until the encroachments of Western imperialism in the 19th century. In this long period, autocracy (*khudkamegi*) and tyranny (*taghalub*) comprised the common features of political institutions and the spirit of politics in all Islamic lands and periods, despite their differences in other respects.[19] The third period began with the domination of Western imperialism and continues to our time.[20]

In the second period, Khatami suggests, the cultural/intellectual domain in the Muslim world can be divided into three more or less distinct categories: orthodoxy (*tasharu'*), mysticism (*tasawuf*) and reason (*ta'qul*). Among these, what was more influential and had most determining impact on the masses was the orthodoxy.[21] Mysticism, Khatami contends, became prevalent among some of the Muslim elites who were disgruntled with the status quo, but who could not see any way out. Philosophy and reason, on the other hand, were marginalized as orthodoxy became the dominant component of Muslim culture.[22] While philosophy in general was marginalized, political philosophy and social thought never had a chance to develop in Muslim lands. The only philosopher in the Muslim world who made any substantial effort in this direction was al-Farabi (d. circa 950) who, by describing the different kinds of "city" as different ideal types of polity, paved the way for the potential development of political philosophy. However, al-Farabi's efforts were not continued by later philosophers, and Khatami believes that one of the major historical reasons for the "bitter and dark destiny of Muslims," should

17. *Az Donya-ye Shahr ta Shahr-e Donya*, 149.
18. Mohammad Khatami, *Ai'in va Andisheh dar Dam-e Khodkamegi: Seyri dar Andisheh-ye Siyasi Moslamanan dar Faraz va Forud-e Tamadon-e Islami* (Religion and thought in the snare of autocracy: a study in the political thought of Muslims during the ascent and descent of Islamic civilization), (Tehran: Tarh-e nou, 1999), 423.
19. *Ai'in va Andisheh dar Dam-e Khodkamegi*, 10.
20. *Ai'in va Andisheh dar Dam-e Khodkamegi*, 11.
21. *Ai'in va Andisheh dar Dam-e Khodkamegi*, 72–73.
22. *Ai'in va Andisheh dar Dam-e Khodkamegi*, 90.

be sought in their "lack of reflection and contemplation on the nature of society and its fate, specifically in its political dimensions."[23]

In the absence of proper political theory, Khatami argues, political thought in the Muslim world turned toward attempts to justify autocracy.[24] The Persian tradition of monarchy in the pre-Islamic period and its lore provided the model for the development of tyranny and its theoretical underpinnings.[25] The *speculum principium* ("mirror for princes"; Persian, *siyasatnameh*) of the Persian monarchical tradition played a significant part in this process, according to Khatami. These books, which were written for the edification of the tyrants, were not against Islam, but their interpretations of Islam were in the service of the power of the autocrat.[26] Thus, Islamic political thought never addressed the question of people's rights and at most just exhorted the Sultan to treat his people with kindness, to avoid God's wrath, or for the practical purpose of maintaining power.[27] As a result, Khatami argues, in the political episteme of medieval Muslims, the monarch is God's trustee who is not accountable to anybody except to God. People under him have no say in the discharge of his office, nor do they have any right to call him to account for his behavior.[28]

In summary, Khatami concludes, the Prophet, attempting to realize the divine nobility of man in this situation:

> turned Yathrib into "*Madinatulnabi*" [City of the Prophet] and opened up a new and promising horizon to the man who sought honor. But the historical fate of the Muslims was such that after half a century of the rise of the Islamic sun, the sinister clouds of "tyranny" and "autocracy" darkened the sky of the social lives of Muslims. In this darkness, the vision of Muslim thinkers was closed to the nature of politics and power, as serious contemplation on the political affairs and on the social and political system, which had begun with the efforts of the founder of Islamic philosophy, al-Farabi, was eclipsed after his death. [As a result] political thought fell into the precipice of justifying and sanctifying, or at most explicating, the status quo.[29]

Khatami's own discourse, it seems, is intended to reverse this trend.

Power as Respect

After his election to the presidency in 1997, Khatami expressed his views mostly in the form of formal speeches that he gave on numerous and different occasions. Many of these speeches were collected by his supporters and published in thematically organized monographs shortly after they were delivered. One theme that often appears in these speeches and seems to occupy a very significant place in his thought is that of *ezzat* (Arabic *izza*). The

23. *Ai'in va Andisheh dar Dam-e Khodkamegi,* 233.
24. *Ai'in va Andisheh dar Dam-e Khodkamegi,* 240.
25. *Ai'in va Andisheh dar Dam-e Khodkamegi,* 240.
26. *Ai'in va Andisheh dar Dam-e Khodkamegi,* 328.
27. *Ai'in va Andisheh dar Dam-e Khodkamegi,* 385.
28. *Ai'in va Andisheh dar Dam-e Khodkamegi,* 308–9.
29. *Ai'in va Andisheh dar Dam-e Khodkamegi,* 423.

Perso-Arabic term *ezzat* has the meaning of respect and esteem, and for this reason, Khatami uses another Perso-Arbaic term, *hurmat* (Arabic *hurma*) synonymously. Yet, in his discourse the connotation of power, which is the original meaning associated with the Arabic term *izza*, is clear. The Iranians made the revolution of 1979, Khatami asserted in one his speeches, because they were seeking *hurmat* and *ezzat*.[30] The first Imam of the Shiites, Ali, Khatami argues in another speech, was the leader of people with *ezzat*, not abject and servile (*zalil*; Ar. *dhalil*) people.[31] He has even said that, "the greatest achievement of our revolution has been '*ezzat*'. That means people decided to stand on their own feet under the auspices of Islam and did not give in to any [form of] bullying [...] Tens of thousands of people sacrificed and endured imprisonment and bondage for many years [during the Iran-Iraq war]. Old men, teenagers and young men all strode in the path of God and risked their lives in the war front. This is the price we paid for our *ezzat* and therefore we cannot afford to lose it."[32]

The reason why Ayatollah Khomeini could command so much reverence among the people, Khatami argues, is that he was the promulgator of an Islam that was restoring their *ezzat*.[33] Beyond Islam, even the pre-Islamic Iranian spirit, in his view, is very much imbued by *ezzat*, as one can observe, for example, in the story of Rustam and Isfandiar in the national epic of Iran, *Shahnamah* by Firdawsi.[34] Khatami has gone as far as saying that *ezzat* and dignity override the Islamic principle of *sadaqa* or charity, and instead has urged the establishment of a system of social security that guarantees the esteem of the citizens.[35] Khatami even interprets the expectation of the Mahdi, in terms of respect and dignity derived from power: "[What underlies] the philosophy of Mahdisim [*mahdaviyat*] is that man deserves respect [*hurmat*], justice and freedom and will achieve them".[36]

There is very little doubt that Khatami's analysis of respect and esteem in terms of power is closely related to the notion of human empowerment and subjectivity discussed earlier. Freedom, understood in its positive sense, is but the ability to act upon the world, the freedom of agency and subjectivity. For this reason, as I will try to demonstrate, Khatami's notion of freedom is not distinct from the notion of power discussed above.

Freedom and its Limits

In a speech addressing the people of Hamadan in 1999, Khatamai rhetorically asks, "Is it not true that the prophets came to lift the internal and external bonds of servitude from the hands and feet of God's servants [i.e., the people]? Has freedom not been the noble desire of all humans throughout history? And is it not true that nothing has claimed

30. *Gozideh Sokhanraniha-ye Rai'is Jomhur*, 110–11.
31. *Islam, Rohaniyat va Enqelab-e Islami*, 42.
32. *Islam, Rohaniyat va Enqelab-e Islami*, 43.
33. *Islam, Rohaniyat va Enqelab-e Islami*, 156
34. *Hozureh Goftogu va Ttafahom*, 68–69.
35. *Gozideh Sokhanraniha-ye Rai'is Jomhur*, 140.
36. *Islam, Rohaniyat va Enqelab-e Islami*, 17. *Mahdi* means the "rightly guided one" and refers to the expected restorer of religion and justice who, many Muslims, particularly the Shiites, believe, will rule the world before it comes to an end. *Mahdaviyat* refers to such a doctrine.

as much sacrifice as did freedom?"[37] Whatever has come into conflict with freedom, Khatami often told his audiences, has been impaired or vanquished. Even righteousness, when it countered freedom, was damaged. Religion, justice, development, social justice: when they opposed freedom, they all suffered. Then Khatami mentions the examples of medieval Christianity and communism, in which religion and the idea of social justice opposed freedom, and they were both vanquished.[38]

Khatami's vision of freedom is very much grounded in the monotheistic metaphysics, which as I tried to explain above, attempts to carve out an indirect path of liberation of subjectivity for humans. According to Khatami, only faith can bring about human liberation from the clutches of our "existential conditions," that is, determinism and contingence. Similarly, faith is possible only because of human freedom to choose:

> Whether [one believes that] man is trapped in the labyrinth of the eternal repetition of existence, or whether [we believe man is caught] in the cycle of historical calamities; and, whether [we might think] history is moved by history itself, or by our sensual drives, or by the mode of production, or by superhuman individuals, what is certain is that only with the elixir of faith, which is [nothing but] the removing of new and old shackles from humans, can we be emancipated from the eternal circle [of existence] and the determinism of history and arrive in the open space of freedom and liberation. In the same way, it is only with the life-confirming breath of freedom that [humans can] choose spirituality and faith.[39]

Yet, freedom, Khatami pointes out, should not be considered a mere philosophical category and political slogan: "Freedom means the freedom to oppose." The state has the duty to provide the conditions for its opponents to have the freedom to express their opposition peacefully.[40]

Nevertheless, freedom, Khatami argues, has certain limits and boundaries. The law sets the limits on freedom. In an Islamic state, no one has the freedom to say anything he or she pleases; no other state allows such a freedom. In an Islamic state:

> the limit of freedom of speech is the disruption of the foundations of Islam and contravention of public rights. Within these limits, everybody is free to express their views. And we should not be parsimonious; [we should not] define the foundations of Islam so narrowly that it only agrees with our own taste and anyone who opposes our taste, would be accused of opposing the fundamentals of Islam.[41]

To protect Islam and maintain freedom, while preventing freedom from turning into chaos, Khatami argues, it is necessary to demonstrate the compatibility of Islam and freedom. It is impossible, according to Khatami, to set Islam in contrast to freedom in

37. Mohammad Khatami, *Mardomsalari* (Democracy) (Tehran: Tarh-e Nou, 2001), 99.
38. *Gozideh Sokhanraniha-ye Rai'is Jomhur,* 117–18.
39. *Hezareh Goftogu va Tafahom,* 52.
40. *Gozideh Sokhanraniha-ye Rai'is Jomhur,* 120.
41. *Islam, Rohaniyat va Enqelab-e Islami,* 143.

the contemporary world. If Islam is placed in opposition to freedom, "Islam would be vanquished."[42]

Most important for Khatami, given his tendency to underline the intellectual and cultural dimensions of life, which is grounded in turn in his cosmology, is freedom of thought. Humans' advantage over animals is their ability to think, and thought is nothing but generating questions and making the effort to answer them.[43] To question is the right of every citizen. One can never force people with a mind, especially young people, not to ask questions, as one cannot "command a hungry person not to be hungry."[44] "There are no forbidden zones," Khatami told a group of teachers, when it comes to "inquiry, whether it is in regard to dogmas, customs and culture or in regard to social affairs or natural and physical issues. Similarly, one can question whether or not atom exists; or whether there is a God or not; or whether God possesses certain attributes or He does not."[45] In fact, Khatami argues, a civilization which cannot question freely has "no thought" and therefore is doomed to be subjugated by others.[46]

This attitude leads Khatami to broach the idea of reflexivity in culture. A culture that is unable to reflect upon itself and takes all of its past as sacred and therefore not amenable to questioning, is a stagnant culture whose soul is dead.[47] One cannot claim that whatever has the color of one's culture is sacred and has to be maintained at any cost, or that anything that comes from outside has no value. Our understanding of the world, social relations, institutions and customs are human affairs, and as such it is possible that they are partly wrong or belong to a bygone time. Only a culture that constantly critiques and purifies itself can develop and stay alive.[48] We must know our past well, not to return to it and stagnate in it, which is the very essence of regression, but in order to understand the types of mentality and habits that are very much temporally and spatially relative and in order to conduct a rational critique of the past to find a foundation for the dignity of our today and a future that is even more glorious than our past.[49]

Freedom of thought in Khatami's discourse also entails the notion of pluralism in a society that has not so far genuinely embraced the idea that multiple sets of beliefs and practices could be legitimate simultaneously. When a state is genuinely powerful, Khatami argues, it accepts that in a human society, "there are differences of opinion." God has "created humans different [...] Those who wish to homogenize society, especially with directives and from above, are moving in a direction opposed to the course [intended by]

42. *Mardomsalari*, 72.
43. *Gozideh Sokhanraniha-ye Rai'is Jomhur*, 134.
44. *Zanan va Javanan*, 105.
45. *Zanan va Javanan*, 103.
46. *Islam, Rohaniyat va Enqelab-e Islami*, 22.
47. *Zanan va Javanan*, 106.
48. *Zanan va Javanan*, 118–19. It is interesting to note that Jürgen Habermas thinks it is only in the conditions of modernity that cultures can be reflexive and critique themselves and their mores. See, for example: Habermas, *The Theory of Communicative Action. Vol.1. Reason and the Rationalization of the Society* (Boston: Beacon Press, 1981), 52.
49. *Islam, Rohaniyat va Enqelab-e Islami*, 23.

creation."[50] Because humans possess thought and the instrument of thought is logic, we should use logic in our dialogues with people who may have different worldviews.[51] This frame of mind allows Khatami to propose a level of tolerance toward different and unorthodox ideas and practices hitherto not exhibited by the Islamic establishment in Iran.

In the social world, Khatami seems to insist, freedom needs to be concretized as a right, and for this reason he pays a considerable degree of attention to the idea of rights and social participation.

People's Rights to Participate

One of the major differences between the modern and premodern world, in Khatami's estimation, is that today humans are deemed to be bearers of rights, whereas in the past people were construed to be carriers of obligations and duties.[52] The most salient feature of tyranny is that people living in such a system are presumed to be merely "duty-bound" (*mukalaf*) to be ruled over, and not right-bearing citizens.[53] Imam Ali, Khatami emphasizes, taught that both the people and the state have certain rights. As soon as it is admitted that people possess rights, it means that the state is accountable to the people, because people's rights and state's accountability are mutually complementary.[54] In an Islamic state, Khatami avers, the rulers are accountable to God and the people at the same time.[55]

It is significant that Khatami, at least in his discourse, attempts to expand these rights, approaching a universality of sorts. In Ayatollah Khomeini's thought, Khatami contends, "the forgotten, unrecognized and trampled rights of man are revived. This means that in [the] Imam's movement, despite its religious nature, man [is presumed to] possess the right to determine his own destiny, [and he is] not a mere duty-bound person [*mukalaf*] who receives commands from above to obey. The Imam believed in the rights of humans to determine their fate and participate in [the social and political aspects of] life. The other significance of this point is that this right is to be universalized, that is, the right to participate in determining one's life does not belong only to a segment of the population, i.e., the men, but it belongs to the public, men and women."[56]

Khatami is one of the few officials of the Islamic Republic to pronounce formally that rights of citizenship should be expanded to non-Muslims, even though it is not clear whether all non-Muslims, such as the persecuted Baha'is, would receive them and whether non-Muslims would enjoy exactly the same rights as Muslims. He writes:

50. *Gozideh Sokhanraniha-ye Rai'is Jomhur,* 60.
51. *Islam, Rohaniyat va Enqelab-e Islami,* 101.
52. *Gozideh Sokhanraniha-ye Rai'is Jomhur,* 85.
53. *Gozideh Sokhanraniha-ye Rai'is Jomhur,* 86.
54. *Gozideh Sokhanraniha-ye Rai'is Jomhur,* 87.
55. *Islam, Rohaniyat va Enqelab-e Islami,* 51.
56. *Hezareh Goftogu va Tafahom,* 177–78.

> In fact our judicial system protects the rights of the believer as well as the person who lives in [our] society. The believer has exalted rights, but every citizen who lives in the Islamic Republic, even though he may not be a Muslim, or even be a sinner [*fasiq*], possesses certain rights which the Islamic State is obligated to realize. This means that we are not only responsible to realize the rights of the believers and religious people. Every person who has accepted this state and lives by [the rules of] this state, as a citizen, possesses rights; even, if these rights [of non-believers] are trampled by a believer, [the state] would confront the believer.[57]

Khatami has specifically addressed the question of the rights of women. "Women," says Khatami, "have always been oppressed in history. We have always said that the Islamic revolution has liberated women from their oppression, yet we believe that women in Islamic and non-Islamic countries are suffering from a historical form of oppression. Indeed, whenever there is a discussion of rights, it has mostly addressed the rights of husbands or men over women [...] We have witnessed that even the *fiqhi* [Islamic jurisprudential] rights have not been observed in many families. I believe that even the rights granted [to women] by *fiqih* [Islamic jurisprudence] were not just, taking into account the temporal and spatial factors."[58] On numerous occasions Khatami has proposed to establish institutions such as political parties, trade unions and associations to realize the rights of citizens, even though, as we will see later, his success in practice has been severely limited.[59]

Since the advent of Islamic revolution in Iran, the notion of people's participation in the political and social affairs of the country has been promoted by many revolutionaries and state actors. The logic of revolution and eight years of mobilization for war required the wide-spread participation of the populace in the political and to some extent social life of the country. Khatami's own discourse similarly posits the idea of participation as a necessary accompaniment of rights of citizenship, but with certain twists that make it distinct from the ideas of his revolutionary predecessors. As he put it, "[t]he heartfelt presence of all segments of the population in the [political] sphere [*sahneh*] paved the way for Iran to become independent and proud. [...] The secret of human progress lies in trial and error. What is important is that the people themselves should be present in the [social and political] spheres."[60] One of the distinguishing features of Khatami's ideas on social participation is his emphasis on a reduced role for the state in economic and cultural spheres. Iranian history and social conditions, Khatami contends, have not been encouraging Iranians to participate in their social affairs. The government should endeavor to guarantee people's participation in their social affairs. The more people

57. *Gozideh Sokhanraniha-ye Rai'is Jomhur*, 280. On different occasions Khatami has mentioned the rights of three religious minorities, Zoroastrians, Christians and Jews. He doesn't seem to have mentioned the Baha'is specifically, who constitute the largest religious minority in Iran and who have been most severely persecuted since 1979.

58. *Gozideh sokhanraniha-ye rai'is jomhur dar bareh-ye tose'h-ye siyasi, tose'eh eqtesadi va amniyat*, 83.

59. Given the expectations that Khatami and his cohorts aroused among the populace, even their limited success in certain practical spheres appears as a failure to many of those who had hoped for reforms in real life.

60. *Gozideh Sokhanraniha-ye Rai'is Jomhur*, 40.

participate in their own affairs, the more the government's burden is reduced, allowing it to focus on essential issues such as education, health and providing security.[61]

The implications of this frame of mind for the economic sphere are also very significant. In order for the people to truly participate in the economic affairs of their country, the government should drastically reduce its vast role in the state monopolies that were created in the aftermath of 1979 revolution.[62] This means that the private sector must become more active and productivity and investment must be considered a positive value.[63] The government employees must also be encouraged to participate in the running of the state organizations.[64] Moreover, Khatami argues, another way to promote people's participation in their own economic activities is the expansion of the cooperatives.[65]

The "Paradox" of Women's Participation in the Public Sphere

Another distinct characteristic of Khatami's thought on social participation is that he devotes considerable attention to the issue of women's participation in an Islamic society. His thoughts on women's participation are informed by his ideas about women:

> In order to have a better future, the women of our society should abandon the notion that woman is the second sex and man the first sex and superior. Of course, woman is woman and man is man and any attempt to ignore the differences between them is an injustice to women, men and to society. Women and men are different, but woman is not the second sex and man is not the superior sex. They are both the parts of the same humanity; each occupies her or his own particular position [in society] and both are dignified humans. We desire a proud society and only proud women and men can guarantee such a society. In the past it was presumed that men were superior to women in creation and that religion had endorsed this [alleged superiority]. It was because of this erroneous view that women, men and society were all oppressed.[66]

In order for women to realize their human potential, Khatami argues, they need to increase their presence in the public sphere and become active in determining their own personal and social affairs. However, Khatami believes there is "an apparent contradiction," and "a paradox" in women's participation in the public sphere. On the one hand, asserts Khatami, human character develops in interactions with others and human rational and emotional faculties and skills grow as a result of intense social relations found chiefly in the public sphere. On the other hand, "God has placed woman

61. *Islam, Rohaniyat va Enqelab-e Islami,* 127–28.
62. *Gozideh Sokhanraniha-ye Rai'is Jomhur,* 224.
63. *Gozideh Sokhanraniha-ye Rai'is Jomhur,* 224. This is in sharp contrast to the statist policies pursued by the Islamic Republic in the first decade and half of its existence.
64. *Gozideh Sokhanraniha-ye Rai'is Jomhur,* 102–3.
65. *Gozideh Sokhanraniha-ye Rai'is Jomhur,* 224–25. The cooperatives were envisioned in the constitution of the Islamic Republic to work side by side with the public and the private sectors, but have not developed anywhere near as the state-managed segment of the economy.
66. *Zanan va Javanan,* 21.

in a special position because of her outstanding role in the fate of mankind and society, making her ahead of man [...] [that is] the woman is the mother and the merciful God has endowed her with certain natural characteristics making her the pivot and center of the family."[67] In other words, Khatami maintains:

> The paradox consists of the question whether accepting the central role of woman in the family means that she would be marginalized, and that being distant from the public sphere denies her development? [Secondly] does her presence in the public sphere and enjoying equal social opportunities and her consequent development entail that she would be deprived from a healthy and strong family? I think today our central question about women is to reflect upon this paradox and find an appropriate solution for it. How can we have women in the public sphere without the disintegration of the family?[68]

Khatami never provides a satisfactory solution to the "paradox" he broaches. The only partial solution that he seems to propose is that for women who choose not to have a career outside the home, to get involved in associations of various sorts such as artistic, technical, social, scientific, athletic and religious organizations where they may be able to develop their own agency and subjectivity.[69]

State Controlled by the People

The obverse side of the notion of popular participation in Khatami's discourse is the idea that state ought to be under the people's control and that the state officials ought to be their servants. In one of his early addresses to the members of his campaign team after his first election to the presidency, Khatami reminded his audience that the Majlis and government ought to be under people's supervision. The society is protected, he advised his supporters, only if people's participation in the social and political affairs is uninterrupted, organized and appropriately channeled. This, in turn, is possible only if civil institutions are formed to ensure people's right to determine their fate.[70] In a similar vein, the reason why state officials deserve respect is not because they are superior to the people, but because they have been elected by the people. It is the people's vote that creates legitimacy for the state and state actors.[71]

Khatami's ideas about the state and its mode of legitimation are very much informed by the paradigm of mediated subjectivity discussed in this volume. Khatami believes that there are different types of democracies, supported by different types of philosophical foundations, and an Islamic democracy is differently grounded than Western democracies:

> Of course democratic systems do not have one form and shape; [it is not true] that what has appeared in the West will certainly appear in other types of society. [Different] societies

67. *Zanan va Javanan*, 32–33.
68. *Zanan va Javanan*, 32–33.
69. *Zanan va Javanan*, 38.
70. *Gozideh Sokhanraniha-ye Rai'is Jomhur*, 43–44.
71. *Gozideh Sokhanraniha-ye Rai'is Jomhur*, 38.

> have desires, identities, predispositions, and beliefs of their own. In an Islamic society the characteristics of a democratic system are in some respects different from the democratic systems in other parts of the world. The essence [of democracy] is that power belongs to the people. [The question is] whether this power directly belongs to the people; that is, whether the only source of political and social power are the people, or whether the source of power and sovereignty is God and He has delegated sovereignty to the people. [The latter] is the Islamic version [of democracy], which was recognized in our revolution, stated in our constitution, emphasized by the Imam [i.e., Ayatollah Khomeini], and approved by the supreme leader [i.e., Ayatollah Khamenei].[72]

The paradigm of mediated subjectivity, or in this case mediated sovereignty, is very much prone to precariousness and subject to vacillations that can both affirm and negate human subjectivity and sovereignty at the same time.[73] As if Khatami were aware of this possibility, he attempts to make this conceptualization of people's sovereignty more stable by insisting that God's sovereignty and people's sovereignty are not opposed and one does not deny the other: "In [the] Imam's view [i.e., Ayatollah Khomeini's view], the people, the ordinary people, and God are not opposed to one another. People do not impinge upon God's turf. [Ayatollah Khomeini] is not concerned that if people gain sovereignty and participate in the [sociopolitical] sphere, God would be harmed. [...] People's sovereignty is not contrary to God's absolute sovereignty over people and universe."[74] This type of conditional humanism finds a particular articulation in Khatami's discourse that views humans at its center.

---

72. *Gozideh Sokhanraniha-ye Rai'is Jomhur*, 44–45. In close proximity to grounding people's sovereignty in the paradigm of mediated subjectivity as the indirect path toward human empowerment, Khatami attempts to base the notion of freedom on a particular interpretation of the concept of monotheism or *tawhid.* Khatami has proposed that human autonomy and freedom can be deducted from the concept of monotheism because, in one sense, monotheism is submission to God and defiance of whatever is non-God. In Khatami's words, "The [type of] society that Islam desires has two characteristics: 1) belief in the oneness of God [monotheism]; and 2) social autonomy. If we analyze the concept of monotheism [*tawhid*] then [we find that] the notion of autonomy is embedded in it. Refusal to capitulate to tyrants, oppressors and infidels can be deduced from the notion of monotheism, because monotheism is not merely a belief in oneness of God. Immanent in the idea of monotheism are notions of autonomy, freedom, progress, construction, and the creation of the conditions for the growth of all humans and justice. [...] By negating reliance on oppressors, Monotheism confers autonomy to human character." See, Khatami, *Islam, Rohaniyat va Enqelab-e Islami*, 81. Khatami has expressed the same idea somewhat differently elsewhere: "The essence of freedom consists in the ability to be liberated from whatever is less than, or equal to, the self. This is not possible except by submission to the Absolute Truth. . Human station necessitates that only God rules over man." Mohammad Khatami, *Ehyagar-e Haqiqat-e Din: Majmo'eh Maqalat* (The Reviver of the Truth of Religion: Collection of Essays), (Tehran: Zekr, 2001), 141–42.
73. For a discussion of the precariousness and the simultaneous affirmation and negation of human agency that is peculiar to the paradigm of mediated subjectivity see, Farzin Vahdat, *God and Juggernaut.*
74. *Ehyagar-e Haqiqat-e Din*, 173.

Humans as the Focal Point of Development

In the first decade after the victory of the Islamic Revolution, Iranian society lost much of its economic vitality primarily due to the devastation of eight years of war with Iraq and the mismanagement of the economy by the theocratic regime. After the end of the eight-year war with Iraq in 1988, Iranians expressed the desire for development, and the regime's elites attempted to address this need both on the theoretical and practical levels, without much success at the practical level. On numerous occasions, Khatami has thematized a notion of development that he characterizes as "human-centered." It is significant that, in conformity with his conditional humanism, Khatami defines development in anthropocentric terms: "I do not think anybody would not concur that the focal point [*mehvar*; Arabic, *mihwar*, literally meaning "axis"] of a comprehensive development is man. It is man who creates development and moves it forward, and enjoys its fruits."[75] In a speech at the Congress of the National Association of Parents and Teachers, Khatami urged that development is not a one-way process, allowing the teachers to ignore the desires and judgments of young people, because as humans they are at the center of the process of development.[76] In "Islam and the Qur'an," Khatami argues, "the central topic is man." God sent the prophets so that man may develop.[77]

Khatami's approach to the notion of development leads him to underline the political and cultural aspects of development more than the economic and technological dimensions. Development, Khatami insists, should not be reduced to economic aspects. Since we assume that human kind is at the center of development, the political/cultural dimensions become essential to growth: "[if] society is developed politically and culturally, man, with his creativity, can generate a dynamic economy and power and security. I believe that without political growth, development is incomplete and unsuccessful. That means that without political development, we cannot even grow in the economic sphere.[78]

The subjectivity that Khatami derives from the paradigm of mediated subjectivity allows him to envision a system of international relations that articulates the desire of subaltern nations to be considered as agents on par with powerful nations. Responding to Samuel Huntington's controversial idea of "clash of civilizations," Khatami has proposed the notion of "dialogue of civilization."[79] For this reason, he criticized the imperialist nations for treating subaltern nations as objects:

> The dialogue of civilizations is founded upon the [idea that] the two sides of dialogue would accept the reality of each other, and upon give and take. Dialogue of civilizations means that dialogue would replace monologue. For four centuries only one voice has been heard around

---

75. *Gozideh Sokhanraniha-ye Rai'is*, 53.
76. *Zanan va Javanan*, 48–49.
77. *Zanan va Javanan*, 48.
78. *Gozideh Sokhanraniha-ye Rai'is*, 129.
79. In 1998 the General Assembly of the United Nations declared the year 2001 as the "United Nations Year of Dialogue among Nations."

> the world; a voice that subalterns should hear and accept. Conflict and warfare are inherent in this [type of] relationship. Humans are not objects, but regrettably one of the weak points of the modern civilization is that it considers itself the pivot and center of the universe and treats the Other as an object [to be] appropriated. They [the imperialists] treat the East or Islam as a historical object to be known; [they treat the East and Islam as] an "entity" that today is a historical and museum object at their disposal.[80]

This analysis leads Khatami to the exploration of the dark side of modernity. The reverse side of the process of the empowerment of the subject as the self is the disempowerment of the other and domination.[81] In a speech to a group of Italian academics at the European University at Florence, Khatami analyzed Western imperialism in terms of the dual nature of modernity. The modern attitude of the domination of nature, Khatami argues, plagued human societies also. What later became known as imperialism, Khatami argues, was the result of the extension of the hegemonic approach toward nature imbedded in natural and human sciences. For this reason, one cannot study modernity without taking into account the human and moral side of the issue.[82]

Yet, Khatami does not reduce modernity and the Western experience to its hegemonic dimension. In a speech addressing a group of German intellectuals, Khatami recognizes that some Western epistemologies have distinguished between the hegemonic attitude prevalent in natural sciences which is based on subject-object relationships on the one hand, and human sciences based on intersubjectivity on the other.[83] There is no doubt, Khatami emphasizes, that Western modernity has given rise to much-valued democracy; yet, the achievements of democracy and world peace can only be preserved when international relations are based on intersubjective relations and democratic relations among nations can become a reality.[84]

So far I have tried to analyze Khatami's discourse in the context of Iran's post-revolutionary religious attempts to accommodate the forces of modernity. In the concluding section I will briefly discuss the more practical aspects of Khatami's presidency in light of above analysis.

80. Muhammad Khatami, *Goftogu-ye Tamdon-ha* (Dialogue of Civilizations). (Tehran: Tarh-e Nou, 2001), 97–98.

81. One of the most forceful critiques of the dominatory and dark side of the modern world remains *Dialectic of Enlightenment* by Theodor Adorno and Max Horkheimer.

82. Babak Dad (ed.), *Khatami dar Italia 99: Yaddasht-haye Safar Ra'is Jomhur be Uropa be Hamrah Matn Kamel du Sokhanrani va yek Mosahebeh* (Khatami in Italy 99: notes on the President's trip to Europe with the full texts of two lectures and an interview), (Sazman-e Chap va Entesharat-e Vezarat-e Farhang va Ershad-e Islami, 1999), 82. It is interesting to note that despite his critique of the hegemonic aspect of subjectivity as the dark side of modernity, Khatami does not recognize that his own notion of *ezzat* as de facto modern subjectivity encompasses the same duality of emancipation and domination imbedded in modern human empowerment.

83. *Goftogu-ye Tamdon-ha,* 52.

84. *Khatami dar Italia,* 67 and 74.

Conclusion: Dilemmas and Failures of Khatami's Discourse and Practice

As a philosopher and a social thinker, Khatami's impact on Iranian social thought and therefore political culture seems to have been much more successful than the concrete achievements of his presidency in legal reform and constitutional politics. Yet, although his thought has created a new vocabulary in the political culture of Iran, the dilemmas that his discourse exhibits at the theoretical and practical levels are significant.

Despite his attempt to derive a genuine discourse of modern subjectivity from his interpretation of Islamic metaphysics as well as modern Western thought, in Khatami's thought the carrier and beneficiary of subjectivity is not the individual. Very much like his revolutionary intellectual forefather, Ali Shariati, Khatami has fulminated against the individual in his writings and speeches. In a typical critique of "Western liberalism," Khatami, like some other Islamic modernists in Iran, equates individuality (*esalat-e fard*) with license and denounces it as capitulating to the appetites and desires of the individual:

> Of course there are serious critiques, theoretical as well as practical, that may be leveled at liberalism. Philosophically, the West considers the individual to be essential. When the material and worldly aspects of the individual become authentic, freedom becomes equivalent to the liberty of the desires, inclinations, and urges. [In modernity] the transcendental values of religion have been undermined. [Thus] it is natural that such a freedom is defective. The undesirable state that was produced for the family, morality and values in West, is the result of this understanding of freedom. Moreover, from the bosom of individuality, utilitarianism was derived and material interests became the foundation of social and interstate relations. But the West cannot be reduced to individualism [*fard grai'i*] and utilitarianism.[85]

Khatami's anti-individual stance is complemented by his tendency to emphasize collectivity. In a speech to the students of a technical college in Tehran shortly after his first election to the Presidency of Iran, Khatami warned the students that the individual should "view himself in the context of society. He should seek his good in the good of society; [the individual should] seek autonomy, freedom, progress, spirituality and justice in and for the society."[86] Khatami even attributes the roots of the hegemonic aspects of modern subjectivity to individualism: "it is natural that when individualism, which gives rise to utilitarianism, encounters the other, an attempt is made to negate the other and use him instrumentally."[87]

There is no doubt that modern individualism is responsible for many ills of contemporary world, and for this reason many social thinkers have attempted to reconcile the individual and society.[88] Yet, it is very difficult to think of citizenship rights and civil

---

85. Khatami, *Mardomsalari*, 28.
86. *Mardomsalari* , 110. To be sure, Khatami has rejected the notion of collectivism in some of his works also (see for example, *Khatami dar Italia*, 80). However, his harsh anti individual approach leaves no other possibility but a tendency toward at least a mild for of collectivism.
87. Khatami, *Hezareh Goftogu va Tafahom*, 71.
88. Hegel's attempt to bring about reconciliation between the individual and the collectivity in modernity remains one of the most inspiring. See G.W.F Hegel, *Hegel's Philosophy of Right*

society without the individual as the carrier of the rights and benefits of the modern world. Moreover, any understanding of subjectivity as one of the essential pillars of the modern world should grant the indispensability of the individual. Because subjectivity is founded upon thought and ultimately it is only the individual who is capable of thinking, it is impossible to envision subjectivity attributed to any other entity than the individual. Khatami's attempt to forge an Islamic notion of freedom of subjectivity while negating the individual as its carrier and beneficiary constitutes one of the core conundrums of Khatami's discourse, which has significant practical implications. The youth and women's movements in Iran have increasing (sometimes even excessive) tendencies toward prioritizing the individual, and an approach such as Khatami's will further alienate these very dynamic and demographically highly significant segments of the Iranian society.[89]

As we saw above, Khatami's discourse delineates a scheme for people's rule in a civil society where the state officials and actors are accountable to the people. However, one highly significant obstacle for the achievement of these goals is never fully discussed in Khatami's writings and speeches, namely the notion and institution of Guardianship of the Jurist (*velayat-e faqih*). According to the constitution of the Islamic Republic the Supreme Leader of the Republic is selected by an Assembly of Experts which is itself elected by the people. Once the Supreme Leader (i.e., the Guardian Jurist) is selected he receives vast powers such as delineation of the general policies of the state, supreme command of the armed forces, and declaration of war and peace. He also assumes the authority for the appointment, dismissal, and acceptance of resignation of the Jurists on the Guardian Council, the supreme judicial authority of the country, the head of the radio and television network, the chief of the joint staff, and the chief commander of the Islamic Revolution Guards Corps. While it is true that theoretically the Leader can be dismissed by the Assembly of Experts, the Leader's accountability to the people is minimal because of the indirect nature of the involvement of them in the entire process.

Khatami has chosen not address this issue in any detail. In fact in much of his discourse he has approved of the vast and unaccountable powers of the Guardian Jurist.[90] At most he has declared that discussion of the notion of Velayat Faqih is permissible, while opposing the principle would be tantamount to opposing the very foundation of the regime.[91] Such a neglect of the Achilles' heel of the Islamic state and the key to success of the reform movement has not remained unnoticed by Khatami's base and pro-reform forces.

Another great dilemma that has plagued Khatami's reform attempts originates in his notion of the law and his failure to discuss the prerequisites for adherence to the law. There is not doubt that for civil society to be viable, it is necessary to establish

---

(Oxford: Oxford University Press, 1967). See also two essays by Durkheim on the question of individuality and society: Emile Durkheim, "Individualism and the Intellectuals," in *Emile Durkheim on Morality and Society*, ed. Robert Bellah (Chicago: University of Chicago Press, 1973); and, Emile Durkheim, "The Dualism of Human Nature and its Social Conditions," in *Emile Durkheim on Morality and Society*, ed. Robert Bellah (Chicago: University of Chicago Press, 1973).

89. About sixty percent of Iran's population is under 30 years of age.

90. See for example, *Islam, Rohaniyat va Enqelab-e Islami*, 125 and 170.

91. Khatami, *Islam, Rohaniyat va Enqelab-e Islami*, 170.

the rule of the law and move within the legal parameters. However, when there are some inherently anti-democratic features built into the law, the insistence upon strict observance of the law contradicts the promise of civil society. This dilemma, it seems, has been at the core the disparities between the promises of Khatami's discourse and the failures to realize them.[92]

Yet, to speak of total failure is also inaccurate. During Khatami's two terms of in office, the dissemination of democratic ideas through the burgeoning of a freer press became widespread, and as a result of liberal policies toward book publications, many channels for the deepening of these ideas became available, despite the intense efforts of anti-democratic forces to suppress them. The impact of the people hearing their own voices demanding individual and citizenship rights cannot but have honed the desire for more democracy. The current political system in Iran is attempting to contain the rising tide of the demand for universal subjectivity and citizenship in various ways. What is often ignored, however, is that once a nation reaches the stage that Iranians have reached in terms of consciousness of their citizenship rights, as they voice the demand for more rights and their institutionalization, it would be very difficult, if not impossible, to reverse this trend.[93]

92. The examination of the failures of Khatami's practice in terms of the dilemmas depicted here should not be construed as a comprehensive analysis of his administration's shortcomings. There are many other factors involved. One important factor is Khatami's personal temperament. On several occasion he has described himself more as a scholar and a philosopher than a politician.

93. Since the end of Khatami's tenure as the President of Iran in 2005, the Green Movement that was formed in 2009 in response to the attempt by the conservative establishment in the Islamic Republic to suppress the democratic demands of large segments of Iranian society, very much corroborates the insights presented here.

Chapter Eight

SEYYED HOSSEIN NASR: AN ISLAMIC ROMANTIC?

Very few contemporary Islamic thinkers have exhibited such a paradoxical relation with the modern West as does Seyyed Hossein Nasr. In most of his works the notions, conditions and phenomena associated with the modern West have occupied a central position. In fact, one may say that his concerns with Islam and Islamic issues are secondary and in response to his intellectual and personal preoccupation with what he considers to be the disastrous conditions of the post-Renaissance world. Modern humans, in Nasr's view, having sold their souls, in the manner of Faust, to gain control over nature, are facing not only "ecocide" but ultimately suicide.[1] The solution to this predicament, Nasr has been arguing since he started his career in the 1960s, is what he often calls "traditional Islam," or more accurately a particular interpretation of Islamic heritage which he believes is not much different from other traditional outlooks such as Hinduism, Buddhism and traditional Native American religions.

As such, it is not surprising that Nasr's appeal has been geared more toward the Westerners and the westernized Muslims who have been either educated in the West or have had a high level of Western education and exposure to Western culture in their homelands. Ironically, Nasr believes that Westerners, having a first-hand experience of modernity, have developed a higher discernment of its "calamitous" rule to appreciate the message of Islam that he has extracted for them.[2] Accordingly, Nasr has set two primary goals for himself. First, it is from Eastern metaphysics, that is Nasr's reading of it, that the Westerners must relearn how to prevent the domination of nature from turning into self-destruction. Secondly, perceiving a great danger posed to the "citadel of Islam" by the modern world, Nasr has undertaken to shoulder the task of inoculating the Islamic world against the threat of modernity.

As a result, it would be a grave error to place Nasr in the category of contemporary Islamists, or what in popular parlance is often referred to as a fundamentalist, despite some of his fervent views on Islam as a total way of life. In fact, as Nasr himself has pointed out, the "revivalists," as he calls the contemporary Islamist thinkers and forces, have embraced certain aspects of modernity such as Western science and technology as

1. Nasr, Seyyed Hossein, *Islam and the Plight of Modern Man* (London: Longman, 1975), 4.
2. In his *Islam and the Plight of the Modern Man*, Nasr wrote: "It is this man —obliterated temporarily by the progressive and evolutionary theories of the past few centuries in the West—to whom tradition addresses itself and it is this inner man whom tradition seeks to liberate from the imprisonment of the ego and the suffocating influence of the purely externalized and forgetful aspect of man." (50).

well as different types of Western managerial skills and administrative institutions and outlooks, which come with the modern technology.[3] As such, contemporary Islamist movements, in Nasr's view, are a form of "reform opposed to traditional Islam," which in some instances, have combined with Islamic millenarian trends to create a form of utopianism which is very "alien to the integral Islamic tradition."[4]

As I will try to demonstrate below, Nasr's prolific, but often repetitious, discourse is a *Western* critique of the West itself in some of its most bitter and harshest forms dressed in an Islamic garb. Arguably, at the core of Nasr's discourse lies a one-dimensional criticism of the modern world that is inspired first and foremost by Traditionalism, a European discourse and movement inspired by Romantic attacks on modernity whose aim has been the rescission and reversal of the modern world.[5]

The Life of a Modern Anti-modern

Seyyed Hossain Nasr was born in Tehran in 1933 into a prominent family, some of whose members have played significant roles in the history of twentieth century Iran. His father side included men who were physicians of the court both during the late Qajar (1794–1925) period and during the first Pahlavi monarch.[6] His mother was the granddaughter of Sheikh Fazllolah Nuri (d. 1909), the archconservative high-ranking cleric who vehemently opposed the liberal constitutional movement of early 20th century in Iran, and who was executed after the anti-constitutionalists were defeated. Since early years of childhood Seyyed Hossein was exposed to classical Persian poets and thinkers, as well as ancient and modern European thought, using his father's large collection of books.[7] He attended a primary school near his home in Tehran, and in addition, at home studied not only subjects in Persian and Islamic topics but received tuition in French. At age 12, however, his family, apparently because they did not wish him to see the gradual demise of his father, who had been seriously injured in an accident, sent Seyyed Hossein to the United States to continue his education there.

According to Nasr himself, he received rigorous discipline from his father, while at the same time he seems to have had a close relationship with him and early intellectual

3. Seyyed Hossein Nasr, *A Young Muslim's Guide to the Modern World* (South Elgin, IL: Library of Islam, 1994), 126.
4. Nasr Seyyed Hossein, *Islamic Philosophy from Its Origin to the Present: Philosophy in the Land of Prophecy* (Albany: State University of New York Press, 2006), 270.
5. For a history of traditionalism and the role of Nasr in it, see: Mark Sedgwick, *Against the Modern World: Traditionalism and the Secret Intellectual History of the Twentieth Century* (Oxford: Oxford University Press, 2004).
6. Most of the information on Nasr's biography is taken from: Zailan Moris, "The Biography of Seyyed Hossein Nasr," in *Knowledge is Light: Essays in Islamic Studies Presented to Seyyed Hossein Nasr by his Students in Honor of his Sixty-Sixth Birthday*, ed. Zailan Moris., (ABC International Group, 1999); and from *Dar Jost-o Ju-ye Amr-e Qodsi: Gofto-Gu-ye Ramin Jahanbegloo ba Seyyed Hossein Nasr* (In search of the sacred: Ramin Jahanbegloo's conversation with Seyyed Hossein Nasr) (Tehran, Nashr-e Ney, 1386, 2007).
7. "The Biography of Seyyed Hossein Nasr," 10.

engagement with his father.[8] Nasr seems to have a close relationship with his mother also and says she played an important role in his early upbringing, but he did not like her modern ideas and feminist views and tendencies.[9] In this period Nasr seems to have become closely familiar with modern Western thought, as he read Shakespeare, Victor Hugo and both Alexandre Dumas père and fils, at an early age at home.[10]

On 7 December 1945, after a two-month journey from Iran, Nasr arrived in New York. He has related how this long and difficult journey has had a lasting impact on him and taught him to rely on no one except himself.[11] From 1945 to 1950, Nasr attended the Peddie School in Highstown, New Jersey and graduated from there as the valedictorian of his class. At Peddie, where he had to attend the services on Sundays, he became familiar with Protestant theology but was not interested in it. Later he noted that being a Muslim and attending Protestant services did not create any tensions in him.

In 1950 Nasr attended Massachusetts Institute of Technology (MIT), studying physics. In his sophomore year, however, Nasr became disillusioned with physics, because he came to the realization that it could not answer his metaphysical questions. He even entertained the idea of abandoning physics and leaving MIT and the United States. Yet, because of the discipline that his father had inculcated in him, he endured and finished MIT, but he took many courses in the humanities and philosophy. It is interesting that at MIT, Nasr continued to play American football, a sport that embodies the extreme of modern human's aggressiveness, which as we will shortly see, Nasr has denounced as the blight that is modernity. It was also at MIT that Nasr became familiar with the writings of René Guénon, one of the founders of the Traditionalist movement, which defined itself in terms of rejection and rebellion against modernity. Nasr has described his reading of Guénon in terms of an earthquake that shook everything for him, while finding in Guénon's teachings what he had been missing in life.[12] After this period Nasr gradually immersed himself thoroughly in the writings of other European Romantic opponents of modernity such as Titus Burckhardt, Marco Pallis, Martin Lings, and especially Frithjof Schuon. Schuon's work seems to have had a lasting influence on Nasr, who wrote of Schuon, "I believe this work to be the most outstanding ever written in a European language on why Muslims believe in Islam and why Islam offers to man all that he needs religiously and spiritually."[13]

Upon graduation from MIT, the same institution offered Nasr a scholarship for postgraduate studies, but instead he enrolled at Harvard and began studying geology and geophysics, receiving a Master's degree in 1956. He then enrolled in a PhD program at Harvard in the field of history of science. He wrote his dissertation, called *Conceptions of Nature in Islamic Thought*, which was published in 1964 under the title *An Introduction to Islamic Cosmological Doctrines* six years after he completed his PhD.

8. *Dar Jost-o Ju-ye Amr-e Qodsi*, 14.
9. *Dar Jost-o Ju-ye Amr-e Qodsi*, 19–20.
10. *Dar Jost-o Ju-ye Amr-e Qodsi*, 18.
11. *Dar Jost-o Ju-ye Amr-e Qodsi*, 47–48.
12. *Dar Jost-o Ju-ye Amr-e Qodsi*, 65.
13. Nasr, Seyyed Hossein. *Ideals and Realities of Islam* (Boston: Beacon Press, 1972), 10.

In 1958 Nasr returned to Iran to assume the position of Associate Professor of philosophy and the history of science at the University of Tehran at the age of 25. He became a full professor within five years at the same institution. In 1968, when he was only 35 years of age, Nasr became the Dean of Faculty at Tehran University, a position he occupied until 1972. In 1972, Mohammad Reza Shah appointed him as the President of Aryamehr University, which was established on the model of MIT to serve the grand technoscientific ambitions of the Shah. In 1973 Farah Pahlavi, the wife of the Shah, appointed Nasr as the head of Imperial Iranian Academy of Philosophy, which became a de facto center for the propagation of Traditionalist views and works.[14] In 1978 Nasr was appointed by Farah Pahlavi to be the head of her Special Bureau, a position that he kept until he chose exile in the aftermath of the 1979 Islamic Revolution in Iran.

After the revolution of 1979 Nasr has lived in the West, first briefly in Britain and then in the United States. Since 1984 Nasr has been at George Washington University in Washington D.C. as a professor of Islamic studies. Because of his close relations to the Pahlavis, Nasr has not been able to go back to Iran, but he has also refused to live in any other Islamic or non-modern country, despite the respect and welcome extended to him in some parts of the Islamic world. When asked why he preferred to live in the modern West, given his antimodern ideas and sensibilities, Nasr has responded that because of availability of positions and the better conditions for the dissemination of his ideas in the United States, he has opted not live in the Muslim world.[15]

Nasr's upbringing, his education and social connections, his disciplined and rigorous personality, his considerably large ego and ambitious personality are reflected in his impressive achievements. All are indicative of a modern person, replete with a sense of agency and subjectivity. But, ironically, he has utilized all these to declare war on modernity, without distinguishing between its positive and negative aspects.

Critique of Modernity

The primary feature of Nasr's critique of modernity relates to the idea that the devastation of the nature and natural environment is the direct effect of the renegade modern subject. The modern man has first reduced nature to "brute facts," and then perpetrated acts of "ferocious rape and plunder" against it, for which he is paying dearly now.[16] The environmental crisis that humanity faces, in the form of major oil spills, the burning of tropical forests, or the depletion of the ozone layer, are all the consequences of the aggressive attitude of modern people toward nature.[17] In fact the ferocious wars of the contemporary period, according to Nasr, are but an epiphenomenon of the belligerent attitude of modern people toward nature: "The official state of war is no more than an occasional outburst of an activity that goes on all the time within the soul of men, human society and towards nature. It is no more than a chimerical dream to

14. *Against the Modern World*, 155–56.
15. *Dar Jost-o Ju-ye Amr-e Qodsi*, 189–93.
16. *Islam and the Plight of Modern Man*, 19.
17. *Islam and the Plight of Modern Man*, 3.

expect to have peace based upon a state of intense war toward nature and disequilibrium with cosmic environment."[18]

The premodern Islamic attitude toward nature, Nasr argues, was very different from that of modern people. There is no doubt, according to Nasr, that Muslims pursued a vigorous science of nature with branches such as physics, astronomy and medicine in the medieval period. Yet, these inquiries into nature were in harmony with it and with the "total structure of the Universe."[19] In Islam, "[f]rom the bosom of nature man seeks to transcend nature and nature herself can be an aid in this process provided man can learn to contemplate it, not as an independent domain of reality but as a mirror reflecting a higher reality."[20] The root cause of all these problems, however, should be traced back to the profound changes that took place in the make up of modern humans, namely, "a pollution of the human soul which came into being the moment Western man decided to play the role of the Divinity upon the surface of the earth and chose to exclude the transcendent dimension from his life."[21]

This "pollution" of the human soul accomplished by the modern humanist sense of agency, therefore, is a main target of Nasr's diatribes to redeem the true essence of humanity. Thus, on numerous occasions Nasr has severely assailed the humanism that has characterized the post-Renaissance world in the West:

> This new [Renaissance] conception of an earth-bound man, which is closely tied to the humanism and anthropocentrism of this period, coincided with the destruction and gradual disappearance of what was left of the initiatic and esoteric organization of the Middle Ages.[22]

In a related vein, Nasr argues, the Copernican revolution did not by any means remove man from the center of the universe. This was merely an outward appearance. The real effect of the heliocentric worldview, despite its supplanting of the earth, the abode of man, for the sun as the center of universe, was the promotion of humanistic spirit because it was now the human reason that could determine the true order of things.[23] Similarly,

18. Seyyed Hossein Nasr, *Man and Nature: The Spiritual Crisis of Modern Man* (London: Unwin Paperbacks, 1976), 135. This view of nature expressed by Nasr is directly based upon Frithjof Schuon's (1907–1998) writings, one of the central figures of Traditionalism, whom Nasr quotes: "Utterly untouched nature has of itself the character of a sanctuary and this is considered to be [so] by most nomadic and semi nomadic peoples, particularly the Red Indians [...] For Hindus the forest is the natural dwelling-place of sages and we meet with a similar valuation of the sacred aspect of nature in all traditions which have even indirectly, a primordial and mythical character." (Frithjof Schuon, *Spiritual Perspectives and Human Facts* (London: Faber and Faber, 1954), 46; quoted in Seyyed Hossein Nasr, *Sufi Essays* (London: George Allen and Unwin, 1972), 152.)
19. *Islam and the Plight of Modern Man*, 147.
20. *Man and Nature*, 95. It is noteworthy that here, as in many other occasions as we will see below, Nasr cannot ignore the proto-subjectivist metaphysics of Islam which is largely based on human ascendancy over nature.
21. *Islam and the Plight of Modern Man*, 12.
22. *Man and Nature*, 64.
23. *Man and Nature*, 67–68.

Descartes, in Nasr's reading, created modern humanism by building his anthropocentric philosophy on the foundations of the Christian humanists of the late medieval period and the Renaissance, such as Petrarch, Gerhard Groot, Erasamus, Telesio, Campanella and Adriano di Corento.[24] The end result of this process of unfolding humanism has been the "total alienation of man from his natural environment," which combined with a theory of action as a violent realization "of human agency with the aim of indiscriminately raping and plundering nature."[25]

Interestingly, in his account of the process of the appearance of humanism, Nasr attempts to deflect attention from its roots in monotheistic metaphysics:

> Modern man [...] turns his gaze to the Book of Genesis and the rest of the Bible as the source of the crisis [engulfing the environment] rather than looking upon the gradual de-sacrilization of the cosmos, which took place in the West and especially the rationalism and humanism of the Renaissance which made possible the Scientific Revolution and the creation of a science whose function, according to Francis Bacon [...] was to gain power over nature, dominating her and forcing her to reveal her secrets not for the glory of God but for the sake of gaining worldly power and wealth.[26]

Totally ignoring the roots of human subjectivity in monotheistic ontology, Nasr leaps to the Renaissance as the starting point of the human wish for the domination over nature:

> With the Renaissance, European man lost the paradise of the age of faith to gain in compensation the new earth of nature and natural forms to which he now turned his attention. Yet it was a nature, which came to be less and less a reflection of a celestial reality. Renaissance man ceased to be the ambivalent man of the Middle Ages, half angel, half man, torn between heaven and earth. Rather he became wholly man, but now a totally earth-bound creature. He gained his liberty at the expense of losing the freedom to transcend his terrestrial limitations.[27]

With this leap to the Renaissance, ignoring the roots of human subjectivity in monotheistic religions, Nasr distorts the long and tortuous process of the development of human subjectivity and modernity for his own ideological purposes. Yet, at times, Nasr could not gloss over the forces of Christian metaphysics in its drive toward human agency and anthropocentrism that paved the way for the arrival of the modern world.

24. *Man and Nature*, 69.
25. *Islam and the Plight of Modern Man*, 75.
26. *Man and Nature*, 6. Nasr conveniently omits any references to Genesis 1.26, that at the outset of the text lays the foundation of human subjectivity and sovereignty over nature: "And God said, 'Let us make man in our own image, after our likeness, and let them have dominion over the fish of the sea, and over the birds of air, and over the cattle, and over all the earth, and over every creeping thing that creeps upon the earth. So God created man in his own image, in the image of God he created him; male and female he created them. And God blessed them, and God said to them, 'Be fruitful and multiply, and fill the earth and subdue it; and have dominion over the fish of the sea and over the birds of the air and over every living thing that moves upon the earth.'"
27. *Man and Nature*, 64.

For this reason, Nasr occasionally laments the proto-humanism of medieval Christian thought: "It [Christian theology] succeeded [...] in creating both an artisanal tradition that could construct the medieval cathedrals which are a microcosmic model of the Christian cosmos, and a total science of the visible universe which depicted this universe as a Christian one. *When man stands in a medieval Cathedral he feels himself at the center of the world* [...] [Christian theology] is too rationalistic and man oriented to be concerned with the spiritual essence and symbolism of cosmic phenomenon, unless we understand by theology the apophatic and contemplative theology which is more metaphysical than rationalistic and philosophical."[28]

It is in Protestantism, however, that Nasr finds the most hideous representation of modernity. As a result of the Protestant revolution, the Christianity of Jesus, who owned only a shirt, became a religion of acquiring riches and domination over nature. This form of modern religiosity, in Nasr's view, is most perfectly manifested in American Evangelicalism that was also followed by the Catholics later. In fact he posits a direct causal relation between religious worldviews, their emphases on human agency and relative poverty in certain parts of the world such as the southern Europe compared to northern Europe.[29] Based on this view, the modern conceptualization of human beings, Nasr maintains, is totally opposed to Islamic envisioning of what it means to be a human:

> The Homo Islamicus is innately aware of the fact that his or her consciousness does not have an external, material cause but that it comes from God [...] Obviously such a conception of humanity differs profoundly from that envisioned in most schools of contemporary philosophy and in modern thought, which sees human beings as beings who are purely earthly creatures of nature, masters of nature, but responsible to no one but themselves. No amount of wishy-washy apologetics can harmonize the two different conceptions of being human. The Islamic conception of man removes the possibility of a Promethean revolt against Heaven and brings God into the minutest aspect of human life. Its effect is therefore the creation of a civilization, an art, a philosophy and a whole manner of thinking and seeing things that is completely non-anthropocentric but theocentric and that stands opposed to anthropocentrism, which is such a salient feature of modernism as well as postmodernism.[30]

Thus in Nasr's view modernity is nothing but replacing God's sovereignty with that of humans, which in turn is based upon rationalism, empiricism, this-worldliness and anthropocentrism.[31] His negative views on humanism have led Nasr to vituperate against even human rights, which he dubs as the tragic outcome of modern anthropocentrism: "Today, this forest is destroyed because of man's rights; that sea is polluted because of man's supposed needs. Man is made absolute, his 'rights' dominating over both God's

28. *Man and Nature*, 58–60. Emphasis added.
29. Nasr, Seyyed Hossein and Jahanbegloo, Ramin. *Dar Just-u Ju ye Amr-e Qudsi: Guft-u Gu-ye Ramin Jahanbegloo ba Seyyed Hussein Naṣr* [In search of the Sacred: Ramin Jahanbegloo's conversation with Seyyed Hussein Nasr. Theran: Nashr-e Ney, 1386 (2007)], 251–52.
30. *Islamic Philosophy from Its Origin to the Present*, 266.
31. *Dar Just-u Ju-ye Amr-e Qudsi*, 298.

rights and the rights of His Creation."[32] In order to better understand Nasr's discourse we need to delve further into his views on human beings.

On Being Human

To be a human in Nasr's discourse is a tension-ridden proposition. On the one hand he cannot deny the prevalent Islamic emphasis on human subjectivity that is contingent upon God's subjectivity. On the other hand, Nasr attempts to utilize all his rhetorical skills to debunk any notion of human subjectivity and agency. Thus, in *Islam and the Plight of Modern Man*, he wrote: "In the traditional Islamic view, absolute freedom belongs to God alone and man can gain freedom only to the extent that he becomes God-like. All the restrictions imposed upon his life by the Shariah or upon his art by the traditional canons are seen not as restrictions upon his freedom but as the indispensable aid which alone makes the attainment of real freedom possible."[33] As this passage demonstrates, Nasr is forced to acknowledge the contingent form of human agency that is firmly established in Islamic metaphysics. Neither can he deny the notion of human free will that is often, but not always, posited in the Qur'an. It is true, Nasr believes, that God is "at once the Origin and End of all things and His majesty causes all that is beside Him to melt into nothingness," yet this same God has endowed humans with free will to pursue their own lives and to choose the "right path" of their own accord, without any external compulsion.[34] In fact, "the secret of man's life lies between these two logically contradictory assertions of the absolute omnipotence of Allah and of man's free will and responsibility before Him as the Supreme Judge."[35] At one point Nasr even explicitly acknowledged the notion of human subjectivity that is contingent upon that of God:

> God created man "upon His own image" (*ṣurah*) by virtue of which he has this theomorphic nature that so many men ignore although it exists within them. As a result of possessing this nature, man is given certain qualities which, in their fullness, belong to God alone. God is Alive (*hayy*), therefore man is given life. He has Will, therefore man is given free will, and He has the Quality of Speech or the Word (*kalimah*), so that man is given the power of speech. The Tariqah [the Sufi path] bases its technique on those very Divine Qualities which are reflected in man but which, in their perfection, belong to God alone.[36]

32. *Man and Nature*, 6.
33. *Islam and the Plight of Modern Man*, 21.
34. *Islam and the Plight of Modern Man*, 105.
35. *Islam and the Plight of Modern Man*, 105–6.
36. *Ideals and Realities of Islam*, 141. It is very interesting to note that early in his career Nasr became quite familiar with Islamic metaphysics, especially its core, the notion of elevation and empowerment of humans as God's vicegerent or Khalifa on earth. Thus in one of his earliest works which was based on his doctoral dissertation, Nasr summarized Al-Biruni's human ontology as follows: "Man, the caliph of God on earth, who is given all these gifts and above all is endowed with intelligence, is put here on earth in order to administer to all creatures as a caliph rules over his realm. It is for man to use sight to see "the signs of God in the horizon," and to use his reason in order to journey from the company of creatures to that of the Creator. Only in this way does he realize his noble nature and purpose for which he was created." (Nasr,

Yet, most of Nasr's effort in his career has been focused on diminishing the notion of human empowerment and agency by interpreting the very Qur'anic notions that support human subjectivity as well as those found in Islamic philosophy and the Sufi tradition, away from human agency. One highly significant aspect of this effort is the attempt to interpret the Qur'anic verses that deal with humans as God's vicegerent or successor on earth (Qur'an 2: 30–34) in a manner that would diminish the idea of human agency. Thus he interpreted the notion of being God's successor of earth, as a mere "protector" of the natural order, which is very far from the spirit of the Qur'an in which there are at least thirteen verses that God makes all of nature *subservient* (Arabic root *sakhr*) to humans.[37] Similarly, although Nasr has, on several occasions, referred to the notion of

---

Seyyed Hussein. *Introduction to Islamic Cosmological Doctrines: Concepts of Nature and Methods used for its Study by the Ikhwan Al-Safa, Al-Biruni, and Ibn Sina* (Cambridge, MA: Belknap Press of Harvard University Press, 1964), 150.) But, as we will see later, one of the main efforts of Nasr in his career has been to interpret this type of metaphysics in a manner that minimizes the notion of human empowerment and agency.

37. See the following verses:

[2.29] He it is Who created for you all that is in the earth, and He directed Himself to the heaven, so He made them complete seven heavens, and He knows all things.

[13.2] Allah is He Who raised the heavens without any pillars that you see, and He is firm in power and He made the sun and the moon subservient (to you); each one pursues its course to an appointed time; He regulates the affair, making clear the signs that you may be certain of meeting your Lord.

[14.32] Allah is He Who created the heavens and the earth and sent down water from the clouds, then brought forth with it fruits as a sustenance for you, and He has made the ships subservient to you, that they might run their course in the sea by His command, and He has made the rivers subservient to you.

[14.33] And He has made subservient to you the sun and the moon pursuing their courses, and He has made subservient to you the night and the day.

[16.12] And He has made subservient for you the night and the day and the sun and the moon, and the stars are made subservient by His commandment; most surely there are signs in this for a people who ponder;

[16.14] And He it is Who has made the sea subservient that you may eat fresh flesh from it and bring forth from it ornaments which you wear, and you see the ships cleaving through it, and that you might seek of His bounty and that you may give thanks.

[22.36] And (as for) the camels, We have made them of the signs of the religion of Allah for you; for you therein is much good; therefore mention the name of Allah on them as they stand in a row, then when they fall down eat of them and feed the poor man who is contented and the beggar; thus have We made them subservient to you, that you may be grateful.

[22.37] There does not reach Allah their flesh nor their blood, but to Him is acceptable the guarding (against evil) on your part; thus has He made them subservient to you, that you may magnify Allah because He has guided you aright; and give good news to those who do good (to others).

[22.65] Do you not see that Allah has made subservient to you whatsoever is in the earth and the ships running in the sea by His command? And He withholds the heaven from falling on the earth except with His permission; most surely Allah is Compassionate, Merciful to men.

[31.20] Do you not see that Allah has made what is in the heavens and what is in the earth subservient to you, and made complete to you His favors outwardly and inwardly? And among men is he who disputes in respect of Allah though having no knowledge nor guidance, nor a book giving light.

humans having been created in the image of God, instead of reading this proposition as a form of human subjectivity, has tried to deflect the idea by saying that, "This well-know Hadith of the Holy Prophet which means 'God created man according to His form' must not [...] be understood in a an anthropomorphic sense."[38]

As such, Nasr sets out for himself the life-long task of diminishing the ontological status of human beings as much as possible, an undertaking which runs into major difficulties, to say the least, given the complexity of the issue in various Islamic epistemic domains such as the Qur'anic text, Islamic philosophy and the Sufi tradition.

Subverting the Subject

Given the partially positive attitude of the Islamic epistemic domains such as the Qur'an, *Kalam* (speculative theology), philosophy, and parts of Sufi tradition, toward human subjectivity, Nasr is forced to acknowledge it at times. Thus Nasr recognizes the core Qur'anic notion of centrality of human beings in the universe: "The purpose and aim of creation is in fact for God to come 'to know Himself through His most perfect instrument of knowledge that is the Universal Man. Man therefore occupies a particular position in this world. He is the axis and center of the cosmic milieu, at once the master and custodian of nature. By being taught the names of all things he gains dominion over them.'" Having said this, Nasr immediately adds that, "but he is given this power only because he is the vicegerent (*khalifa*) of God on earth and the instrument of His Will."[39] In much of his writing, Nasr equates God's power with the lack of power of every other entity, a ploy that is meant to diminish the agency of human beings. Thus, Islamic cosmology, in Nasr's view, "is a world view based on the supremacy of the blinding reality

[31.29] Do you not see that Allah makes the night to enter into the day, and He makes the day to enter into the night, and He has made the sun and the moon subservient (to you); each pursues its course till an appointed time; and that Allah is Aware of what you do?
45.12] Allah is He Who made subservient to you the sea that the ships may run therein by His command, and that you may seek of His grace, and that you may give thanks.
[45.13] And He has made subservient to you whatsoever is in the heavens and whatsoever is in the earth, all, from Himself; most surely there are signs in this for a people who reflect. (Shakir's trnalation)

38. *Islam and the Plight of Modern Man*, 23.
39. *Man and Nature*, 96. In another passage Nasr is forced to acknowledge the subjectivity that is attributed to humans in the Qur'an even more explicitly, but again attempts to diminish human stature as much as possible: "There is something God-like in man as attested to by the Quranic statement (Pickthall translation): 'I have made him [Adam] and have breathed into him my spirit (Quran xv, 29) and by the tradition 'God created Adam, the prototype of man, upon "His own form," i.e., as a mirror reflecting in a central and conscious manner His Names and Qualities. There is therefore, something of a "divine nature" (*malakuti*) in man; and it is in the light of this profound nature in man that Islam envisages him. This belief is not, however, in any way anthropomorphic, for the Divine Essence (*al-dhat*), remains absolutely transcendent and no religion has emphasized the transcendent aspect of God more than Islam. The Islamic concept of man as a theomorphic being is not an anthropomorphism." (*Ideals and Realities of Islam*, 18)

of God before whom all creatures are literally nothing."[40] This is manifested, according to Nasr, in the quotidian culture also: "In the daily life the formula Allahuakbar [God is the greatest] demonstrates also the insignificance of the human before the Divine, the weakness of the mightiest human power before the Divine Omnipotence and the awe which comes into being in the heart of a Muslim at the sight of wonders of creation and of human life that reveal this omnipotence."[41] In a similar manner, Nasr interprets the Islamic belief that Prophet Muhammad was "unlettered" (*nabi al-ummi*) to symbolize the nothingness of humans before the God: "The unlettered nature of the Prophet means most of all the extinction of all that is human before the Divine."[42]

In order to justify such an anti-humanist outlook, Nasr also resorts to a one-dimensional reading of the Sufi tradition in which he highlights those elements that lend themselves to the negation of human subjectivity. Nasr thus rejects an interpretation of the ontological doctrines of *wahdat al-wujud* (unity of existence) in which human status can be elevated by the symbolic journey towards the Divine realm: "The pantheistic accusations against the Sufis are doubly false because, first of all, pantheism is a philosophical system, whereas Muhyi al-Din [Ibn 'Arabi] and others like him never claimed to follow or create any "system" whatsoever; and secondly, because pantheism implies a substantial continuity between God and the universe [including humans], whereas the Shaikh [Ibn 'Arabi] would be the first to claim God's absolute transcendence over every category, including that of substance."[43] Running into difficulties in his interpretation of the notion of "unity of existence" Nasr further wrote that *wahdat al-wujud* is neither pantheism, nor panentheism, nor existential monism; rather it means "that while God is absolutely transcendent with respect to the Universe, the Universe is not completely separate from Him; that the 'Universe is mysteriously plunged in God.' It signifies that to believe in any order of realty as autonomous apart from the Absolute Reality is to fall into the cardinal sin of Islam, namely polytheism (*shirk*)."[44] Most significantly, Nasr attempted to diminish the significance of humans in the doctrine of *wahdat al-wujud* by reducing the import of all non-divine beings by means of a flagrant paralogism:

> The relation between God and the order of existence is not just a logical one in which if one thing is equal to another the other is equal to the first. Through that mystery that lies in the heart of creation itself, everything is, in essence, identified with God while God infinitely

40. *Islam and the Plight of Modern Man,* 18.
41. *Ideals and Realties of Islam*, 64.
42. *Ideals and Realities of Islam*, 77.
43. Nasr, Seyyed Hossein. *Three Muslim Sages: Avicenna, Suhrawardi, Ibn 'Arabi* (Cambridge, MA: Harvard University Press, 1964), 105. It is crucial to note that here, as in the overwhelming majority of his claims, Nasr does not engage in any analysis of the text with which he is dealing (here with Ibn 'Arabi,) and merely arbitrarily asserts his own views. At most he makes reference to some European authors that happen to agree with his views– or more accurately by whom he has been inspired. In this particular case Nasr merely makes a reference to a H.A. Wolfson, one of his professors at Harvard, to support his interpretation of Ibn 'Arabi's text.
44. *Three Muslim Sages*, 106.

> transcends everything. To understand this doctrine intellectually is to possess contemplative intelligence; to realize it fully is to be a saint who alone sees 'God everywhere.'[45]

In a related vein, Nasr attempted to interpret Ibn 'Arabi's concept of Perfect Man[46] (*insan kamil*), which maybe considered as a precursor to the notion of human subjectivity in Sufi tradition, in a manner that is confined to a small elite and not humans in general: "Next in importance to the Unity of Being is the doctrine of Universal Man (*al-insan al-kamil*) which is its concomitant [...] *Only the saint realizes the totality of the nature of Universal Man* and thereby becomes the perfect mirror in which God contemplates Himself."[47]

In his attempt to undermine the metaphysical foundations of human subjectivity, Nasr also interprets Ibn Sina's ontology, in which God is conceived as the Necessary Being and the Universe as contingent upon it, in a much more radical fashion than Ibn Sina (d. 1037) intended, and in disfavor of humans:

> We saw how in his ontology Ibn Sina clearly separated Being from all particular beings, while in his cosmology he considers the Universe as an effusion (*faid*) of Being. This apparent contradiction, and more generally the whole question of creation, or manifestation, has always remained among the most debated aspects of Ibn Sina's philosophy and the one which has been attacked most severely. The Islamic perspective can be said to have its particular raison d'être *in integrating the particular in the Universal and in leveling into nothingness all that is creaturely before the absolute transcendence of the Divine Principle.*"[48]

As we have seen in other chapters, many Islamist thinkers derive the notion of human agency and selfhood from the Agency of the Divine, but they do not attempt to annihilate the human subjectivity as forcefully as Nasr does. Thus, by invoking Ibn Sina and Omar Khayyam (d. 1122), Nasr posits the idea of human selfhood by virtue of its contingency upon that of God, but immediately proceeds to destroy the same human self:

45. *Ideals and Realities of Islam*, 137. In another passage Nasr further attempted to interpret Ibn 'Arabi's central notion of *wahdat al-wujud* in an anti-human direction. For Ibn 'Arabi, Nasr wrote, "the aim of all Sufism is union with the Divine which comes as a result of the love created in man for Divine Beauty. This union is generally conceived in terms of a gradual purification of the heart and the attainment of various spiritual virtues leading finally to the state of "annihilation" (*fana*) and "subsistence (*baqa*) in the Divine. According to him [Ibn 'Arabi], knowledge of God and union with Him in the supreme state of contemplation does not mean a ceasing to exist individually (*fana*), or ceasing of that of ceasing (*baqa*), as most gnostics have asserted. Rather, it means to realize that our existence from the beginning belonged to God, that we had no existence to start with which could cease to be. It means the realization that all existence as such is a ray of the Divine Being and that nothing else possesses any existence whatsoever." (*Three Muslim Sages*, 114)
46. Nasr's translation of *insan kamil* into English as "Universal Man" instead of Perfect Man which is the usual translation, could be interpreted as another indication of his attempt to diminish human agency.
47. *Ideals and Realities of Islam*, 137–38. Emphasis added.
48. *An Introduction to Islamic Cosmological Doctrines*, 212. Emphasis added.

> In Avicennan language, which Khayyam confirms in prose philosophical works, man, like all beings in this world, is "contingent" (*mumkin*) and received his reality from the source of Being through that process of *fayadan* [effusion] discussed above. This and similar quatrains [by Khayyam] can be read with perfect logic as poetical assertions of the status of contingency, which is complete poverty of existence or nothingness of the world [read humans], in contrast to the Necessary Being (*wajib al-wujud*) which alone possesses and bestows *wujud* [being] upon all that exists.[49]

To the same extent that Nasr tried to depreciate human selfhood, he has attempted to apotheosize "Being," a category that he sometimes equates with God but often identifies with Nature. As such, one of the most significant aspects of Nasr's discourse is comprised of the idea that modern people have neglected and marginalized Being. Occidental philosophy since Descartes, Nasr complains, has had "difficulty in understanding Being." As a result, this neglect of Being has been carried to such a point that "certain contemporary schools of European philosophy have placed individual existence, rather than Universal Being, as the foundation of their thought."[50]

Passivity as Virtue

The result of subverting the subject in Nasr's discourse has been, no doubt, encouraging a form of human passivity. In one of his earlier works, Nasr opined that one of the chief problems of modern humans is the "divorce between contemplation and action, and in fact the almost complete destruction of the former by latter."[51] Nasr's understanding of "contemplation" gives a strong inert character to this notion as he equates it with *shuhud* (intuition as opposed to active cogitation), *ta'amul* (pondering) and *tafakkur* (meditation).[52] However, again facing the strong agentic and subjectivist element in Islamic epistemic domains such as the Qur'an, Islamic philosophy and some aspects of Sufism, Nasr cannot deny the irrefutable emphasis on action in the Islamic traditions: "In the Islamic context, this contemplation has always been wedded to action understood in its traditional sense.

49. *Islamic Philosophy From Its Origin to Present*, 181. Nasr has expressed the idea of human annihilation before the Divine very unequivocally in the following passage: "Man in Islam thinks and makes in his function of *homo sapiens* and *homo faber* as the *'abd* [Arabic, servant, slave] of God and not as a creature who has rebelled against Heaven. His function remains not the glorification of himself but of his Lord, and his greatest aim is to become "nothing" before God, to undergo the experience of *fana* [annihilation] that would enable him to become as the perfect *'abd*, the mirror in which God contemplates the reflection of His own Names and Qualities and the channel through which His grace and the theophanies of His Names and Qualities are reflected in the world in a central manner." (*Islamic Philosophy From Its Origin to Present*, 266–67)

50. Nasr, Seyyed Hossein. *Islamic Studies: Essays on Law and Society, the Sciences, and Philosophy and Sufism* (Beirut: Librairie du Liban, 1967), 134. Nasr has repeatedly denied having been much influenced by Heidegger, yet the pedigree of the Romantics' fascination with nature and what they call "Being" seems to be closely related, but not identical, between Martin Heidegger and Nasr, as well as his Western mentors such as René Guénon and Frithjof Schuon.

51. *Islam and the Plight of the Modern Man*, 67.

52. *Islam and the Plight of the Modern Man*, 68.

The contemplative form of Islamic spirituality has never been opposed to correct action and has in fact often been combined with an irresistible inner urge to action. It is this inner unity that made Islamic civilization at the height of its power one of the most virile and active in human history at the same time that it harboured within itself a most intensive contemplative life."[53] But, almost immediately after having paid lip service to the ideal of a complementarity relationship between action and contemplation, Nasr gives much more weight to the passivity of what he considers to be Sufi contemplation:

> In the light of the innate relationship between contemplation and action contained in the formulae of the *adhan* [Islamic call to prayer] it can be said that although contemplation and action are complementary, they are not on an equal footing. Contemplation and meditation, which is closely related to it, stand above action, as the *hadith* about an hour of meditation being more worthy than sixty years of acts of worship reveals [...] Thus the contemplative man is held in higher esteem in traditional Islamic society than man of action, as the famous *hadith* testifies [...] "The ink of the man of knowledge is more worthy than the blood of the martyr."[54]

Fracas against Reason and Modern Science

As a thinker who rejects, for the most part, the notion of human selfhood and agency, it is not surprising that Nasr also disdains the actions of the human mind and most anything related to rationality. Early in his career, Nasr assailed the futility of ratiocination and highlighted the value of intuition by frequently footnoting his mentors such as Frithjof Schuon.[55] For this reason, in his various works Nasr has paid a significant amount of attention to the development of rationality in the West as well as the Muslim world. With Aristotle, Nasr argued, rationalism commenced in the West and continued in expressions such as stoicism and epicureanism that became prevalent in the Roman Empire. However, this type of rationalism contributed little to the development of natural sciences and showed slight sympathy, to Nasr's chagrin, for metaphysical and theological concerns.[56]

In the Islamic world, Nasr considers the rationalism of Farabi acceptable, because the latter's studies of mathematics, geography and astronomy, albeit rational in nature, ultimately led to the "affirmation of some attributes of the Creator." The highlighting of "this noble aspect of reason as a natural bridge to the supernatural realities and to religious faith, rather than as an obstacle against them, is a profound aspect of the Islamic spirit."[57] Ibn Sina, on the other hand, combined an Aristotelian rationalism with the "tenets of Islam," while Ibn Rushd's (Averroës) rationalism was "much more pure and radical" than of other Muslim philosophers.[58] Even more radical was the medieval European appropriation of Ibn Rushd's rationalism, which led to the secularization of

53. *Islam and the Plight of the Modern Man*, 68.
54. *Islam and the Plight of the Modern Man*, 69–71.
55. *Three Muslim Sages*, 164.
56. *Man and Nature*, 54
57. *An Introduction to Islamic Cosmological Doctrines*, 115.
58. *Man and Nature*, 61–62.

the intellectual environment and paved the way for the Copernican revolution.[59] But it was with Descartes that Western rationalism totally severed its ties from Divine sources and declared itself a completely human endeavor:

> If by rationalism one means an attempt to build a closed system embracing the whole of reality and based upon human reason alone, then this begins with Descartes, since for him the ultimate criterion of reality itself is the human ego and not the Divine Intellect or Pure Being. His *cogito ergo sum* places a limitation upon human knowledge by binding it to the level of individual reason and to the consciousness of the individual ego. It is this tendency which reaches its culmination with the eighteenth and nineteenth century rationalism, before the very heaviness of the rationalist system begins to produce cracks in its own protective wall, through which irrational elements begin to flow in from below.[60]

Thus, according to Nasr, rationalism as it developed in the West—a West in which the traditional Christian was closely bound to God in the medieval time—"became a veil which separated man from God and marked the human revolt against heaven."[61] Moreover, and to Nasr's horror, this form of Western rationality became an unstoppable invading force, which has assailed the Muslim world relentlessly since the 19th century.

In the Islamic world itself, on the other hand, the trajectory of thought, in Nasr's view, has been different from that of the West. It is interesting to note that Nasr pursues this line of argument not from the Qur'anic or Hadith position, but from the standpoint of Neoplatonic discourse that was adopted in the Muslim world in early medieval period. Thus, reading Nasr's argument a bit more closely than he would himself present it, it is not Mecca, Medina or Baghdad that should be considered the intellectual foundation of Islamic civilization, but the Greco-Roman Alexandria of Neoplatonism:

> In Alexandria [...] mystical and religious schools of philosophy developed during a period of intense activity in the mathematical and physical sciences. It was here that Neoplatonic metaphysics, Neopythagorean mathematics and Hermeticism were developed and where the study of mathematical and natural sciences was often carried out in the matrix of a metaphysics that was aware of the symbolic and transparent nature of things. It is of significance that the immediate background of Western civilization, in its external and formal aspect, is Roman, while that which Islam received from the Greco-Hellenistic heritage comes mostly from Alexandria.[62]

As a result of these influences, Nasr suggests, Islamic epistemology and hence civilization lean much more toward "direct knowledge" and inspiration than ratiocination. Islam "is based on gnosis or direct knowledge that however cannot by any means be equated with rationalism, which is only an indirect and secondary form of knowledge. Islam leads to that essential knowledge which integrates our being, which makes us know what we are

59. *Man and Nature*, 62.
60. *Sufi Essays*, 53.
61. *Sufi Essays*, 53.
62. *Man and Nature*, 54.

and be what we know or in other words integrates knowledge and being in the ultimate unitive vision of Reality."[63]

Furthermore, for Nasr, the Islamic belief of the putative unlettered character of the Prophet, serves as a crucial model of the passive and intuitive nature of knowledge:

> The Word of God in Islam is the Quran; in Christianity it is Christ. The vehicle of the Divine Message in Christianity is the Virgin Mary; in Islam it is the soul of the Prophet. The Prophet must be unlettered for the same reason that the Virgin Mary must be virgin. The human vehicle of a Divine Message must be pure and untainted. The Divine Word can only be written on the pure and "untouched" tablet of human receptivity. If this Word is in the form of flesh the purity is symbolized by the virginity of the mother who gave birth to the Word, and if it is in the form of a book this purity is symbolized by the unlettered nature of the person who is chosen to announce this Word among men [...] The unlettered nature of the Prophet demonstrates how the *human recipient is completely passive* before the Divine. Were this purity and virginity of the soul not to exist, the Divine Word would become in a sense tainted with purely human knowledge and not be presented to mankind in its pristine purity. The Prophet was purely passive in the face of the revelation he received from God. He added nothing.[64]

It is significant to note that again in the face of emphasis in many Islamic epistemic domains on the significance of human reason and rationality, at times Nasr is forced to acknowledge the importance that for example the Qur'an places on human reason and tries to reconcile it with his own Romantic biases.[65] But as we have seen above with regard to similar issues, Nasr's effort in this regard is also to minimize, to the extent possible, humans' selfhood, in this case with reference to human intellectual endeavor.

Nasr's attempt to devalue human reason has also spilled over into the realm of modern science as he has often engaged in fulminating against post-Renaissance natural sciences and quixotically attempted to undermine their philosophical foundations. For example, in his earliest published work, Nasr disputed one of the essential tenets of modern sciences, namely the notion of constancy in the principles governing natural phenomena across time and space, without adducing any reason or evidence:

63. *Ideals and Realities of Islam*, 22.
64. *Ideals and Realities of Islam*, 43–44. Emphasis added.
65. Thus in one of his earlier works Nasr wrote: "Islam has always considered the positive aspect of the intellect (*'aql*) and man's ability to reach the cardinal doctrine of Islam, i.e., the doctrine of Unity (*tawhid*), through his *'aql*. In fact the Quran often describes those who have gone astray from religion as those who cannot intellect (*la ya'qilun*). But this is no license for rationalism and an *ad hoc* treatment of the Shari'ah as judged by human reason, because man can reach *tawhid* through his own *'aqle* only under the condition that his *'aql* is in a wholesome state (*salim*). And it is precisely the Shari'ah whose practice removes the obstacles in the soul which prevent the correct functioning of the intellect and obscure its vision." (*Islamic Studies: Essays on Law and Society*, 28–29) In a somewhat later work, Nasr wrote: "As a matter of fact one of the great services that Islam can render to the modern world, in which the dichotomy between reason and revelation or science and religion has reached such dangerous proportions, is to represent this possibility of the union between revelation and reason as found in the Quran." (*Sufi Essay*, 54)

> The modern assumption of the uniformity of Nature throughout time, which has been made the basis of the study of past, considers that the forces acting in Nature, observable by the human senses at the present moment in the particular conditions chosen for the study of these forces by modern scientists, have been acting in the same manner throughout the history of the word. Moreover, it is assumed that any forces which cannot be observed now could not have acted in the past.

And based on this contention Nasr concludes that, "The 'laws of Nature' are therefore not valid throughout the history of cosmos, like the law of the rotation of wheels inside a watch, but themselves change during the life of the world as the form and function of an organism alter during various periods of its life."[66]

Nasr has reserved his most vehement attacks on modern science, however, for the theory of evolution, a relatively rare phenomenon among contemporary Islamic thinkers compared to, for example, American conservative Evangelicals.[67] One of the basic tenets of Nasr's discourse seems to be the notion of constancy of human nature, an assumption that the theory of evolution could allegedly seriously undermine. Were it not for the theory of evolution, it would become manifest that "human nature," is "something constant and permanent."[68] Indeed, as far as Nasr is concerned, the theory of evolution is one of "modern man's most insidious pseudo-dogmas," that was created to "enable man to forget God."[69] Given Nasr's proclivity to view things modern quite negatively, it is not surprising that he makes a close link between the theory of evolution and the desire for social change and condemns both.[70] As a result, Nasr has categorically rejected the idea of evolution as a dangerous innovation on the part of the modern world:

---

66. *An introduction to Islamic Cosmological Doctrines*, 118. Again, when faced with realities of the contemporary world, Nasr has expressed more moderate views on the acceptability of modern science: "If it be asked what one is to do in a practical manner in the present context, it can be answered that on the plane of knowledge one must seek a higher science of nature into which the quantitative sciences of nature can be integrated. This in turn can only be achieved through a knowledge of the indispensable metaphysical principles upon which these sciences are ultimately based." (*Sufi Essays*, 162)
67. For one of the few academic studies of the impact of Darwinism on the Islamic world see: Adel A. Ziadat, *Western Science in the Arab World: The Impact of Darwinism 1860–1930* (St. Martin's Press, New York, 1986).
68. *Islam and the Plight of Modern Man*, 9.
69. *Islam and the Plight of Modern Man*, 139.
70. *Islam and the Plight of Modern Man*, 139. Once more, Nasr is forced to recognize the Qur'anic emphases on notions of change in nature explicitly and in history and society by implication, without any serious attempt to integrate it into his discourse: "Aside from such a specifically modern concepts such as the Darwinian theory of evolution, there are many modern geological ideas, such as change of land and sea, sedimentation, rise of mountains, and so on, which are to be found in various medieval Muslim treatises, particularly those of al-Biruni. Undoubtedly this conception of great changes in the structure of the surface of the earth, and even the disappearance of such things as mountains which seem so solid and firm, is due not only to the ability of Muslim natural historians to travel over great distances and observe diverse geological conditions, but also to the emphasis of the Islamic perspective *supported by many Quranic verses, upon the transitory nature of all that is in this world.*" (*An Introduction to Islamic Cosmological Doctrines*, 141. Emphasis added)

> Throughout the world today, particularly in the Orient where there are still societies that remain faithful to their religious principles and the social structure based upon them, men are asked to evolve and change simply because evolution is in the nature of things and is inevitable. A more objective assessment of the findings of biology would insist that as long as man has been living on earth he has not evolved at all; nor has his natural environment changed in anyway. The same plants and animals are still born, grow, wither and die and regenerate themselves, except for the unfortunate species that modern man who believes to belong to the process of evolution has made extinct.[71]

Given Nasr's stance against what he calls "reason" and modern science and the putative disasters caused by them, the next step for him has been the extravagant task of restoring the lost magic to the world.

Re-enchanting the Modern World

Like some of the 19th and 20th century critics of modernity, Nasr has mourned the loss of enchantment in the world from which meaning has allegedly disappeared. In the modern world, Nasr asserts, "[t]he cosmos which had been transparent thus became opaque and spiritually meaningless—at least to those who were totally immersed in the scientific view of nature—even if individual scientists believed other wise. The traditional sciences, such as alchemy, which can be compared to the celebration of a cosmic mass, became reduced to a chemistry in which the substances had lost all their sacramental intelligibility."[72] Yet, according to Nasr, the disenchantment of the world has had a long history and is the product of centuries of desacralization and objectification of nature in the West which goes back to the Greeks. With the Greek deities abandoning their natural habitat in Western history, the divine which was dwelling within nature was severed from it, starting a process that led to the emergence of the philosophical and scientific worldview:

> The ancient Greeks possessed a cosmology similar to that of other Aryan peoples of Antiquity. The elements, and nature itself, were still inhabited by the Gods. Matter was alive with spirit and spiritual and corporeal substances had not as yet become distinct. The rise of philosophy and science in the sixth century BC was not so much the discovery of a new realm as an attempt to fill a vacuum created by the fact that the Olympian Gods had deserted their earthly abode. The basic ideas of *phusis, dike, nomos* and the like which are fundamental to Greek science and philosophy are all terms of religious significance which have been gradually emptied of their spiritual [i.e., sacral] substance [...] With the gradual increase in decadence of Greek Olympian religion, more and more the substance of nature itself became divorced from its spiritual significance, and cosmology and physics tended toward naturalism and empiricism. In the same way that from the Orphic-Dionysian dimension of Greek religion there developed the Pythagorean-Platonic school of philosophy and mathematics, so from the body of Olympian religious concepts, emptied of their meaning, arose a physics and a natural philosophy which sought to fill the vacuum and to

71. *Man and Nature*, 128.
72. *Man and Nature,* 21.

> provide a coherent explanation for a world no longer inhabited by the gods. The general movement was from symbolic interpretation of nature to naturalism, from contemplative metaphysics to rationalistic philosophy.[73]

In Europe, it was the adoption of Averroesism into the medieval Latin culture which led to major intellectual transformations and, during the period from the 11th century to 13th century, replaced the contemplative and respectful attitude toward nature with rationalism and hostility toward nature.[74] Christianity itself, according to Nasr, was largely responsible for the alienation from nature, because it made rationality the handmaid of faith, "ignoring the supernatural essence of natural intelligence within man." This was necessary to sustain civilization by preserving its intellectual integrity, but "in the process an alienation took place towards nature which has left its mark upon the subsequent history of Christianity," and which is one of the "deep-lying roots of the present crisis of modern man in his encounter with nature."[75]

As we have seen above, however, Nasr believes that it is in the post-Renaissance period, especially after the Protestant Reformation, that the process of secularization and desacralization of the world culminated in the total disenchantment with and alienation from nature. For this reason, Nasr thinks that the process of salvation cum re-enchantment must start with the resacralization of nature. Thus for Nasr, nature is in need of redemption as much as humans:

> In the writings of this small group of theologian who have devoted some attention to the question of man's relation with nature [...] all creation must somehow share in the act of redemption in the same way as all creation is affected by the corruption and sin of man as asserted by St. Paul in the Epistle to Romans (Chap.VIII). The total salvation of man is possible when not only man himself but all creatures are redeemed. This point of view above, which could have the profoundest significance in modern man's relation to nature, has however, rarely been understood and accepted. Even those who have devoted themselves most to a sacramental theology have, for the most part, failed to apply it to the world of nature. *As a result, those who still feel and understand the meaning of the sacred, at least in religious rites, fail to extend it to the realm of nature.*[76]

As such, Nasr has advocated the idea of resacralization of nature using Islamic symbols quite cleverly:

> In revealing the central rite of daily prayers to the Prophet, *God allowed not only nature to become once again the temple of worship*, as it had been for primordial man, without the danger of naturalism or idolatry, but also permitted the *sanctification of the earth* itself through the *sujud*

73. *Man and Nature*, 53–54. It is not very often that one finds a Muslim thinker lamenting the loss of Greek gods!
74. *Man and Nature*, 61.
75. *Man and Nature*, 55. Thus, in Nasr's view, "[i]t was left to St. Francis of Assisi to express, within the bosom of Christian spirituality, the profoundest insight into the sacred quality of nature." (*Man and Nature*, 60)
76. *Man and Nature*, 34–35. Emphasis added.

> [prostration] of the Perfect Man [Muhammad]. By touching the ground with his forehead the Prophet bestowed a special significance upon the floor of his house, through it upon the first mosque, and through the Medina mosque upon the whole of Islamic architecture as far as the floor and the experience of space from the floor is concerned [...] When one enters a traditional mosque or home the very emptiness of the space draws attention to the Invisible [*ghayb*] as does the experience of the ground upon which one can only walk after taking off one's shoes. This touching of the ground with one's hands and face in prayer creates the awareness of the *hallowedness of the earth* by virtue of the act of that most Perfect of Creatures who, in touching the earth with his forehead in total submission to God, sacralized it for all subsequent generation of Muslims.[77]

For Nasr, modern humans have denuded nature from its "subjectivity" and of possessing a spirit that makes it a living being capable of action. Invoking the Brethren of Purity (*Ikhwan al-Safa*, a secretive group of Islamic intellectuals of the 10th and 11th centuries), Nasr wrote, "The Rasail [the treatises of the Brethren of Purity] emphasize the importance of understanding and accepting the presence of this spiritual force called Nature which is the performer of all actions. In fact, they often identify as materialists those who deny Nature [...] The universe for Ikhwan acts more like a live organism whose motions come from a force within rather than a cadaver to which external motion has been added."[78] In the West of antiquity also, nature was an active spirit, as "the water of Thales was still full of the animating spirit of nature and in fact symbolized the psycho-physical substratum of things. It was very far from the post-Cartesian dead matter with which Lavoisier was experimenting twenty four centuries later."[79]

To reverse this long process of alienation from nature, Nasr proposes of proffering subjectivity to nature by resacralizing it:

> The thesis presented in this book is simply this: that although science is legitimate in itself, the role and function of science and its application have become illegitimate and even dangerous because of the lack of a higher form of knowledge into which science could be integrated and the destruction of the sacred and spiritual value of nature. To remedy this situation the metaphysical knowledge pertaining to nature must be revived and the sacred quality of nature given back to it once again.[80]

In this spirit of restoring the sacral character of nature, Nasr has proposed some measures to achieve the goal of re-enchanting the world. The most important of these ideas is the attempt to restore the validity of two the traditions of Hermeticism and

77. Nasr, Seyyed Hossein. *Islamic Art and Spirituality* (Albany: State University of New York Press, 1987), 39; 47. Emphasis added. It is quite significant that Nasr alludes to the "danger of naturalism or idolatry" when referring to resacralization of nature in this passage. The Islamic banning of the depiction of animate beings and its hostility toward any possibility of any form of idol worship are undoubtedly rooted in the fear of treating nature as sacred, to which Nasr seems to be oblivious.
78. *An Introduction to Islamic Cosmological Doctrines*, 61.
79. *Sufi Essays*, 91.
80. *Man and Nature*, 14.

alchemy, as he defines them. Alchemy, for Nasr, is the reversal of modern science, a major culprit in the disenchantment process, "[a]lchemy is neither a premature chemistry nor a psychology in the modern sense, although both of these are to be found in alchemical writings. Alchemy is a symbolic science of natural forms based on the correspondence between different planes of reality and making use of mineral and metal symbolism to expound a spiritual science of the soul. For alchemy, nature is sacred, and the alchemist is the guardian of nature considered as a theophany and reflection of spiritual realities. A purely profane chemistry could come into being only when the substance of alchemy became completely emptied of the sacred quality."[81]

Through most phases of his career, Nasr has written on and championed the cause of Hermeticism as an enchanted alternative to the modern outlook. Hermeticism's putative reliance on magical approaches, their antirational views and their alchemical attitudes toward nature have made it a very attractive body of thought for Nasr: "The Hermetic school, cultivated an illuminationist school in philosophy and considered inner purification as the means of attaining the truth as opposed to the rationalistic tendencies of the Peripatetics. In the sciences of nature, this school distrusted the syllogistic method and sought to rely on knowledge of concrete causes which could be observed and experienced."[82] In his attempt to remagicalize the world, it is very important to mention that Nasr went even as far as praising not only Taoism and Shinto religion, but also Shamanism for its "particular emphasis upon the significance of nature in a cultic sense."[83]

It is very significant that Nasr attempts to produce an interpretation of Islamic art which represents a more subdued component of his attempt to re-enchant the world. First, however, Nasr attempts to debunk the modern (i.e., post-Renaissance) Western art in conception as well as corpus. The art of the Renaissance, Nasr asserted, reflects

81. *Man and Nature*, 104–5.

82. Nasr, Seyyed Hossein. *Islamic Studies: Essays on Law and Society, the Sciences, and Philosophy and Sufism* (Beirut: Librairie du Liban, 1967), 77. It is interesting that Nasr speaks about a concept that he attributes to Hermeticism that has a peculiar resemblance to the notion of human subjectivity. Both in his early Persian and later in his English writings on Hermeticism Nasr has mentioned the notion of "Perfect Nature" (Ar. *taba'Q tam*) as "each person's divine truth and celestial selfhood (*ana'iyat asmani*)". This Perfect Nature is said to have been the cause of Alexander's victory over the Persians. See Seyyed Hossein Nasr, *Hermes va neveshteha-ye hermesi dar jahan-e Islam* (Hermes and Hermetic Writings in the Islamic World) (Tehran University Press 1341, 1962), 20–24.

83. *Man and Nature*, 87. It seems that throughout his discourse Nasr is oblivious to the Qur'anic condemnation of any form of magic, *sihr*, in most vehement terms. See the Qur'an, 2:102; 4: 51; 6:7; 10:77, 81; 11:7; 20:73. On the other hand, as if realizing that his views on nature are in sharp contrast to the Qur'anic position, Nasr has written: "Nor is the re-discovery of virgin nature a return to paganism from a theological point of view. There is a profound difference between the paganism of the Mediterranean world, this idolatry of created things against which Christianity has fought, and the "naturism" of modern European people for whom nature possessed a symbolic and spiritual significance. The re-discovery of virgin nature with the aid of traditional principles would mean a reunification of the symbolic meaning of natural forms and the development of a spiritual sympathy (*sym-pathia*) for nature which has nothing to do with either paganism and idolatry or the modern individual revolt." (*Man and Nature*, 118)

worldly concerns rather than the beauty of the spiritual world, which exposed art to purely human art at the expense of doing away with sacred and divinely inspired art of the medieval period, despite the works of geniuses such as Leonardo da Vinci, Raphael and Michelangelo.[84] At the center of Nasr's criticism of art in the modern world is his persistent denunciation of humanism as we saw above:

> In fact Renaissance art reflects more directly than any other aspect of Renaissance culture the new humanism which placed man rather than God at the center of the scheme of existence. Although religious themes continued to be treated, the art of the Renaissance was no longer the sacred or traditional art of the earlier centuries. Even the Vatican, the center of Catholicism to this day built on the older building which was destroyed during the Renaissance, displays not the heavenly beauty of the medieval cathedrals but the atmosphere of a palace which reflects the power of the world and the humanistic characteristics of the age in which it was built.[85]

Another aspect of Nasr's antimodern position that has been implicit in his discourse all along, comes to life especially in his discussion of art, namely his denunciation of the individual: "It is important to note that much of modern Western art is based on individualism, subjectivism and psychological impulses of the individual painter rather than the Divine norm which would transcend the individual artists, whereas, of course, Islamic art as all traditional art, has been the source of art to be above and beyond the individual."[86] As such, in Nasr's view, "[i]f a traditional Muslim finds the titanesque statues of a Michelangelo crushing and Rococo churches stifling, it is because of that sense of submission to God created in his soul by Islamic spirituality and his horror of human self-aggrandizement at the expense of Divine Presence."[87] With regard to contemporary artistic expressions as the application of modern science of nature and as reflecting the eclipse of the esoteric dimension of the premodern world manifested, for example, in the subway architecture and skyscraper, Nasr obviously finds modern art appalling and frequently denounces it.[88]

Significantly, however, Nasr believes, rather arbitrarily, that Western classical music, including the music of Mozart, Beethoven and Brahms, remained non-humanist and

84. *A Young Muslim's Guide to the Modern World*, 218.
85. *A Young Muslim's Guide to the Modern World*, 218.
86. *A Young Muslim's Guide to the Modern World*, 221. Nasr has further expressed his opposition to the significance of the individual in modern art, by denouncing the novel as a major form of literary expression in modernity: "There is a special emphasis in Islamic civilization upon poetry which holds an exalted position among all Islamic peoples [...] Certain forms of literature such as the novel which are prevalent in the West today were, however, never developed by Muslims. The reason is that such forms of literature, especially as they developed in the nineteenth and twentieth centuries, are in reality in most cases attempts to create a subjective and fictitious world in which the reader journeys in forgetfulness of the reality of Allah, a world which Islam has always opposed in principle." (*A Young Muslim's Guide to the Modern World*, 109)
87. *Islamic Art and Spirituality*, 11.
88. Nasr, Seyyed Hossein, *Knowledge and the Sacred: The Gifford Lectures* (Edinburgh: Edinburg University Press, 1981), 267.

retained its "mystical" effect, while "It was only in the [...] twentieth century that classical music, like pictorial arts, experienced a dissolution of forms 'from above' as one sees in the twelve-tone music associated with Schoenberg, minimalism and many others of contemporary classical music which often sound strange even to the ear of trained Western listeners."[89] Since even modern classical music can be interpreted as "enchanted," it seems, it can be useful in Nasr's paradigm, even though it is no longer linked to the sacred directly: "In any case, classical Western music is one of the richest aspects of the art of the West with many diverse developments that make it a unique musical tradition, and for that very reason it has been deeply appreciated on a wide scale by non-Western cultures throughout the world *although much of this music, in fact, is not conducive to interiorization of remembrance of God.*"[90] Even contemporary popular music has some utility in Nasr's scheme, because despite its origin in the "lower impulses of the soul," it is in "a sense, a way of destroying that rationalism and the cerebral treatment of all things with which so much of European culture has been associated since Descartes and an attempt to rediscover the significance of the body as a reality in addition to the mind."[91]

However, it is in music as such that Nasr finds one of the most direct paths to re-enchanting the world. In fact, Nasr often goes beyond the Islamic world to make his points as long as the source of evidence is premodern and "traditional" it will suffice. When it comes to music this tendency is even more evident. "Music," he wrote, "is not only the first art brought by Šiva into the world, the art through which the *asrar-i alast* or the mystery of the Primordial covenant between man and God in that pre-eternal dawn of the day of cosmic manifestation is revealed, but it is also the key to the understanding of the harmony that pervades the cosmos. It is the handmaid of wisdom [i.e., non-rational inspired knowledge] [...] The gnostic hears in music the melodies of the Paradise whose ecstasies the music brings about once again. That is why music is like the mystical wine."[92]

Dance, a taboo subject in most mainstream Islamic circles, is another very important vehicle for Nasr's project of re-enchantment:

> As for dance, it, like music, is a direct vehicle for the realization of union. The sacred dance unifies man with the Divine at the meeting point of time and space at the eternal now and immutable center which is the locus of Divine presence. From the sacred art of dance is born not only those great masterpieces of Hindu art in which Šiva performs the cosmic dance upon the body of his consort Parvati, but also the temple of dances of Bali, the cosmic dances of the American Indians and the native Africans, and on the highest level, those esoteric dances connected with initiatic practices leading to Union.[93]

There is little doubt that these attempts by Nasr to present more amiable aspects of religious experience to the Islamic world, especially since the late 20th century, is salutary. However, the larger framework in which this attempt is taking place, namely, his

89. *A Young Muslim's Guide to the Modern World*, 222–23.
90. *A Young Muslim's Guide to the Modern World*, 223. Emphasis added.
91. *A Young Muslim's Guide to the Modern World*, 224.
92. *Knowledge and the Sacred*, 272.
93. *Knowledge and the Sacred*, 272.

attempt to largely dispense with the modern world, with all its negative as well as positive aspects, must not be overlooked. This attempt to do away with modernity is very closely related to an overall conservatism that highlights the discourse of Seyyed Hossein Nasr. In fact, Nasr's predominantly conservative ethos manifests itself so vividly that it eclipses any attempts by him to bring about reform in Islamic world, be it inspired by European Romanticism or by the Sufi tradition.

Conservative Ethos

For Nasr the cultural patterns from the past, regardless of being Islamic, Hindu, Buddhist, Christian or Jewish, are sacred and must be preserved at all cost. The Muslims living in the contemporary world ought to, according to him, wage a *jihad* in order to protect the "marvelous spiritual and artistic heritage" that their forebears have bequeathed to them and transmit it to the next generations.[94] This *jihad* also includes the preservation of the notion of law as an immutable divine category that is not amenable to relativistic and changing social conventions.[95] These views are, in turn, based on Nasr's larger view of humans as having a fixed nature, "[i]n reality, the needs of man, as far as the total nature of man is concerned, remains for ever the same, precisely because of man's unchanging nature [...] [because] the situation of man in the universal hierarchy of being, his standing between the two unknowns which comprise his state before terrestrial life and his state after death, his need for a 'shelter' in the vast stretches of cosmic existence and his deep need for certainty (*yaqin* in the vocabulary of Sufism) remain unchanged."[96]

Thus, in general Nasr has opposed most forms of change in the Islamic society and Muslim culture.[97] For Nasr Islamic society has no need for any change, and the best

94. *Islam and the Plight of Modern Man*, 18.
95. *Islam and the Plight of Modern Man*, 19.
96. *Islam and the Plight of Modern Man*, 49–50.
97. This is not to say that Nasr does not recognize the reality of historical change, but for him factual changes in history are merely non-essential: "Of course when all is said concerning the permanent needs of man [...] it must be remembered that these needs concern only one pole of man's being, namely the essential pole. As far as the other pole is concerned, the pole which involves man's temporality and historico-cultural conditions that colour the outer crust of his being, it can be said that man's needs have changed. They have changed not in their essence but in their mode and external form." (*Islam and the Plight of Modern Man*, 51). It is also very important that Nasr notes the central notion of Mulla Sadra, the eminent Iranian philosopher of the 17th century of whom Nasr considers himself a follower, the idea of "substantive motion" (*al-harakat al-jawhariyyah*) which is diametrically opposed to Nasr's views regarding lack of any essential change in human affairs: "It is well known that the Muslim Peripatetics [...] believed that motion was possible only in the categories of accident and not in the substance of things [...] By asserting the unity and principality of existence (*wujud*) over quiddity (*mahiyah*) Mulla Sadra makes possible a conception of the cosmos in which there is substantial change, i.e., one in which things change not only in their accidents (*'ard*) but also in their substance (*juhar*). Everything is in a process of becoming until it reaches the plenum of its archetypal reality. There is in fact, a "vertical" evolution in the cosmos." (*Islamic Studies: Essays on Law and Society*, 60) Despite these admissions, as we will see shortly, Nasr's conservative ethos makes him oppose most forms (but not totally) of cultural change.

prescription for it is the eternal recurrence of the old. "A true Islamic renaissance," Nasr wrote, "is not just the birth or rebirth of anything that happens to be fashionable at a particular moment of human history, but the re-application of principles of a truly Islamic nature."[98]

Furthermore, according to Nasr, to a Muslim history is a "series of accidents that in no way affect the nontemporal [permanent] principles of Islam. He [the Muslim] is more interested in knowing and 'realizing' these principles than in cultivating originality and change as intrinsic virtues. The symbol of Islamic civilization is not a flowing river, but the cube of the Ka'ba, the stability of which symbolizes the permanent and immutable character of Islam."[99]

As such, Nasr has for the most part opposed change in the orthodox Islamic law, the Sharia, despite his many heterodox views, "Divine Law is an objective transcendent reality, by which man and his actions are judged, not vice-versa [...] To attempt to conform the Divine Law to the 'times' is therefore no less than spiritual suicide because it removes the very criteria by which the real value of human life and action can be objectively judged and thus surrenders man to the most infernal impulses of his lower nature."[100] On the issue of the reform of personal law in Islam (such as marriage, divorce, child custody and inheritance), however, Nasr has shown some flexibility, but with extreme caution:

> All reforms and changes—especially in matters of personal law—proposed today should be with the aim of preserving and building rather than destroying this equilibrium [between human material needs and spiritual strivings] whose chief symbol in Islam is the square Ka'ba. The question of changing Muslim personal law should be approached with the spirit of belief in the Shari'a, as well as an attempt to apply and preserve it to the extent possible in the modern world, and to build the life of a Muslim society according to it."[101]

In Nasr's conservative agenda there is little space for human freedom in general and for individual freedom in particular. On the theoretical level, he has even gone as far as faulting the notion of indeterminacy in quantum physics because it putatively accords with the idea of human freedom: "The principle of indeterminacy is made to mean freedom of the human will or lack of a nexus of causality between things [...] How often has one heard in classroom and from pulpits that physics through the principle of indeterminacy "allows" man to be free, as if the lesser could ever determine the greater, or as if human freedom could be determined externally by a science which is contained in human consciousness itself."[102] By the same token, Nasr condemns the idea of individual freedom, "[t]he concept of *hurriyah* (the word into which "freedom" is usually translated today in modern Arabic) is taken from the Post-Renaissance idea of individual freedom, which means ultimately imprisonment within the narrow confines

98. *Islam and the Plight of Modern Man*, 127.
99. Nasr, Seyyed Hossein. *Science and Civilization in Islam* (Cambridge, MA. Harvard University Press, 1968), 21.
100. *Islamic Studies*, 28.
101. *Islamic Studies*, 32.
102. *Man and Nature*, 28–29.

of one's own individual nature. This totally Western idea is so alien to traditional Islam that this word cannot be found in any traditional text with the same meaning it has now gained in modern Arabic."[103]

Yet, despite his rhetoric against individuality, Nasr has often expressed the view that only a small group of individuals as the elite of society are capable of comprehending the metaphysical truths that he and his fellow Traditionalists have articulated.[104] Thus the elitism to which Nasr and his co-Traditionalists subscribe predisposes them to advocate a caste system that militates against the modern ideas of equality. In this regard Nasr explicitly maintains that humans exhibit four proclivities that divides them into four types, namely, intellectual, warrior, merchant and masses. "In any case," Nasr writes, "as far as the study of human types is concerned, they [the four types] are to be found everywhere in all times and climes where men and women live and die. They represent the fundamental human types complementing the tripartite Neoplatonic division of human beings into the pneumatics, psychics and "*hylics*" (the *hylikoi* of the Neoplatonists). To *understand the deeper significance of caste* is to gain an insight into a profound aspect of human nature in whatever environment man might function and live."[105] Any change in the hierarchy of this order, any disturbance of the caste system in which the lower castes rebel against the higher caste, in Nasr's view, are signs of entering Kali Yuga, or the Dark Age, into which we have actually slipped as a result of modernity.[106]

Another very important feature of Nasr's conservatism is to be found in his views on women. In his interviews with Ramin Jahanbegloo, Nasr has referred to his disapproval of his mother's feminist tendencies since a young age.[107] Occupying the traditional role of mother and wife is the what Divine Will and the hands of destiny has provided for women, according to Nasr: "Putting aside certain female ascetics like Rabiah, who is one among many female saints and mystics in Islam, most contemplative Muslim women, have, like men, found the possibility of the contemplative life within the matrix of the Muslim social order itself. To accept one's destiny as the wife and mother who is of necessity concerned with daily problems and to submit oneself to one's social position and duties with the awareness that this is in reality submitting oneself to the Divine Will have led many Muslim women to an intensely contemplative inner life amidst, and integrated into, the type of active life imposed upon her by the hands of destiny."[108]

In some of his earlier writings, Nasr has explicitly and unabashedly praised patriarchy:

> From the point of view of social structure, the teachings of the Shariah emphasize the role of the family as the unit of society, family in the extended sense not in its atomized modern form [...] The Muslim family is the miniature of the whole of Muslim society and its firm basis. In it the man or father functions as the *imam* [leader] in accordance with patriarchal nature of Islam. The religious responsibility of the family rests upon his shoulders. He is in a sense

103. *Islam and the Plight of Modern Man*, 21.
104. *Ideas and Realities of Islam*, 136.
105. *Knowledge and the Sacred*, 179. Emphasis added.
106. *Dar Just-u Ju-ye Amr-e Qudsi*, 268.
107. *Dar Just-u Ju-ye Amr-e Qudsi*, 19–20.
108. *Islam and the Plight of Modern Man*, 73.

> the priest, in that he can perform the rites which in other religions is reserved for the priestly class. In the family the father upholds the tenets of the religion and his authority symbolizes that of God in the world. The man is in fact respected in the family precisely because of the sacerdotal function that he fulfills. The rebellion of Muslim women in certain quarters of Islamic society came when men themselves ceased to fulfill their religious function and lost their virile and patriarchal character. By becoming themselves effeminate they caused the ensuing reaction of revolt among certain women who no longer felt the authority of religion upon themselves.[109]

It is quite significant that in the philosophical aspects of his discourse Nasr attempts to play down, as much as possible, human agency as such. However, in regard to gender relations, he is willing to posit a rather potent form of autonomy and self-sufficiency of human subjectivity for men and denying it to women: "Man possesses certain privileges such as social authority and mobility against which he has to perform many heavy duties. First of all he bears all the economic responsibilities [...] A woman in traditional Islamic Society does not have to worry about earning a living. There is always the larger family structure in which she can find a place and take refuge from social and economic pressure even if she has no husband of father [...] Secondly, a woman does not have to find a husband for herself. She does not have to display her charms and make the thousand one plans through which she hopes to attract a future mate [...] Being able to remain more true to her own nature she can afford to sit at home and await the suitable match."[110] In fact in some passages Nasr celebrates men's agency as masculinity and virility, while attributing the quality of being "receptive" to women and lamenting about their reversal in the modern world: "In a society in which the machine crushes the very possibility of the full growth of human nature, whether it be the male or the female, or one in which existing pressures are such that men become ever less masculine and virile and women less feminine and receptive, stands at the very antipode of the Islamic social ideal."[111]

On the issues of polygyny and veiling, Nasr has endorsed the traditional positions. He argues that covering of women's hair in Islamic societies is based on the "Sunnah [tradition] of Islam and on social practices," therefore closed to the possibility of newer interpretations.[112] Similarly, Nasr believes the practice of polygyny is a source of stability in Islamic society, implying any changes in marriage institutions would lead to social chaos, a much feared condition in many Muslim societies, "The traditional family is also the unit of stability in society and the four wives that a Muslim can marry, like the four-sided Ka'bah, symbolizes this stability."[113]

Nasr's discourse does not engage overtly political themes in much detail, despite, or perhaps partly because of, his close involvement in the Pahlavi state when he lived in Iran. Yet the very similar conservative patterns can be observed in the mostly, but not entirely, casual pronouncements that he has made regarding political issues. One

109. *Ideals and realities of Islam*, 110.
110. *Ideals and Realities of Islam*, 112.
111. *Islamic Life and Thought*, 212.
112. *A Young Muslim's Guide to the Modern World*, 244.
113. *Ideals and Realities of Islam*, 111.

political theme that Nasr has dealt with consistently is the issue of secularism, which he has doggedly tried to debunk. In conformity with his overall ideology, Nasr refers to secularism as, "everything whose origin is merely human and therefore non-divine and whose metaphysical basis lies in this ontological separation between man and God."[114] As such, Nasr blames some well-known, and some less known, Islamic thinkers, such as Seyyed Jamal al-Din Afghani, Muhammad Abduh, Shari'at Sangilaj, Sir Ahmad Khan, Ali Abd al-Raziq and Taha Hussein for introducing secular ideas to the Muslim world since the 19th century. He also censures the Baha'i faith for introducing Western and therefore secular "ideas in a religious dress," among certain classes of society in Iran and elsewhere in the Islamic world.[115] Later in his life, however, Nasr has, implicitly rejected the direct rule by clerics, as in Iran, as unprecedented in both Sunni and Shii traditions, while also rejecting the separation between religion and the state as in the United Sates.[116]

Nasr has promulgated the notion of Islamic unity embodied in the Islamic Ummah (the universal Muslim community) to contain all the components of a Muslim ideal polity: "On the social plane Unity [*tawhid*] expresses itself in the integration of human society which Islam has achieved to a remarkable degree. Politically it manifests itself in Islam's refusal to accept as the ultimate unit of the body politic anything less than the totality of the Islamic community or the Ummah."[117] This form of polity may entail the institution of the overarching Caliphate to bring all the different Islamic societies together, a measure that Nasr does not seem to advocate universally. On the practical level and in the earlier phases of his career, however, Nasr identified monarchy as the most suitable type of polity for an Islamic society, especially in a Shii context: "As to the question of who the ruler in Islamic society should be, Sunnism and Shi'ism differ. For Twelve-imam Shi'ism there is no perfect government in the absence of the Mahdi or Twelfth Imam. In such a situation a monarchy or sultanate that rules with the consent of the Ulama is the best possible form of government in circumstances which by definition cannot be perfect."[118] In the Sunni world, Nasr suggests, it is the Caliphate that would be the ideal form of state because the duty of the Caliph is to protect and implement the Sharia, and he serves as a symbol of the rule of Divine Law among people. Yet, Nasr emphasizes, the Caliphate is not a theocracy but a "nomocracy" where society is run on the basis of God's law.[119]

Earlier in his career Nasr made strong pronouncements against any form of parliamentary democracy. First, humans are not capable of legislation in general because, "in the Islamic view God is the only legislator. Man has no power to make laws; he must obey the law God has sent for him. Therefore, any ideal government from the point of view of the Shari'ah is devoid of legislative power in the Islamic sense. The function of the political ruler is not to legislate but to execute them [laws]."[120] Even in

114. *Islamic Studies*, 15.
115. *Islamic Studies*, 23.
116. *Dar Just-u Ju-ye Amr-e Qudsi*, 437–39.
117. *Ideals and Realities of Islam*, 29.
118. *Ideals and Realities of Islam*, 106–7.
119. *Ideals and Realities of Islam*, 107.
120. *Ideals and Realities of Islam*, 106.

situations where the Qur'an and Hadith, the two sources of Islamic law, have not clarified certain aspects of the law, ordinary people cannot be involved in law making, because this function has traditionally belonged to the learned men of Islamic jurisprudence: "the view of Muslims over the centuries has been that giving opinion on a problem of Law should be the function of the Ulema, who alone are well-versed in the science of Law."[121] The reason for this intellectual monopoly by the Ulema, in Nasr's view, is that, "the sciences connected with the Shariah are complex and require study before one can claim to be an authority in them. One could do no more than ask the consensus of a body of laymen on the diagnosis of a certain disease than on the legitimacy of a certain Law."[122] However, later in his career Nasr seems to have somewhat ameliorated his views and tentatively supported a form of democracy, without finding any solution for human intervention in legislation which lies at the center of any modern democracy:

> There are certainly advantages on a certain level to the political institutions in the West based on the idea of democracy, advantages which do not exist in many parts of the Islamic world where political confrontation and tensions are so great that they affect negatively all facets of social life and people do not have the freedoms envisaged for them by the Shariah and traditional Islamic institutions. Still, young Muslims should never simply submit to the idea that democracy, as crystallized in Western political institutions, is simply the ideal norm of government everywhere, especially in the form that it has taken in the West. They must realize that popular participation in the government always existed in the Islamic world before the modern period but through other means than simply casting of votes in a box and that the Islamic world must be given its own space and freedom of choice to be able to develop its own political institutions in conformity with the principles of Islam and the structure of Islamic society, an opportunity which, in fact, is not provided for Muslim countries at the present moment often because of the actions of those very nations which criticize political practices in those countries.[123]

It is important to note here the contradiction of Nasr's remarks above with the overall gist of his discourse. It is not clear how it would be possible to create democracy without its main building block, namely, the individual agency, which Nasr has devoted his life to suppressing as much as possible.

Even more recently, in what seems to be a response to the rise of the reform movement and the presidency of Mohammad Khatami in Iran, Nasr has expressed more positive views on the notion of Islamic democracy in Iran, in which both people and God would be content, and articulated the hope that it would serve as a model for the rest of the Muslim world.[124]

On the other hand, Nasr seems to have persistently maintained his position on a view of political economy in which private property is deemed to be inviolable: "The emphasis on the sacrosanct nature of private property is also clearly stated in the Quran.

---

121. *Ideals and Realities of Islam*, 100.
122. *Ideals and Realities of Islam*, 100.
123. *A Young Muslim's Guide to the Modern World*, 247.
124. *Dar Just-u Ju-ye Amr-e Qudsi*, 442.

In fact the economic legislation of the Quran could not be applied where there to be no private property. According to the Shari'a man is given the right to own property by God and the possession of property is necessary for the fulfillment of his soul in this world provided he keeps within the teachings of the Shari'a. Those who interpret the teachings of Islam in a purely socialistic sense oppose the very text of the Quran, which instructs man as to what he should do with his possessions. The Quran could not legislate about property if it did not accept the legitimacy of private property."[125] On this issue also Nasr seems to be unaware that closely related to the question of private property is the notion of an autonomous individual agent. These tensions in Nasr's thought, in fact, are merely the tip of iceberg that pale when compared to the much deeper aporias that are rooted in his discourse.

Antinomies of Orthodox Sufism

In his protracted pursuit of fulfilling the Western Romantics' agenda of undoing modernity by undermining human agency and subjectivity, Nasr has attempted to utilize Islamic epistemic domains to the maximum possible extent. Of these domains Nasr has made most utility of the Sufi tradition and the Sharia-based orthodoxy by selectively combining certain aspects of two, the result of which is a discourse that exhibits strong strains of contradiction. As such, while attempting to negate the human subject using the Sharia orthodoxy, he has retained, and in fact accentuated, the dogmatism of the orthodoxy. From the Sufi tradition also, he has highlighted those aspects that deny human subjectivity and has remained silent on the aspect of Sufism that that are more positive toward the notion of human agency.

Thus, as we saw before, with respect to the central Sufi doctrine of Unity of Being (*wahdat al-wujud*), Nasr has attempted to interpret it in a fashion that minimizes the notion of human subjectivity. This doctrine with roots in Neoplatonic tradition and Ibn Arabi's thought can be used to elevate human ontological status by perceiving the journey toward the divine realm as a process of human empowerment and acquiring of agency. This Sufi ontology can also be interpreted as a negation of human selfhood by way of dissolving the ego in "Being" or the "Divine Essence." Nasr has attempted to do just the latter by emphasizing what may be called the "negative Sufism," that part of Sufi tradition that negates human subjectivity and agency. On the other hand, Nasr tries to appropriate the element of Sharia-based orthodoxy in his battle against the modern world. In itself, the attempt to combine Sharia orthodoxy and Sufi tradition is nothing new and has been attempted often before. Neither are the contradictions resulting from such an attempt something new. What is the distinct in Nasr's discourse is the peculiar combination of antihumanist elements of these two domains to uphold a desire to overcome modernity that caters to *Western* disillusionment with the modern world.

In general terms, the Sharia-based orthodoxy, because of its logocentric tendency, has tried to elevate the mind (often codified as "spirit" in religious discourse) by debasing the matter and body. Negative Sufism as represented here by Nasr, on the other hand,

125. *Ideals and Realities of Islam*, 108–9.

contains a component that highly valorizes the matter and the body. The result of the combination of these two has been Nasr's attempt to base his discourse on the two elements of matter and spirit at the same time, giving rise to a profound contradiction at the very foundation of his discourse.

Thus, one of the foundations of Nasr's discourse focuses on valorization of the spiritual and the demonization of the physical. "History," Nasr contends, "consists of cycles of decay and rejuvenation. Decay comes from the corrupting influence of the terrestrial environment, from the earth which pulls all things downward and makes every spiritual force decay as it moves away gradually from its original source. Rejuvenation comes from heaven through the prophets who through successive revelations renew the religious and spiritual life of man."[126] On the other hand, one of the tenets of Nasr's ontology consists of the valuing of nature/matter and the body. First, following the footsteps of his European Romantic mentors, Nasr laments the devaluation of matter by the modern cerebral subject: "Cartesian dualism divided reality into the material and the mental, positing a non-material substance which somehow engulfs all the levels of non-material existence and reduces them to a single reality."[127] Then, in a later work, Nasr invokes a Taoist text to prescribe that the spiritual man become natural: "the aim of the spiritual man is to contemplate nature and become one with it, to become 'natural'".[128]

A very significant extension of this approach by Nasr is manifested in his emphasis on the human body, which is quite unusual from the perspective of Sharia-based orthodoxy:

> Man possesses an incorruptible body as well as a radiant spiritual body corresponding to the other "earth" of the higher states of being [...] The human body is not the seat of concupiscence but only its instrument. Although asceticism is a necessary element of every authentic spiritual path, for there is something in the soul that must die before it can reach perfection, the *body itself is the temple of God*. It is the sacred precinct in which the Divine presence or the Divine Light manifests itself as asserted not only in the Oriental religions but also in Hesychasm within Orthodox Christianity where the keeping of the mind within the body and the Divine Name within the center of the body, which is the heart, plays a crucial role."[129]

126. *Ideals and Realities of Islam*, 33.
127. *Islam and the Plight of Modern Man*, 52. As we saw before, Nasr has even gone as far as blaming Christianity, and therefore implicitly monotheism, for valorizing the spirit qua mind and devaluing nature.
128. *Man and Nature*, 84–85.
129. *Knowledge and the Sacred*, 172–73. Emphasis added. Nasr's main mentor, Frithjof Schuon, took this attitude to its logical conclusion and praised human nudity: "Given the spiritual degeneration of mankind, the highest possible degree of beauty, that of the human body, plays no role in ordinary piety; but this theophany may be a support in esoteric spirituality [...] Nudity means inwardness, essentiality, primordiality and thus universality [...] Nudity means glory, radiation of spiritual substance or energy; the body is the form of the essence and thus the essence of the form." Quoted in Mark Sedgwick, *Against the Modern World*, 174. See also Sedgwick 174–75 for the charges against Schuon in early 1990s for his alleged sexual misconducts when he was living in Indiana.

Thus, as a result of wishing to do away with human subjectivity which is founded upon the mind and its activity, Nasr, very similar to his Romantic mentors, has embraced a materialism and valuation of the body, at the expense of the mind, which is very far from the spirit of the Islamic emphasis on human intellect. Nasr has expressed this idea in very unequivocal terms: "modern man, in quest of the sacred and the rediscovery of pontifical man [premodern humans presumably unsevered from nature and the Divine] seek, on the one hand, techniques of meditation which would allow the agitated mind to simply be and to overcome that excessive cerebral activity which characterized modern man and on the other hand, to rediscover the wisdom and intelligence of the body through yoga, oriental forms of medicine, natural foods and the like."[130] This attitude leads Nasr to embrace dance, which in the view of Islamic orthodoxy would be impossible to imagine. Thus, Nasr has succinctly expressed some of the most important elements of his thought, his Romantic concerns to annihilate the subject, his negative Sufism and his views on the body and the mind/spirit by interpreting the dance of Rumi Dervishes: "The Mawlavi dance begins with the nostalgia for the Divine but develops into a gradual opening up towards the grace of Heaven finally resulting in annihilation (*fana*) and absorption in the Truth. Through this dance man journeys from the periphery to the Center which is at once the center of the Universe and the Center of man's own being. The dance also "actualizes" the spirit in the body, making the body the temple of the spirit and a positive element in that spiritual alchemy which certain masters have described as the 'spiritualization of the body and corporealization of the spirit.'"[131]

On a more positive side, however, Nasr's interests in Traditionalism have enabled him to express views that are very tolerant of other religions (at least premodern religions), despite his avowed adherence to Sharia-based orthodoxy. Throughout his long career Nasr has shown a generous level of sympathy for not only other monotheistic religions (with the exception of Protestantism which Nasr censures for its role in the emergence of the modern world), but also Taoism, the Zen tradition, Confucianism, Buddhism, Zoroastrianism and Hinduism, among others.

Conclusion

There is no doubt that many of the ills to which Nasr's discourse responds are serious problems that are closely related to the modern world. These problems as Nasr and his Traditionalist colleagues have observed include human alienation from nature, both the outer nature and the inner nature, which has made the scenario of destruction of the environment and ourselves a possibility, to say the least. His discourse has also depicted the loss of certain elements of beauty and artistic achievements that existed in the premodern world, although perhaps in an exaggerated manner. These are not

130. *Knowledge and the Sacred*, 174.

131. *Islamic Art and Spirituality*, 128. The tension between being a materialist and a "spiritualist" at the same time is indeed profound in Nasr's discourse. However, on a more personal level, one of the most substantive contradictions is Nasr's attempt to suppress the idea of human subjectivity as much as possible, while he has lived the life of an autonomous, self-willing agent to the maximum extent that an individual can expect to achieve in modern times.

new problems and, since the dawn of the modern world, various groups of thinkers and philosophers, poets and artists have been engaged with them. What would be new about Nasr's thought is that he deals with these issues from what he considers to be an Islamic point of view. In fact even this is not new, and the foundations of his discourse are based those of older European Traditionalists such as Rene Guenon and Frithjof Schuon, who tried to graft their Romantic views to Sufi Islam. As such, the solutions offered by Nasr do not seem viable. The very profound contradictions in his discourse indicate that his solutions often run into impasses on the theoretical and practical levels from which Nasr often has to reverse himself. More importantly, it is not clear how solutions offered for the problems of the modern world that explicitly or implicitly reject human freedom and advocate a caste system and the subordination of women could be appealing to anyone.

At the core of Nasr's solutions to the problems of the modern world is the attempt to destroy or at least minimize the notion of human agency and subjectivity. It is the assertive and self-assured human of the post-Renaissance world that has rebelled against the order of nature, the sanctity of "Being" and the absolute sovereignty of God. For this reason, this modern man has to be annihilated and the Sufi path offers itself to achieve this goal. However, in this attempt Nasr reduces Islam to the Sufi tradition and further sacrifices the multifaceted Sufi tradition to what I have designated as "negative Sufism," those elements of Sufism that can be interpreted as the negation of human subjectivity and dissolution in God. In doing so, Nasr ignores those elements of Sufi tradition that constitute a human journey toward the Divine and the elevation of human beings to the status of subjectivity. Similarly, Nasr's discourse, for the same reason, largely contravenes the protosubjectivist elements of mainstream Islam and Qur'anic conception of being human.

As a result, the most incongruous aspect of Nasr's discourse is his attempt to destroy the human subject in the Islamic context that seems to be in the process of formation but is not even born yet in most areas of the Muslim world. As we have seen above, at the deepest level his effort is to destroy, or at least severely weaken, human subjectivity and agency. This is ironic and untimely because in the Muslim world, individual human subjectivity has not come of age yet. In fact Nasr's discourse is aimed primarily at a Western audience or those few extremely westernized Muslims who feel the angst of modern alienation. It is a discourse deeply rooted in Western anguish to overcome the ills of modernity without paying attention to the needs of the Islamic world. But because it is couched in an Islamic idiom, it has been appealing to significantly large groups of Muslims in areas such as Malaysia and other English-speaking parts of the Muslim world. These types of discourse may have very significant negative consequence for these parts of the Islamic world because they merely focus on the detrimental aspects of modernity and are oblivious to the positive achievements of the modern world such as democracy, more equal life opportunities, individual freedoms and rights, and women's rights. Nasr's project and agenda essentially belong to the Western Romantic movement that ironically has been taken up by an Islamic intellectual, and for this reason is largely irrelevant to the Muslim world. At best it can serve as a warning for the negative aspects of modernity, but it ought not do so prematurely.

On the other hand many but not all[132] of Nasr's solutions to remedy the ills of the modern world are at best quixotic efforts to remagicalize the world. By introducing traditions such as "alchemy" and Hermeticism, Nasr and his Traditionalist colleagues hope to address what Max Weber called the disenchantment of the modern world. Combined with the rejection of modern scientific principles, however, these attempts are not going to bring beauty and the sublime to modern world, but will only be used to tranquilize a very small segment of the elite in the West and even smaller number of individuals in the Muslim world.

132. For example, Nasr's emphasis on art, music and dance, could direct modern people's attention to the beautiful and the sublime.

Chapter Nine

MOHAMMED ARKOUN AND THE IDEA OF LIBERAL DEMOCRACY IN MUSLIM LANDS

Few of the thinkers treated in this volume can qualify as steadfast theorists and advocates of liberal democracy in Muslim parts of the world the way Mohammed Arkoun does. In the past four decades he has created a large corpus to broach the idea of pluralism, tolerance of difference and free thinking, all aimed at shifting the discourses of Muslims. Arkoun is a staunch advocate of social and political transformation in a liberal direction in the Muslim world, and for him the key way to achieve this revamp is through change in cultural and ideational spheres. Even though he is an eminent scholar of Islam and Islamic history, he insists that scholarship should not be confined to descriptive and narrative presentation of facts, beliefs and rituals in the past or contemporary period of Muslim lives. Rather, Arkoun maintains, the task of thinkers and scholars of Islam is to problematize the domain of knowledge and to reflect on historical conditions in order to dismantle and debunk cognitive systems and related ethico-juridical norms and codes to free the Muslims from the ideological traps in which they have been incarcerated for centuries. In Arkoun's discourse, knowledge is the foundation upon which norms and legal institutions are built and, as such, to change the latter, the former has to undergo a fundamental transformation. For this reason he has devoted his considerable intellectual ability to bringing about change in the sphere of knowledge and epistemology in the context of Muslim societies.

In its classical period, Arkoun argues, Islamic civilization was sufficiently self-confident to integrate intellectual elements from foreign cultures such as Iran, Greece, Mesopotamia and India, which enriched its thinking and assured its creativeness and vibrancy by keeping its intellectual channels open and alive. But beginning in the 13th century, Islamic intellect embarked upon a process of stagnation that culminated in its loss of intellectual pluralism and humanist momentum, which has intensified since the 19th century encounter with Western imperialism even after the emergence of post-colonial nation states in the Muslim world. As such, Arkoun maintains, the Islamic world is in a dire need of an intellectual renaissance to bring it into the modern world and reinvigorate its vital pulse. He has been very active in the examination and critique of Islamic thought and Muslims' consciousness in order to contribute to a true renaissance of intellect among Muslims around the world.

Epistemology Prevails over Ontology

Human existence for Arkoun is very much defined and determined by knowledge, and to bring about change to the human situation, it is necessary to transform the cognitive system that gives rise to it. Islam, in this view, is but a cognitive system that is in much need of a comprehensive overhaul to update the worldview of its adherents—a process that, if successful, would not leave the Muslims with their traditional belief system recognizable. In this chapter, I delve into Arkoun's attempt to fundamentally shake the traditional Muslim episteme.

Mohammed Arkoun (1928–2010) was born in Taourirt-Mimoun, a town in Grande Kabylie in Algeria. He received his primary education in Taourirt-Mimoun and his secondary education in Oran (Ar. Wahran), which is currently Algeria's second largest city. He studied philosophy in Algeria and then in France at the Sorbonne, obtaining his PhD in philosophy from the Sorbonne in 1968. From 1961 to 1991 Arkoun was a lecturer at the Sorbonne and a visiting lecturer at several universities in France and other countries. Arkoun was initially interested in the history of Islamic thought, and his earliest work included a French translation of Ibn Miskawayh's (d.1030) classical work *Tahdhib al-Ahlaq*, one of the earliest major books on ethics in the Muslim world. Later Arkouns's focus shifted from the classical period to contemporary issues, and he has written prolifically on contemporary issues pertaining to Islam and modernity.

Re-interpreting Fundamental Texts

Logically, the first step for someone who wishes to change the direction of Muslim thought would be the reinterpretation of fundamental Islamic texts, that is the Qur'an and Hadith. Thus, in one of his seminal works, Arkoun complained that no attempt has been made by Muslim thinkers to study and reinterpret the fundamental texts of Islam utilizing the contemporary approaches that recent scholars of Judaism and Christianity, such as André Neher, Jean Daniélou, Karl Barth and Rudolf Bultmann among others, have adopted. What Muslims have done so far has been the emotional repetition and reaffirmation of the truth, eternity and perfection of the message of the Prophet, which amounts to nothing more than a "defensive apology" instead of a new understanding that is appropriate for the contemporary needs of Muslims.[1] Yet, Arkoun promptly rejects the idea of engaging in a definitive and objective interpretation of the Qur'an. Contemporary interpretation of the Qur'an must start with demystification, which means that the Qur'an must be "cleansed" of the different layers of intellectual sediments that are results of speculative reason.[2] The mythical structure of the Qur'anic language has resulted in linear and formulaic reasoning, abstract and dogmatic binaries, sterile and useless controversies and esoteric constructions.[3] Reinterpreting the Qur'an, thus, involves the reversal of the consequences of the "mythical" language of the Qur'an without engaging in another form of dogma resulting from allegedly objective interpretations of the text.

The Qur'an, according to Arkoun, is a homogeneous body and not a selective and arbitrary collection of inquiries. The Muslims have developed a science to determine the "occasion of revelation" (*asbab al-nuzul*) for each of the verses of

1. Arkoun, Mohammed, *Lectures du Coran* (Paris: G.-P. Maisonneuve et Larose, 1982), 2.
2. *Lectures Du Coran*, 4.
3. *Lectures Du Coran*, 15.

the Qur'an, but these occasions cannot address the circumstances of the utterance of all the verses. On the contrary, the coherence of the Qur'anic corpus relies upon a vast network of words and patterns of action that are unchangeable. Yet, the Qur'an is open to the most variegated types of interpretation, because when the Qur'anic text broaches something, it makes communication necessary, which in turn makes the person as its addressee think. Furthermore, even though from a theological point of view the Qur'an might be construed as irrevocably closed, from the historical perspective the modification of the text based on a critical philological approach has always been open.[4]

At times Arkoun's promotion of the idea of reinterpretation of fundamental Islamic texts takes an extreme radical turn in which the only criterion for interpretation seems to be the "unbridled creativity" of the interpreter:

> As regards the Qur'an more directly, it is clear that what is called for here is a protocol of interpretation that is free from both the dogmatic orthodoxy and the procedural discipline of modern scholarship which is [...] no less constraining. It is an interpretation which wanders, in which every human, Muslim or non-Muslim, gives free rein to his or her dynamic of associating ideas and representations, starting out from the freely chosen interpretation of a corpus whose alleged disorder, so often denounced, favours peripatetic freedom and unbridled creativity.[5]

In order to expand his ideas on the reinterpretation of fundamental Islamic texts, Arkoun has utilized a tripartite concept, what he calls "the thinkable, the unthinkable, and the unthought." The "thinkable" is that which, at a given time, is possible to be thought about and explicated with the help of extant intellectual tools in a given linguistic community.[6]

---

4. *Lectures Du Coran*, 43–44.
5. Arkoun, Mohammed, *The Unthought in Contemporary Islamic Thought* (London: Saqi, 2002), 65. It should be noted that Arkoun attempts to refute the arbitrary element in such an impetuous approach to interpretation of texts by asserting that, "[t]his approach is able to extricate itself definitively from every kind of arbitrary rhetorical, artificial and allegedly logical reconstruction, and deluded 'coherence' later imposed by legal, theological, apologetic, ideological and fantasmatic interpretations. One potential model here is, of course, the creative freedom of the likes of Ibn 'Arabi, but in the case we are presenting, the desired freedom is more subversive, since it would include all forms and experiences of subversion ever attempted by mystics, poets, thinkers and artists." (*The Unthought in Contemporary Islamic Thought*, 65) In what seems to be a further attempt to deflect the idea of arbitrary interpretation of fundamental texts, Arkoun has proposed the method of using a "progressive-regressive" approach to understand the Qur'an and Hadith: "We go back to the past not to project on fundamental texts the demands and needs of the present Muslim societies—as the *islahi ulama* do—but to discover the historical mechanisms and factors which produced these texts [the Qur'an and Hadith] and assigned them such functions (regressive procedure). At the same time we cannot forget that these texts are still alive, active as ideological system of beliefs and knowledge shaping the future. We have, then, to examine the process of transformation of initial contents and functions into new ones (progressive procedure)." ("The Concept of Authority in Islamic Thought," in *Islam: State and Society*; eds Kalus Ferdinarnd and Mehdi Mozaffari (Curzon Press, 1988), 56)
6. *Lectures Du Coran*, xiii.

The issues that a community can discuss, explicate and reflect upon in a given period fall into this category. The "unthinkable," by contrast, is what the members of a sociocultural community at a given time cannot fathom, because of the limits of the cognitive order, the self-censorship of the speaker, or the constraints imposed by the dominant ideology.[7] The third part of Arkoun's concept, the "unthought" seems to be closely related to the second, but refers more to a historical situation in which major elements of Islamic tradition that have not been critically evaluated and analyzed but accepted at face-value.[8] The unthinkable and unthought, in Arkoun's view, are the mechanisms by the means of which a community prevents certain key concepts from being thematized and evaluated critically:

> To control the epistemological validity of any discourse, it is necessary to discover and analyze the implicit postulates. This work has never been done for any discourse in Islamic thought [...] This is why I must insist here on the new episteme implicit in the web of concepts used in human and social sciences since the late sixties. It is not possible, for example, to use in Arabic the expression "problem of God," associating Allah and *mushkil* (problem); Allah cannot be considered as problematic. He is well-known, well-presented in the Qur'an; man has only to meditate, internalize, and worship what Allah revealed of Himself in His own words. The classical discussion of the attributes [of God] has not been accepted by all schools; and finally the attributes are recited as the most beautiful names of Allah [...] but are neglected as *subjects of intellectual inquiry*. This means that all the cultures and systems of thought related to pagan, polytheistic, *jahili* (pre-Islamic), or modern secularized societies are maintained in the domain of the unthinkable and, consequently, remain unthought in the domain of "orthodox" Islamic thought or thinkable.[9]

Historically, Arkoun argues, one of the most significant reasons for the expansion of the unthinkable and the unthought was the process of the elimination of philosophy by all Islamic Sunni regimes starting in 848 by the Caliph Mutawakkil, and the suppression of Mu'tazilite theology, which employed rational discourse in its approaches.[10] In the contemporary period, revolutionary Islam has reinforced the perpetuation of the unthinkable and the unthought under the threat of political violence.[11] The expansion of the sphere of the unthinkable and the unthought, Arkoun correctly observes, results in the shutting of the mind and closure of intellect, "[w]hen the field of the unthinkable is expanded and maintained for centuries in a particular tradition of thought, the intellectual horizons of reason are diminished and its critical functions narrowed and

---

7. *Lectures Du Coran*, xiii.
8. See Robert D. Lee's introduction to Arkoun's book, *Rethinking Islam: Common Questions, Uncommon Answers*, 5.
9. Arkoun, Mohammad, "Rethinking Islam Today," *The Annals of the American Academy of Political and Social Science*, vol. 558, July 2003, 20. Emphasis added. Arkoun provides more concrete instance of the unthought in Islamic context by pointing out the refusal of the majority of Muslims to acknowledge the validity of historical and anthropological approaches to rites such as the Hajj pilgrimage and the revered narratives about the Ka'ba, Ibrahim, Ismail, and Isaac. (*Lectures Du Coran*, 158)
10. *The Unthought in Contemporary Islamic Thought*, 89.
11. *The Unthought in Contemporary Islamic Thought*, 139.

weakened because the sphere of unthought becomes more determinate and there is little space left for the thinkable."[12] In fact this is what happens to a "mature" civilization such as Islamic civilization:

> Any system of thinking […] reaches its final stage of development and becomes fully organized by fixing the necessarily limited concepts and procedures of thought of the system. But by that very fact, it delimits the *thinkable* within the system and thus by contra-distinction, also demarcates the sphere of what is *not thinkable* within the system. Arab theology, for example, has perfected a polemical strategy rather than a heuristic model for an open-minded discussion; consequently, modern Arab thought offers a vast domain of the, for the time being, still unthought.[13]

In order to open up the horizon of thought among the Muslim populations, Arkoun has proposed the project of "thinking" and "rethinking" Islam, which are responses to two basic needs: first, to encourage Muslim people to "think for the first time about their own problems," which the triumph of the orthodoxy had rendered unthinkable; secondly, in the thought of the contemporary globalized world in general, and Muslim thought in particular, benefits from new fields of inquiry and new horizons of knowledge can be harvested from "a systematic cross cultural approach to the fundamental problems of human existence."[14] In this connection, it is very important to note that Arkoun recognizes the close relation between what is selected as thinkable and unthinkable and the processes of power in any society:

> Any proposition is an act of power whether followed by a result or not; for a proposition implies selection from the range of significations in any tradition […] To that may be added the selective pressures brought to bear by all protagonists in positions of power in every political and linguistic context. From clan leader, tribal chief or village mayor to king, caliph, sultan, emperor, or president, for the smallest republic or kingdom to today's Unites States; from bishop, rabbi, village imam to pope, chief mufti or chief rabbi: all of these exercise control over the thinkable and the unthinkable, over the selection of what is thought in the orthodox line and over what has to be eliminated and remain unthought if intellectually subversive.[15]

---

12. *The Unthought in Contemporary Islamic Thought*, 12.
13. Arkoun, Mohammed, *Arab Thought* (New Delhi: S. Chand, 1988), 42. It is important to note that Arkoun's idea of intellectual stagnation is not confined to Islam and includes academic endeavors also. He writes: "scholars are not always innovative in their methodology, approaches to aspects of reality, vocabulary and systems of thought and interpretation; they tend to reproduce the substance and cognitive framework of what is already available, supported and imposed by the academic establishment. This attitude has clear repercussions on the shape of government, the style of governance and the type of civil society that is necessarily depended on the scientific culture and the space of the thinkable created and transmitted from behind the scenes on the highest level. (*The Unthought in Contemporary Islamic Thought*, 305–306) One can think of the innumerable academic infantry who write, after a paradigm becomes the establishment in Western academia, largely to reproduce and corroborate the ideas of a handful of generals.
14. "Rethinking Islam Today," 28.
15. *The Unthought in Contemporary Islamic Thought*, 20–21.

Logocentrism and Dogmatism

Arkoun has coined the phrase "Official Closed Corpus" that seemingly partially parallels and partially serves as a foil to his tripartite notion of "the thinkable, unthinkable and unthought." The Qur'an and Hadith began as oral phenomena and only later they were transformed into written form and solidified with orthodox exegeses and theology. With this transformation, the thinkable with regard to these fundamental texts was set, while the unthinkable and unthought came to constitute what Arkoun refers to as a "dogmatic enclosure" that encompassed and restricted Muslim intellect early on in their history.[16] Arkoun has yet another set of concepts to elucidate his ideas about the historical closing of the Muslim mind. He refers to "Qur'anic fact" and "Islamic fact" to distinguish between the historical, linguistic and discursive stage of early Islamic civilization, and the subsequent stage when the political, theological, juridical, mystical, literary and historiographical expansions, elaborations and doctrinal disputes took place.[17] The Qur'anic fact is the early stage of the revelatory phenomenon through which "man must strive to attain the level of perfection embodied by God." In other words, Arkoun seems to suggest, the Qur'anic fact had the promise of human emancipation through an empowerment derived from perfection. But this promise was not fulfilled because of what he calls the development of "Islamic fact." The Islamic fact, Arkoun argues, retains, and in fact exploits, the promise of human perfection, but then hardens and defeats the revelatory hope by rendering it far beyond the human world through processes of "sanctification, spiritualization, transcendentalization, and ideologization," resulting from "all the doctrinal schemes, all the legalistic, ethical and cultural codes, all the systems of legitimation put in place by the ulama [doctors of Islamic theology and law]."[18] Historically the emergence of Islamic dynasties gave rise to Islamic fact whereby various regimes appropriated revelation to promote their political agenda and the creation of state religion:

> "Islam-as-fact" refers to the state appropriation of religion, already apparent with the Umayyids, richly augmented both culturally and intellectually under the 'Abbasids, taken up again by the Ottomans, and finally seen in the modern states with their growing determination to promote populist religion at the expense of the great theoretical and doctrinal confrontations (*munazarat*) of classical times. The administrators of the sacred (*ulama*) were subordinated to state power, and religious confraternities sprang up wherever the central power was weak; these are the two main characteristics of Islam-as-fact from at least the 13th century onwards.[19]

16. See, *The Unthought in Contemporary Islamic Thought*, 61; and *Rethinking Islam: Common Questions, Uncommon Answers*, 32–33.
17. *The Unthought in Contemporary Islamic Thought*, 262.
18. *The Unthought in Contemporary Islamic Thought*, 262–63. Again, Arkoun realistically associates this historical development with the processes of power, as he continues the same passage: "The 'Islamic fact,' like the Christian, Jewish and Buddhist fact, or any other, cannot be dissociated from the exercise of political power in that the state, in all its historical forms, attempts to direct for its own benefit the spiritual ethos of the 'Qur'anic fact,' yet the Qur'anic fact's connection with the 'Islamic fact (notably ethical and legal codes) resists any total, irreversible annexation."
19. Arkoun, Mohammed. "Islam, Europe, the West: Meanings-at-stake and the will-to-power," in *Islam and Modernity: Muslim Intellectuals Respond*, eds. John Cooper, et al. (London: I.B. Tauris, 2000), 176.

Conceptually, Arkoun connects these historical and cultural developments and formations to what he calls "logocentrism" in the cultural history of Islamic civilizations. Apparently influenced by poststructuralist theory in general and Derrida's work in particular, Arkoun utilizes terms such as "logocentrism" and "difference" to further his conceptualization of the closure of Muslim mind. An attempt to combine the Qur'an and philosophical reason lies at the crux of the matter. "It is easy to show how," he wrote "the whole of Islamic thought in its anxiety to represent fully and faithfully both the revealed truth and the sapiential [philosophical] Greco-Persian tradition very rapidly walled itself in a logocentric enclosure principally delineated by the decisive concept of *asl* (source, root, origin, foundation). *Asl* means referring from the outset to the [...] revealed given [the Qur'an] which must be endlessly consulted to verify the legitimacy of any human endeavour and of the discourse that express it."[20] The trouble with the use of philosophical reason, in Arkoun's view, is that once the mind starts seeking logical coherence it will lose touch with the ability to innovate, promote or even accept heterogeneity, that is linguistic, cultural, social and political heterogeneity and difference. "Consequently, while maintaining the requirements for a return to the roots (*usul* [pl. of *asl*]), reason has, in practice, enclosed *ijtihad* [deriving new religious ideas, precept and legal injunctions] within the rigid confines of a scholastic methodology [...] Any attempt to know the truth (*al-haqq*) therefore consists in practice of total submission (*taqlid*) to the authority of the Qur'anic text whose linguistic pre-eminence is inevitably confounded with the transcendence of God's will."[21] The social and political implications of logocentrism are, in Arkoun's view, of course, quite detrimental:

> The religion, culture and state that [are] constructed within the logocentric confines become its supports and constitute regulating and unifying forces. These forces tend to predominate over the forces of differentiations: ethnic differences, heresies and the customs, beliefs and folk traditions of minority groups, excessively independent individuals, etc. Instead of favouring attempts to find a way out of the enclosure, religion and culture are transformed into codes and institutions that apply themselves to the defence of an "official" legitimacy. The quest for meaning is then reduced to a simple repetition (*taqlid*) of meanings already established and assimilated into a specific type of discourse.[22]

Given his use of the notion "logocentrism" in this context, it might easily be perceived that Arkoun's analysis here is a condemnation of reason and rationality as such for being responsible for the dogmatism that characterizes religion in general and Islamic tradition in particular. Yet, Arkoun often recognizes the exploitation and abuse of reason that is frequently committed by dogmatic systems of thought and power. He points out that Islamic law needed to adopt and adapt to the regulating principles of Greek science, and this explains why disciplines of logic, linguistics, theology and ethics converged relatively early on in Islamic tradition. "But," he argues, "the faculty of reason has to pay for

20. *The Unthought in Contemporary Islamic Thought*, 174.
21. *The Unthought in Contemporary Islamic Thought*, 174.
22. *The Unthought in Contemporary Islamic Thought*, 177.

the satisfaction obtained from these exercises by accepting the role of *handmaid* to the revealed Text; its sole function is to shape, bend and systematize reality in accordance with the ideal meanings it recognizes in God's 'signs'."[23] In fact Arkoun seems to praise the Qur'an for endorsing and encouraging reason itself while he condemns the medieval abuse of reason for forging an essentialist and rigidified approach to understanding and the world: "The Qur'an insists on the necessity of man to listen, to be aware, to reflect, to penetrate, to understand, and to mediate. All these verbs refer to intellectual activities leading to a kind of rationalization based on existential paradigms revealed with the history of salvation. Medieval thought derived from this an essentialist, substantialist and unchangeable concept of rationality guaranteed by a divine intellect."[24]

In fact, Arkoun's analysis of dogmatism and the complex relations that he finds between dogmatism and reason, disposes him to dwell extensively on notions of rationality that constitute a significant part of his discourse overall.

Rationality and Muslim Intellect

Arkoun's relations to notions of rationality are quite complex. In general, Arkoun is very much supportive of the humanism of the European Enlightenment and its attempts at human emancipation, but he also is aware and critical of its hegemonic and dominatory aspects. In one passage Arkoun rhetorically shows his solidarity with the ideals of the Enlightenment, such as the universal emancipation of human conditions and rational realism (as opposed to, for example, sentimental imagination and "nostalgic reminiscences"):

> In the name of a historical realism that implies a philosophy of history yet to be validated, should we assume that any attempt to explore or reactivate the question of meaning, which is so alive in the Mediterranean arena, is doomed to capsize among spiritualist imaginings, idealistic speculation, nostalgic reminiscences? Or, despite the triumphant march of a globalization bereft of a humanistic project, can we identify, in the Mediterranean history of thought and culture, stances of reason, objectives from the mind, works of creative imagination, the words of civilizing prophets, saints, thinkers, artists, heroes that might fertilize, illuminate, inspire, provide some additional soul for the new struggles to emancipate the human condition such as they are borne in urgently on all the citizens of a world that is chained to the same destiny?[25]

Yet, he immediately adds that, "I have always distinguished between the legitimacy of the fight against a certain Europe's colonial, racist, fascist domination and my intellectual solidarity with the progress made by humanistic culture, whether in Islamic or Christian or European secular contexts."[26]

23. *The Unthought in Contemporary Islamic Thought*, 175.
24. "Rethinking Islam Today," 36.
25. Arkoun, Mohammed. "Thinking the Mediterranean Arena Today," *Diogenes* 2005; 52; 99, 99.
26. "Thinking the Mediterranean Arena Today," 100. Arkoun has expressed similar ideas somewhat differently: "There is progress and a new departure of code [compared to the

With regard to reason itself, Arokoun has also articulated views that may appear to be in high tension with each other, but in fact capture the nuances and complexity of categories such as reason. Historical research, Arkoun contends, clearly demonstrates the tragic consequences of the jettisoning of the "philosophical standpoint of reason" from the Islamic intellectual sphere, while revealing the vital role it played in the development of scientific rationality and the formation of democracy in modern Europe.[27] The predicaments of contemporary Muslim societies, Arkoun implies, are due to the replacement of critical reason by superstitious emotionality that took place long ago: "We suggest that fresh research should be undertaken to determine how evocations of the miraculous and supernatural, of strong personal and collective emotions, of anxiety, of impatience for the arrival of the Messiah, of eschatological visions and the like came to replace the attitudes typical of the period of growth of Arab [i.e., Muslim] thought, to wit, rational criticism, the experimental method, scientific curiosity, philosophical audacity, and the will to influence events [...] Such a study in historical psychology, if undertaken, would present the additional advantage of throwing light on many a phenomenon pertaining to the Arab societies of our own day."[28] In reality, Arkoun emphasizes the vitality of the idea of critical reason time and time again in his discourse.[29]

Yet, Arkoun is quite cognizant of the dark side of reason that has been revealed after the early and unconditional celebration of rationality became more sober and somber, witnessing the tragedies of the 19th and 20th centuries. "Today," he wrote, "reason is in a more skeptical and critical position. It strives to return to the euphoria of the Enlightenment, but it cannot pass over in silence the resounding setbacks it suffered since the 19th century: colonial domination, Communist despotism, Nazism [...] the dismissal of ethical and spiritual concerns, the support of the selfish individual citizen to the detriment of the person, the triumph of pragmatic liberal philosophy using the mechanism of the free market, the destructive genesis of meaning and so on."[30]

---

ancien régime] with the reason of the Enlightenment because it liberated the intellectual field from false knowledge, as well as arbitrary political and juridical orders, accumulated by the clerical institutions of all regimes. But in its turn, this liberating reason quickly exhausted its ethical and spiritual ethos by becoming conquering, dominating and dogmatic. Particularly in France, the anti-clerical struggle, which was so necessary and fruitful but also violent and radical, engendered a secularist religion that reveals its dogmatism and incapacity to mange cultural pluralism after two centuries of rich and powerful experiences." ("Present-Day Islam between its Tradition and Globalization" in Farhad Daftari [ed.], *Intellectual Traditions in Islam* (I.B. Taruis, 2000), 210)

27. *The Unthought in Contemporary Islamic Thought*, 14.
28. *Arab Thought*, 72.
29. For example: "We see all we can learn from the progress-regressive analysis. Without it, the concept of orthodox Islam with its subsequent heresiographical vision of sects, true and false religions, believers and non-believers, Islamisation of knowledge and foreign, Western knowledge, will continue to obscure and alienate the critical, creative, [and] emancipating use of reason." (*The Unthought in Contemporary Islamic Thought*, 220)
30. *The Unthought in Contemporary Islamic Thought*, 119. Arkoun does not delve completely into the dialectic of modernity to reveal the Janus-faced nature of human subjectivity which ultimately accounts for the both the liberatory and dominatory moments of subjectivity.

Without elaborating much, Arkoun has implicitly associated positivism with the dark side of rationality. The "no-nonsense" unsentimental approach to society and history, adopted by, for example, historical figures such as Ataturk and currents such as French *laïcité* is a necessary phase in the process to emancipation but itself is a problem to overcome. For example, Arkoun maintains that the practice of *taqlid* (following the precedent and the beaten path set by earlier authorities and the fundamental texts) has promoted a mystical worldview to the detriment of "positivist knowledge of man and his history" and to the development of personal observation and experimentation in the Muslim world.[31] Similarly, the prevalence of "the supernatural and the irrational [in the Muslim world] did have the effect of creating insurmountable resistance to the adoption of a positivist attitude based on reason. The nefarious consequences of this development continue to make themselves felt in the Arabian Muslim world of our own day."[32]

On the other hand, in Arkoun's estimation, some of the revolutions in the Muslim world, such as the Ataturk revolution, were tantamount to the victory of positivist thought in a Muslim society, which radically ruptured, with mostly negative consequences, the traditional milieu in which the Muslim masses and the elite used to live and act.[33] The general negative impact of positivism on intellect is that it ultimately closes human thought, which is manifested in the ignorance and intolerance toward religion, myths and by implication religious people such as Muslims in a country such as France. Thus, the positivist approach and secularist thought, "on the pretext of neutrality, has eliminated from the public schools all scientific instruction in the history of religions understood as a permanent and universal dimension of human societies. The general public has thus become illiterate in all that touches religious life and expression, especially in France. A positivist, scientific rationalism has made it impossible for many to even think about myths, symbols, symbolic capital and metaphors that have played a decisive role in all religious expressions."[34]

Subjectivity, to put it rather prosaically, at the bottom entails human empowerment and power and when power is involved it means emancipation for the power-holder as well as domination of the Other. Yet, Arkoun gets close enough: "It should not be forgotten that the reason of the Enlightenment liberated mankind from what Voltaire called a 'wild beast' (meaning the dogmatic theological reasoning employed by the institution of the Church as a way of wielding its power over souls and bodies). By the same token, this reasoning ratified recourse to the violence of war in order to impose a new political legitimacy—a historical fact which is not without bearing on the barbarous instances of violence in the 19th and 20th centuries and on what has been stated here about 'modern' terrorism." (*The Unthought in Contemporary Islamic Thought*, 270)

31. *Arab Thought*, 49.
32. *Arab Thought*, 68. In addition to positivist reason, Arkoun sometimes speaks of "tele-technico-scientific reason," which is closely related to the notion of instrumental rationality and its concrete manifestation in the economic and technical spheres. "So-called 'tele-technico-scientific reasoning' is spreading a new pragmatic instrumental form of reasoning lead by principles of 'just do it,' as long as doing ensures concrete, significant technological and economic success." (*The Unthought in Contemporary Islamic Thought*, 40)
33. *Rethinking Islam: Common Questions, Uncommon Answers*, 25.
34. *Rethinking Islam: Common Questions, Uncommon Answers*, 20.

Reason, Arkoun suggests, should not undergo the same fate as religion did; it should not become dogmatic. For this reason he underlines the critical function of reason that has to be applied to itself. "The crucial point," Arkoun writes "is that the critical function applied to concrete existential, social, political, ethical and legal debates should first focus on the suspicion of reason itself, just as the scientist remains suspicious of the result of his experiment in the laboratory."[35] In the later period of his thought, Arkoun introduced the notion of "emerging reason" that seems to be built on, but not a simple continuation of, the idea of critical reason. The first characteristic of the emerging reason is that it "will be continuously emerging to reassess its function."[36] The emerging reason, Arkoun argues, does not simply represent a linear progress of positivist reason, but at the same time it does not discount the plentiful accomplishments of the modern period. Most significantly, the emerging reason does not, "disqualify a priori all the legacies of the living cultural traditions still linked to religious inspiration."[37] In other words, the emerging reason does not dismiss non-Western and nonmodern epistemes as positivist reason does. As such, Arkoun argues, because the emerging reason is built on the emancipatory aspects of Enlightenment reason, minus its hegemonic and dominatory facets, it is well suited to serve as the cultural and educational foundation for the socialization of Muslim minorities in the West, as well as enabling the Muslims in their own lands to transform their traditions without totally alienating them from their past:

> Here ER [emerging reason] faces two tasks. It points out the ideological solidarity of social and political sciences with hegemonic reason, and it undertakes the neglected duties of the state in the fields of education, cultural activities, relevant criticism of the "return of religion," the resurgence of the sacred, all of which mean, in fact, a dialectic response to an arbitrary policy or a total lack of effective policy. These tasks are not only required for the migrants in European/Western contexts, they are all the more urgent in Islamic contexts where many "national" states are even more cynical and obscurantist in their religious, cultural and social policy. In other words, ER carries on several battles simultaneously in all contemporary contexts, namely the epistemological battles in the West, the didactic battles in the traditional, marginalized societies, and political battles with all categories of establishments that monopolize the decision-making process in academic, bureaucratic, governmental and economic institutions. It is interested in all types of silenced voices throughout history, like all those voices silenced today in Islamic contexts, either by official censorship or by the pressures of public opinion manipulated by political activists; it reactivates the persecuted innovative mind.[38]

---

35. *The Unthought in Contemporary Islamic Thought*, 325.
36. *The Unthought in Contemporary Islamic Thought*, 23.
37. *The Unthought in Contemporary Islamic Thought*, 28.
38. *The Unthought in Contemporary Islamic Thought*, 29. Arkoun insists that his notion of "emergent reason" should not be conflated with postmodern reason: "I have explained why the concept of post-modernity cannot be used here: as a result of all the criticism it has attracted from various disciplines and schools of thought in the West itself. It had some relevance for a while in the 1970s and 1980s in the elimination of limited, abstract postulates used by the rationale of the Enlightenment—the formalistic, vacuous humanism, especially during the period of the conquering liberal bourgeoisie on the one side and the Socialist-Communist

Overcoming Positivist and Traditional Reason

Arkoun's notion of emergent reason sounds quite utopian; nevertheless it points to Arkoun's efforts to pave the way for overcoming both the traditional and positivist approaches toward reason. The tensions that exist in Arkoun's thought on reason in general, are also visible in his approaches toward conceptual thinking on the one hand, and imagination on the other. In his writing, especially during the earlier phases, Arkoun vehemently criticizes anything that might resemble mythologization and mystification of the world. He refers to the necessity of immense efforts to demystify and demythologize the religions of humanity, including the greatest theological works, utilizing scientific methodology.[39] In another context, Arkoun denounces the explicit resorting of the religious outlook to "[an] enchanted world of mystery, the supernatural, transcendence and the miraculous, where the operation of sanctification, mythification, sublimation, transfiguration, and ontologisation, and even mystification take place."[40] The Qur'an itself, Arkoun points out, rejects the notion of miracles and provides the "coordinates" for the positive recognition in space and time.[41] On the other hand, Arkoun insists that nonconceptual and nondiscursive knowledge is a part of human epistemology that needs to be recognized and accommodated duly in any epistemological scheme such as his: "The irrational and imaginary dimensions of mind have been negated by classical theology and metaphysics because man is created in the image of God and man strives to resemble God [...] The operative forces of the irrational and the imaginary remained and still remain hidden, unknown, unthought of even in our most sophisticated, rationalist, [and] scientific culture."[42]

For this reason Arkoun introduces the notion of the "imaginary" (sometimes he uses "imagination"). Arkoun describes the imaginary as possessed by both the individual and the collectivity at the group or national level. In traditional settings, the imaginary is the collection of images carried by that culture about itself or another culture and is the product of categories such as religious discourses, poetry and epics, and in contemporary settings it is produced primarily by the media and secondarily by the education system.[43] As such Arkoun declares that the rational and the imaginary both are legitimate and therefore must be reconciled:

> The rational and the imaginary must assume more flexible definitions and more realistic functions in cognitive activity and cultural production. Reason must give up its arrogant sovereignty and recognize the portion of imagination to be found in its most rigorous exercises, especially in the domain of the human and social sciences [...] The rational and

---

proletarian revolution on the other. The definition and the tasks assigned to post-modern reason have remained limited to the European/Western historical perspective." (*The Unthought in Contemporary Islamic Thought*, 26)

39. *Lectures Du Coran*, 21.
40. *The Unthought in Contemporary Islamic Thought*, 62.
41. *Lectures Du Coran*, 93.
42. *The Unthought in Contemporary Islamic Thought*, 88.
43. *Rethinking Islam: Common Questions, Uncommon Answers*, 6.

the imaginary are two interdependent aspects of any cognitive action undertaken by the mind, and they exist in fruitful tension with each other. By recognizing this fact, scholars can free themselves from dichotomous thought, which has long pitted reason against imagination, logos against *mūthos*, concept against metaphor, proper meaning against figurative meaning, science against religion, diverse beliefs against superstitions, religion against magic, modern against archaic or traditional, civilized against primitive, developed against underdeveloped.[44]

The above epistemological attempt at reconciling logos and mythos is in turn grounded in a view of being human that is common among many modern Islamic thinkers (as we have seen in previous chapters): "Two poles of the same reality, man is both matter and spirit, engendered from the earth and destined to return to the earth, man is nevertheless capable of appreciating divine things, to which end his mind and his heart, the twin powers of perception and immediate intellectual apprehension on the one hand and intense affective participation, on the other, are both insistently solicited. The preceding remarks explain why Arab thought developed in two opposite directions, the one emphasizing discursive reasoning and the other faith and the intuitive grasp of reality."[45] Even at a deeper level, Arkoun argues, since the 17th century a rupture between the aspects of human knowledge, and consequently human modes of existence, has intensified in which logos (conceptual languages and logic and mathematical language) and mythos (religious, poetic, artistic languages, metaphor and symbol) have been alienated from one another. In fact, Arkoun argues, this rupture and alienation goes back to Plato and Aristotle and has marked the Islamic civilization both among the Sunnis and Shii reaching its apex today. For this reason, Arkoun prescribes a reconnecting, or what he calls "*rememberment*," of the two ruptured, crucial elements of human knowledge and life.[46]

44. *Rethinking Islam: Common Questions, Uncommon Answers*, 128. It is interesting that Arkoun compares what he calls contemporary anthropological emphasis on the imaginary with the Qur'anic mythos found in the notion of the heart: "We must abandon the dualist framework of knowledge that pits reason against imagination, history against myth, true against false, good against evil, and reason against faith. We must postulate a plural, changing, welcoming sort of rationality, one consistent with the psychological operations that the Qur'an locates in the heart and that contemporary anthropology attempts to reintroduce under the label of the imaginary." (*Rethinking Islam. Common Questions, Uncommon Answers*, 37) In conformity with his notion of logocentrism that has putatively mired *learned* Islamic epistemology, Arkoun, also criticizes the overemphasis on rationality, at the expense of the imaginary, by some Islamic trends: "the prejudice of rationality which commands the pious as well as the modern historical reading of holy founding texts, has eliminated the marvelous as the anthropological dimension of the type of knowledge produced and expanded by imagination interacting with reason. This dimension opens rich possibilities for a more inclusive psychology of religious and poetic knowledge beyond the prevailing irrelevant opposition between reason and imagination." (*The Unthought in Contemporary Islamic Thought*, 233–34)

45. *Arab Thought*, 51.

46. *Lectures Du Coran*, 175.

Modern Social Sciences Modifying Islamic Reason

Interestingly one of the implicit corollaries of the reconciliation that Arkoun proposes above is the possibility of modifying the Islamic worldview by means of modern social sciences. The controllers of the Orthodoxy in Islam, Arkoun declares, constantly exercise an intense badgering of scientific reason, while promoting an idea of religion that is prior to all human experiences and effectively penetrates and controls all aspects of individual and collective life. He then proposes opening up the Islamic intellect by utilizing modern and methodical sociological and historical explorations to correct its claims of being transcendental and beyond change. Sociology, Arkoun continues, is a very important tool in examining religious symbolisms related to social transformation and historical action.[47] Contemporary Islamic beliefs accuse modern science of attempting to dissolve the religious reality in a barren relativism. In fact, however, scientific research purifies religion from the dross that is imposed on it by the numerous regulators of the sacred.[48] The intellectual field in all Muslim lands, Arkoun argues, has been in decline since the period of the three late medieval empires—the Ottomans, the Safavids in Iran and the Moguls in India. Islamic thought has been isolated from the great intellectual and scientific achievements of the modern period. In fact Muslim intellect has been indifferent, suspicious and even hostile to many of the discoveries and inventions of modernity. Even during the so-called Arab Renaissance (*Nahda*), which stretched from middle of the 19th century to the early 20th century, Arkoun argues, the Muslims failed to spread the achievements of modernity in any substantial manner.[49]

For these reasons, Arkoun believes that modern fields of study, such as social sciences, linguistics, and modern historical studies, should be utilized to contribute to the reinterpretation of received religious and theological notions, but without conceding to the arrogance of positivistic approaches:

> What is received, taught, interpreted and lived as Revelation in Jewish, Christian and Muslim traditions needs to be revisited, re-read and re-interpreted as social, linguistic and literary constructs enhanced and consolidated over time by shared historical solidarity, a sense of belonging to a common history of salvation [...] This means that we *suspend* any theological statement about Qur'anic Discourse as the word of God until all of the linguistic, semiotic, historical and anthropological problems raised by the Qur'an, as text, are clarified. I say "suspend," rather than "disqualify," "ignore" or "eliminate," as modern linguists and historians arrogantly do when they refuse even to listen to the rightful demands of believers who are rejected in a non-scientific category. By so doing, they substitute and oppose a positivist, pseudo-scientific, self-promoting interpretation to the dogmatic, theological one which, over the centuries, has imposed its own form of arrogant self-entitlement to the exclusive Truth.[50]

47. Arkoun, Mohammed, and Louis Gardet, *L'Islam Hier-Demain* (Paris: Buchet/Chastel, 1978), 220.
48. *Lectures Du Coran*, 174.
49. *The Unthought in Contemporary Islamic Thought*, 159.
50. *The Unthought in Contemporary Islamic Thought*, 73. Arkoun largely excludes from this process the Orientalists and the majority of experts on Islamic studies whom he views as non-critical thinkers with regards to study of Muslim societies: "It remains true that the most admirable

In this way Arkoun strives to cleanse the religious episteme of its dogmatism through the use of social sciences that have presumably been paved by emergent reason: "The objective of a consistent critique of religious reason is to use all the sources of intelligibility provided by the human and social sciences to remove the issue of Revelation from the epistemic and epistemological posture associated with the dogmatic spirit to the fields of analysis and interpretation opened up by emergent reason."[51] In a related vein Arkoun argues that Muslim scholars should learn to contribute to the new approaches to the religious issues, by means of increasing the possibilities for the exchange and confrontation of ideas, to make progress in what is bound to be a long-term enterprise with the ultimate goal of engaging in critical thought, knowledge and action.[52] Among the methodologies of human and social sciences, Arkoun has emphasized the notion of "historicity" as an indispensible tool in the attempts to reinterpret and revise religious thought. By historicity he means the insights of moral, religious, political values, norms and institutions are subject to historical change and are thus of relative value. All these products of human intellectual activity, Arkoun contends, are semiotic productions that fall in the category of historicity.[53]

With the popularity of postmodernist thought and notions such as deconstruction in the human sciences in the past two decades, Arkoun's interest in modification of Islamic thought by means of the social sciences has also evolved to incorporate the

---

scholars who limit their search and their 'writings' to the erudite accumulation of factual knowledge, neglect to read and enhance their critical thinking with the conceptualisations and the epistemological shifts imposed by those scholars-thinkers who contributed so efficiently to the successive 'scientific revolutions' of intellectual modernity. The unique, valid point in discussion here is how to bring Islamic thought and studies to the level of fertile criticism we have witnessed since the seventeenth-eighteenth century in European scholarship and historical development." (*The Unthought in Contemporary Islamic Thought, 36*)

51. *The Unthought in Contemporary Islamic Thought*, 95. Another task that Arkoun assigns to modern social sciences is that of contributing to the "deconstruction" of Islamic orthodoxy and dogma by strengthening the local and popular forms of religiosity in Muslim lands, which combined a large portion of popular culture with a low dose of formal Islam: "Despite this official written, 'learned' Islam, a popular Islamic culture developed under the leadership of many local saints who were able to share the dialects, beliefs and customs of the various ethnic groups, which the remote government was unable to control politically. An ethno-sociological survey is needed of this neglected but exuberant Islam, so often condemned as 'superstition' and illiterate by the official 'orthodox' Islam concentrated in the urban social classes." (*The Unthought in Contemporary Islamic Thought*, 159)
52. *The Unthought in Contemporary Islamic Thought*, 48.
53. For example he wrote: "All semiotic productions of a human being in the process of his social and cultural emergence are subject to historical change, which I call historicity. As a semiotic articulation of meaning for social and cultural uses, the Qur'an is subject to historicity. This means that there is no access to the absolute outside the phenomenal world of our terrestrial, historic existence [...] This line is opposed to all medieval thinking based on stable essences and substances. The concept of Revelation should be reworked in the light of semiotic systems subjected to historicity. The Mu'tazili theory of God's created speech deserves special consideration along this new line [...] The Aristotelian definition of formal logic and abstract categories also needs to be revised in the context of the semiotic theory of meaning and historicity of reason." ("Rethinking Islam Today," 24)

idea of deconstruction in his discourse. Thus, in close conformity with his idea of a critical approach to all aspects of human knowledge, Arkoun thinks that the task of researchers is to problematize all systems that are active in producing meaning and knowledge, both contemporary and the historical.[54] Arkoun believes it is time to engage in a "deconstruction of the axioms, tenets and themes that hold together and establish the 'adventurous cohesion' of every faith."[55] The point, however, is not to engage in a "scientific" demonstration of the validity or irrationality of the articles of the faith of given religion or system of value, but to engage in Nietzschean genealogical criticism of values and their roles in the formation of human personality.[56] "It is important," Arkoun posits, "to show all the discourses derived from the revealed word of God [...] contributed to shaping the anthropological structure of the religious, political and social imaginaries (*imaginaires*). Deconstructing these structures is the task of the historian who is able to retrace the psychological, cultural, political process initiated by the impact of Revelation, carried on through the recurrent rivalry between the driving forces in two related fields [...] the quest for meaning and the will-to-power."[57] What Arkoun means by "deconstruction" of religious structures and social imaginaries seems to pertain to what he calls "Islamic fact," as we saw above: "One rarely finds in the most critical writing [...] about Islam [...] the concepts of state control over religion, sacralization, transcendalization, spiritualization, ontologization and mythologization of religion. All this has made it necessary for the analyst to undertake the reverse process of de-sacralization, etc.—in other words: unveiling, deconstruction, de-historization; laying bare the reality which has been constructed by and for the social *imaginaire*."[58]

---

54. *The Unthought in Contemporary Islamic Thought*, 42.
55. Arkoun, Mohammed, *Islam: To Reform of to Subvert* (London: Saqi, 2006), 87.
56. *The Unthought in Contemporary Islamic Thought*, 61–62.
57. *The Unthought in Contemporary Islamic Thought*,77.
58. "Present-Day Islam Between its Tradition and Globalization," 202–03. It is significant that Arkoun's notion of deconstruction is closely linked to the idea of critique of power and violence, be it violence linked to religious traditions or Western hegemony. "The critique of Islamic, Christian, Jewish, Buddhist, Hindu, Marxist, liberal, etc. reason will take the form of an effort to identify the unthought and unthinkable, not with reference to a modernity which is conceptually one with the recurrent aspirations of European-Western hegemony, but by making the epistemological resolution to move towards an intellectual outlook based on the principles of overcoming, surpassing, and removing all constructions, all affirmations of identity, all truths deriving from or spread by violence." ("Islam, Europe, the West: Meaning-at-Stake and will-to-power," 174–75) Arkoun has extrapolated this form deconstruction to all values that are in one way or another related to domination and exploitation: "Values become dangerous in all cultures and all contexts when they are used as a cloak for inadmissible and reprehensible ventures motivated by the desire to dominate, exploit and profit from those without whose help the powerful of this world would not enjoy the monopoly that they do. Values must be constantly recreated because of the actions of the very people who are supposed to be the stewards and protectors of so-called sacred, divine, humanist or universal values and who appropriate them for their own ends so long as they are shielded from the subversive criticism of non-conformist thinkers." (Arkoun, Mohammed, "For a Subversive Genesis of Values," in *The Future of Values: 21st Century Talks*. Jerome Binde, ed. New York: Berghahn Books, 2004, 49.)

The State of Contemporary Islamic Thought

Arkoun's attempt to revitalize the Islamic intellect should be viewed in relation to what he portrays to be the actual state of contemporary Islamic thought. Ironically some of Arkoun's critiques of contemporary Muslim intellect partially resemble some of the positivistic points of view that he generally criticizes. Thus, he criticizes contemporary Muslim thought for, on the one hand, lack of internal coherence and objectivity to discover the "inner truth of things" with regard to the natural world, and on the other hand, lack of respecting the rights of Muslims in the sociopolitical sphere.[59] Even during its most successful phase, that is during the reform (*islah*) period of mid-19th to mid-20th century, Islamic thought was not able to transcend the religious paradigm. Secularly oriented thinkers such as Taha Hussein (d. 1973), Salama Musa (d. 1958), and Ali Abd al-Raziq (d. 1966), according to Arkoun, did try to generate fruitful discussions among Muslims, but ultimately they failed to create a durable school of thought free of religious constraints.[60] The conditions of Islamic thought, in Arkoun's view, have further deteriorated since mid-20th century with attempts to Islamicize knowledge: "Muslim scholars feel that they can dispense, as Ibn Khaldun did, with any need to point to other traditions of thought and knowledge. This cognitive posture is expressed today in a more arrogant style by those who endeavor to *Islamise Modernity*. With this attitude, the tradition of thought is doomed to miss all enabling opportunities in order to avoid accumulating false knowledge and an increasing number of epistemological obstacles."[61] In fact, Arkoun contends, contemporary Muslim intellectual scenes are much more barren compared to the classical period (661–1258) in which a form of doctrinal pluralism was respected and exercised. This lack of doctrinal diversity today has to do, to a large extent, with the political situation in many contemporary Islamic contexts in which the state imposes a rigid ideology and appeals to and uses the history of official religion propagated as true religion.[62]

---

59. *L'Islam Hier-Demain*, 187.
60. *The Unthought in Contemporary Islamic Thought*, 88.
61. *The Unthought in Contemporary Islamic Thought*, 221–22. Arkoun has summarized the historical conditions undergirding the current state of Muslim thought in more concrete terms than he usually does in the following passage: "After the death of Ibn Rushd (1198), the creative interface between theology, religious law and philosophy was disrupted; theology as a rationalizing attempt at faith building or even criticism, disappeared after the thirteenth-fourteenth centuries; schools of law stopped their disputations (*munazara*) and became isolated from each other; ethic elevated by Miskawayh (1020) [sic] to the rank of a key discipline in the curriculum of a learned humanist human subject, was disregarded as well as a critical, rationalizing endeavuor to consciously discern the positive, operative, emancipating virtues from the traditional, uncriticized, unthought collective habits ritually reproduced in patriarchal societies." (*The Unthought in Contemporary Islamic Thought*, 317) Arkoun's estimation of the Shia history is somewhat more optimistic, "We shall simply point out that, as a consequence of the Shi'ite notion of Tradition, enlarged to include the teachings of the Imams, the Shi'ite reading of the Qur'an was more interpretive, made more place for the imagination and postulated a different philosophy of language [compared] to that implied by the more literal reading of the Qur'an of the Sunnites." (*Arab Thought*, 57)
62. Arkoun, Mohammad, "History as an Ideology of Legitimation: A Comparative Approach to Islamic and European Contexts," in Martín Muñoz, Gema, ed. *Islam, Modernism and the West:*

This state of affairs, in turn, has to do with the strength of traditionalist modes of cultural patterns in which the idealization of the founding figures of Islam are extremely obdurate:

> The values of human conduct and, in a more general way, that of the historical development of a people since 632 AD, is considered to depend solely upon conformity to the text-source-model [the Qur'an] or to the examples and behests of the idealized figures of the Prophet, the Companions and the Imams [among the Shia]. Any falling away from those models is felt and thought of as personal degeneration and communal decadence. Consequently, the doctors of every social school have, to this day, preached the return to the true pattern of all genuinely human existence; this is what is meant by the reformist attitude or *islah.* [63]

As such, Arkoun thinks that the challenge of contemporary Islamic thought, in order to achieve its rightful status, is not merely to fight against official ideology and outmoded ideas, but more importantly, to overcome its conformism and self-censorship, which is more harmful than the official censorship. Such an undertaking, of course, faces many obstacles given the strong cultural barriers that Muslim intellectuals face.[64] Another challenge that the contemporary Muslim thought faces in the processes of transforming itself, Arkoun often remarks, is the label of Western cultural hegemony that many groups in the camps of political Islam attach to efforts to bring about change to Muslim thought and culture.[65]

Orientalism and Islam

Western scholarship, in Arkoun's estimation, especially the Orienatalist type, not only does not contribute to the transformation of Muslim intellect, but in fact it prevents such a change. The mere accumulation of knowledge and historical facts about the

---

Cultural and Political Relations at the End of the Millennium (London: I.B. Tauris, 1999), 29.

63. *Arab Thought*, 16. It is very important to note that while Arkoun's project is to overcome centuries of tradition accumulated in Islamic contexts, he is ultimately loyal to the philosophical views expressed in the Qur'an on human conditions (more on this issue below): "If Arab thought has today reached the stage at which these questions [of the usefulness of modern branches of knowledge] can no longer be eluded, that is so because she has travelled a long distance in the last 150 years in the discovery of modernity. One cannot speak of her backwardness without taking into consideration the disillusionment she suffered at the time when she stood most in need of her self-confidence. Like Christian thought, she must learn to overcome the temptation, to which she yielded for centuries, of setting up ideas reflecting transitory situations as transcendental truths. Like profane thought she must learn *to look at man as he is without in any way renouncing the will to continue the great debate opened by the Qur'an.*" (*Arab Thought*, 101; emphasis added)
64. *Arab Thought*, 98.
65. In one instance Arkoun wrote: "The Islamic discourse claims to be scientific while at the same time human and social sciences are rejected as the product of Western societies and tools for cultural aggression (*al-ghazwa al-fikri*). It is difficult to explain to Muslim militants, or to Ulama trained in traditional sciences, that human and social sciences are the vital counterpart of the ideologies produced in industrialized as well as in developing countries." ("The Concept of Authority in Islamic Though," 68)

Islamic world, Arkoun argues, perpetuates the traditional Islamic dogmatic discourse. He takes the Orientalists to task for their "refusal to epistemologically commit their accumulated knowledge to a criticism of religious reasoning that would include all known examples in the societies of the Book-book. The refusal of historian, anthropologist, sociologist, psychologist, literary critic and semiotician to identify and answer the challenges of prophetic discourse [the Qur'an and Hadith] and the logic of existential feelings and emotions [...] it generates, will maintain the gap between the 'reductive, positivist' scientific posture of mind and the 'dogmatic,' 'subjective,' 'emotional' attitude of religious mind."[66] As Arkoun correctly observes, one of the most significant reasons why the Orientalist traditions do not and cannot commit themselves to a critical and evaluative approach is that they are incapable and unwilling to engage in any theoretical and epistemological discussions, which could putatively affect the orthodox rules that dominate the Islamic studies in Western academia.[67] And the reason why nontheoretical works preserve the status quo, with regard to dogmatic Islamic intellect, is that such works do not in any way encourage free and creative thought. For this reason Arkoun complains that "[t]hose who criticize me for giving more place to the setting up of theoretical and methodological frameworks than to substantial monographs can measure to what extent Islamic studies suffer from weakness, rather absence, of theoretical and epistemological debates fitting, of course, into concrete historical, sociological and anthropological frameworks. We are well aware that the accumulation of scholarly knowledge (which remains an indispensible step) does not necessarily generate critical, inventive, liberating thought."[68] A related problem, Arkoun argues, is that in its static approach, Orientalism treats Islam as static, essentialist and incapable of change:

> All the polemics recently directed against Orientalism show clearly that so-called modern scholarship remains far from any epistemological project that would free Islam from the essentialist, substantialist postulates of classical metaphysics. Islam, in these discussions, is assumed to be a specific, essential, unchangeable system of thought, beliefs, one which is superior or inferior (according to Muslims or non-Muslims) to the Western (or Christian) system. It is time to stop this irrelevant confrontation between two dogmatic attitudes—the theological claims of believers and the ideological postulates of positivist rationalism.[69]

66. *Islam: To Reform or to Subvert*, 89.
67. *The Unthought in Contemporary Islamic Thought*, 82.
68. *The Unthought in Contemporary Islamic Thought*, 142.
69. *Rethinking Islam Today*, 19. Arkoun further complains that, "The Muslim intellectual must today fight on two fronts: one against a disengaged social science merely concerned with narrative and descriptive style; the other against the offensive/defensive apologia of Muslims who compensate for repeated attacks on the authenticity and the identity of the Islamic personality with dogmatic affirmation and self-confirming discourse." (Arkoun, Mohammed, "The State, the Individual, and Human Rights: A Contemporary View of Muslims in a Global Context" in *Muslim Almanac*, 1995, 456.)

Political Philosophy

Despite his overwhelming emphasis on thought and intellect in his discourse—at the expense of a direct discussion of core political issues—Arkoun sometimes attempts to demonstrate the close relationship between thought and power in general, and Islamic reason and political reason in particular. From very early on in Islamic history, when the Qur'an was compiled into an official corpus, Islamic reason became intertwined with state reason in a dialectical fashion.[70] In all religions, Arkoun maintains, religious discourse and revelation have functioned to enunciate and represent God's Supreme Authority as being transferred to the emperor, the Caliph, the sultan and now the president.[71] The question that Arkoun poses is that is it ever possible to separate and free the state power from religious discourse and revelation and vice versa?[72] Arkoun finds the answer to this essential question in secular political liberalism and democracy, as we will see in the discussion of his political theory.

At the core of Arkoun's rather succinct political theory is the notion of a relationship between power, authority and legitimacy. In his view, the distinction and yet the relations between authority (*hukm, hakimiyya*) and power (*sulta, sultan*) in Islam are crucial. The most recent studies by both Muslim thinkers and Orientalists on authority and power in Islamic contexts, Arkoun argues, are largely focused on power in its political expression through the state, effectively sidelining the question of authority, which for Arkoun undergirds the concept and fact of power.[73] In the Islamic context from early stages until today, the orthodoxy finds authority in established sources, be they religious or philosophical. The notion of *taqlid* (following the authority of established religious sources) in Islam vests authority in following the sacralized texts and personalities, which is antithetical to modern sensibilities:

> Although philosophers in classical Islam contributed to the enrichment of political thought, they did not initiate a cognitive shift from their Greek sources and higher authorities. Aristotle, in particular, was promoted to the rank of "first master," Farabi being the "second." Intellectually, they used the same attitude of *taqlid* as theologians and Jurists, if we understand *taqlid* as the active intellectual search for identifying among the known respected authorities in a field of knowledge, the most stable, reliable source of authority. I have shown in my *Humanisme Arabe* how this intellectual convergence on the problem of authority is one of the distinctive characteristics of the medieval mindset and cognitive practice. For this reason,

70. *Lectures Du Coran*, 147–48.
71. At one point Arkoun declares the Umayyid and Abbasid states as all secular except in appearance: "The Umayyid-'Abbasid state is secular in its sociological and anthropological basis, its military genesis and expansion, its administrative practice, its ideological discourse of legitimacy. The theological and jurisprudential endeavour developed by ulema contributed to concealing behind a religious vocabulary and sacralizing conceptualization, literary devices, ideological basis of the so-called 'Islamic' polity and governance." (*The Unthought in Contemporary Islamic Thought*, 248) One might argue that even the most theocratic state in essence is secular along the lines that Arkoun describes here.
72. *The Unthought in Contemporary Islamic Thought*, 77.
73. *The Unthought in Contemporary Islamic Thought*, 205.

> we cannot confuse the medieval political philosophy that was not yet emancipated from the theological categories and modern political philosophy that has deliberately strived for full emancipation from any concession to theology.[74]

Power, authority and legitimacy, in Arkoun's view, are ultimately conditioned by perceptions of truth in all societies. In premodern societies, orthodox truth defined and legitimized authority in terms of revelation or precepts derived from it, whereas in modern liberal democratic society, authority is legitimized based on popular sovereignty. "In all cultures, Truth with capital T, refers to the Truth imagined, constructed, articulated and projected back by the historiographical literature produced *post facto* under the pressures and the specific needs of several social, ethnic, competing groups, as is clearly shown during the Ummayid and Abbasid rule. Each group defends and promotes its own 'orthodox Truth,' using the same literary device of projecting back to the same Inaugurating Time when Revelation or revelatory discourse attributed to ancient wisdom in 'non-revealed' religions, occurred. This collective process of building the supreme instance of Authority is repeated everywhere through history and is also present in the secular theory of popular sovereignty on which is based our democratic legitimacy."[75] The crucial difference is that, in modernity, truth derives from the collective will of the people and manifested in popular sovereignty. Thus Arkoun prescribes and approves of popular sovereignty as the truth of modern liberal democracy that legitimizes politics.

The next logical step is, of course, the embracing of secular liberal democracy. Liberal democratic thought, in its heyday in the Muslim world, roughly from mid-19th century to mid-20th century, was popular among a small group of urbane people, but in the time since the anti-colonial struggle lost its appeal, especially among the revolutionaries and the multitude of their followers. Arkoun finds this state of affairs not salutary and prescribes liberal democracy as "a universalizable model in the present context of globalization," as well as separation of religion and state affairs.[76]

---

74. *The Unthought in Contemporary Islamic Thought*, 205.

75. *The Unthought in Contemporary Islamic Thought*, 216.

76. *The Unthought in Contemporary Islamic Thought*, 240. After the contested election results between Al Gore and George W. Bush in 2001, Arkoun expressed the concern that such an event can further damage the legitimacy of liberal democracy in some parts of the Muslim world and contribute to the solidification of political Islam. (*The Unthought in Contemporary Islamic Thought*, 240) On the issue of separation of state and religion, while he is emphatic, Arkoun warns of the extremism found in the French form of *laïcité* because this radical form in fact impoverishes the general culture by marginalizing the critical approach toward the examination of religions and traditions. In Arkoun's own words, "[t]his combative secularism employed in the service of a specific political project—construction in France of a republic that is 'one and indivisible' neglects one of its own founding principles, that of philosophical openness to the study of all human channels for the production of meaning. By 'privatizing' religion, through its elimination from the teaching syllabus in state schools in the name of "national education,' the French Republic's 'compulsory, secular and free' principles for schooling equally all citizens has generated a lack of religious culture and abandoned religious affairs to the exclusive responsibility of the various 'churches.'" (*The Unthought in Contemporary Islamic Thought*, 96)

In order for democracy to work, Arkoun argues, critical debate and competing voices must be allowed to function in society: "I have shown the decisive role played by the philosophical postulates which, implicitly or explicitly, govern all religious, legal, moral and political thought. For this reason, I would maintain that there is no viable democracy without open, free, fruitful, critical debate, initiated in each society; and these debates cannot attain the humanistic aims of democracy unless they incorporate philosophical interrogation of the prevailing systems of thought used by competing protagonists."[77] Thus, Arkoun's political philosophy is very much grounded in the notion of a pluralistic ethos that he has contrasted with the principles of monotheism. The notion of single truth that constitutes the backbone of a monotheistic religion and of nonreligious totalitarian systems, is antithetical to the principles of pluralistic society:

> The founding religious texts have contributed extensively to the establishment of a structural violence that erupts frequently in all societies in which, along with a single God, the idea has spread of an equally single Truth, one that excludes all competing versions, and is held up as the obligatory source of all laws, all political and jurisprudential order, all ethical, semantic and cultural values, and all the legitimation procedures that differ therefrom, however slightly. We know, of course, how this ultimate form of control, that becomes totalitarian and oppressive in many historical contexts, has led in several of today's European societies to serious, so-called revolutionary confrontations."[78]

In other words, Arkoun maintains, the exclusive monopoly over truth that the three monotheistic religions have created is the most important obstacle for the development of a pluralistic ethos. "A reciprocity of consciousness as a base for an exchange of rights and duties on a level of legal equality would come only after there occurred an epistemological, hence mental, break with the concept of theological truth developed in the three revealed religions."[79]

---

77. *The Unthought in Contemporary Islamic Thought*, 273.
78. *The Unthought in Contemporary Islamic Thought*, 283. It is very important to note that while Arkoun is a staunch supporter of pluralism, he is quite cognizant of the deleterious consequences of an extreme form of relativism, which could be derived from post-modernist sensibilities. He continues in the same passage: "In the light of these recurrent devastating conflicts, in which the will to power hides its violence behind meaning-related objectives as attractive as they are ill-defined (cf. the French Revolution with its substitution of the Supreme Being to the God of Abraham and Jacob; or the eschatological promises of the Khomeinist revolution), the pertinent and urgent question is how can there be progress beyond, on the one hand, the potentially totalitarian structure of religious Truth [...] and on the other, the generalized corrosive, demobilizing relativism that is just as liable to generate violence, which has resulted from a certain practice of modernity." (*The Unthought in Contemporary Islamic Thought*, 283)
79. *Rethinking Islam: Common Questions and Uncommon Answers*, 54. As we have seen above, Arkoun's political theory is rather brief and very much overshadowed by his emphasis on epistemology. His economic philosophy is even briefer and merely speaks in generalities such as, "the economic task is to institute and carry out changes based on fairness and openness." (Arkoun, Mohammed. "Islam and the Hegemony of the West," in *God, Truth and Reality: Essays in Honour of John Hic*. Arvind Sharma ed. (New York: St. Martin's Press, 1993), 84)

Political Islam

Arkoun's views on political Islam, or what he often refers to as fundamentalism, are quite abundant and negative, if not very sophisticated. Most of Arkoun's ideas on political Islam, it seems, are informed by al-Ikhwan al-Muslimun (the Muslim Brotherhood), which was created in Egypt by Hasan al-Bana and Sayyid Qutb, and to some extent by the Iranian Islamic movement and the Islamic Republic that was built on that movement. One of the most important characteristics of Islamic fundamentalism, according to Arkoun, is that its social base of support and appeal are the uneducated masses that have been increasing in most Muslim countries because of demographic changes that have been favoring their augmenting numbers. What Arkoun thinks of Hasan Al-Banna, the founder of the Muslim Brotherhood, is very telling of his low opinion of political Islam in general: "'Islam,' Al-Banna peremptorily declares, 'is dogma and cult, fatherland and nationality, religion and state, spirituality and action, the Qur'an and the sword'; this is a dangerous hotchpotch of ideas violating at once the Word of God and scientific reason. Yet it must be admitted that it is the language of the Brothers that most surely stirs the masses just as did, in other times and places, that of the Ismaili popular preachers, the story-teller and local saints."[80]

True to his epistemological interests, Arkoun launches his critique of fundamentalists by targeting their position on knowledge. The Islamists, Arkoun observes, have closed the range of interpreting the fundamental texts of Islam to the narrow band of their knowledge and interests: "The fundamentalist posture in religion amounts to a philosophical option concerning the genesis of meaning through the interaction of language and thought; the vast philosophical expanse opened up by the revealed Word of God for a continuously renewed thinkable is closed and reduced to the unthinkable. That is exactly what has happened in the case of the debate opened up by the Mu'tazili

80. *Arab Thought*, 86. Sometimes Arkoun acknowledges the positive role that some groups among fundamentalists play in representing the aspirations of the poor and subaltern. "Present-day Islam," he wrote, "continues to guarantee to the social masses, excluded from the liberties and comforts reserved for limited privileged groups, a hope mixed with traditional expectation of eternal salvation, the possibility of attaining moral dignity in intimate encounter with the Just and Merciful God of the Qur'an, a belief in a promise of imminent justice to be accomplished by their charismatic leader, a 'modern' substitute for the ancient Imam Mahdi. Or it demands obedience to the divine injunction to eliminate by a just and holy war (*jihad*) all the 'pharaohs' who sow disorder and corruption on earth." ("Present-Day Islam Between its Tradition and Globalization," 190) Interestingly Arkoun argues that Islamic fundamentalists and militants are essentially secular (but not liberal): "Islamic societies are more involved than ever in a secular history; since the colonial impact, enlarged by the ideology of development, they have adopted all the attributes of material modernity; this total involvement is precisely the reason for the success of fundamentalist movements claiming a total application of Islamic Law and teaching. These movements are themselves secular in their daily life, their professions and their basic needs; the majority of militants come from the lower classes, cut off from the traditional culture and unable to reach the modern urban culture; they rightly ask for more justice, less brutal oppression, possibilities to participate in the new history; but they express these basically secular hopes in a religious language, the only one at their disposal." ("The Concept of Authority in Islamic Thought," 70.)

thinkers."[81] The other side of the coin, for Arkoun, is that political Islam (in its broadest sense) has reduced religion to a vehicle for attaining power, neglecting religion's important capacity for generating meaning and spiritual creativity that is mediated through the idea of the divine:

> Just after the emergence of post-colonial states—including Israel—the ideological euphoria of liberation helped conceal the cultural and social cost to be paid for later economic, institutional, political, cultural, educational, intellectual failures. Religious authority, related to the horizon of meaning and spiritual creativity of the human experience of the divine, has been and continues to be practically deleted by the opposite face of religion as the clerical institutionalization of political struggle for power; in other words, the will to power with its intrinsic violence, has deviated from and overridden any quest for meaning or pretention to reach and give it a sustainable status.[82]

For this and other reasons, Arkoun finds political Islam very much akin to the communist movements and states in the 20th century. In fact the affinity between Islamic movements and "socialism," in Arkoun's views are quite deep. The ideologically driven actions against oppressors are common to both:

> The struggle for the hegemony between the cognitive models [ideologies] cannot be separated through ongoing political competition between social groups in the same society as well as by the nation-states on the geopolitical level. The most recent example of the struggle is provided by the well-known, redeeming role of an industrial proletariat dogmatically opposed to the corrupt and oppressive action of the capitalist bourgeoisie. This is nothing more than a "modern" version—an atheist one, of course—of the semiotic *actantial* model of the prophetic discourse, of which the Qur'an is an Arabic language variant introduced in a cultural context already steeped in the messianic preaching common to all the people of the Book. So no one should be surprised by the consonances between Islam and socialism now being emphasized in the so-called Arab socialist revolution, followed and defeated by the so-called Islamic Revolution initiated by Khomeini.[83]

In Arkoun's view the switch from socialist revolution in the Muslim world, which emphasized the collectivity, to Islamist politics and movements is merely the substitution of Islamic terminology for socialist terminology. The problem with both Islamist movements and socialism, Arkoun declares, is that in both cases, "liberal philosophy and political institutions are rejected and maintained in the domain of the unthinkable order."[84]

---

81. *The Unthought in Contemporary Islamic Thought*, 75.
82. *The Unthought in Contemporary Islamic Thought*, 123–24.
83. *The Unthought in Contemporary Islamic Thought*, 110.
84. *The Unthought in Contemporary Islamic Thought*, 304. Arkoun's most critical comments on political Islam are kept for the Islamic revolution in Iran, which in his estimation, took the country back to the Middle Ages. The European revolutions took them forward, toward the modern world and introduced alternatives to religious norms. The case of Iran is most puzzling to Arkoun and, "one of the most challenging issues not yet really considered by social scientists,

Gender Inequality

For Arkoun one of the areas in contemporary Muslim culture that is in dire need of rethinking and change is gender relations. Although Arkoun's thoughts on women in Muslim contexts are not very elaborate, he deplores the status of women and gender inequality in Muslim societies in general. He argues that while women may be considered to be equal in spiritual matters to men, the legal status of male children, non-Muslim men and even male slaves is potentially higher than that of Muslim women: "In Muslim law, the full blown status of person is reserved for the orthodox Muslim who is male, free (as opposed to being a slave) and entitled in law to respect the rights of God and human rights. Children, slaves and non-Muslims are potentially entitled to gain access to this status (the child when he reaches the age of responsibility [*mukallaf*], the slave when freed, the non-Muslim when converted). Woman, however, while raised to a spiritual dignity equal to that of a man, is kept in an inferior ritual and legal status, since the Qur'an itself did not succeed in removing all the taboos and restrictions weighing on the female condition in what it called the *Jahilliya*."[85]

Arkoun's analysis of the situation of women in Muslim contexts attributes the intolerable status of women to a few factors. While Islam broke down the tribal solidarity and created a community based on faith open to all humans, the socially conservative practice of matrimony remained, and the personal status laws derived from the Qur'an that regulate gender relations acquired sacred characteristics. Women's fate was sealed as a result of their involuntary role in preserving the foundations of social solidarity (i.e., the process of socialization of children), which imposed significant constraints on women. As a consequence, the social status of women as preservers of conservative values and traditions was fixed through Islamic laws that were developed after the seventh century.[86] The role of women as primary agents of socialization and preservers of social cohesion, and therefore tradition as well as individual and social virtues, Arkoun argues, is the major reason for confining women to the home, which is deemed to be essential in the formation of women's identity in the Muslim world. This process also explains the extraordinary sensitivity of Muslim societies with regard to the question of women's chastity, which is allegedly compromised in the modern world.[87]

Another factor that contributes to the status of women in Islam, Arkoun maintains, is to be found in the fundamental texts: "I will be careful not to spirit away the true issues

political scientists, philosophers and theologians." ("The Concept of Islamic Reformation," in *Islamic Law Reform and Human Rights: Challenges and Rejoinders*. Tore Lindholm, and Kari Vogt eds. (Copenhagen: Nordic Human Rights Publications, 1993), 23) The Iranian revolution, just like the socialist revolution in its Nasserist and Algerian manifestations, Arkoun complains, did not engender an enlightened scientific and philosophical discourse unlike the transformations in 18th century Europe, which brought about the French Revolution. (*Rethinking Islam: Common Questions, Uncommon Answers*, 12) What Arkoun is neglecting is that Islamist movements, especially the Iranian case, should not be compared to the French Revolution, but loosely speaking its precursor, the Protestant Reformation.

85. *The Unthought in Contemporary Islamic Thought*, 265.
86. *L'Islam Hier-Demain*, 166–67.
87. *L'Islam Hier-Demain*,227.

by reasserting that the Qur'an improved the status of women, raising them to the same spiritual dignity as men or that women in 'Islam' are not subjected, as their sisters in the West, to fierce social and economic competition with men. Muslims militating for an Islamic model of human rights often advance such arguments."[88]

To remedy and redress the status of women in Muslim societies, Arkoun has advanced some rather scant ideas that should be discussed briefly. One of the factors that contributes to the situation of women in general is "biological," according to Arkoun, which modern technology, such as modern medicine, can remedy:

> Biological make up of women engages them in the reproduction of life and hence in the distribution of the most precious good in any society. Everywhere women have been the "object" of strategies on the part of men, who have a monopoly of control over the distribution of goods and power relationships among families, clans, and tribes. It was only with the appearance of biological means of liberation such as the contraceptive pill that the emancipation of the feminine condition could reach down to the level of the strategies as old as human societies.[89]

But in an Islamic context, the backlash to such a sexual revolution reinforces and even intensifies the old taboos and certain aspects of human sexuality in Islam, which render this option not very viable.[90]

As regards the confinement of women to the private sphere, the obvious remedy is the facilitation of women's participation in the public sphere, and Arkoun seems to encourage it. Yet, he also seems to be skeptical about the actual, or even the potential, possibility of women's participation in the public sphere in Muslim societies. Although there are significant numbers of female students and workers of different social class backgrounds in these societies, their population is not large enough to organize a movement that could help women achieve a modern intellectual ability and political consciousness to express their opposition to the status quo effectively.[91]

For these reasons the only viable solution that Arkoun seems to propose is legislation to change the general culture, which would prepare new attitudes regarding women as well as new mindsets regarding legal issues related to women: "it will be difficult to make progress in women's emancipation, unless legislators speed up the evolution of mentalities

88. *Rethinking Islam: Common Questions, Uncommon Answers*, 60. On the other hand, Arkoun warns, the Westerners' prejudices toward Muslim women should be countered. Continuing in the same passage, he adds: "Westerners, inversely, emphasize the intolerable inferiority of women in Muslim societies, citing polygamy, divorce by repudiation, the wearing of the veil, segregation of the sexes, imprisonment in household tasks, strict dependence on the husband and lack of legal rights. Those who have generated these images, positive or negative, have neglected to begin by considering the givens of the feminine condition common to all societies, givens that persist in our time despite numerous efforts at emancipation, especially in the modern West."
89. *Rethinking Islam: Common Questions, Uncommon Answers*, 61.
90. *Rethinking Islam: Common Questions, Uncommon Answers*, 61.
91. *L'Islam Hier-Demain*, 226.

by introducing not only audacious reforms that will have educational effects on all social categories and all levels of culture, but also a subversive philosophy of Law."[92]

Women's conditions in Islamic societies is not a central concern in Arkoun's discourse, but it is significant enough that he thinks gender relations that constitute the foundation of many institutions in Islamic societies have retarded the attempts to bring about modernity, a central concern in his thought.

Islam and Modernity

One of the central problematics in Arkoun's discourse is the question of modernity. Arguably, many of his considerable intellectual endeavors in the past few decades have focused on redirecting Islamic ethos on the path toward the modern world. In his approach to the notion and conditions of modernity, Arkoun recounts some of the most familiar markers of the modern world: the passage from a closed world to an open world, from divine power to secular power, from a regime of privileges and ascribed statuses to the declaration of rights of humans and citizens, from subsistence economy to an economy driven more and more by productivity and based on technology that has transformed all facets of human existence.[93] Yet, as a theorist, Arkoun is very much interested in the philosophical foundations of modernity also. Thus, Arkoun finds the proposal by Philo of Alexandria (d. 54) that humans are created in God's image reflected in the Qur'anic notion of humans as God's vicegerents on the earth, conferring to them the consciousness of being a subject and a volition that makes them capable of walking in the path of liberation.[94]

At the deepest level of his analysis, Arkoun subscribes to a theory of human subjectivity that constitutes the cornerstone of his discourse. Arkoun, in subtle ways, interprets the bulk of Islamic metaphysics in terms of an undertaking to construct the human subject, which he thinks has not developed very successfully in historical reality. By referring to the Qur'anic verses in which God appoints Adam, symbolizing humans in general, as his vicegerent or representative on earth,[95] Arkoun invokes the notion of human subjectivity and agency (being a "person" in Arkoun's parlance) that is mediated by God's Subjectivity and Agency: "Thanks to the revelatory richness of 'prophetic discourse,' man raises himself to the dignity of person through internalizing God as an inner protagonist, with the help of prayer, thanksgiving and a meditative deciphering of all the signs (*ayat*) of creation and of that mark of Benevolent Care whereby man is singled out among all creatures to receive the heavy responsibility of directing a just order as 'God's representative on earth.' All this leads to the emergence of *consciousness of self* in relation to the Absolute of a God who is the ultimate Criterion and inevitable

92. *The Unthought in Contemporary Islamic Thought*, 23. It is interesting that, in this regard at least, Arkoun resorts to reform from above in Muslim societies in general, a practice that is closely related to "Ataturkism" and reform from above, of which he is generally critical.
93. *L'Islam Hier-Demain*, 124.
94. *L'Islam Hier-Demain*, 127.
95. Qur'an, 2:29; 3:72.

Referent for all the various activities of the 'person-creature' [potential human subject]."[96] What Arkoun seems to be saying here is that humans, by approximating themselves to God, are seeking to acquire subjectivity and agency and to achieve self-consciousness, that is, to recognize the autonomy of their own selves, but this is a process that would potentially unfold in history. In other words, modernity is achieved when the potential and contingent human subject is transformed into a self-sufficient, autonomous agent who lives as the citizen of a democratic state. As Arkoun continues his argument in the previous passage, "[t]he change to be wrought by modernity to this mode of awakening and realization of consciousness of self will lie in moving from the 'person-creature' of God, bound to him by a debt of sense [owing one's consciousness to God] and loving acceptance of His commandments, to the 'person-individual-citizen' [fully self-sufficient subject] bound to the state by a social and legal contract."[97]

In Islamic civilization, Arkoun maintains, the notion of human subjectivity, often rendered as "Perfect Human" [*al-insan al-kamil*] has been a central theme, even though it has been mediated by and contingent on God's Subjectivity: "The cultural, intellectual, and spiritual patrimony accumulated in the Islamic tradition has always nourished the aspiration for the ideal person, the perfect human being, *al-insan al-kamil*. God established the characteristics and the path toward [its] realization. Saints, mystics, and thinkers drew up the itinerary both in their personal lives and in the reports of their experience they left behind."[98] Yet, historically speaking, Arkoun observes, in Muslim lands this form

---

96. *The Unthought in Contemporary Islamic Thought*, 260–61. Emphasis original. In fact Arkoun has articulated the passage toward attaining subjectivity in terms of what may be called "theomorphism," or the attempt by humans to achieve some of the attributes of the Divine. Arkoun also explains the Sufi notion of *ishq* (parallel to agape) in terms of this theomorphic path to become a subject and agent: "At the stage of the 'Qur'anic fact,' God presents Himself to man in a discourse articulated in the Arabic language. He sets himself to perceive, receive and listen as the Person par excellence, possessing a fullness of fundamental attributes whose acquisition is only effectively possible for man through what mystics and philosophers have long called *ta'alluh*, 'the imitation of God.' Man must strive to attain the level of perfection embodied by God who reveals Himself in order to guide man in the fulfillment of this *essential Desire*, the celebrated *ishq*, that powerful motive for the moral, spiritual and intellectual search for the status of person (or, as it was known, Perfect Man, *al-insan al kamil*)." (*The Unthought in Contemporary Islamic Thought*, 262; emphasis original) Arkoun has further explained the notion of "love" toward God in terms of theomorphic subjectivity: "Usually the word *islam* is translated as 'submission,' 'submission to God,' or 'resignation.' 'Resignation' is quite inappropriate. Believers are not resigned before God. They experience outpourings of love toward God, a transformation pulling toward acceptance of that which God proposes, because God, by revelation, raises human beings to his level. This elevation elicits a human feeling of gratitude toward a Creator who has helped creatures with good things. There is thus established a relationship of loving and grateful obedience between Creator and creature [...] To move toward God is to move toward the absolute, toward transcendence; it is to feel promoted to a higher level of existence. All these connotations attach to the word *islam*." (*Rethinking Islam: Common Questions, Uncommon Answers*, 15)
97. *The Unthought in Contemporary Islamic Thought*, 261.
98. *Rethinking Islam: Common Questions, Uncommon Answers*, 103. Arkoun also sometimes points out the potential of the individual as the carrier of subjectivity in the Qur'an. He thus reads the story of Joseph in the Qur'an as the seed of individual subjectivity, even though it is

of mediated subjectivity has not developed into a fully fledged, autonomous and self-sufficient human subject that is the *sine qua non* of modernity and the related institutions of civil society:

> The inroads that prophetic discourse attempted to make with regard to the emancipation of the person in law, have been only partially successful, either in time or space, since kinship solidarities continue to this day to interfere with the modern construction of the social bond and the emergence of a civil society, the rule of law and the person-individual-citizen as interactive dimensions of the human subject in the historical march towards intellectual, spiritual, ethical and political modernity, all linked indissolubly together.[99]

It is clear that Arkoun is very interested in the emergence of the modern subject. However, his approach to the formation of human subjectivity suffers from a one-sided idealism, which pays little attention to the experiential dimension of the development of subjectivity. In conformity with his lopsided emphasis on epistemology and ideational factors, Arkoun grossly neglects that the formation of the subject historically involves political, economic, social and gender-based struggle. Ideas about human subjectivity do not evolve by themselves; rather ideas in interaction with historical experience that

---

contingent and mediated by the Divine Subjectivity: "each choice made by Joseph is shown to be *a personal one*; but all these choices together are part of a destiny controlled by one superior, unfathomable but emancipating Will. Joseph, with his trust-hope in God, does come up against obstacles, intrigues and lies from his opponent: the brothers united by jealousy and greed against their father and his two favourite sons; the seductress; the polytheists; the ancient social order represent the forces of Evil in conflict with those of good (what we call today, the social dialectic). It is at the heart of this dialectic that we see, emerging with the figure of Joseph, a new liberty; one that breaks with the old world, substitutes *personal merit for tribal support*, absolute preference for the birth right, self-confirmation in a foreign milieu [...] for conformist concentration on the importance of the group." (Arkoun, Mohammed. "Religion and Society: The Example of Islam," in *Islam: Critical Concepts in Sociology*. Turner, Bryan S. [ed.] (London: Routledge, 2003), 349. Emphasis added)

99. *The Unthought in Contemporary Islamic Thought*, 263. In fact Arkoun believes that subjectivity qua "spiritual autonomy" has been confiscated "by the top (the state) and by the bottom (lay believers, mobilized by 'saints' in brotherhoods) that began in 661 and has lasted until today." (*The Unthought in Contemporary Islamic Thought*, 248) On the other hand, Arkoun correctly observes that even in secular societies not all segments of the social body have acquired self-sufficient subjectivity and remained in the stage of mediated subjectivity, while instrumental rationality assails the achievements of the autonomous subject: "Even in the most secular societies, competition remains open between a 'humanism' centered on God, on whom man's salvation depends in this world and the next, and a 'humanism' centered exclusively on man. Note the first borrows more from the second than the second from the first; but it should be added that the second increasingly distances itself from the classical concept of humanism, as the tele-techno-scientific reason behind the process of globalization, is asserting its hegemony over the theological and philosophical stage of reason." (*The Unthought in Contemporary Islamic Thought*, 265) Moreover, Arkoun continues, now human subjectivity and autonomy are threatened by postmodern attacks as well: "The concept of humanism itself is also disputed [...] it has almost fallen into disuse. The status of the person thus finds itself fought over from several points of reference, ancient, traditional and new, while current debates and social scientific research fail to provide all the necessary enlightenment." (*The Unthought in Contemporary Islamic Thought*, 265)

often involves some type of struggle, strife, resistance and effort lead to the emergence of a human subject, which is the very foundation of the modern world. Thus, not paying heed to these experiential factors necessary for the development of human subjectivity, Arkoun complains about the lack of emergence of subjectivity in the Muslim world, in contrast to Europe:

> [T]he human person including women, as defined in the Quran, in the Prophetic traditions and in legal codes as the 'Divine Law' (Shari'a), has barely begun to open itself to necessary revisions and discussions inaugurated in Christian Europe, with the emergence, in the 16th century, of a humanist reason open to the pagan cultures of Greco-Roman Antiquity and increasingly desirous of carving out its philosophical autonomy in the face of the dogmatic sovereignty of theological reason. This development continued with the reasoning of the Enlightenment, the philosophy of human rights and the establishment of a democratic rule of law, bound by renewable contract, within a civil society from which political sovereignty derives. This is how the citizen-individual, protected both in his relationships with other citizens and the free legalistic construction of his private person, emerges as a human subject.[100]

As the above passage clearly demonstrates, Arkoun is very much negligent of the more experiential aspects of the historical process of the formation of the subject. He merely focuses on the cultural dimensions of the process, which is absolutely necessary, but at the expense of the more pragmatic and existential dimensions. With regard to the formation of the subject in the West, Arkoun thus neglects all the struggles against terrestrial and celestial powers in the Reformation, the political and social struggles in the English and the French revolutions, the economic struggle of the working classes in the 19th and 20th centuries, and women's struggle for their rights since the 19th century, among others. Thus for Arkoun, it seems, the construction of subject merely involves educational and cultural reform:

> [W]e shall start by identifying the many obstacles we need to remove in order to give research new contributions to programmatic epistemology, offer education systems [that pose] more challenging critical questions and introductions that are more open to the practice of interculturality and intercreativity, create the irreversible conditions for a reversal of the relationship between the de facto priority given to technological culture inseparable from the desire for power and rightful *primacy* of humanistic culture devoted to construction of a human subject capable of carrying out all the responsibilities—which remain to be defined by the culture—involved in governing on a worldwide scale.[101]

Conclusion: Would Culturalism Work?

Arkoun's hyperidealism leads him to overemphasize the role of culture and cultural reform from above to bring modernity in Muslim world. For example Arkoun wrote:

100. *The Unthought in Contemporary Islamic Thought*, 253.
101. "Thinking the Mediterranean Arena Today," 106–7.

> Struggle for respect for the rights of man, woman and child are joined in every country and every regime in which Islam, Islamic Tradition and Sharia remains points of reference that are impossible to bypass. The spiritual, moral and cultural wholeness of the person can be ensured only by way of a democratic regime, a rule of law, monarchical or republican, according to the history of each country and a civil society recognized as a partner from which the sovereignty of the state derives. It has been conclusively shown, since the 1950s, that movement towards these institutors is more strongly conditioned by the acquisition and diffusion of a *culture of democracy* than by material prosperity, which nevertheless remains a trump card when managed with the democratic participation of all the participants.[102]

To be sure Arkoun is quite cognizant of the limitations of a path to modernity that relies primarily on cultural reform from above. But he thinks that is the only hope, given the failure of the radical politics of 1950s and 1960s in the Arab world and the looming or actual threat of fundamentalism more recently. "The enterprise of thinking Islam today," Arkoun writes, "can only be achieved—if ever—by dynamic thinkers, writers, artists, scholars, politicians and economic producers. I am aware that long and deeply rooted traditions of thinking cannot be changed or even revised through a few essays or suggestions made by individuals. But I believe that thoughts have their own force and life. Some, at least, could survive and break through the wall of uncontrolled beliefs and dominating ideologies."[103] Arkoun admits the necessity of historical experience for the development of modernity in Muslim societies that have to undergo the experience themselves; it cannot be simply imported:

> [I]deas and representations [such as democracy, rule of law, human rights, citizenship, justice, liberal philosophy, and free market] can be transferred from one culture to another; but the concepts will remain abstract, cut off from their initial existential, historical content as long as the process of conceptualization has not become rooted [and] initiated by the historical experience that shapes the living collective memory of each social group, community or nation. This collective memory also needs to be expressed and transmitted in the original language used through all the historical experience of the group.[104]

Arkoun sometimes even explicitly rejects the notion of idealism,[105] yet he believes that ideas are the ultimate foundations of subjectivity and personhood: "what is at stake in the comparison [between Islamic thought and modern thought] now as before, is the *ultimate foundation of values that establish the person* and shape his or her thought and action. Traditional religions located this foundation and succeeded in rooting it in the beliefs of everyone. Scientific thought has corralled the expressions and carriers testifying to

102. *The Unthought in Contemporary Islamic Thought*, 273. Emphasis original.
103. "Rethinking Islam Today," 19.
104. *The Unthought in Contemporary Islamic Thought*, 300.
105. "The history of thought cannot be detached from social history, as I have shown in my book *Arab Humanism in the Tenth Century*. Unfortunately too many Arabic-speaking scholars remain prisoners of an idealist framework for the history of ideas." (*Rethinking Islam: Common Questions, Uncommon Answers*, 76)

the mental existence of this foundation."[106] While this is—in a sense—correct, it is only because of their mental capacity that humans can develop subjectivity and personhood. These latter do not emerge spontaneously and, as Arkoun sometimes acknowledges, historical experience is necessary for their development.

A part of Arkoun's rather unbalanced emphasis on intellectualism and culturalism should be traced back to his own personal experience, academic training and background. Islamic fundamentalism, however, also seems to be very important. As we saw above, Arkoun is very critical of the Islamic fundamentalist movements because of their trampling of the ideals of freedom, democracy, certain essential aspects of human rights, and women's rights. Notwithstanding its populism, political Islam has engaged the populace of many Islamic societies in activities that could, in the long term, create a sense of agency and subjectivity among the masses. But the path is long, hazardous and possibly catastrophic, and there is no guaranteeing that fundamentalism, even in the long term, could indeed engender a sense of agency among the populace. For these reasons, it seems, Arkoun opts for the path of education and cultural change, which inevitably has to be attempted from above and without much of the active participation of those millions involved.

No matter how much one values and shares Arkoun's views on liberal and democratic norms and institutions, one cannot ignore that a strong trend has started in the Muslim world, which seems to be on the path of bringing the masses to the political and social arenas. The process of subject formation, which is the foundation of liberal and democratic norms and institutions, is indeed tortuous and torturous, precisely because it has to go through the mobilization and empowerment of popular strata and the subaltern in any society. For this reason, any attempt to think of an alternative path, as Arkoun does, must be appreciated, but the question remains whether it would be effective to bring about modernity and democracy on a large scale in the Muslim world.[107]

---

106. *Rethinking Islam: Common Questions, Uncommon Answers*, 101. Emphasis added.

107. It should be noted that in a society such as Iran's, in which a large portion of the population has gone through the process of subject formation to a significant degree, discourses such as Arkoun's are very important in the building of the institutions of civil society and democracy, as evidenced by the translation of his work into Persian and the embracing of his ideas by some of the intellectuals of the reform movement in that country.

CONCLUSION

Many scholars of modernity, including Jürgen Habermas, have conceptualized the foundation of modernity in terms of the notions of human empowerment, agency and subjectivity. The transformation of humans from a state of passivity and subservience to a state of action and agency has been responsible for the emergence of modernity in the West, as well as other parts of the world. Without active and self-assertive individuals, there cannot be a democracy, a modern economy or human rights and women's rights. Only when a large segment of the population acquires agency and subjectivity as individuals can these fruits of modernity become attainable.

A vision of human agency constitutes one of the major themes of the Qur'an. In the Qur'anic tradition, the notion of humans as God's vicegerent (*khalifah*) on earth contains the seeds of human subjectivity, notwithstanding its retardation during the Islamic medieval period. In a similar vein, in contemporary Islamic thought, human agency is chiefly conceptualized in terms of a vicarious and indirect notion of subjectivity and agency, mediated through the Divine Agency. I call this the paradigm of mediated subjectivity, since human agency is believed to be circuitous and indirect.

Most of the Islamic thinkers I analyzed in this book have broached this notion of indirect human agency as the cornerstone of their responses to modernity. This approach, however, often entails contradictions on issues such as human rights, citizenship and individual rights and freedoms, fundamentally because human agency and subjectivity can easily be perceived as annulling God's subjectivity and supremacy. Despite their vast differences, a majority of the thinkers discussed in this book exhibit this aporia as a common thread connecting their discourses. In their formulations of new visions for Muslims, they frequently envision a new Islamic person who is empowered and who possesses agency, but they very often simultaneously deny these building blocks of the modern world. This approach to the understanding of Muslim consciousness in relation to modernity explains the vacillations and contradictions of modernist Muslim thinkers on the main markers of the modern world that were elaborately discussed in the chapters of this study.

As I have tried to demonstrate, all of the thinkers and intellectual trends treated in this study have made significant contributions to the making of Muslims' consciousness and to the debate on relations between Islam and modernity. Since the mid-19th century, these intellectual trends and approaches have encountered the forces and ideas of the modern world such as democracy, Western science and technology, economic development and new conceptions of women and ethnic and religious minorities. Within the paradigm of what I call mediated subjectivity (or vicarious agency), the responses by modern Muslim intellectuals discussed in this book have varied from one society to another and over time. Each intellectual responded to some of the most urgent issues that defined their time.

Among these responses, the discourses of Muhammad Iqbal and Sayyid Qutb were crucial in the formation of the contemporary Islamic consciousness. Iqbal was well versed in modern Western discourses as well as in classical Islamic thought. His notion of the Islamic "self" (*khudi*) as the modern subject constitutes the very foundation of current Islamic discourses in many parts of the world. Iqbal revived and reinterpreted certain aspects of the Sufi tradition to lay the foundations of Muslim agency and subjectivity, which had major impacts in the Muslim world in the 20th century.[1]

Sayyid Qutb and Abul 'Ala Maududi were also highly influential thinkers of the 20th century, whose thought has had major impacts on contemporary radical Islamist discourses and movements, especially in their relations with the West. Qutb's major contribution to contemporary Islamic discourse was the introduction of an Islamic totality that was designed to challenge and replace not only liberal democracy but also the now-defunct Marxist totalitarian systems. I tried to show how Qutb's sociopolitical discourse was meant to create a totalizing modernity, and how he attempted to ground it in the Qur'an and Hadith. Maududi, on the other hand, emphasized discipline in the creation of Muslim subjectivity, which in turn had major implications for gender relations, because his idea of discipline was based on the confinement of women, who would otherwise interfere with the process of disciplining of men, supposedly through seduction. Fatima Mernissi has extensively addressed the issue of women's subjectivity and its historical roots, as well as the resistance to women's empowerment in contemporary Muslim societies. I closely analyzed Mernissi's discourse to shed light on what she considers to be the foundations of women's agency and the possibilities of more egalitarian gender relations in Muslim lands.

Some of the Iranian thinkers treated in this study have taken the debate on Islam and modernity to a different register. Thus, Mehdi Haeri Yazdi (an Ayatollah and a philosopher trained in the West) devoted his career to investigating the compatibility of Islamic philosophical principles with the fundaments of the modern world. He meticulously (sometimes belaboring some issues) analyzed the canon of modern Western philosophy and Islamic philosophy and jurisprudence to forge the foundations of human rights and democracy in Iran, informing some of the postrevolutionary Muslim modernists in Iran.

Mohammad Khatami, Iran's ex-president, attempted to forge a practical bridge between Islam and modernity, especially the idea of civil society and democratic rule of law. On the other hand, Mojtahed Shabestari has been trying to demonstrate that there is no conflict between human subjectivity and God's sovereignty, hence creating a milestone in reconciling the Islamic culture with one of the fundamental foundations of the modern world. Seyyed Hossein Nasr, by contrast, has been trying to posit the reverse view, opposing the modern world by its roots and branches. In the last chapter of this study I analyzed the discourse of the late Mohamad Arkoun, who was a major theorist of liberal democracy in many Muslim societies, and whose thought has inspired liberal individuals and social movements in recent years across the Muslim world.

1. Ali's Shari'ati (d. 1977) was one of the major architects of 1979 revolution in Iran who was significantly influenced by Iqbal.

As I am writing these lines, many of the countries in the Middle East and North Africa are undergoing political and social changes that may prove to have long-lasting impacts on the history of the region and the world. Apparently, so far, the role of groups with an overt Islamic ideology has not been very prominent in the upheavals that are taking place in this very important part of the Muslim world. Yet, we do not know what the future might hold. It is possible that as a result of these changes, some states could emerge that take up one or another form of Islamic ideology as their guide in social and political action. The middle classes in these areas are relatively small, and the proportion of the "downtrodden" is relatively high. In the absence of a viable socialist option, the Islamist groups with various ideologies could easily take up the cause of the majority of the subaltern. Even if such an outcome would not be forthcoming, contemporary Islamic thought has already had sufficient impact on the current political culture of Muslim societies to contribute to the shaping of state and society in the Muslim world.

The discourses we encountered in this volume provide the intellectual framework and cultural boundaries within which change in the Muslim world may take place.[2] The most important question is: What would be the fate of democracy and freedom? Throughout this book, I have implied that achieving the fruits of modernity, i.e., democracy, human rights, women's rights and equality, individual rights and the betterment of the quality of life for the society as a whole, are the result of the development of human subjectivity and agency, and their universalization. Yet, there are serious perils in the path toward such outcomes. The road toward modernity often passes through a totalitarian phase, that of the early formation of the disciplined subject. The processes of the subjectification of the populace in different parts of the world in the postmedieval period have so far been accomplished through the mobilization of the multitudes in revolutions and revolutionary wars, including civil wars, lead by ideological elites. Often revolutions and revolutionary wars are also followed by years, and in fact decades, of harsh discipline mixed with repression and demobilization of the same populace. These experiences bring with them horror and devastation, affecting millions. As a consequence, very large numbers of people are killed and displaced, and the physical infrastructures of many communities are destroyed. Moreover, many of the experiences involving the process of subjectifcation get mired in this totalitarian phase. The horrors of the communist movements across the world and the states created by these movements in the 20th century are good cases in point.

The contemporary Islamist ideologies are largely influenced by the discourses discussed in the chapters presented in this volume. In the Sunni world, in the event that Islamic movements resulting in the creation of a state would appear, it is possible that the thought of Sayyid Qutb and Abul 'Ala Maududi, who in turn integrated or reflected some aspects of the vast discourse of Muhammad Iqbal, would shape the contours of

2. The phrase "Muslim world" is indeed an abstraction, but a necessary one. Islamic civilization should be conceptualized as a historical constellation, consisting of different stars that have changed and will change, but that belong to the same configuration with certain shared characteristics. In my analysis presented in this study, the most important and deep-seated shared characteristic in the contemporary constellation is the idea of mediated subjectivity that can give rise to powerful (and militant) social and political systems that are more (but not totally) resistant to foreign influences and prone to developing their own dynamics from inside.

their ideas and actions. As we have seen, a closed system such as that of Qutb can easily lead to a form of totalitarianism, which may produce some sort of subjectivity for the downtrodden but at the same time repress the development of full human subjectivity, and more importantly, individual subjectivity and intersubjectivity.

In this book I have often discussed subjectivity and agency synonymously for the sake of accessibility and convenience. Yet, the two are somewhat different and have important practical consequences. In a way, we can think of subjectivity in terms of the empowerment of the individual autonomous self, who through her/his free will can act upon the world and thus exercise agency. Yet, the human mind is the source of all these actions. Animals also act upon the world, but they do not have not subjectivity. The human mind and its elaborations embodied in various forms of discourse, literature, theology and other cultural expressions grounds human agency. The question of subjectivity is particularly pertinent to odd phenomena such as the Taliban movement in Afghanistan. There are, at least on the surface, some of the manifestations of acting upon the world in the Taliban movement. The war machine of this antihuman movement must have created at least a rudimentary sense of agency among its followers. Yet, one can hardly think of the Taliban as even the precursors of any form of modernity, except in their use and abuse of modern technology and technoscientific rationality to promote their misogynistic and misanthropic agenda.

Another very important issue in the Islamic discourses we encountered is the question of who would be the carrier of subjectivity. In most of the discourses presented in this volume, the carrier of the inchoate subjectivity is the collectivity, rather than the individual. One can hardly expect the emergence of individual subjectivity in the early stages of the formation of the subject, because most of the characteristics associated with individuality, such as narrow self-interest, consumerism and even narcissism, militate against the emergence of disciplinary subjectivity, which involves the sacrifice of the individual self. However, at the end of long road to human empowerment, the ultimate beneficiary of subjectivity is the individual. In the Muslim world and in the Islamic discourses discussed here, this process is ongoing while there are still powerful barriers against the development of the individual subject. Yet, I contend, once there is a critical mass of the sense of agency in a society, the path for the individual may also open up, because ultimately it is the individual who has to make choices in the social and political spheres.

The same dialectical relation is found between the notion and the reality of subjectivity and freedom. Subjectivity qua empowerment and agency is the foundation of freedom, and yet the process of subjectification can, and often does, suppress freedom itself. It is not possible to conceive of freedom without agency as its underpinning. One can be a vagabond and feel "free" about it. But without the ability to act upon nature, society and politics, freedom cannot be conceivable. Most of the thinkers we have encountered in this work are concerned with the notion of subjectivity, or in fact with what I call mediated subjectivity. While Arkoun was very much concerned with freedom, he failed to connect it to the evolution of the human subject that is emerging in the Muslim context. Mojtahed Shabestari, on the other hand, expanded the notion of mediated subjectivity and is arriving at more or less the idea of the autonomous self-subsisting subject and (very explicitly) human rights. Yet, the notion of freedom per se has not been thoroughly theorized and thematized by the thinkers we encountered in this volume. In a similar vein, the dialectic of subject-object has not been overcome to yield universalization of subjectivity, or intersubjectivity. The transition from subject-object relation to intersubjectivity is first and foremost a social and political process. Once a critical mass of society acquires a sense of agency and subjectivity it is possible that it would arrive at the universal recognition of the subjectivity of all, which is sine qua non for the establishment of democracy. In this long and arduous societal process, theories of intersubjectivity can facilitate and expedite the development of democratic ethos.

Modernity is a long and tortuous process that reveals the naïveté of development/underdevelopment discourses of previous decades. Yet, some new versions of these discourses are being articulated as the "solution" to the quest for modernity and democracy in the Muslim world. Thus, in his recent work Vali Nasr basically argues for the promotion of capitalism for the multitude to bring about modernity and democracy in the Muslim world. By invoking Max Weber's notion of the elective affinity between the Reformation and capitalism, Nasr believes it is possible to just wish away the Puritanism of the former and adopt its dialectical outcome, that is capitalism: "If European history is any guide, only this robust breed of capitalism will bring true modernizing change to the Muslim world. The modern world was invented by children of the Reformation, but it was not their puritanical and intolerant faith that transformed the world—far from it—but rather trade and commerce that took hold in unlikely backward corners of Europe like Scotland, home to the early Industrial revolution and the likes of Adam Smith, David Hume, and Sir Walter Scott [...] The road to human rights, social freedoms, and democracy runs through business and economic progress."[3] What Nasr ignores here is the intervening process of mass subjectivity that Puritanism brought about with itself. What distinguishes modern capitalism from its premodern versions is that the humans involved in its various aspects—entrepreneurs, labor force, the managerial groups and consumers—are all modern agents who see the world differently and have different expectations of their lives. One cannot put the cart before the horse. Human agency gives rise to capitalism, or they develop through interaction with one another; one cannot force the development of modern industrial capitalism without the development, or a concurrent expansion, of a sense of subjectivity and agency on a large scale. Modernity is a long and dialectical process with contradictory phases; the discourses of development/underdevelopment and its newer variations are naïve because they see modernity mostly in terms of a quick, historically speaking, economic transformation, paying no heed to the fact that the *process* of modernity, painfully, is anything but quick. Yet, once the process of subjectification is underway, it is possible to channel the energy that is released by human agency toward economic activity that would benefit the individual and the collectivity simultaneously.[4]

---

3. Nasr, Seyyed Vali Reza. *Forces of Fortune: The Rise of the New Muslim Middle Class and What It Will Mean for Our World* (New York: Free Press, 2009), 24–26.
4. The most significant recent case in point is that of China. The Chinese revolution, through genocidal bloodshed, transformed a critical mass of the Chinese people into subjects and agents that made the economic development of the last two decades possible. Similar events in other communist countries, equally bloody and genocidal, largely failed. It is important to observe that the quest for agency in the Islamic world, like many other parts of the world,

The transition from the earliest stages of protosubjectivity to freedom and its universalization in democratic institutions in the West, from Puritanism to the Enlightenment, took a long time. But in the Muslim world it may not take as long, because it is surrounded by the forces of the modern world in the midst of globalization. The powerful discourse of democracy, the unstoppable vigor of mass media and the Internet would undoubtedly expedite the process of subjectification. The facility of the development of democratic movements in the Muslim world also depends on the ability of contemporary discourses to absorb democratic ideas from outside. As the case of Iran since the Islamic Revolution of 1979 demonstrates, the internal dynamics of the development of subjectivity in that country, as well as the ability of its intellectual sphere to integrate the modern discourse from outside, have combined to give voice to a democratic movement that was manifested in the reformist movement of 1990s and later in the civil society movement that has come be known as the Green Movement since the crisis of the presidential election of 2009. Yet, modernity as a process of subjectification is Janus faced. It can give rise to intersubjectivity, which is the foundation of democratic ethos and institutions, or it can engender the monopolization of power, concentrating it in the hands of a few. Power and empowerment that constitute the core of the formation of the subject and subjectivity in practice often result in the formation of an elite who, having experienced the taste of power, attempt to perpetuate it for themselves by excluding the others and preventing the universalization of subjectivity. Thus, some segments of the postrevolutionary elite in Iran, represented by different groups such as those around Mahmoud Ahmadinejad, Ali Khamenei and their cohorts, the Basij, the poltical clerics and the security forces, have been attempting to confine power and empowerment to their own inner circles and their clients, while trying systematically to disempower and demobilize the new middle classes of Iran, who comprise large segments of society represented by the Green Movement.

The dynamics of subjectivity constitute empowerment. The other side of the coin of empowerment is power and domination. Whenever there is power, it is over someone or something. In his master-slave dialectic, Hegel posited that the downtrodden's rebellion against, and defeat of, the oppressors would culminate in a state of universal subjectivity. It seems, however, that he grossly overlooked that when the subaltern overthrows the ancien régime, a group within it develops an addiction to power. Hailing from the lowest rungs of society, this relatively small group fights tooth and nail against, and vanquishes, its former master by spilling its own blood and that of others. It perceives itself to be in the right no matter what, because it was once wronged and oppressed. Thus, this group pretends that it deserves the power and the appurtenant wealth that comes with victory. The very idea of going back to its former status of have-not and can-not is anathema to this small group. It construes itself, and later pretends, to represent the poor and disempowered. It monopolizes power in its own name as the "oppressed" and on behalf of the underdog. The process of dominatory power dynamics in postrevolutionary Iran is very much contained in this paradigm.

---

has been a political affair, because it consists largely of a reaction to colonialism, imperialism and domestic despotism. Thus far Islamic discourses have not yet adequately turned toward economic agency.

Subjectivity qua power is also domination over nature, that is, external and internal nature. The modern subject has achieved its status in the crucible dominating its own inner nature, which is the domain of discipline. The disciplinary self-control often leads to individual and collective neuroses that could be quite severe, at least among the first few generations of those who undergo the rigors of disciplining the body and the psyche. A case in point is again postrevolutionary Iran, where mass depression, addiction to drugs among a vast number of people and other types of social and personal malaise have become prevalent. In a similar vein, human agency and empowerment mean control and domination over the outer nature. In dealing with the "thing," modern subjects often come to the brink of annihilating the physical nature. Industrialization, over-exploitation of natural resources and over-consumption are rooted in the emergence of the modern self-centered individual, and they represent potential mortal blights for nature and our habitat. Nevertheless, mature subjectivity and intersubjectivity can and are addressing these vital issues.

In other parts of the Islamic world, such as Egypt, political Islam has exhibited the potential for both the dissemination of agency in society at large and its restriction to the elite, which could morph into a further consolidation and authoritarian monopoly of political power. The militant extremist groups in Egypt and elsewhere often engage in the practice of *takfir*, that is regarding every Muslim outside their group as infidels. On the other hand, groups such as the Muslim Brotherhood, despite their narrow and fanatical views on many social and political issues, have been able to create a sense of agency among the lower-middle and middle classes that would be a necessary, but not sufficient, condition for the development of democratic ethos.[5]

One question that is often raised with regard to modernity is whether we should speak of modernity or modernities. Is Islamic modernity different from Western modernity? As far as the foundations of modernity are concerned, that is generalization of human subjectivity within society, there cannot be much difference. Human empowerment and agency are not different in the East and the West. Yet, there are other factors involved. For example, given the central emphasis on collectivity in Islamic history and discourses, the space for individual liberty would be contingent on and in tune with the welfare of the group. Similarly, the process of disenchantment, as Max Weber referred to it, could be slower than or not quite as radical as in the West. As we saw in chapter one, Iqbal deliberately expressed his powerful modernist views largely in poetry, as if to retain the "enchanted" aspect of his thought. Thus, categories such as secularity, rationality, desacralization and attenuation of passion, emotionality and sensuality might be less pronounced, at least in the initial phases of modernity in Muslim societies. What is certain, though, is that the transformation of the specter of modernity into a spirit and ethos of democracy in the Muslim world would be arduous and long, very much like in other parts of the world.

5. On the process of agentification by Islamist groups in Egypt see, for example: Rosefsky Wickham, Carrie. *Mobilizing Islam: Religion, Activism, and Political Change in Egypt* (New York: Columbia University Press, 2002); and Baker, Raymond William. *Islam without Fear: Egypt and the New Islamists* (Cambridge, MA: Harvard University Press, 2003).

BIBLIOGRAPHY

Akhavi, Shahrough. "Qutb, Sayyid." In *Oxford Encyclopaedia of the Modern Islamic World.* New York: Oxford University Press, 1995, v. 3.

Amir Arjomand, Said. "Civil Society and the Rule of Law in the Constitutional Politics of Iran under Khatami." *Social Research,* Vol. 67 Issue 2 (Summer 2000).

Arkoun, Mohammed. *Arab Thought.* New Delhi: S. Chand, 1988.

______. "The Concept of Authority in Islamic Thought." In *Islam: State and Society,* edited by Ferdinand, Klaus, and Mehdi Mozaffari. London: Curzon Press, 1988.

______. "The Concept of Islamic Reformation." In *Islamic Law Reform and Human Rights: Challenges and Rejoinders,* edited by Tore Lindholm and Kari Vogt. Copenhagen: Nordic Human Rights Publications, 1993.

______. "For a Subversive Genesis of Values." In *The Future of Values: 21st Century Talks,* edited by Jerome Binde. New York: Berghahn Books, 2004.

______. "History as an Ideology of Legitimation: A Comparative Approach to Islamic and European Contexts." In *Islam, Modernism and the West: Cultural and Political Relations at the End of the Millennium,* edited by Gema Martín Muñoz. London: I.B. Tauris, 1999.

______. "Islam and the Hegemony of the West." In *God, Truth and Reality: Essays in Honour of John Hic,* edited by Arvind Sharma. New York: St. Martin's Press, 1993.

______. "Islam, Europe, the West: Meanings-at-Stake and the Will-to-Power." In *Islam and Modernity: Muslim Intellectuals Respond,* edited by John Cooper, et al. London: I.B. Tauris, 2000.

______. *Islam: To Reform or to Subvert.* London: Saqi, 2006.

______. *Lectures du Coran.* Paris: G.-P. Maisonneuve et Larose, 1982.

______. "Present-Day Islam between its Tradition and Globalization." In *Intellectual Traditions in Islam,* edited by Farhad Daftari. London: I.B. Taruis, 2000.

______. "Religion and Society: The Example of Islam." In *Islam: Critical Concepts in Sociology,* edited by Turner, Bryan S. London: Routledge, 2003.

______. *Rethinking Islam: Common Questions, Uncommon Answers.* Boulder: Westview Press, 1994.

______. "Rethinking Islam Today." *The Annals of the American Academy of Political and Social Science,* vol. 558 (July 2003).

______. "The State, the Individual, and Human Rights: A Contemporary View of Muslims in a Global Context." In *Muslim Almanac,* 1995.

______. "Thinking the Mediterranean Arena Today." *Diogenes* (2005); 52; 99.

______. *The Unthought in Contemporary Islamic Thought.* London: Saqi, 2002.

Arkoun, Mohammed, and Louis Gardet. *L'Islam Hier-Demain.* Paris: Buchet/Chastel, 1978.

Baker, Raymond William. *Islam without Fear: Egypt and the New Islamists.* Cambridge, MA: Harvard University Press, 2003.

Beck, Lewis White. *Essays on Kant and Hume.* New Haven: Yale University Press, 1978.

Berman, Marshal. *All That Is Solid Melts into Air: The Experience of Modernity.* New York: Penguin Books, 1988.

Binder, Leonard. *Islamic Liberalism: A Critique of Development of Ideologies.* Chicago: University of Chicago Press, 1988.

Calvin, Jean. *Institutes of the Christian Religion,* vol. 3. Philadelphia: Philip Nicklin, 1816.

Carre, Oliver. *Mysticism and Politics: A Critical Reading of Fi Zilal al-Qur'an by Sayyid Qutb.* Leiden: Brill, 2003.

Chehabi, Houchang. *Iranian Politics and Religious Modernism: The Liberation Movement of Iran under the Shah and Khomeini.* Ithaca: Cornell University Press, 1990.

Dabashi, Hamid. *Theology of Discontent: The Ideological Foundation of Islamic Revolution in Iran.* New York: New York University Press, 1993.

Dad, Babak, ed. *Khatami dar Italia 99: Yaddasht-haye Safar Ra'is Jomhur be Uropa be Hamrah Matn Kamel du Sokhanrani va yek Mosahebeh* (Khatami in Italy 99: notes on the President's trip to Europe with the full texts of two lectures and an interview). Sazman-e Chap va Entesharat-e Vezarat-e Farhang va Ershad-e Islami, 1999.

Dupré, Louis. *Passage to Modernity: An Essay in the Hermenutics of Nature and Culture.* New Haven: Yale University Press, 1993.

Durkheim, Émile. "The Dualism of Human Nature and its Social Conditions." In *Emile Durkheim on Morality and Society*, edited by Robert Bellah. Chicago: University of Chicago Press, 1973.

______. *The Elementary Forms of the Religious Life.* New York: Free Press, 1965.

______. "Individualism and the Intellectuals." In *Emile Durkheim on Morality and Society*, edited by Robert Bellah. Chicago: University of Chicago Press, 1973.

(Yusefi) Eshkvari, Hasan. *Nougarai Dini* (Religious modernity). Tehran: Qasideh, 1998.

Gheissari, Ali and Vali Nasr. "Iran's Democracy Debate." *Middle East Policy*, Vol. XI, No.2, (Summer 2004).

Giddens, Anthony. *Modernity and Self-identity: Self and Society in the Late Modern Age.* Stanford: Stanford University Press, 1991.

Habermas, Jürgen. *Between Facts and Norms: Contributions to a Discourse Theory of Law and Democracy.* Cambridge, MA: MIT Press, 1996.

______. "Communicative Versus Subject-Centered Reason." In *Rethinking the Subject: An Anthology of Contemporary European Thought*, edited by James Faubion. Boulder: Westview Press, 1955.

______. *The Theory of Communicative Action Vol.1. Reason and the Rationalization of the Society.* Boston: Beacon Press, 1981.

Haddad, Yvonne Y. "Sayyid Qub: Ideologue of Islamic Revival." In *Voices of Resurgent Islam*, edited by Esposito, John L. New York: Oxford University Press, 1983.

Haeri Yazdi, Mehdi. *Hekmat va Hukumat* (Philosophy and the state). London: Shadi, 1995.

______. *Heram-e Hasti: Taḥlili az Mabadi-e Hasti Shenasi-e Taṭbiqi* (Pyramid of Existence: an analysis of the foundations of comparative ontology). Tehran: Mu'assesehe Muṭale'at va Tahqiq-e Farhangi, 1983.

______. *'Ilm-e Kulli* (Universal knowledge). Tehran: Intesharat-e Ḥekmat, 1970.

______. *Kavoshha-ye 'Aql-e 'Amali: Falsafeh-ye Akhlaq* (Investigations of practical reason: Philosophy of Ethics). Tehran: Mu'asseseh-ye Muṭale'at va Taḥqiqat-e Farhangi, 1982.

______. *Kavoshha-ye 'Aql-e Nazari* (Investigations of pure reason). Tehran: Amir Kabir, 1982.

______. *Khaṭerat-e Mehdi Ḥaeri Yazdi* (Memoires of Mehdi Haeri Yazdi). Cambridge, MA: Center for Middle Eastern Studies, Harvard University, 2001.

______. *Metafizik: Majmu'eh-ye Maqalat-e Falsafi-Manṭeqi* (Metaphysics: a collection of philosophical and logical essays). Tehran: Nehẕat-e Zanan-e Musalman, 1982.

______. *The Principles of Epistemology in Islamic Philosophy: Knowledge by Presence.* Albany: State University of New York, 1992.

Hegel, G.W.F. *Hegel's Philosophy of Right.* Oxford: Oxford University Press, 1967.

______. *The Phenomenology of Mind* (Tr. J.B. Baillie). New York: Harper and Row, 1967.

Horkheimer, Max and Theodor Adorno. *Dialectic of Enlightenment.* New York: Herder and Herder, 1972.

Hume, David. *A Treatise of Human Nature*, edited by David Fate Norton and Mary J. Norton. Oxford: Oxford University Press, 2000.

Hyppolite, Jean. *Genesis and Structure of Hegel's Phenomenology of Spirit.* Evanston: Northwestern University Press, 1974.

Ibn Khaldun. *The Muqaddima: An Introduction to History*. Pantheon Books: 1958.

Iqbal, Muhammad, *Armaghan-i Hijaz*. Lahore: Sediqi, 1972.

———. *Asrar-i Khudi*. Tehran: Moaseseh Farhang va Amuzesh-e 'Ali, 1991.

———. *Complaint and, Answer (Shikwaand, and Jawab-i-shikwa): Iqbal's Dialogue with Allah*. Delhi: Oxford University Press, 1981.

———. *The Development of Metaphysics in Persia; A Contribution to the History of Muslim Philosophy*. Lahore: Bazm-i Iqbal, 1964.

———. *Gulshan Raz-i Jadid*, N.P.N.D.

———. *Islam as an Ethical and a Political Ideal: A Lecture Delivered in 1908*. Lahore: Muhammad Ashraf, 1940.

———. *Javidname*. Lahore: Sediqi, 1972.

———. *Mathnavi Mosafer*. Lahore: Sediqi, 1972.

———. *The New Rose Garden of Mystery, And The Book of Slaves*. Lahore: Sh. Muhammad Ashraf, 1969. Alternative translation: *Gulshan-i Raz-i Jadid* (translated by Bashir Ahmad Dar). Lahore: Institute of Islamic Culture, 1964.

———. *A Message from the East*. Karachi: Iqbal Academy, 1971.

———. *Pas Che Bayad Kard Ey Aqvam-i Sharq*. Lahore: Sediqi, 1972.

———. *Payam-i Mashriq*. Lahore: Sediqi, 1972.

———. *The Reconstruction of Religious Thought in Islam*. Lahore: Ashraf, 1999.

———. *The Rod of Moses* (Versified English Translation of Iqbal's Zarb-i-Kalim), translated by Syed Akbar Ali Shah. Lahore: Iqbal Academy, 1983.

———. *Rumuz-i Bikhudi*. Tehran: Moaseseh Farhang va Amuzesh-e 'Ali, 1991.

———. *Secrets of Collective Life*. Lahore: Islamic Book Service, 1977.

———. *Speeches and Statements of Iqbal*. Lahore: Al-Manār Academy, 1948.

———. *What Should be Done O People of the East*. Lahore: Iqbal Academy, 1977.

———. *Zabur-i Ajam*. N.P. N.D.

Iqbal, Muhammad, and A. J. Arberry. *Persian Psalms* (Zabur-i Aajam) Parts I & II. Lahore: M. Ashraf, 1948.

Iqbal, Muhammad, and Reynold Alleyne Nicholson. *Secrets of the Self: A Philosophical Poem*. New Delhi: Arnold-Heinemann, 1978.

Jahanbegloo, Ramin. *Dar Jost-o Ju-ye Amr-e Qodsi: Gofto-Gu-ye Ramin Jahanbegloo ba Seyyed Hossein Nasr* (In search of the sacred: Ramin Jahanbegloo's conversation with Seyyed Hossein Nasr). Tehran: Nashr-e Ney, 2007.

———. "The Deadlock in Iran: Pressures, from Below," *Journal of Democracy*, Vol. 14, No, 1, (January 2003).

Jansen, J.J.G. "Sayyid Kutb." In *Encyclopedia of Islam II*.

Jay, Martin. *Marxism and Totality: The Adventures of a Concept from Lukacs to Habermas*. Berkeley: University of California Press, 1984.

Kadivar, Muhsin. *Nazariyahha-yi dawlat dar fiqh-e Shi'ah* (Theories of state in Shia jurisprudence). Tehran: Nashr-e Nay, 1997.

Kant, Immanuel. *Critique of Pure Reason*. New York: St. Martin's Press, 1965.

Khatami, Mohammad. *Ai'in va Andisheh dar Dam-e Khodkamegi: Seyri dar Andisheh-ye Siyasi Moslamanan dar Faraz va Forud-e Tamadon-e Islami* (Religion and thought in the snare of autocracy: a study in the political thought of Muslims during the ascent and descent of Islamic civilization). Tehran: Tarh-e nou, 1999.

———. *Az Donya-ye Shahr ta Shahr-e Donya: Seyri dar Andisheh-e Siyasi Gharb* (From the World of the City to World-City: A Study of Political Thought in the West). Tehran: Nashr-e Ney, 1999.

______. *Ehyagar-e Haqiqat-e Din: Majmo'eh Maqalat* (The Reviver of the Truth of Religion: Collection of Essays). Tehran: Zekr, 2001.

______. *Goftogu-ye Tamdon-ha* (Dialogue of Civilizations). Tehran, Tarh-e Nou, 2001.

______. *Gozideh Sokhanraniha-ye Rai'is Jomhur dar bareh-ye Tose'h-ye Siyasi, Tose'eh Eqtesadi va Amniyat* (A selection of President's speeches on political and economic development, and security). Tehran: Tarh-e Nou, 2000, 270.

______. *Hezareh Goftogu va Ttafahom: Gozareshe-e Safar-e Mohamad Khatami be Sazman-e Melal-e Motahed* (The Millennium of Dialogue and Understanding: The Report of Mohamad Khatami's Trip to the United Nations). Tehran: Nashr-e Resanesh, 1999.

______. *Islam, Rohaniyat va Enqelab-e Islami* (Islam, the clergy, and Islamic Revolution). Tehran: Tarh-e Nou, 2000.

______. *Mardomsalari* (Democracy). Tehran: Tarh-e Nou, 2001.

______. *Zanan va Javanan* (Women and the Youth). Tehran: Tarh-e Nou, 2000.

Kitch, Sally. *Chaste Liberation: Celibacy and Female Cultural Status*. Urbana: University of Illinois Press, 1989, 36.

Kojève, Alexander. *Introduction to the Reading of Hegel: Lectures on the Phenomenology of Spirit*. Basic Books, 1969.

Malik, Hafeez. *Iqbal, poet-philosopher of Pakistan*. New York: Columbia University Press, 1971.

Maududi, Syed Abul 'Ala. *Capitalism, Socialism, and Islam*. Kuwait: Islamic Book Publishers, 1977.

______. *Correspondence between Maulana Maudoodi and Maryam Jameela*. Lahore: Mohammad Yusuf Khan, 1969.

______. *First Principles of the Islamic State*. Lahore: Islamic Publications, 1974.

______. *Four Basic Qur'anic Terms*. Lahore: Islamic Publications, 1979.

______. *Fundamentals of Islam*. Lahore: Islamic Publications, 2000.

______. *Human Rights in Islam*. Leicester: Islamic Foundation, 1976.

______. *Islam and Ignorance*. Lahore: Islamic Publications, 1976.

______. *The Islamic Movement: Dynamics of Values, Power, and Change*. Leicester: Islamic Foundation, 1984.

______. *Islamic State: Political Writings of Maulana Sayyid Abul 'Ala Maudoodi*. Karachi, Pakistan: Islamic Research Academy, 1986.

______. *Jihad in Islam*. Lahore: Islamic Publications, 1980.

______. *Life after Death*. Lahore: Islamic Publications, 1968.

______. *Political Theory of Islam*. Lahore: Islamic Publications, 1993.

______. *The Process of Islamic Revolution*. Ichhra, Pakistan: Markazi Maktaba Jama'at-e-Islami, 1955.

______. *The Punishment of the Apostate According to Islamic Law*. Mississauga (Canada): N.P., 1994.

______. *Purdah and the Status of Women in Islam*. Lahore: Islamic Publications, 1979.

______. *The Religion of Truth*. Delhi: Markazi Maktaba Jamaat-e-Islami Hind, 1970.

______. *A Short History of the Revivalist Movement in Islam*. Lahore: Islamic Publications, 1972.

______. *System of Government under the Holy Prophet*. Lahore: Islamic Publications, 1978.

______. *Towards Understanding the Qur'an* (vol. 1). Leicester: Islamic Foundation, 1988.

______. *West versus Islam*. Lahore, Pakistan: Islamic Publications, 1991.

______. *Worship in Islam*. Karachi: Islamic Research Academy, 1977.

Martin, Vanessa. *Creating an Islamic State: Khomeini and the Making of a New Iran*. London: I.B. Tauris, 2000.

Mernissi, Fatima. *Beyond the Veil: Male-Female Dynamics in Modern Muslim Society*. Indiana University Press, 1987.

______. *Dreams of Trespass: Tales of a Harem Childhood Reading*. Addison-Wesley, 1994.

______. *The Effects of Modernization on the Male-Female Dynamics in A Muslim Society: Morocco.* Dissertation, Brandeis University (Sociology Department), 1973.

______. *The Forgotten Queens of Islam.* University of Minnesota Press, 1991.

______. *Islam and Democracy: Fear of the Modern World.* Addision-Wesley, 1992.

______. *Women's Rebellion and Islamic Memory.* Zed Books, 1996.

Mitchell, Richard. *The Society of the Muslim Brothers.* New York: Oxford University Press, 1993.

Mojtahed Shabestari, Mohamad. "Fetrat-e Khoda Jouy-e Ensan dar Qur'an" (The God-seeking nature of man in the Qur'an). *Andishe-ye Eslami* 1 (1979), no. 7.

______. "Fetrat-e Khoda Jouy-e Ensan dar Qur'an" (The God-seeking nature of man in the Qur'an), *Andishe-ye Eslami* 1 (1979), no. 9.

______. *Hermenutik, Ketab va Sunnat: Farayand-e Tafsir-e Vahy* (Hermeneutics, the Book and the Sunna: process of interpreting revelation). Tehran: Tarh-e Naw, 1996.

______. *Iman va Azadi* (Faith and freedom). Tehran: Tarh-e Naw, 1997.

______. "Qarat-e Rasmi az Din" (Official reading of religion). *Rah-e Naw*, no. 19, Shahrivar 7 (August 29, 1998): 19.

Moris, Zailan. "The Biography of Seyyed Hossein Nasr." In *Knowledge is Light: Essays in Islamic Studies Present to Seyyed Hossein Nasr by his Students in Honor of his Sixty-Sixth Birthday*, edited by Zailan Moris. ABC International Group, 1999.

Morris, James. *The Wisdom of the Throne: An Introduction to the Philosophy of Mulla Sadra.* Princeton: Princeton University Press, 1981.

Nasr, Seyyed Hossein. *Hermes va neveshteha-ye hermesi dar jahan-e Islam* (Hermes and Hermetic Writings in the Islamic World). Tehran: Tehran University Press, 1962.

______. *Ideals and Realities of Islam.* Boston: Beacon Press, 1972.

______. *An Introduction to Islamic Cosmological Doctrines; Conceptions of Nature and Methods Used for its Study by the Ikhwan Al-Ṣafa, Al-Biruni, and Ibn Sina.* Cambridge, MA: Belknap Press of Harvard University Press, 1964.

______. *Islam and the Plight of Modern Man.* London: Longman, 1975.

______. *Islamic Art and Spirituality.* Albany: State University of New York Press, 1987.

______. *Islamic Life and Thought.* London: George Allen and Unwin, 1981.

______. *Islamic Philosophy from Its Origin to the Present: Philosophy in the Land of Prophecy.* Albany: State University of New York Press, 2006.

______. *Islamic Studies: Essays on Law and Society, the Sciences, and Philosophy and Sufism.* Beirut: Librairie du Liban, 1967.

______. *Knowledge and the Sacred: The Gifford Lectures.* Edinburgh: Edinburg University Press, 1981.

______. *Man and Nature: The Spiritual Crisis of Modern Man.* London: Unwin Paperbacks, 1976.

______. *Science and Civilization in Islam.* Cambridge, MA: Harvard University Press, 1968.

______. *Sufi Essays.* London: G. Allen and Unwin, 1972.

______. *Three Muslim Sages: Avicenna, Suhrawardi, Ibn 'Arabi.* Cambridge, MA: Harvard University Press, 1964.

______. *A Young Muslim's Guide to the Modern World.* South Elgin, IL: Library of Islam, 1994.

Nasr, Seyyed Hossein and Jahanbegloo, Ramin. *Dar Just-u Ju-ye Amr-e Qudsi: Guft-u Gu-ye Ramin Jahanbegloo ba Seyyed Ḥussein Naṣr* (In search of the Sacred: Ramin Jahanbegloo's conversation with Seyyed Hussein Nasr). Tehran: Nashr-e Ney, 2007.

Nasr, Seyyed Vali Reza. *Forces of Fortune: The Rise of the New Muslim Middle Class and What It Will Mean for Our World.* New York: Free Press, 2009.

______. *Mawdudi and the Making of Islamic Revivalism.* New York: Oxford University Press, 1996.

Norton, David Fate. *The Cambridge Companion to Hume.* Cambridge: Cambridge University Press, 1993.

Qutb, Sayyid. *Al-Taṣwīr al-fannī fī al-Qur'ān*. Cairo: Dār al-Ma'ārif, 1959.

______. *Islam and Universal peace* [translation of Salām al-ālamī wa-al-Islām]. American Trust Publications, 1977.

______. *Islam, the Religion of the Future* [translation of *Islam, al-Mustaqbal li-hādhā al-dīn*]. Delhi: Markazi Maktaba Islami, 1990.

______. *The Islamic Concept and its Characteristics* [translation of *Khasa'is us Tasawwur al-Islami wa Muqawwamatihi*]. American Trust Publications, 1991.

______. *Milestones* [translation of *Mālim fī al-tarīq*]. Dehli: Marakazi Makataba Islami, 1991.

______. *This Religion of Islam* [translation of hadha'd-din]. Dehli: Marakazi Makataba Islami, 1974.

Quṭb, Sayyid, and William E. Shepard. *Sayyid Qutb and Islamic Activism: A Translation and Critical Analysis of Social Justice in Islam*. Leiden: E.J. Brill, 1996.

Rahaman, Fazlur. "Muhammad Iqbal and Atatürk's Reforms." *Journal of Near Eastern Studies*, Vol. 43, No. 2. (Apr., 1984).

______. *The Philosophy of Mulla Sadra*. Albany: State University of New York, 1975.

Razavi, Masoud, ed. *Afaq-e Faslafeh: Az Aql-e Nab ta Hekmat-e Ahkam* (Horizons of Philosophy: From Pure Reason to Philosophy of Law). Tehran: Farzan Ruz, 2000.

Rhouni, Raja, *Secular and Islamic Feminist Critiques in the Work of Fatima Mernissi*, Brill, 2009.

Rosefsky Wickham, Carrie. *Mobilizing Islam: Religion, Activism, and Political Change in Egypt*. New York: Columbia University Press, 2002.

Rustum, Shehadeh Lamia. "Women in the discourse of Sayyid Qutb." *Arab Studies Quarterly*, vol. 22, no. 3.

Sabbah, Fatna A. (Fatima Mernissi). *Women in the Muslim Unconscious*. Pergamon Press, 1984.

Sadri, Ahmad. "The Varieties of Religious Reform: Public Intelligentsia in Iran." *International Journal of Politics, Culture, and Society*, Vol.15, No.2, (Winter 2001).

Schuon, Frithjof. *Spiritual Perspectives and Human Facts*. London: Faber and Faber, 1954.

Sedgwick, Mark. *Against the Modern World: Traditionalism and the Secret Intellectual History of the Twentieth Century*. Oxford: Oxford University Press, 2004.

Shepard, William E. *Sayyid Qutb and Islamic Activism: A Translation and Critical Analysis of Social Justice in Islam*. Leiden: Brill, 1996.

Sorush, Abdulkarim. *Hekmat va Ma'ishat* (Philosophy and life). Tehran: Serat, 1984.

______. "Modara va Modiriyat-e Mo'menan: Sokhani dar Nesbat-e Din va Demokrasi" (Conciliation and administration of the faithful: a discussion of the relation between religion and democracy). *Kiyan* 4, no. 21 (Sep–Oct 1994): 7.

______. *Tafarruj-e Sun'* (Promenading creation). Tehran: Entesharat-e Sorush, 1987.

Tibi, Bassam. *Islam's Predicament with Modernity: Religious Reform and Cultural Change*. London: Routledge, 2009.

Vahdat, Farzin. *God and Juggernaut: Iran's Intellectual Encounter with Modernity*. Syracuse: Syracuse University Press, 2002.

______. "Religious Modernity in Iran: Dilemmas of Islamic Democracy in the Discourse of Mohammad Khatami." *Comparative Studies of South Asia, Africa and the Middle East*, volume 25, no. 3, (2005).

Walzer, Micheal. *The Revolution of the Saints: A Study in the Origins of Radical Politics*. New York: Atheneum, 1974.

Weber, Max. *The Protestant Ethic and the Spirit of Capitalism*. New York: Routledge, 2001.

Wilber, James B. and Allen, Harold J. *The Worlds of Hume and Kant*. Buffalo: Prometheus Books, 1982.

Ziadat, Adel A. *Western Science in the Arab World: The Impact of Darwinism 1860-1930*. New York: St. Martin's Press, 1986.

INDEX